Contents

UNIT 1
Perspectives on Teaching

The concepts in bold italics are developed in the article. For further expansion, please refer to the Topic Guide and the Index.

UNIT 2
Development

UNIT 3
Exceptional and Culturally Diverse Children

The concepts in bold italics are developed in the article. For further expansion, please refer to the Topic Guide and the Index.

UNIT 4
Learning and Instruction

Unit Overview   74

The concepts in bold italics are developed in the article. For further expansion, please refer to the Topic Guide and the Index.

The concepts in bold italics are developed in the article. For further expansion, please refer to the Topic Guide and the Index.

UNIT 5
Motivation and Classroom Management

The concepts in bold italics are developed in the article. For further expansion, please refer to the Topic Guide and the Index.

UNIT 6
Assessment

The concepts in bold italics are developed in the article. For further expansion, please refer to the Topic Guide and the Index.

The concepts in bold italics are developed in the article. For further expansion, please refer to the Topic Guide and the Index.

Topic Guide

This topic guide suggests how the selections in this book relate to the subjects covered in your course. You may want to use the topics listed on these pages to search the Web more easily.

On the following pages a number of Web sites have been gathered specifically for this book. They are arranged to reflect the units of this *Annual Edition.* You can link to these sites by going to the DUSHKIN ONLINE support site at *http://www.dushkin.com/online/.*

ALL THE ARTICLES THAT RELATE TO EACH TOPIC ARE LISTED BELOW THE BOLD-FACED TERM.

Adolescent development
7. What Empathy Can Do
8. Differing Perspectives, Common Ground: The Middle School and Gifted Education Relationship

Alternative assessment
39. Working Inside the Black Box: Assessment for Learning in the Classroom

Behaviorism
20. Caution—Praise Can Be Dangerous
29. Intrinsic Versus Extrinsic Motivation in Schools: A Reconciliation

Block-scheduling
25. Constructivism and Block Scheduling: Making the Connection

Brain-based education
16. Students Remember...What They Think About
17. Beyond Learning By Doing: The Brain Compatible Approach

Character education
22. Invitations to Learn
23. Promoting Academic Achievement Through Social and Emotional Learning

Child development
5. Shaping the Learning Environment: Connecting Developmentally Appropriate Practices to Brain Research
6. To Be Successful—Let Them Play!
7. What Empathy Can Do
8. Differing Perspectives, Common Ground: The Middle School and Gifted Education Relationship

Classroom assessment
39. Working Inside the Black Box: Assessment for Learning in the Classroom
40. Classroom Assessment for Learning
41. How Classroom Assessments Improve Learning

Classroom management
32. When Children Make Rules
33. The Key to Classroom Management

Cognitive development
5. Shaping the Learning Environment: Connecting Developmentally Appropriate Practices to Brain Research
6. To Be Successful—Let Them Play!

Cognitive learning
16. Students Remember...What They Think About
17. Beyond Learning By Doing: The Brain Compatible Approach
21. Webs of Skill: How Students Learn
24. Teachers Bridge to Constructivism

Constructivism
21. Webs of Skill: How Students Learn

24. Teachers Bridge to Constructivism
25. Constructivism and Block Scheduling: Making the Connection
28. Using Data to Differentiate Instruction
32. When Children Make Rules

Deep understanding
25. Constructivism and Block Scheduling: Making the Connection

Developmentally appropriate practices
5. Shaping the Learning Environment: Connecting Developmentally Appropriate Practices to Brain Research

Differentiated instruction
21. Webs of Skill: How Students Learn

Disabilities
9. 'Mom, Will Kaelie Always Have Possibilities?'—The Realities of Early Childhood Inclusion
10. Into the Mainstream: Practical Strategies for Teaching in Inclusive Environments

Discipline
34. Twelve Practical Strategies to Prevent Behavioral Escalation in Classroom Settings
35. Corporal Punishment: Legalities, Realities, and Implications

Diversity
3. What Urban Students Say About Good Teaching
13. Celebrating Diverse Minds
14. When Should Bilingual Students Be in Special Education?
15. Cultural Influences on the Development of Self-Concept: Updating Our Thinking

Early childhood
5. Shaping the Learning Environment: Connecting Developmentally Appropriate Practices to Brain Research
6. To Be Successful—Let Them Play!

Educational issues
4. Helping Children Cope With Loss, Death, and Grief: Response to a National Tragedy
26. What is High-Quality Instruction?

Effective teaching
1. Good Teachers, Plural
2. Teachers as Leaders
3. What Urban Students Say About Good Teaching
4. Helping Children Cope With Loss, Death, and Grief: Response to a National Tragedy
24. Teachers Bridge to Constructivism
26. What is High-Quality Instruction?
28. Using Data to Differentiate Instruction
39. Working Inside the Black Box: Assessment for Learning in the Classroom

World Wide Web Sites

The following World Wide Web sites have been carefully researched and selected to support the articles found in this reader. The easiest way to access these selected sites is to go to our DUSHKIN ONLINE support site at *http://www.dushkin.com/online/*.

AE: Educational Psychology 05/06

The following sites were available at the time of publication. Visit our Web site—we update DUSHKIN ONLINE regularly to reflect any changes.

General Sources

American Psychological Association
http://www.apa.org/topics/homepage.html

By exploring the APA's "PsychNET," you will be able to find links to an abundance of articles and other resources that are useful in the field of educational psychology.

Educational Resources Information Center
http://www.eric.ed.gov

This invaluable site provides links to all ERIC sites: clearinghouses, support components, and publishers of ERIC materials. Search the ERIC database for what is new.

National Education Association
http://www.nea.org

Something—and often quite a lot—about virtually every education-related topic can be accessed at or through this site of the 2.3-million-strong National Education Association.

National Parent Information Network/ERIC
http://npin.org

This is a clearinghouse of information on elementary and early childhood education as well as urban education. Browse through its links for information for parents.

U.S. Department of Education
http://www.ed.gov/pubs/TeachersGuide/

Government goals, projects, and grants are listed here, plus many links to teacher services and resources.

UNIT 1: Perspectives on Teaching

The Center for Innovation in Education
http://www.center.edu

The Center for Innovation in Education, self-described as a "not-for-profit, non-partisan research organization," focuses on K–12 education reform strategies. Click on its links about school privatization.

Classroom Connect
http://www.classroom.net

This is a major Web site for K–12 teachers and students, with links to schools, teachers, and resources online. It includes discussion of the use of technology in the classroom.

Education World
http://www.education-world.com

Education World provides a database of literally thousands of sites that can be searched by grade level, plus education news, lesson plans, and professional-development resources.

Goals 2000: A Progress Report
http://www.ed.gov/pubs/goals/progrpt/index.html

Open this site to survey a progress report by the U.S. Department of Education on the Goals 2000 reform initiative. It provides a sense of the goals that educators are reaching for as they look toward the future.

Teacher Talk Forum
http://education.indiana.edu/cas/tt/tthmpg.html

Visit this site for access to a variety of articles discussing life in the classroom. Clicking on the various links will lead you to electronic lesson plans, covering a variety of topic areas, from Indiana University's Center for Adolescent Studies.

UNIT 2: Development

Association for Moral Education
http://www.amenetwork.org/

AME is dedicated to fostering communication, cooperation, training, curriculum development, and research that link moral theory with educational practices. From here it is possible to connect to several sites on moral development.

Child Welfare League of America
http://www.cwla.org

The CWLA is the United States' oldest and largest organization devoted entirely to the well-being of vulnerable children and their families. This site provides links to information about issues related to morality and values in education.

Pediatric Behavioral Health Resources
http://www.earlychildhoodbehavioralhealth.com/index.htm

This Web site is dedicated to serving the needs of those working with young children and their families who are experiencing mental health or behavioral issues. Find information on Abuse & Neglect, Mental Health Disabilities, Classroom & Behavior Management, and Discipline Reactive Attachment Disorder.

The National Association for Child Development
http://www.nacd.org

This international organization is dedicated to helping children and adults reach their full potential. Its home page presents links to various programs, research, and resources into such topics as ADD/ADHD.

National Association of School Psychologists (NASP)
http://www.nasponline.org/index2.html

The NASP offers advice to teachers about how to help children cope with the many issues they face in today's world. The site includes tips for school personnel as well as parents.

Scholastic News Zone
http://www.scholasticnews.com

At this site, Scholastic Classroom magazines provide up-to-date information to children, teachers, and parents online to help explain timely issues.

UNIT 3: Exceptional and Culturally Diverse Children

The Council for Exceptional Children
http://www.cec.sped.org/index.html

This page will give you access to information on identifying and teaching gifted children, attention-deficit disorders, and other topics in gifted education.

www.dushkin.com/online/

Global SchoolNet Foundation
http://www.gsn.org

Access this site for multicultural education information. The site includes news for teachers, students, and parents, as well as chat rooms, links to educational resources, programs, and contests and competitions.

International Project: Multicultural Pavilion
http://curry.edschool.virginia.edu/curry/centers/multicultural/papers.html

Here is a forum for sharing stories and resources and for learning from the stories and resources of others, in the form of articles on the Internet that cover every possible racial, gender, and multicultural issue that could arise in the field of multicultural education.

Let 1000 Flowers Bloom/Kristen Nicholson-Nelson
http://teacher.scholastic.com/professional/assessment/100flowers.htm

Open this page for Kristen Nicholson-Nelson's discussion of ways in which teachers can help to nurture children's multiple intelligences. She provides a useful bibliography and resources.

Multicultural Publishing and Education Catalog
http://www.mpec.org

This is the home page of the MPEC, a networking and support organization for independent publishers, authors, educators, and librarians fostering authentic multicultural books and materials. It has excellent links to a vast array of resources related to multicultural education.

National Association for Multicultural Education
http://www.nameorg.org

NAME is a major organization in the field of multicultural education. The website provides conference informantion and resources including lesson plans, advice for handling touchy issues, and grant information.

National Attention Deficit Disorder Association
http://www.add.org

This site, some of which is under construction, will lead you to information about ADD/ADHD. It has links to self-help and support groups, outlines behaviors and diagnostics, answers FAQs, and suggests books and other resources.

National MultiCultural Institute (NMCI)
http://www.nmci.org

NMCI is one of the major organizations in the field of diversity training. At this Web site, NMCI offers conference data, resource materials, diversity training and consulting service information, and links to other related sites.

UNIT 4: Learning and Instruction

Education Week on the Web
http://www.edweek.org

At this page you can open archives, read special reports, keep up on current events, and access a variety of articles in educational psychology. A great deal of this material is helpful in learning and instruction.

Online Internet Institute
http://www.oii.org

A collaborative project among Internet-using educators, proponents of systemic reform, content-area experts, and teachers who desire professional growth, this site provides a learning environment for integrating the Internet into educators' individual teaching styles.

Teachers Helping Teachers
http://www.pacificnet.net/~mandel/

This site provides basic teaching tips, new teaching-methodology ideas, and forums for teachers to share their experiences. It features educational resources on the Web, with new ones added each week.

The Teachers' Network
http://www.teachers.net/

Bulletin boards, classroom projects, online forums, and Web mentors are featured on this site, as well as the book *Teachers' Guide to Cyberspace* and an online, 4-week course on how to use the Internet.

UNIT 5: Motivation and Classroom Management

Canada's Schoolnet Staff Room
http://www.schoolnet.ca/home/e/

Here is a resource and link site for anyone involved in education, including special-needs educators, teachers, parents, volunteers, and administrators.

UNIT 6: Assessment

Awesome Library for Teachers
http://www.neat-schoolhouse.org/teacher.html

Open this page for links and access to teacher information on everything from assessments to child development topics.

Kathy Schrocks's Guide for Educators: Assessment
http://school.discovery.com/schrockguide/assess.html

Sponsored by Discovery School.com, this webpage has a comprehensive compilation of sites about classroom assessment and rubics.

Phi Delta Kappa International
http://www.pdkintl.org

This important organization publishes articles about all facets of education. You can check out the online archive of the journal, *Phi Delta Kappan,* which has resources such as articles having to do with assessment.

Washington (State) Center for the Improvement of Student Learning
http://www.k12.wa.us/

This Washington State site is designed to provide access to information about the state's new academic standards, assessments, and accountability system. Many resources and Web links are included.

We highly recommend that you review our Web site for expanded information and our other product lines. We are continually updating and adding links to our Web site in order to offer you the most usable and useful information that will support and expand the value of your Annual Editions. You can reach us at: *http://www.dushkin.com/annualeditions/.*

UNIT 1
Perspectives on Teaching

Unit Selections

1. **Good Teachers, Plural**, Donald R. Cruickshank and Donald Haefele
2. **Teachers as Leaders**, Richard F. Bowman
3. **What Urban Students Say About Good Teaching**, Dick Corbett and Bruce Wilson
4. **Helping Children Cope With Loss, Death, and Grief: Response to a National Tragedy**, National Association of School Psychologists

Key Points to Consider

- What questions would you like to see educational psychologists study?

- Describe several characteristics of effective teachers. How is effective teaching viewed by different constituents?

- As we move into the twenty-first century, what new expectations should be placed on teachers and schools? What expectations will fade?

 Links: www.dushkin.com/online/
These sites are annotated in the World Wide Web pages.

The Center for Innovation in Education
http://www.center.edu

Classroom Connect
http://www.classroom.net

Education World
http://www.education-world.com

Goals 2000: A Progress Report
http://www.ed.gov/pubs/goals/progrpt/index.html

Teacher Talk Forum
http://education.indiana.edu/cas/tt/tthmpg.html

The teaching-learning process in school is enormously complex. Many factors influence pupil learning—such as family background, developmental level, prior knowledge, motivation, and, of course, effective teachers. Educational psychology investigates these factors to better understand and explain student learning. We begin our exploration of the teaching-learning process by considering the characteristics of effective teaching.

In the first three articles, perspectives on effective teaching are presented—the variety of professional perspectives as well as the urban students' perspective.

The fourth article discusses the range of reactions that children and adolescents have experienced in response to the terrorism attacks of September 11, 2001, and suggests ways that educators can help them to cope and continue their schooling.

Educational psychology is a resource for teachers that emphasizes disciplined inquiry, a systematic and objective analysis of information, and a scientific attitude toward decision making.

The field provides information for decisions that are based on quantitative and qualitative studies of learning and teaching rather than on intuition, tradition, authority, or subjective feelings. It is our hope that this aspect of educational psychology is communicated throughout these readings, and that, as a student, you will adopt the analytic, probing attitude that is part of the discipline.

While educational psychologists have helped to establish a knowledge base about teaching and learning, the unpredictable, spontaneous, evolving nature of teaching suggests that the best they will ever do is to provide concepts and skills that teachers can adapt for use in their classrooms. The issues raised in these articles about effective teaching, and the issues facing teachers in the twenty-first century, help us understand the teaching role and its demands. As you read articles in other chapters, consider the demands they place on the teaching role as well.

Good Teachers, Plural

What makes a teacher good? Looking at the ways we have answered that question in the past century may place the current evaluation craze in perspective.

Donald R. Cruickshank and Donald Haefele

There are as many kinds of good teachers in our schools as there are varieties of good apples in supermarkets. Unfortunately, we tend to recognize and honor only one kind of teacher at a time. We currently glorify teachers whose students pass standardized tests (Bradley, 2000). In the 1990s, we admired those who had proven they could bring about greater student achievement. In the 1980s, good teachers were those who followed Madeline Hunter's prescriptions for teaching success (Garman & Hazi, 1998). And the list goes on.

For the first half of the 20th century, school principals, supervisors, and education professors determined the attributes of good teachers.

Let us identify some of these visions of good teachers. Only then can we begin to explore how we can value them all and how school districts can support the development of many kinds of teachers and create ways to evaluate them.

Visions of Good Teachers

Ideal teachers. For the first half of the 20th century, school principals, supervisors, and educational professors determined the attributes of good teachers. Schools, school districts, and colleges cranked out checklists and rating scales that scored such traits as professional attitude, understanding of students, creativity, control of class, planning, individualization, and pupil participation. During this period, scholar Dwight Beecher (1953) developed the popular Teaching Evaluation Record, and Arvil Barr and his associates (1961) drew up a comprehensive list of ideal attributes that included buoyancy, emotional stability, ethical behavior, expressiveness, forcefulness, and personal magnetism.

Thus, an ideal teacher met subjective standards of excellence determined by selected, significant others. Because the standards were subjective, many disagreements developed over what the standards meant and which teachers met them (Mitzel, 1960; Morsh & Wilder, 1954).

Analytic teachers. By the early 1960s, administrators encountered problems associated with measuring the attributes of ideal teachers (Cruickshank, 1990). In a search for some other way to judge teacher quality, experts soon began describing good teachers as analytic.

Analytic teachers methodically inspected what they did in the classroom. They recorded and examined their classroom practice using a variety of observation techniques (Simon & Boyer, 1968). Many teachers and observers used the Flanders System of Interactional Analysis (Flanders, 1960) to make a detailed record of the teacher-student interactions occurring during a lesson: how much and about what the teacher talked, how much and about what students talked, and the extent and nature of student silence or confusion. Teachers modified their practice on the basis of these analyses. Becoming an analytic teacher required being investigative and self-correctional. Over time, the work involved in being analytical seemed to overwhelm even proponents of this vision of good teachers.

Effective teachers. In 1966, the influential Coleman Report asserted that students' socioeconomic backgrounds influenced their learning more than their teachers did (U.S. Department of Health, Education, and Welfare). Immediately, dozens of educational researchers set out to show that teachers made a crucial difference in student achievement. First, researchers identified teachers whose students scored higher on tests than did comparable students taught by others. Next, they examined these overachieving teachers, referred to as *outliers* or *effective teachers*, to determine exactly what they were like and what they did so that other teachers might benefit from such knowledge.

The findings of many studies (Rosenshine, 1971; Rosenshine & Furst, 1971) consistently found that effective teachers carefully monitor learning activities and are clear, accepting and supportive, equitable with students, and persistent in challenging and engaging them. Nonetheless, researchers disagreed about the methods used in the studies and about whether student gain is the most important outcome of teaching (Cruickshank, 1990).

Paralleling the development of the concept of the effective teacher has been a significant increase in the amount of student-achievement testing. As a result, we have become more focused on the product—better student scores on standardized tests—and on rewarding teachers who succeed in teaching to the test. In many states, teachers and principals are deemed effective and are rewarded monetarily when students demonstrate satisfactory gains on standardized tests. Opposition to this narrow definition of teacher effectiveness is mounting (Hoff, 1999; Kohn, 1999).

Dutiful teachers. Those less than satisfied with the attributes originally assigned to effective teachers argued that teachers who do not display the typical attributes of effective teachers, such as enthusiasm, may yet bring about student learning. They asserted that studying the attributes of effective teachers can be useful, especially for guiding preservice and inservice development, but these attributes should not be used as standards for judging teacher quality. Rather, we should evaluate teachers according to how well they understand and perform their duties: knowledge of the subject matter, school, and community; demonstrated classroom skills, including testing and grading; personal characteristics that encourage learning; and service to the profession (Scriven, 1990).

Competent teachers. The U.S. accountability movement in the 1970s spurred an effort in education to identify competencies that teachers should possess. Specifically, the public wanted to know what teachers needed to know and be able to do.

To identify teacher competencies, scholars studied the early research on teacher effectiveness, analyzed what teachers do, and obtained the opinions of expert teacher practitioners and other educators. The most thorough compilation (Dodl et al., 1972) organized competencies in the areas of planning instruction, implementing instruction, assessing and evaluating students, communicating, and performing administrative duties.

The public also wanted to make certain that teachers used their knowledge and performed well in the classroom. Consequently, the teacher-testing movement was born, soon to be given a boost by the 1983 publication of *A Nation At Risk* (National Commission on Excellence in Education). Thereafter, teachers or teachers-to-be had to pass tests developed by state education departments or by such national organizations as the Educational Testing Service and the National Board for Professional Teaching Standards.

The Educational Testing Service developed the Praxis teacher competency series of tests for use in teacher preparation programs and entry into the teaching profession. Praxis assesses three areas: reading, writing, and math skills near the beginning of a preservice teaching program; professional academic and pedagogical knowledge near the end of a teaching program; and on-the-job classroom performance. Thirty-eight states currently require some Praxis testing.

The National Board for Professional Teaching Standards provides national certification for experienced teachers who meet competencies set forth by discerning teachers (King, 1994). Teachers seeking National Board certification submit portfolios that include lesson plans, videotapes of lessons taught, and samples of student work. They also come to regional sites for further inspection and testing. States now offer incentives for teachers to obtain Board certification. For example, in Massachusetts, the Veteran Teachers Board offers up to $50,000 over 10 years to any public school teacher who receives National Board certification (Bradley, 1998).

Even the National Council for Accreditation of Teacher Education is moving toward assessing the competence—the knowledge and skills—of preservice teachers and away from merely reviewing their programs of study (Bradley, 1999).

Expert teachers. In the 1980s and into the 1990s, many scholars decided that what makes a teacher good is expertise. Expert teachers are different from nonexperts in three ways: they have extensive and accessible knowledge that is organized for use in teaching; they are efficient and can do more in less time; and they are able to arrive at novel and appropriate solutions to problems (Sternberg & Horvath, 1995). Thus, expertise is more than experience. Teachers could be experienced and have less expertise than some novices.

Reflective teachers. The definition of the reflective teacher was developed at Ohio State University in the late 1970s. Reflective teachers are students of teaching, with a strong, sustained interest in learning about the art and science of teaching and about themselves as teachers (Cruickshank, 1987, 1991). Reflective teachers are introspective, examining their own practice of teaching and seeking a greater understanding of teaching by reading scholarly and professional journals and books, including teachers' autobiographies. Because they want to be thoughtful practitioners, they constantly monitor their teaching—for example, by using videotape or audiotape.

Satisfying teachers. Satisfying teachers please students, parents or caregivers, teaching colleagues, administrators, and supervisors by responding to their needs. In Rochester, New York, for example, parents rate their children's teachers on the basis of 20 questions that inquire about such qualities as the teacher's accessibility, clarity, responsiveness, and optimism (Janey, 1997).

School or parent organizations recognize satisfying teachers by presenting them with awards for good teaching. More often, however, admiration shows up in daily responses to the teacher: students advise one another to take this teacher's courses, fellow teachers look to this teacher for guidance and inspiration, most parents want their children in this teacher's class, and administrators trust this teacher to respond positively to difficult students.

Of course, knowing and meeting the expectations of others is a daunting task, and considerable disagreement can develop about what expectations are appropriate. We can all think of instructors who did or did not satisfy us or others but who were nonetheless effective teachers.

Diversity-responsive teachers. Diversity-responsive teachers take special interest in and are particularly sensitive to students who are different culturally, socially, economically, intellectually, physically, or emotionally. For example, Jacqueline Irvine and James Fraser (1998) believe that African American students are best served by "warm demanders" (p. 56). Warm demanders use a culturally specific pedagogical style that is substantively different from the approaches described in effective teaching research. Such teachers perceive themselves as parental surrogates and advocates, employ a teaching style filled with rhythmic language and rapid intonation, link students' everyday cultural experiences to new concepts, develop personal relationships with the learners, and teach with authority.

Diversity-responsive teachers are also dedicated to bettering the lives of students both inside and outside the classroom. Often working with children who have special needs, this kind of teacher demonstrates great tenderness, patience, and tact. A well-known exemplar is Annie Sullivan, Helen Keller's teacher (Peterson, 1946).

Respected teachers. Respected teachers, real and fictional, sometimes are idolized in books and films. Some of the real ones include LouAnne Johnson in *Dangerous Minds*, Jaime Escalante in *Stand and Deliver*, and Marva Collins in *The Marva Collins Story*. Fictional, virtuous teachers have been crafted in *Mr. Holland's Opus; The Prime of Miss Jean Brodie; Up the Down Staircase; To Sir, with Love;* and *Goodbye, Mr. Chips*.

Historian Richard Traina (1999) explored the autobiographies of some 125 prominent Americans to determine what qualities in teachers they valued. He notes that three attributes stand out: subject-matter competence, caring about students and their success, and distinctive character. Respected teachers possess and demonstrate virtuous qualities, including honesty, decency, fairness, devotion, empathy, and selflessness. Most such teachers also have determination, overcoming great odds to ensure student success.

Moving Forward

None of these categories is mutually exclusive. And no variation, by itself, has proven or is proving to be just right: None satisfies all education stakeholders. In a utopian world, teachers would demonstrate all aspects of teacher "goodness" and possess the attributes of all 10 visions. In the real world, we must learn how to recognize and appreciate the many models that teachers can follow to be good teachers.

Further, we need to answer some questions. Have we identified all of the possible exemplars of good teaching?

Variations of a Good Teacher

IDEAL teachers meet standards set by school principals, supervisors, and education professors.

ANALYTIC teachers use observation techniques to record how well they are meeting their instructional intentions.

EFFECTIVE teachers bring about higher student achievement.

DUTIFUL teachers perform assigned teaching duties well.

COMPETENT teachers pass tests that indicate they possess requisite teacher attributes.

EXPERT teachers have extensive and accessible knowledge and can do more in less time.

REFLECTIVE teachers examine the art and science of teaching to become more thoughtful practitioners.

SATISFYING teachers please students, parents or caregivers, colleagues, supervisors, and administrators.

DIVERSITY-RESPONSIVE teachers are sensitive to all students.

RESPECTED teachers possess and demonstrate qualities regarded as virtues.

To what extent do the exemplars overlap? Are some models more valuable than others? Who decides which exemplar is more valuable? Should all teachers be good teachers according to at least one of the 10 or so models? What should be the standard for good teachers within each vision of a good teacher? How can we prepare teachers and help them become good by some criteria? How can teachers document what kind of good teachers they are? How can we reward good teachers?

Tests for teachers were a direct result of the push to describe the competent teacher and to determine to what extent teachers measure up.

In addition, we need to conduct research. To what extent do various education stakeholders agree on what makes teachers good? How do perceptions of good teachers differ by age, gender, socioeconomic background, educational level, geographic area, and political persuasion? Which exemplars of good teachers are related to which educational outcomes? To what extent can good teachers be readily distinguished from bad teachers?

Evaluating Different Kinds of Teachers

School districts that appreciate multiple kinds of good teachers need to create teacher evaluation systems corresponding to the full range of teaching exemplars. To meet legal requirements, an evaluation system must be both formal (guided by public, written policies and procedures) and standardized (applied evenly and fairly). For example, all teachers must meet the criteria of one of the exemplars. Evaluations of *effective teachers* should require that teachers demonstrate such attributes as clarity and enthusiasm— qualities associated with student achievement. *Dutiful teachers* should be judged on such criteria as knowledge of subject matter and classroom skills.

Clearly, to judge each vision of a good teacher, we must use valid criteria that are related to the particular exemplar that the teacher strives to emulate. A good teacher evaluation system should also have predictive validity and make the desired impact on students; an evaluation of a *satisfying teacher*, for example, should include surveys of students and parents. Of course, any teacher evaluation system should require that evaluators—administrators, supervisors, teaching peers, or others—receive training so that each evaluation is objective and would result in approximately the same outcome if done by another evaluator.

Accepting Many Exemplars

Substantiating that there are all kinds of good teachers serves several useful ends. First, it dispels the traditional notion that there is only one kind of good teacher. Second, it permits teachers to describe which kind of good teacher they are and, when necessary, submit evidence to that effect. Third, it provides positive direction for teachers and persons responsible for teachers' continuing development. Finally, such knowledge enables the teaching profession to identity and remove teachers who are unable to meet any definition of what makes teachers good.

Meanwhile, Wyoming Governor Jim Geringer, chairman of the Education Commission of the States, whose membership consists of governors and top state education officials, reports that he hopes to work with the states to define what it means to be a good teacher (Sandham, 1999). Is the time right for educators, educational researchers, and elected officials to join hands in broadening the scope of this ambitious and important task?

References

Barr, A., Worcester, D., Abell, A., Beecher, C., Jenson, L., Peronto, A., Ringness, T., & Schmidt, J. (1961). Wisconsin studies of the measurement and predictability of teacher effectiveness. *Journal of Experimental Education, 30*, 1–156.

Beecher, D. (1953). *The teaching evaluation record.* Buffalo, NY: Educators Publishing Company.

Bradley, A. (1998, February 25). A better way to pay. *Education Week, 17*(24), 29–31.

Bradley, A. (1999, January 13). NCATE unveils a plan for aspiring elementary teachers. *Education Week, 18*(18), 5.

Bradley, A. (2000, March 22). L.A. proposes linking teacher pay to tests. *Education Week, 19*(28), 3.

Cruickshank, D. (1987). *Reflective teaching: The preparation of students of teaching.* Reston, VA: Association of Teacher Educators.

Cruickshank, D. (1990). *Research that informs teachers and teacher educators.* Bloomington, IN: Phi Delta Kappa Educational Foundation.

Cruickshank, D. (1991). *Reflective teaching.* Bloomington, IN: Phi Delta Kappa Educational Foundation.

Dodl, N., Elfner, E., Becker, J., Halstead, J., Jung, H., Nelson, P., Puriton, S., & Wegele, P. (1972). *Florida catalog of teacher competencies.* Tallahassee: Florida State University.

Flanders, N. (1960). *Teacher influence, pupil attitudes, and achievement: Final report.* Minneapolis: University of Minnesota.

Garman, N., & Hazi, H. (1998, May). Teachers ask: Is there life after Madeline Hunter? *Phi Delta Kappan, 69*(9), 669–672.

Hoff, D. (1999, September 22). Standards at crossroads after debate. *Education Week, 19*(3), 1, 9.

Irvine, J., & Fraser, J. (1998, May 13). Warm demanders. *Education Week, 17*(35), 56, 42.

Janey, C. (1997, October 1). Seeking customer satisfaction. *Education Week, 17*(5), 39.

King, M. (1994). Locking themselves in: National standards for the teaching profession. *Teaching and Teacher Education, 10*(1), 95–108.

Kohn, A. (1999, September 15). Confusing harder with better. *Education Week, 19*(2), 68, 52.

Mitzel, H. (1960). Teacher effectiveness. In C. Harris (Ed.), *Encyclopedia of educational research* (3rd ed.) (p. 1481). New York: MacMillan.

Morsh, J., & Wilder, E. (1954). *Identifying the effective instructor: A review of quantitative studies.* Lackland Air Force Base, TX: Air Force Personnel and Training Center.

National Commission on Excellence in Education. (1983). *A nation at risk.* Washington, DC: U.S. Department of Education.

Peterson, H. (1946). *Great teachers.* New York: Random House.

Rosenshine, B. (1971). *Teaching behaviors and student achievement.* London: National Foundation for Educational Research.

Rosenshine, B., & Furst, N. (1971). Research on teacher performance criteria. In B. O. Smith (Ed.), *Research in Teacher Education* (pp. 37–72). Englewood Cliffs, NJ: Prentice-Hall.

Sandham, J. (1999, August 4). ECS members take closer look at the teaching profession. *Education Week, 18* (43), 23.

Scriven, M. (1990, September). Can research-based teacher evaluation be saved? *Journal of Personnel Evaluation in Education, 4*(1), 19–32.

Simon, A., & Boyer, E. (1968). *Mirrors for behavior: An anthology of classroom observation instruments.* Philadelphia: Research for Better Schools.

Sternberg, R., & Horvath, J. (1995, August/September). A prototype view of expert teaching. *Educational Researcher, 24*(6), 9–17.

Traina, R. (1999, January 20). What makes a teacher good? *Education Week, 18*(19), 34.

U.S. Department of Health, Education, and Welfare. (1966). *Equality of educational opportunity: Summary report* (The Coleman report). Washington, DC: U.S. Government Printing Office.

Donald R. Cruickshank (cruickshank1@osu.edu) is Professor Emeritus and **Donald Haefele** (haefele@osu.edu) is Associate Professor of Education at Ohio State University, 2817 Wickliffe Rd., Columbus, OH 43221.

Teachers as Leaders

RICHARD F. BOWMAN

In an era of dwindling resources, compelling student needs, burgeoning violence, and escalating performance expectations for students and faculty alike, classroom teachers are confronted with new demands that challenge their traditional roles as educators. The leap from a productive individual contributor, working essentially behind a closed classroom door, to a new identity of "teacher as leader" constitutes one of the most engaging transitions in teachers' professional lives. Learning how to accumulate informal power, exercise influence, and reconcile conflicting collegial interests requires nothing less than a profound identity shift for contemporary classroom teachers.

Why Lead?

Effective classroom teachers sense the positive changes they make in the intellectual, socioemotional, physical, and ethical lives of their students. This awareness gives meaning to their lives as professional educators. But to many teachers, leadership demands seem different—so different that many teachers shun the challenge of leadership opportunities altogether. Heifetz and Linsky argue, however, "when they look deep within themselves, people grapple with the challenge of leadership in order to make a positive difference in the lives of others" (2002, 74).

Ironically, when classroom teachers do embrace leadership challenges in his or her schools or school district, fellow teachers often chastise him or her for exhibiting a hunger for importance or a thirst for control. In truth, most professionals have a genuine need to feel impor-

tant and have others confirm that authority (Heifetz and Linsky 2002). Moreover, many of those same professionals also feel they have a responsibility to transform their classrooms and schools for the better.

Instinctively, teachers fear taking leadership roles because the "essence of leadership lies in the capacity to deliver disturbing news and raise difficult questions in a way that moves people to take up the message without killing the messenger" (Heifetz and Linsky 2002, 74). Many teachers often are genuinely frightened to confront hard issues and embrace the sometimes painful solutions that will transform a school or a district (Heifetz and Linsky 2002). But for the teacher as leader, shrinking from these difficult challenges is ignoring one's responsibility as an effective educator. In one of his last addresses before his death, John W. Gardner, former secretary of health, education, and welfare, singled out the pathology of the comfortable indifference that affects too many reluctant leaders in organizational settings: "Who gave them permission to stand aside! I am asking you to issue a wake-up call to those people—a bugle call right in their ear" (Hesselbein 2003, 4). For teachers as leaders, learning to see is life's work. And learning to act upon what one sees is a limitless gift to others.

Teachers as Leaders

Successful teachers as leaders are adept at influencing constituencies over which they admittedly have no formal authority. These teachers as leaders are effective in doing so because they draw on diverse sources of power beyond formal authority: "expertise, appealing personal qualities, position in key networks, and visibility" (Johnson 2003, 10). Against the backdrop of increasingly interdependent professional relationships, teachers as leaders re-engage in workplace politics as they seek to create connections both inside and outside their schools. Perceptively, teachers as leaders recognize that everyday leadership dilemmas are laced with complex motives and are played out on an uneven political terrain (Badaracco 2002). However, they continue to believe that when organizations make an honest, open effort to determine the truth of a situation, the right decisions often become self-evident.

These education leaders create and sustain a developmental culture for their students and themselves by building a range of relationships with colleagues, parents, students, administrators, and community leaders. These relationships help establish and sustain systems that "reinforce a development mentality" within their individual school environments (Johnson 2003, 11). But teachers as leaders "simultaneously develop people and instill disciplined decision-making systems" in their classrooms and their schools, and they use similar techniques within their own classrooms (Belasco and Stead 1999, 15). The result is that teachers as leaders "infuse their entire decision-making process with the brutal facts of reality" (Stauffer 2003, 2).

To create and sustain such a developmental school culture, school leaders must teach not only students but also each other (Flaum 2003). Given that "almost a third of teachers leave the field within the first three years and a half before their fifth year," mentoring systems are increasingly important because they represent a supportive developmental system (Stern 2003, 13). Intensive mentoring for beginning teachers fosters productive development environments. In a school in Columbus, Ohio, for example, mentoring teachers are relieved of their teaching duties entirely to ensure they have time to focus on their caseloads of twelve to fifteen new teachers. Additionally, those mentors are "required to observe each new teacher 20 times in the classroom and schedule 10 conferences" (15). As teachers as leaders, the mentors are committed to creating success for the new teachers. This type of commitment builds relationships, increases job satisfaction, and further develops effective teaching techniques. In short, education leaders guide their colleagues by engaging in collective conversations, invoking symbolic gestures that reveal relationship, modeling professionalism beyond the label of one's role, championing evocative ideas in both the classroom and the workplace, and being "in influence" as opposed to being "in control" (Ellinor and Gerard 1998, xxx).

Leadership: Powerful Processes

In their breakthrough study, *Geeks and Geezers*, Bennis and Thomas (2002) probed the powerful processes through which leaders emerge. They focused on the differences in leadership between those who grew up in the shadows of the Great Depression and World War II versus those who matured in the phosphorescent glow of computer screens. Their research findings suggest that true leaders of any age share a cluster of critical qualities: adaptive capacity, the ability to engage others in shared meaning, a distinctive and compelling voice, and a sense of integrity.

Adaptive capacity is "an almost magical capacity to transcend adversity, with all of its attendant stresses, and to emerge stronger than before" (Bennis and Thomas, 121). Although everyone faces obstacles, "the willingness to climb those walls and the ability to find ways to do so are the real measure of a leader" (92). For teachers as leaders, the core of adaptive capacity is the ability to grasp context. For example, at the conclusion of a recent student teaching observation, a clinical student inquired: "How well did I manage student interactions in class today?" His inquiry is significant on three levels. First, this student teacher internalized the fact that relationships are the key to classroom and organizational success. Second, he had transitioned from theory into practice. That is, he focused on managing relationships rather than individual student behavior. Third, he discovered that social context adds meaning to information. Like Saul Bellow's alter ego in the novel *Ravelstein* (2000), the clinical student was a first-class noticer.

Identifying relationships and skillfully managing them are the foundations for transitioning from teacher to leader. Related research by Bennis and Nanus (1997) suggests that teachers as leaders exhibit four common abilities:

Management of Attention

In Shakespeare's *Henry IV, Part I*, the Welsh seer, Glendower, boasts to Hotspur: "I can call the spirits from the vasty deep" (Knight 1968, 79-80). In response, Hotspur deflates Glendower with, "Why so can I or so can any man; But will they come when you do call them?" Like spirits, students return from the "vasty deep" when the call is enticing enough. Teachers as leaders must devise and maintain an atmosphere in which students can succeed. Their calls must define purpose—a purpose that strikes a chord with students.

Human beings have an innate need to hear and tell stories because those stories provide a lens through which they can view things that happen to them. Stories ignite self-awareness and engender self-confidence. Teachers as leaders recognize the power of stories and often use them in the classroom to focus attention and frame purpose. Stories, metaphors, analogies, and evocative questions capture interest and sustain collective engagement.

Management of Meaning

At a fundamental level, learning, or meaning making, is a social activity. A school or classroom's culture is defined by the "emergence of shared meanings" (Block 1998, 89). Teachers who are adept at turning information into a shared experience lead in the classroom. This transformation is important because "… people change out of experience. They don't change out of words or techniques or manipulation of policies" (Ellinor and Gerard 1998, xi). Thus, effective teachers as leaders find ways to make meaning personal for students by creating a shared experience to which students can relate.

Management of Trust

Trust has two enemies: "bad character and poor information" (Prusak 2003, 12). Leadership is about character. Transparency and openness of action create trust in organizational settings. However, although trust is built over long stretches of time, it is often lost through a single thoughtless act. Teachers as leaders must always remember that "in a professional relationship, never be the cause of a surprise, because doing so inevitably erodes trust." Trust is inextricably linked to honesty and sincerity.

Management of Self

Teachers as leaders need to form a strong identity. Just as writers must find their voices, so too must classroom teachers. Teachers as leaders "must find an individual and persuasive voice, an authentic version of themselves that engages and recruits others. As long-time Girl Scouts of America CEO Frances Hesselbein observed, 'You lead by voice'" (Bennis and Thomas 2002, 137).

In their interactions with students, colleagues, and community, teachers as leaders must model integrity. In contrast, teachers with weak self-awareness or an exaggerated sense of entitlement, create difficulties for themselves because others will perceive their indulgences as neither right nor fair. Teachers who develop an authentic identity founded on genuine principles will become successful leaders.

Summary

The classic view of leadership is captured in the image of the leader of a band. The bandleader, as boss, barks commands, and followers march lock step. More recently, the role of a leader has been reflected in the representation of the conductor of a contemporary orchestra. Although many renowned orchestra leaders are still considered exceedingly autocratic, "they do not see themselves as the boss. They see themselves as the servant of the score" (Drucker 1996, 16). Thus, their authority rests on their ability to communicate with specialists in the orchestra. Today, the role of teacher as leader mirrors the playful novelty of a jazz band, in which leadership flows freely from player to player, refrain to refrain, inspiring others to new levels of achievement, service, and significance. In improvisational dialogue, teachers as leaders search for ways to collaboratively create a story that "wants to be born." Together, they sense that "an idea shared becomes a movement toward inevitable progress. An idea hoarded becomes filled with the stain of personal ambition and idiosyncratic desire" (Flaum 2003, 7).

In short, teachers as leaders do not inflate the importance of their leadership efforts or the likelihood of their success. Unlike heroic leaders who single-handedly save the world, teachers as leaders seek to lead from the middle-inconspicuously and without casualties. (Badaracco 2002).

Key words: developmental culture, leadership, management skills

REFERENCES

Badaracco, J. 2002. *Leading quietly*. Boston: Harvard Business School Press.

Belasco, J., and J. Stead. 1999. The five jobs of leaders. *Leader to Leader* 14: 15-17.

Bellow, S. 2000. *Ravelstein*. New York: Penguin Putnam.

Bennis, W., and B. Nanus. 1997. *Leaders: Strategies for taking charge*. 2nd ed. New York: Harper Business.

Bennis, W., and R. Thomas. 2002. *Geeks and geezers: How era, values, and defining moments shape leaders.* Boston: Harvard Business School Press.

Block, P. 1998. From leadership to citizenship. In *Insights on Leadership,* ed. L. C. Spears, 87-95. New York: John Wiley and Sons.

Drucker, P. 1996. The shape of things to come. *Leader to Leader* (Premier Issue): 12-18.

Ellinor, L., and G. Gerard. 1998. *Dialogue.* New York: John Wiley and Sons.

Etzioni, A. 2004. How character is built. *Kappa Delta Pi Record* 40 (2): 54-57.

Flaum, S. 2003. When ideas lead, people follow. *Leader to Leader* 30: 7-12.

Heifetz, R., and M. Linsky. 2002. A survival guide for leaders. *Harvard Business Review* 80 (6): 65-74.

Hesselbein, F. 2003. A bugle call right in the ear. *Leader to Leader* 30: 4-6.

Johnson, L. K. 2003. Accelerating the new manager's start. *Harvard Management Update* 8, no. 9 (September): 10-11.

Knight, C., ed. 1968. *Comedies, histories, tragedies, and poems of William Shakespeare.* 2nd ed. Vol. V. New York: AMS Press.

Mayer, J. D. 2004. Be realistic. *Harvard Business Review* 82 (1): 28.

Prusak, L., 2003. A matter of trust. *Trends and Ideas* 1, no. 1 (Fall): 11-12.

Stauffer, D. 2003. How to win the buy-in: Setting the stage for change. *Harvard Management Update* 8, no. 6 (June): 1-3.

Stern, S. 2003. The great escape. *Christian Science Monitor,* October 7: 13, 15.

Richard F. Bowman is a professor of educational foundations at the College of Education at Winona State University in Winona, Minnesota.

From *The Clearing House,* Vol. 77, No. 5, May/June 2004, pp. 187-189. Reprinted by permission of the Helen Dwight Reid Educational Foundation. Published by Heldref Publications, 1319, Eighteenth St., NW, Washington, DC 20036-1802. Copyright © 2004.

What Urban Students Say About
Good Teaching

Interviews with these inner-city adolescents show that they want to learn and have a vision of the kind of teacher who can help them excel.

Dick Corbett and Bruce Wilson

What can schools do to encourage students to care more about learning? Make sure that teachers act in ways that demonstrate how much *they* care! At least, that would be the answer of nearly 400 students we interviewed from inner-city, low-income middle and high schools. In fact, the students never wavered in identifying their teachers as the main factor determining how much they learned, and they spoke with one voice when describing good teachers. Good teachers

- Made sure that students did their work.
- Controlled the classroom.
- Were willing to help students whenever and however the students wanted help.
- Explained assignments and content clearly.
- Varied the classroom routine.
- Took the time to get to know the students and their circumstances.

Significantly, students did not confuse teachers' personal qualities with their professional ones. Interviewees described "mean" good teachers and "mean" bad teachers; "funny" good teachers and "funny" bad teachers; and "boring" good teachers and "boring" bad teachers. If a teacher had the six qualities that students identified as those of a good teacher, then demeanor, sense of humor, and charisma—as well as any other personal characteristic—were unimportant.

Interviewing Students About Reform Efforts

In an effort to include students' voices in education reform efforts being implemented in Philadelphia, we interviewed inner-city middle schoolers annually for three years while their schools were undergoing a districtwide reform known as Children Achieving. The adolescents,

selected to reflect a range of attendance and achievement patterns, attended six of the lowest-income schools in the city. Each year, we asked them to talk about their daily instructional routines, the classes in which they learned the most and least (and behaved the best and worst), how they preferred to learn and which classes accommodated this preference, what they thought good teaching was, and where in their schedules they encountered it. We hoped to discover through these conversations whether school reforms had actually changed the educational experiences of students.

We also followed many of the same students into high school. In a serendipitous occurrence, several of the middle schools fed into high schools that had adopted the Johns Hopkins Talent Development Model. Because of this fortunate timing, we were able to get students' descriptions of their high school experiences before and during this reform.[1]

Throughout the years that the students talked with us, they held fast to their view that good teaching was central to the quality of their schooling experiences.

Throughout the years that the students talked with us, they held fast to their view that good teaching was central to the quality of their schooling experiences. Moreover, when they talked about the value of education reforms (specifically, the Talent Development Model's block schedule), they judged such reforms on the basis of their effects on teacher behavior that aided student learning.

What Is a Good Teacher?

Students repeatedly invoked the six qualities of good teaching in answering almost any question we asked. Students talked approvingly about "strict" teachers—those who pushed students to complete their assignments and maintained an orderly classroom. Students added that good teachers were willing to help, explained assignments and content clearly, varied classroom activities, and tried to understand students.

Good Teachers Push Students

These urban students admitted that their default response to most assignments was to ignore them, which understandably gave the impression that they cared little about learning. Nevertheless, students liked teachers who successfully combated this habit. As two students explained (in their words and syntax),

> I like the ones that don't allow excuses. It's my turn to get an education. I need to have someone to tell me when I'm tired and don't feel like doing the work that I should do it anyway.

> If they don't keep after you, you'll slide and never do the work. You just won't learn nothing if they don't stay on you.

Teachers "nagged" students in many ways—by consistently checking homework, offering quiet individual reminders, giving rewards, and calling parents. As one student boasted, "He keeps pressing me until I get it right."

Good Teachers Maintain Order

According to students, their teachers varied tremendously in how well they were able to control students, and the ones who could not maintain control bothered them a lot. As one student succinctly explained,

> The kids don't do the work. The teacher is hollering and screaming, "Do your work and sit down!" This makes the ones that want to learn go slower. It makes your grade sink down. It just messes it up for you. The teacher is trying to handle everybody and can't.

Another student pointed out the difference between strict and not-so-strict teachers:

> Teachers that just let you do what you want, they don't get a point across. Strict teachers get the point across.

And, as was typical of almost everything students had to say about good teaching, everything came back to whether they learned:

> I want a teacher strict enough for me to learn.

Good Teachers Are Willing to Help

Just as research has demonstrated that students have different learning styles, the students we interviewed had different helping styles. Some wanted help after school, some during class, some individually, some through working with peers, some through whole-class question-and-answer sessions, and some without ever having to acknowledge to anyone that they needed it. Being omnisciently adept at knowing how and when to offer help was an indelible part of being a good teacher.

> A good teacher takes time out to see if all the kids have what they're talking about and cares about how they're doing and will see if they need help.

Teachers who offered generous help often hooked students who previously had been reluctant classroom participants into working.

> One boy in the class, he do all his work now. If it wasn't for my teacher, he wouldn't do nothing. At the beginning of the year, he don't do nothing; now he does…. [It's] 'cause the teacher took time out to help him and talk to him.

Teacher help also broke the cycle of failure that we heard about from so many students. One of them explained this phenomenon and the role of teacher assistance in ameliorating it:

> Say, for instance, I didn't come to school. The next day I came in, they went over something new. There wouldn't be like time to show me what they did [the previous day]. And the teacher wouldn't make sure I understood. So, I start moving with them, but I be behind. They should have given extra help…. They could pull me to the side and ask me if I want to do it. Then it would be my choice.

Good Teachers Explain Until Everyone Understands

Many students complained about teachers who moved too fast through material or explained it only once and in one way. They much preferred to have teachers who stayed on an assignment until everyone understood, who offered multiple and repeated explanations, and who, as one student said, "feed it into our head real good; they do it step-by-step and they break it down."

Students seemed most disturbed by teachers who allowed discipline problems to affect the quality of their explanations. For example, many students referred to teachers who would say a variant of "I've already told you this; you should have listened the first time" in response to repeated requests for clarification. Although the teachers may have been justified in feeling frustrated at the lack of attention that prompted the requests, to students this phrase meant "I refuse to teach you."

By contrast, students' faces brightened considerably when they were able to say something like the following:

> The teachers are real at ease. They take the time, you know, go step-by-step. We learn it more. It seems like they got the time to explain it all. We don't have to leave anyone behind.

Good Teachers Vary Classroom Activities

Different activities appealed to different students. Students' preferences included working in groups, listening to the teacher talk, reading from a book, doing worksheets, participating in whole-class discussions, and doing hands-on activities. However, students agreed that learning was the primary reason for liking a certain approach, as the following three statements illustrate:

> I prefer working in groups. You have more fun and you learn at the same time. You learn quickly. So, you have fun and you do the work.

> My favorite subject is math because she made our work into a game and I caught on real fast doing it that way.

> I prefer to work by myself because most people don't read on the same level. I don't like to listen to others read. I might be ahead or behind where they are, whatever the case may be.

Students appreciated teachers who made the effort to see beyond students' behavior and understand who they really were.

Good Teachers Try to Understand Students

Students applauded teachers who did more than just teach content to them. They especially appreciated teachers who made the effort to see beyond students' behavior and understand who they really were. One student explained:

> I heard teachers talking about people, saying "Those kids can't do nothing." Kids want teachers who believe in them.

Students particularly valued teachers who recognized the possibility that students' misbehavior was not automatically targeted at the teachers.

> Sometimes a teacher don't understand what people go through. They need to have compassion. A teacher who can relate to students will know when something's going on with them. If like the student don't do work or don't under-

stand, the teacher will spend a lot of time with them.

Good Teaching = More Learning

Students clearly expressed the belief that good teaching was important because it made them learn better. Understand that when they said "better," students sometimes meant that they learned "something." Unfortunately, it was not unusual for these students to spend a semester or an entire year in a core subject in which they learned nothing, most often because they experienced a revolving door of substitutes or a new teacher who was not equipped to meet the challenges of an urban environment. Indeed, one student's advice to an early-career teacher was, "She should quit this job—it's too hard for her."

Students defined learning "better" as "getting the work right," "understanding something that a teacher already tried to teach," and "getting stuff we haven't had before." Despite the lack of definitional sophistication, students voiced no doubt about doing better in some teachers' classrooms than in others.

And because they cared about learning, it mattered greatly to students how often they encountered good teachers. Nearly every student in all six Philadelphia middle schools could identify a teacher whom they considered to be good; and nearly every one could describe a classroom situation where little learning, if any, took place.

Students' Views on School Reforms

Because good teachers were central in determining students' school experiences, these same students judged the changes that adults implemented in their schools on the basis of whether the reforms increased the number of good teachers. Students were keenly adept at evaluating the effects of significant instructional changes that had been made in their schools in terms of whether these changes promoted better teaching and, by extension, learning.

In that respect, therefore, the students tended to adopt the kind of single-minded, uncomplicated focus on improved school and classroom practices that the experts frequently urge education stakeholders to use when making strategic decisions. An illustration of how students perceived the value of one such change occurred after our original middle school students had moved on to two high schools that adopted a block schedule.

The Block Schedule

The students we had talked to in the middle school project were in the 10th grade when their schools became Talent Development High Schools and switched all of the grades from the traditional seven-period day to a block schedule in which students took four classes each semester, with 80–90 minutes devoted to each class. They saw a difference between their 9th grade and 10th grade experiences. Time seemed to be the theme that ran through many of their comparisons:

> Teachers last year wouldn't take as much time to help you.

> Now the teachers take time with you, and let you know what's got to be done.

Students predictably complained about the length of the classes with this new arrangement. Class got boring, they said—they had to sit too long, and sometimes the teachers talked forever. However, when we asked whether they preferred seven periods to four, 107 out of 148 9th and 10th graders said that they wanted the latter. Of the 41 who did not, six were neutral, and not a single student said that he or she learned better in the shorter classes. Even as they rolled their eyes about the tedium of having to be with one teacher for so long, the students explained their almost reluctant endorsements of the block schedule:

> There is more time for the teachers to help you. They can explain the work. We get to also work in groups and if I don't understand, someone else can help me.

> You learn more with just four classes because the teacher has a longer time to explain it right.

> We get to do more things. We get to work by ourselves, we get to work together, and we get to go over the work more.

> I become more focused. With more classes, oh God, it drove me crazy.

> You can build a relationship with the teacher. We can have more one-on-one interaction.

Readily available help… good explanations… variety… focused attention… closer student-teacher relationships—the block schedule, students felt, had almost single-handedly created a school full of good teachers! In spite of students' complaints about the "boredom" of longer class periods, the implementation of block scheduling had changed teachers' behaviors to correspond more closely with students' notions of good teaching—and that result alone was enough reason for students to support the reform.

Students Do Care

The block schedule has been the subject of intensive debates. Adults argue passionately, relying on research that cannot conclusively bolster either side. Our students exhibited much more single-mindedness in deciding that they supported this change. Unlike adults, they did not raise financial, political, occupational, legal, bureaucratic, or philosophical reasons why something that promoted student learning was nevertheless inadvisable. All that the Philadelphia high school students knew was that with the advent of longer classes, their teachers had changed. Instead of telling the students something once and leaving it up to them to choose to work or not, the teachers prodded, aided, and clarified more. And, over time, students noticed the true benefit of this development—they learned better.

When adults ask what they can do to make students care more about learning, their question implies that students do not care enough now. Adults, quite understandably, allow scowls, yawns, misbehavior, disrespect, and refusal to work to persuade them that apathy is rampant.

But our interviews with students in high-poverty schools suggest that these adolescents do care. The students we talked with cared so deeply about having good teachers that they wholeheartedly embraced a reform about which many adults are deeply divided. Students simply wanted good teachers because such teachers made them learn—often in spite of themselves.

Do students care about learning? Perhaps the question we should be asking is What can schools do to support and reinforce adult actions that demonstrate to students that the adults care as much about learning as the students do? The students' definitions of good teaching provide an excellent starting point for identifying just what those actions might look like.

Note

1. Our discussions with middle schoolers are reported in detail in *Listening to Urban Students: School Reform and the Teachers They Want* (Wilson & Corbett, 2001, State University of New York Press). Additional material from the project that followed students to high school is available in *Students' Perspectives on the Ninth Grade Academy of the Talent Development High Schools in Philadelphia: 1999–2000* (Corbett & Wilson, 2000, Philadelphia Education Fund).

Dick Corbett (610-408-9206) and **Bruce Wilson** (856-662-6424) are independent education researchers. Their most recent book (with coauthor Belinda Williams) is *Effort and Excellence in Urban Classrooms: Expecting and Getting Success with All Students* (Teachers College Press, 2002).

Helping Children Cope With Loss, Death, and Grief: Response to a National Tragedy

The security and safety that was a hallmark of our American society was shattered by the events of September 11th. Never before in our nation's history have so many lives been lost in a single day. Communities are impacted by multiple losses that stretch their capacities to cope. It is difficult to predict how students, adults and schools will be able to deal with the harsh realities of life in the coming weeks, months and years. Children who have experienced the loss of one or both parents, siblings, other relatives, friends, or neighbors are now suffering from profound grief.How can caring adults help these children deal with loss of this magnitude? How can we begin to understand and respond to the depths of their suffering? One thing we do know is that this will be an extremely difficult and painful task. Children and adolescents will need all the support they can get and they will require a long time to recover. Life may not be the same for anyone in this country, but those youngsters who have sustained personal losses may require significant assistance from trained, caring adults.

Expressions of Grief

Talking to children about death must be geared to their developmental level and their capacity to understand the related facts of the situation. Children will be aware of the reactions of significant adults as they interpret and react to information about death and tragedy. The range of reactions that children display in response to the death of significant others may include:

- *Emotional shock* and at times an apparent lack of feelings, which serve to help the child detach from the pain of the moment;
- *Regressive (immature) behaviors*, such as needing to be rocked or held, difficulty separating from parents or significant others, needing to sleep in parent's bed or an apparent difficulty completing tasks well within the child's ability level;

- *Explosive emotions and acting out behavior* that reflect the child's internal feelings of anger, terror, frustration and helplessness. Acting out may reflect insecurity and a way to seek control over a situation for which they have little or no control;
- **Asking the same questions over and over**, not because they do not understand the facts, but rather because the information is so hard to believe or accept. Repeated questions can help listeners determine if the child is responding to misinformation or the real trauma of the event.

Helping Children Cope

The following tips will help teachers and parents support children who have experienced the loss of parents or loved ones. Some of these recommendations come from Dr. Alan Wolfelt, Director of the Center for Loss and Life Transition in Fort Collins, Colorado.

- *Allow children to be the teachers about their grief experiences*: Give children the opportunity to tell their story and be a good listener.
- *Don't assume that every child in a certain age group understands death in the same way or with the same feelings*: All children are different and their view of the world is unique and shaped by different experiences. (Developmental information is provided below.)
- *Grieving is a process, not an event*: Parents and schools need to allow adequate time for each child to grieve in the manner that works for that child. Pressing children to resume "normal" activities without the chance to deal with their emotional pain may prompt additional problems or negative reactions.
- *Don't lie or tell half-truths to children about the tragic event*: Children are often bright and sensitive. They will see through false infor-

mation and wonder why you do not trust them with the truth. Lies do not help the child through the healing process or help develop effective coping strategies for life's future tragedies or losses.

- *Help all children, regardless of age, to understand loss and death*: Give the child information at the level that he/she can understand. Allow the child to guide adults as to the need for more information or clarification of the information presented. Loss and death are both part of the cycle of life that children need to understand.

- *Encourage children to ask questions about loss and death*: Adults need to be less anxious about not knowing all the answers. Treat questions with respect and a willingness to help the child find his or her own answers.

- *Don't assume that children always grieve in an orderly or predictable way*: We all grieve in different ways and there is no one "correct" way for people to move through the grieving process.

- *Let children know that you really want to understand what they are feeling or what they need*: Sometimes children are upset but they cannot tell you what will be helpful. Giving them the time and encouragement to share their feelings with you may enable them to sort out their feelings.

- *Children will need long-lasting support*: The more losses the child or adolescent suffered, the more difficult it will be to recover. This is especially true if they lost a parent who was their major source of support. Try to develop multiple supports for children who suffered significant losses.

- *Keep in mind that grief work is hard*: It is hard work for adults and hard for children as well.

- *Understand that grief work is complicated*: When death results from a terrorist act, this brings forth many issues that are difficult, if not impossible, to comprehend. Grieving will also be complicated by a need for vengeance or justice and by the lack of resolution of the current situation: Perpetrators may still be at large and our nation is at war. The sudden nature of death and the fact that many individuals were considered missing rather than dead further complicates the grieving process.

- *Be aware of your own need to grieve*: Focusing on the children in your care is important, but not at the expense of your emotional needs. Adults who have lost a loved one will be far more able to help children work through their grief if they get help themselves. For some

families, it may be important to seek family grief counseling, as well as individual sources of support.

Developmental Phases in Understanding Death

It is important to recognize that all children are unique in their understanding of death and dying. This understanding depends on their developmental level, cognitive skills, personality characteristics, religious or spiritual beliefs, teachings by parents and significant others, input from the media, and previous experiences with death. Nonetheless, there are some general considerations that will be helpful in understanding how children and adolescents experience and deal with death.

- *Infants and Toddlers*: The youngest children may perceive that adults are sad, but have no real understanding of the meaning or significance of death.

- *Preschoolers*: Young children may deny death as a formal event and may see death as reversible. They may interpret death as a separation, not a permanent condition. Preschool and even early elementary children may link certain events and magical thinking with the causes of death. As a result of the World Trade Center disaster, some children may imagine that going into tall buildings may cause someone's death.

- *Early Elementary School*: Children at this age (approximately 5–9) start to comprehend the finality of death. They begin to understand that certain circumstances may result in death. They can see that, if large planes crash into buildings, people in the planes and buildings will be killed. However, they may over-generalize, particularly at ages 5–6—if jet planes don't fly, then people don't die. At this age, death is perceived as something that happens to others, not to oneself or one's family.

- *Middle School*: Children at this level have the cognitive understanding to comprehend death as a final event that results in the cessation of all bodily functions. They may not fully grasp the abstract concepts discussed by adults or on the TV news but are likely to be guided in their thinking by a concrete understanding of justice. They may experience a variety of feelings and emotions, and their expressions may include acting out or self-injurious behaviors as a means of coping with their anger, vengeance and despair.

- *High School*: Most teens will fully grasp the meaning of death in circumstances such as the

World Trade Center or Pentagon disasters. They may seek out friends and family for comfort or they may withdraw to deal with their grief. Teens (as well as some younger children) with a history of depression, suicidal behavior and chemical dependency are at particular risk for prolonged and serious grief reactions and may need more careful attention from home and school during these difficult times.

Tips for Children and Teens with Grieving Friends and Classmates

Many children and teens have been indirectly impacted by the terrorists' attacks. They have learned of the deaths of people close to their friends and classmates—parents, siblings, other relatives and neighbors. Particularly in areas near the World Trade Center or Pentagon, it is not unusual to find several children in a given classroom who lost a family member—or even multiple family members. Additionally, all over the country, children have been impacted by the death of a family member at either the attack site or on board one of the four hijacked planes. Seeing their friends try to cope with such loss may scare or upset children who have had little or no experience with death and grieving. Some suggestions teachers and parents can provide to children and youth to deal with this "secondary" loss:

- Particularly with younger children, it will be important to help clarify their understanding of death. See tips above under "helping children cope."
- Seeing their classmates' reactions to loss may bring about some fears of losing their own parents or siblings. Children need reassurance from caretakers and teachers that their own families are safe. For children who have experienced their own loss (previous death of a parent, grandparent, sibling), observing the grief of a friend can bring back painful memories. These children are at greater risk for developing more serious stress reactions and should be given extra support as needed.
- Children (and many adults) need help in communicating condolence or comfort messages. Provide children with age-appropriate guidance for supporting their peers. Help them decide what to say (e.g., "Steve, I am so sorry about your father. I know you will miss him very much. Let me know if I can help you with your paper route…") and what to expect (see "expressions of grief" above).

- Help children anticipate some changes in friends' behavior. It is important that children understand that their grieving friends may act differently, may withdraw from their friends for a while, might seem angry or very sad, etc., but that this does not mean a lasting change in their relationship.
- Explain to children that their "regular" friendship may be an important source of support for friends and classmates. Even normal social activities such as inviting a friend over to play, going to the park, playing sports, watching a movie, or a trip to the mall may offer a much needed distraction and sense of connection and normalcy.
- Children need to have some options for providing support—it will help them deal with their fears and concerns if they have some concrete actions that they can take to help. Suggest making cards, drawings, helping with chores or homework, etc. Older teens might offer to help the family with some shopping, cleaning, errands, etc., or with babysitting for younger children.
- Encourage children who are worried about a friend to talk to a caring adult. This can help alleviate their own concern or potential sense of responsibility for making their friend feel better. Children may also share important information about a friend who is at risk of more serious grief reactions.
- Parents and teachers need to be alert to children in their care who may be reacting to a friend's loss of a loved one. These children will need some extra support to help them deal with the sense of frustration and helplessness that many people are feeling at this time.

Resources for Grieving and Traumatized Children

At times of severe stress, such as the trauma of the terrorist attacks on our country, both children and adults need extra support. Children closest to this tragedy may very well experience the most dramatic feelings of fear, anxiety and loss. They may have personally lost a loved one or know of friends and schoolmates who have been devastated by these treacherous acts. Adults need to carefully observe these children for signs of traumatic stress, depression or even suicidal thinking, and seek professional help when necessary.

Resources to help you identify symptoms of severe stress and grief reactions are available at the National Association of School Psychologist's website—*www.nasponline.org*. See also:

For Caregivers

Deaton, R.L. & Berkan, W.A. (1995). *Planning and managing death issues in the schools: A handbook*. Westport, CT: Greenwood Publishing Group.

Mister Rogers Website: *www.misterrogers.org* (see booklet on Grieving for children 4–10 years)

Webb, N.B. (1993). *Helping bereaved children: A handbook for practitioners*. New York: Guilford Press.

Wolfelt, A. (1983). *Helping children cope with grief*. Bristol, PA: Accelerated Development.

Wolfelt, A. (1997). *Healing the bereaved child: Grief gardening, growth through grief and other touchstones for caregivers*. Ft. Collins, CO: Companion.

Worden, J.W. (1996). *Children and grief: When a parent dies*. New York: Guilford Press

For Children:

Gootman, M.E. (1994). *When a friend dies: A book for teens about grieving and healing*. Minneapolis: Free Spirit Publishing.

Greenlee, S. (1992). *When someone dies*. Atlanta: Peachtree Publishing. (Ages 9–12).

Wolfelt, A.(2001). *Healing your grieving heart for kids*. Ft. Collins, CO: Companion.

UNIT 2
Development

Unit Selections

5. **Shaping the Learning Environment: Connecting Developmentally Appropriate Practices to Brain Research**, Stephen Rushton and Elizabeth Larkin
6. **To Be Successful—Let Them Play!**, Sally C. Hurwitz
7. **What Empathy Can Do**, Ernest Mendes
8. **Differing Perspectives, Common Ground: The Middle School and Gifted Education Relationship**, Hilda C. Rosselli and Judith L. Irvin

Key Points to Consider

- How do biology and environment interact to produce an intelligent human being?

- Why is an accurate perception of "self" important to children's self-esteem?

- How can schools and teachers provide an environment that is conducive to adolescent development?

 Links: www.dushkin.com/online/
These sites are annotated in the World Wide Web pages.

Association for Moral Education
http://www.amenetwork.org/
Child Welfare League of America
http://www.cwla.org
Pediatric Behavioral Health Resources
http://www.earlychildhoodbehavioralhealth.com/index.htm
The National Association for Child Development
http://www.nacd.org
National Association of School Psychologists (NASP)
http://www.nasponline.org/index2.html
Scholastic News Zone
http://www.scholasticnews.com

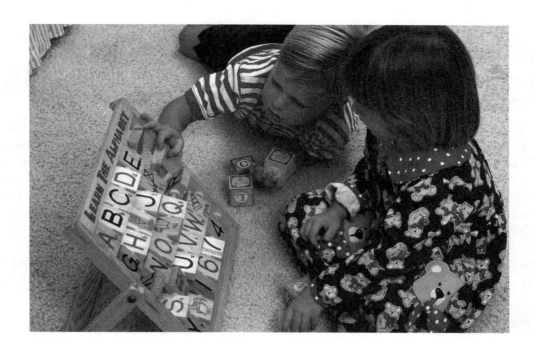

The study of human development provides us with knowledge of how children and adolescents mature and learn within the family, community, and school environments. Educational psychology focuses on description and explanation of the developmental processes that make it possible for children to become intelligent and socially competent adults. Psychologists and educators are presently studying the idea that biology as well as the environment influence cognitive, personal, social, and emotional development and involve predictable patterns of behavior.

The perceptions and thoughts that young children have about the world are often quite different when compared to adolescents and adults. That is, children may think about moral and social issues in a unique way. Children need to acquire cognitive, moral, and social skills in order to interact effectively with parents, teachers, and peers. Human development encompasses all of the above skills and reflects the child's intelligent adaptation to the environment.

Today the cognitive, moral, social, and emotional development of children takes place in a rapidly changing society. A child must develop positive conceptions of self within the family as well as at school in order to cope with the changes and become a competent and socially responsible adult. In "Shaping the Learning Environment: Connecting Developmentally Appropriate Practices to Brain Research," the authors discuss the interaction of biology and environment. The article "To Be Successful-Let Them Play!" discusses the development of cognitive and social skills in children.

Adolescence brings with it the ability to think abstractly and hypothetically and to see the world from many perspectives. Adolescents strive to achieve a sense of identity by questioning their beliefs and tentatively committing to self-chosen goals. Their ideas about the kinds of adults they want to become and the ideals they want to believe in sometimes lead to conflicts with parents and teachers. Adolescents are also sensitive about espoused adult values versus adult behavior. The articles in this unit discuss the unique needs of young adolescents and also suggest ways in which schools and teachers can help meet these needs.

Shaping the Learning Environment: Connecting Developmentally Appropriate Practices to Brain Research

Connections are shown between recent findings in brain research and principles of Developmentally Appropriate Practices to explore the implications for early childhood learning environments and teaching practices. New research on how the growing mind learns appears to bear out the value of NAEYC's constructivist approach to early childhood education where environments are designed to gain the learner's attention, foster meaningful connections with prior understanding, and maximize both short- and long-term memory through patterns and active problem solving. Each unique learner needs to feel challenged, but not fearful, so that stimulating experiences result in an exchange of ideas and promote deeper understanding.

KEY WORDS: early childhood education; brain research; developmentally appropriate practices (DAP); learning environments.

Stephen Rushton and Elizabeth Larkin

INTRODUCTION

The past several years have seen an explosion of published articles, books, and documentaries as well as a proliferation of conferences and workshop seminars focused on connecting recent neuroscientific research findings relating the child's developing brain to educational strategies. President of the James S. McDonnell Foundation, Bruer (1998), questions the validity of this marriage, stating clearly that "brain science has little to offer education practice or policy" (p. 14). He is supported by others who warn the educational community that knowledge gleaned from today's brain science may well be out-dated in several years due to its rudimentary nature. Indeed, many educators are quick to exert pressure on the educational pendulum in order to substantiate their philosophical position. However, although brain science is relatively new, Wolfe (1998), an educational consultant and expert on brain research, postulates that the bridge between neuroscience research and education is not the job of neuroscientists, but instead, that of educators.

Studies about how the human brain learns need to be interpreted in light of the classroom environment, because children spend a great deal of their time in these settings at a critical period in their development, and expectations for our professional success carry high stakes. The good news is that new research appears to be affirming what many early childhood educators have always known about effective learning environments. The bad news is that we have yet to fully explore the implications of this rapidly expanding area of knowledge in terms of generating widely recognized practices in the field of early childhood education. This paper is a beginning attempt to draw some parallels between brain research and the early childhood classroom, and so it should be acknowledged at the outset that the connections we propose here are tentative.

The National Association for the Education of Young Children's position statement on developmentally appropriate practices (DAP) for children birth through age 8 (Bredekamp & Copple, 1997) originally stated two main objectives, namely, (a) to provide "guidance to program personnel seeking accreditation by NAEYC's National Academy of Early Childhood Programs"; and (b) to counter persistent beliefs in the prevailing traditional approach to early childhood education. The educational emphasis was on a didactic, teacher-centered approach to learning that encompassed primarily whole group instructional techniques (Bredekamp & Copple, 1997, p. v). Subsequently, DAP was revised to describe a philosophical orientation that now implies a constructivist approach to teaching young children. It is built on the premise that children are social learners who actively construct meaning and knowledge as they interact with their environment.

Research on what constitutes appropriate early learning experiences has focused during the past decade on both the social-emotional (Burts, Hart, Charlesworth, & Kirk, 1990; Hyson, Hirsh-Pasek, & Rescorla, 1990) and the cognitive (Dunn, Beach, & Kontos, 1994; Sherman & Mueller, 1996) development of young children. Studies indicate that children actively engaged in learner-centered environments score higher on measures of creativity (Hyson et al., 1990), have better receptive verbal skills (Dunn et al., 1994), and are more confident in their cognitive abilities (Mantzicopoulos; Neuharth-Pritchett, & Morelock, 1994; Stopek, 1993). Additionally, Frede and Barnett (1992) reported that children who attended developmentally appropriate programs in preschool performed better in first grade on standardized assessments of achievement. A study by Burts et al. (1993) indicated that children from low socioeconomic home environments who were enrolled in DAP kindergarten classrooms showed higher reading scores in first grade than their counterparts who attended more traditional classrooms.

Unfortunately, even with these studies, there exists a wide discrepancy between what research recommends and how children are currently being taught. Dunn and Kontos (1997) postulated that DAP programs are not the norm in early childhood programs as teachers have difficulty knowing how to implement such practices. They also reported that many parents are unaware of the significant benefits of a DAP program and therefore choose a more traditional learning environment for their children.

During the past decade a parallel body of literature has emerged, one that has potentially important implications for teachers and young children alike. Research in the fields of neuroscience (Diamond & Hopson, 1998; Fitzpatrick, 1995; Sylwester, 1997), cognitive psychology (Gardner, 1993; Goldman, 1995; LaDoux, 1996), and education (Caine & Caine, 1991, 1997; Jensen, 1998; Kovalik, 1994; Wolfe, 1998) has provided some new information for teachers to better understand the learning process with implications for how to create more effective classroom environments. Combining knowledge across these disciplines could benefit teachers seeking ideas about best practices in designing environments that are consistent with what we now know about how the human brain learns. Specifically, brain research will help provide educators with strategies that can stimulate specific areas of the brain (thalamus, amygdala, hippocampus, and the frontal cortex) in order to gain the learner's attention, foster meaningful connections with prior understanding, and maximize both short- and long-term memory.

Brain research also supports the importance of developing and implementing a curriculum that is appropriate for the learner's particular developmental age. Early childhood teachers have been acutely aware for some time now that certain periods in a young child's life are more receptive for some kinds of learning. It is exciting to observe how the literature also indicates that particular "windows of opportunities" for learning do exist when the brain's plasticity, or adaptability, allows for greater amounts of information to be processed and absorbed (Wolfe, 1998).

Many teachers who embrace the early childhood philosophy are already practicing brain research-based strategies. Rushton (in press) describes a typical early childhood setting, for example, encouraging verbal interaction, integrating curriculum content areas, and providing meaningful problem-solving opportunities. Brain research, in and of itself, does not introduce new strategies for teachers; however, it does provide very concrete and important reasons why specific approaches to teaching and certain classroom strategies are more effective than others. As we will show, brain research seems to affirm many DAP principles and the underlying early childhood educational philosophy. With each DAP principle and brain research corollary, examples are provided on how to create, organize, and/or implement a learner-centered classroom that is compatible with both bodies of research. Not all principles are addressed since clear connections are not always evident. Table I outlines the parallels between the DAP standard and what we termed Brain Research principle. Additionally, the chart provides a few classroom strategies [to] connect the two similar bodies of research.

DAP Principle 1

Domains of children's development—physical, social, emotional, and cognitive—are closely related. Development in one domain influences and is influenced by development in other domains.

Educators have known for some time that development in one area is either influenced by, or is influencing another area of development. For instance, Graves (1983), Adams (1990), Weaver (1990), and others have articulated how reading and writing are connected; as a child begins to explore letters, sounds, and writing the desire and capacity to interpret, recognize, and understand these symbols increases simultaneously. And of course, this is conditional on the child's ability to see and hear—two very separate, yet interconnecting physiological functions. With even younger children, becoming mobile increases their ability to explore and understand their immediate environment. This increased activity also helps to stimulate cognitive development as they begin to interact and make sense of their surroundings (Kostelnik, Soderman, & Whiren, 1993; Sroufe, Cooper, & DeHart, 1992).

Each region of the brain consists of a highly sophisticated neurological network of cells, dendrites, and nerves that interconnect one portion of the brain with another. New stimuli entering the body via the five senses are directed immediately to the thalamus. The thalamus acts as a sorting station and reroutes the sensory input to various parts of the brain that deal specifically with each sense. These portions of the brain, called lobes, consist of millions of cells related to the specific sense that is being stimulated. For instance, the occipital lobe relates to the receiving and processing of visual information, and is located near the rear of the brain. The temporal lobe relates to language development, writing, hearing, sensory associations, and, to some extent, memory. It is located in the mid-left portion of the brain. The parietal lobe relates to higher sensory, language, and short-term memory. Finally, the frontal lobe helps us in our ability to judge, be creative, make decisions, and plan. Learning does not take place as separate and isolated events in the brain—all these parts work together.

When a child is engaged in a learning experience a number of areas of the brain are simultaneously activated. Each lobe interacts cohesively, not as separate or isolated organs, but as interdependent collective units (Sylwester, 1997), and all of them are needed in order to read and write. For instance, reading a book requires that the child picks up a book (activating the motor cortex: movement); she looks at the words (activating the occipital lobe: vision); she attempts to decipher words (activating the temporal lobe: language); and finally, she begins to think about what the words mean (activating the frontal lobe: reasoning) (Sorgen, 1999).

We know that learning and memory are strongly connected to emotions, and thus, the learning environment needs to be both stimulating and safe. Classroom experiences can be designed to allow children to investigate, reflect, and express ideas in a variety of ways that are increasingly complex and interconnected. Gardner (1993) proposed that each individual draws on multiple intelligences and generally relies on some more than others. Thus, learners need ample opportunities to use and expand their preferred intelligences, as well as adapt to and develop the other intelligences, which are all interdependent within the one brain. Then, they need opportunities to express what they know and understand in a variety of formats.

Early childhood teachers need to recognize developmental characteristics among children in a group, as well as each learner's unique capabilities. Multiage grouping is one strategy that helps to facilitate learning for a range of abilities (Kasten & Clarke, 1993). Because all the children in the class are not the same age, children can recognize more readily how individual approaches to learning tasks are both distinctive and viable. Here, what a child knows and how he knows it is not so much a factor of age as of prior experience and learning meanings. In this, or any environment, teachers of all ages will want to foster a learning context that builds trust, promotes self-direction, and encourages students to freely exchange their feelings and ideas so that the social/emotional realm is connected positively to cognitive and physical experiences.

Table I. Different Strategies and Principles

DAP position[a]	BR principle[b]	Classroom environment[c]
1. Domains of children's development—physical, social, emotional, and cognitive—are closely related. Development in one domain influences and is influenced by development in other domains.	Each region of the brain consists of a highly sophisticated neurological network of cells, dendrites, and nerves that interconnect one portion of the brain to another. The brain's emotional center is tied to the ability to learn. Emotions, learning, and memory are closely linked as different parts of the brain are activated in the learning process.	Good curriculum naturally engages many of the five senses and activates more than one of Gardner's eight intelligences at the same time. Learning is a social activity, so children need opportunities to engage in dialogue. Multiage grouping is a strategy that can support and challenge a range of learning styles and capabilities. Good learning environments build trust, empower learners, and encourage students to explore their feelings and ideas.
2. Development occurs in a relatively orderly sequence, with later abilities, skills, and knowledge building on those already acquired.	The brain changes physiologically as a result of experience. New dendrites are formed every day, "hooking" new information to prior experiences. An enriched environment increases cell weight and branching of dendrites.	Hands-on activities stimulate the various regions of the brain, and active participation helps young children to form stronger associations with existing understanding. Different stages of play (solitary, parallel, associative, collaborative), for example, can be identified and appropriate activities designed to build increasingly complex ideas through play.
3. Development proceeds at varying rates from child to child as well as unevenly within different areas of a child's functioning.	Each brain is unique. Lock-step, assembly-line learning violates a critical discovery about the human brain: each brain is not only unique, but also is growing on its own timetable.	Environments should allow choices to accommodate a range of developmental styles and capabilities. Large blocks of time, and systems for planning and tracking work, can be organized for children to share responsibility for their activity choices. Teachers need to adjust expectations and performance standards to age-specific characteristics and unique capabilities of learners.
4. Early experiences have both cumulative and delayed effects on individual children's development. Optimal periods exist for certain types of development and learning.	Brain research indicates that certain "windows of opportunity" for learning do exist. The brain's "plasticity" allows for greater amounts of information to be processed and absorbed at certain critical periods (Wolfe, 1998). The critical period for learning a spoken language is lost by about age 10 (Sorgen, 1999).	Children need opportunities to use sensory inputs, language, and motor skills. Young children also require frequent opportunities to interact verbally with peers. Repeated opportunities to interact with materials, peers, and ideas are critical for long-term memory. Second language programs will be most successful before 5th grade and should start as early as possible.
5. Development proceeds in predictable directions toward greater complexity, organization, and internalization.	The brain is designed to perceive and generate patterns. The brain is designed to process many inputs at once and prefers multi-processing. Hence, a slower linear pace reduces understanding (Caine & Caine, 1997).	Finding patterns can be built into math, language arts, science, and other subject area curriculum. Learning environments need to be organized for both low and high order thinking skills. The use of metaphor, and repeated opportunities to compare and contrast through multiple modalities, allow children to differentiate increasingly complex schemas.
7. Children are active learners, drawing on direct physical and social experience as well as culturally transmitted knowledge to construct their own understanding of the world around them.	When a child is engaged in a learning experience, a number of areas of the brain are simultaneously activated. Children raised in nonacademically oriented environments have little experience in using decontextualized language. They are more inclined to reason with visual, hands-on strategies (Healy, 1990).	Learning should be presented in a real life context so that new information builds upon prior understanding, and then generalizes to broader concepts. Field trips, guest speakers, interactive technology, and multicultural units of study will help children better understand themselves and succeed in today's world. In environments where children can interact with diverse populations (various cultures and generations—including grandparents), and use language as well as visual-spatial strategies, their learning will be enhanced.

Table I. Different Strategies and Principles (cont.)

DAP position[a]	BR principle[b]	Classroom environment[c]
8. Development and learning result from interaction of biological maturation and the environment, which includes both the physical and social worlds that children live in.	Each of the senses can be independently or collectively affected by environmental factors that in turn will affect the brain's ability to learn. Enriched environments increase dendritic branching and synaptic responses (Diamond, 1998). The simple act of reading a book may be one of the most challenging tasks the brain must perform. Speech comes naturally, but reading does not (Sorgen, 1999).	Environments should be carefully monitored for appropriate lighting, aromas, ionization (fresh air), and noise. Water and appropriate foods should be made available to children, remembering that each person's internal clock differs. Environments should offer a wealth of materials and activity choices to explore. Children need to understand the relevance of learning to read. Learning to read should be connected to the child's speaking and writing. Reading aloud and reading for meaning are two different processes, and children need opportunities to do both.
11. Children demonstrate different modes of knowing and learning and different ways of representing what they know.	"The mental mechanisms that process music (and rhyme and rhythm) are deeply entwined with the brain's other basic functions, including emotion, perception, memory, and even language" (Sorgen, 1999, p. 56). The most powerful influences on a learner's behavior are concrete, vivid images. The brain has a primitive response to pictures, symbols, and strong, simple images (Jensen, 1995).	A classroom should provide opportunities for individual children to learn via modalities other than just verbal/linguistic or logico-mathematical tasks. Rhyme and rhythm are memory aids. Children should be able to express knowledge in a variety of forms. Dramatization, music, and the visual arts should be made readily available as modes of both learning and expression. Symbolic representation can easily be built into the arts.
12. Children develop and learn best in the context of a community where they are safe and valued, their physical needs are met, and they feel psychologically secure.	Brain research has clearly demonstrated that high levels of stress, or a perceived threat, will inhibit learning (Caine & Caine, 1997). "The brain is primarily designed to survive. No intelligence or ability will unfold until or unless given the appropriate model environment" (Jensen, 1996).	The classroom environment should connect learning experiences to positive emotions. Students need to make decisions and choices about learning that is meaningful to them. The classroom culture should support risk-taking, and view failures as a natural part of the learning process.

[a]NAEYC's positions on Developmentally Appropriate Practices (DAP)

[b]What brain research (BR) suggests about how the brain learns

[c]Strategies that incorporate both BR and DAP

DAP Principle 2

Development occurs in a relatively orderly sequence, with later abilities, skills, and knowledge building on those already acquired.

DAP Principle 3

Development proceeds at varying rates from child to child as well as unevenly within different areas of a child's functioning.

We learn to sit before we crawl, and crawl before we walk. In this way, human development is ordered and sequential. Developmental psychologists have described how stages of physical, cognitive, and social development are stable and predictable over time especially in children during the first 9 years of life. Notable pioneers such as Piaget (1952) and Erikson (1963), for example, proposed different stages of play and socialization that, providing normal development, are observable, predictable, and measurable. In these hierarchies, no stage can be skipped over as the developmental process unfolds.

Wolfe and Brandt (1998) stated that the brain changes physiologically as a result of experience. As the child experiences an event for the first time, either new dendrites are formed, or the experience is associated with a similar past event hooking new information to old understanding. Much of our behavior and development is "hardwired" through a long history of human evolution (i.e., breathing, circulation, and reflexes). However, individual brains are also "softwired" in order to adapt and create new neurological networks in response to the unique environmental stimuli encountered in our individual lives. It is in the interplay between environment and genetics, hardwired automatic behaviors and softwired developing neuronetworks, that we need to be sensitive to differences among children.

Each child's uniqueness is expressed in a number of ways: personality, temperament, learning style, maturation, speed of mastering a skill, level of enjoyment of a particular subject, attention, and memory. These attributes help to identify how a particular child will learn and what style of teaching is best suited for him or her. Further, each brain's growth is largely dictated by genetic timing, and therefore is as individualized as DNA (Sylwester, 1995). In truth, there are no homogeneous groups of children; as no two children are the same, no two brains are the same. Wolfe (1998) put it succinctly when she stated: "The environment affects how genes work, and genes determine how the environment is interpreted" (p. 10).

IMPLICATIONS FOR PRACTICE

Early childhood teachers have learned that children progress through various stages of development, knowing that each child's rate of development (and each brain) is unique and different. Providing hands-on activities that both cater to the differences among children and stimulate various regions of the brain reinforces stronger associations of meaning and makes learning inherently more interesting. Teachers who are trained to observe each child's development can establish a responsive environment for different documented stages of play (solitary, parallel, associative), and carefully design appropriate activities for the child's level. Teachers of older students can pay attention to higher order thinking skills in a similar manner, challenging students with engaging problem-solving opportunities. Teaching complex skills too soon may impede learning, and conversely, not teaching children when they are ready may result in boredom and a lack of interest.

Activities that have different levels of complexity allow every child access both to the content ideas and to conversation with peers. Creating centers around the classroom with a range of problems to solve and materials to use can accommodate the differences among learners. A general overall theme may permeate the activities in each center so that the children see connections across subject areas. A center (Rushton, in press) approach can easily be adapted from preschool to third grade, using planning sheets and individualized contracts to help children discover for themselves what their particular strengths and challenges are.

Because each learner is so different, children should be able to choose activities that fit their level of development, experience, and interest. Thus, teachers will want to use a variety of teaching methods and materials to ensure that every child becomes interested in exploring ideas, so that their auditory, visual, tactile, or emotional preferences are accounted for. More important, teachers need to remember that each child's educational experiences inside the classroom play a part in shaping a lifetime of learning habits. Different children feel challenged by different problems, and threatened by different social circumstances, and these matter in what and how they learn.

DAP Principle 4

Early experiences have both cumulative and delayed effects on individual children's development. Optimal periods exist for certain types of development and learning.

Principle 4 suggests that each learning experience lays groundwork for future learning, either positively or negatively. The child's ability to learn and interpret new information is directly related to the frequency of prior experience with related ideas. Brain research also indicates that certain windows of opportunities for learning do exist (Sorgen, 1999). In some instances, it is vital to development that a particular sense be stimulated. For instance, it has been demonstrated that some animals have had their vision obscured at key times in their development and were unable to ever see again. The blueprint, so to speak, relating to vision simply cannot be reestablished if not stimulated to grow in the first several years (Wolfe, 1998). The same can be said for developing oral language. In extreme cases in which a child has been abused, neglected, and cut off from society, speech pathologists have been unable to help those individuals speak normally.

Language and motor development both require children to actively engage with others. Conversation and physical activity are extremely important for the development of the brain. To facilitate optimal development, young children require opportunities to interact with each other regularly, encounter new vocabulary, construct arguments, express emotions, and stretch their muscles. Thus, learning environments should encourage verbal interactions, moving around the room as children work on projects or pursue a line of inquiry, and plentiful occasions to use manipulative materials including gross motor equipment.

Second language acquisition is most successful prior to fifth or sixth grade when the necessary structures in the brain for language learning are still in place. Young children seem to be particularly adept at mimicry, especially when language is rhythmic and rhyming. Also, the brain looks for patterns and connections, and repetition is critical for long-term memory. Introducing young children to more than one language is extremely beneficial, even if they do not yet understand how language is structured grammatically or written down. This early learning creates a foundation for later, more formal, study of another language.

DAP Principle 5

Development proceeds in predictable directions toward greater complexity, organization, and internalization.

The brain is designed to perceive and generate patterns and is constantly seeking to place new information into existing neurological networks. If no prior network exists, then new dendrites will be formed. Each layer of learning builds upon former networks. It has been suggested that the myelin sheath that surrounds the axons (the long tentacles of a dendrite) thicken with repeated exposure to a thought, idea, or experience. The greater the complexity of an experience, the thicker the myelin becomes. The belief is that thicker myelin results in faster recall of an event and greater memory (Diamond & Hopson, 1998). If this is true, then repetition of activities helps to thicken the myelin and thus, reinforce students' understanding.

Since no two children learn at the same rate, it is crucial that children be given repeated opportunities and ample time to explore, play, and socialize while they work in various curriculum areas (paint, blocks, dramatic play, listening center, water table, science). A typical K–3 classroom covers content in reading, writing, and mathematics, and time permitting, social studies, science, and the arts. Curriculum is often presented as separate subjects in distinct units with little overlap. Information would be better presented in a context of real life experiences where new information can build upon prior knowledge, so that learners understand how it is meaningful to them. Field trips are an excellent strategy to connect new learning to real world applications. When studying pollution, for example, students might visit the landfill, clean water treatment center, recycling plant, or local municipal garbage collection center rather than just viewing pictures and reading texts about the subject. The learner should be able to connect new information to well-established conceptual frameworks in an experiential manner, not as isolated bits of information that have no meaningful connection.

DAP Principle 7

Children are active learners, drawing on direct physical and social experience as well as culturally transmitted knowledge to construct their own understanding of the world around them.

DAP Principle 8

Development and learning result from interaction of biological maturation and the environment, which includes both the physical and social worlds that children live in.

The environment in which a child learns, both the explicit physical surroundings (people, manipulative materials, books) and the implicit cultural norms (alphabet, numerical symbols, values), shapes that child's understanding of the meaning of his or her experiences. Bredekamp and Copple (1997) stated that "young children actively learn from observing and participating with other children and adults" and that they need to "form their own hypotheses and keep trying them out through social interaction, physical manipulation, and their own thought processes" (p. 13).

The human brain is constantly seeking information from a variety of stimuli. These data are interpreted through all the senses and are then organized by the brain. Since each of the senses can be independently or collectively affected by environmental factors, they will affect the brain's overall ability to learn. Therefore, it stands to reason that the learning environment should make children physically comfortable—they need good lighting, fresh air, and a reasonable level of noise. In addition, children cannot learn when they are hungry or tired because their minds will be focused on the body's signals to eat or sleep. They need to move around to oxygenate their blood and exercise their muscles.

The social environment in a classroom relies heavily on language, and the simple act of reading is one of the most challenging tasks the brain performs. But the brain perceives patterns, and so we can help children develop language skills by looking for letter patterns in words, word patterns in sentences such as rhyming or alliteration, patterns in story sequence, and the like. Most importantly, we need to help children see the relevance of learning language and becoming competent readers, so that their motivation to learn and attention to the challenge are both high. The learning environment can reflect children's interests by including them in conversations about which books will be read.

Children who have been raised in nonacademically oriented environments have less experience using decontextualized language than their peers. In other words, they are less apt to rely on words to describe events to others outside the context where they occurred, and oral language skill development will affect later reading ability (Snow, Tabors, & Nicholson, 1995). These children may communicate more readily through using visual images, physical activity, and symbolic representation.

The curriculum can include practice in storytelling as a way to develop oral language skills and to make connections with children's real world experiences at the same time. The more children are exposed to and talk about experiences that are new to them, the more connections they can make to what they already know. Children also need opportunities to express ideas and understanding in physically active ways, such as through visual and dramatic arts. Repeated practice helps children to recall information and master physical tasks. As new information builds on prior understanding, children are able to generalize their own experiences to broader concepts.

DAP Principle II

Children demonstrate different modes of knowing and learning and different ways of representing what they know.

Gardner's (1993) work in multiple intelligences and assessment has pointed to the need for classrooms to provide more occasions for children to use music, bodily-kinesthetic, visual-spatial, and interpersonal domains to learn and express understanding. Brain research has indicated that the "mental mechanisms that process music (and rhyme and rhythm) are deeply entwined with the brain's other basic functions, including emotion, perception,

memory, and even language" (Sorgen, 1999, p. 56). If music and movement can be used to build children's social/emotional experiences in the classroom, and to reinforce memory, language development, or even mathematical skills, we are likely to reach more kinds of learners than we would if we relied solely on narrowly defined subject areas.

Jensen (1998) has said that the most powerful influences on a learner's behavior are concrete, vivid images. The brain, he added, has a primitive response to pictures, symbols, and strong, simple images. It follows, then, that our systems of symbolic representation (the alphabet and numbers) are learned better if they can be connected to concrete, vivid images such as pictures and expressive motions. Children's memories are helped by physically representing what they know in addition to using language, so the arts should hold an important place in the curriculum. Children can draw, paint, construct, and dramatize what they know and understand.

DAP Principle 12

Children develop and learn best in the context of a community where they are safe and valued, their physical needs are met, and they feel psychologically secure.

Research on the brain and learning has clearly demonstrated that high levels of stress, or a perceived threat by the child, inhibits learning (Caine & Caine, 1997). It is the brain's principal job to ensure survival. The brain's emotional center is tied to its ability to learn. The amygdala checks all incoming sensory information first to see if it fits a known impression of danger. If a threat is perceived, the ability to learn is greatly impeded as the entire body automatically gears up to defend itself.

Teachers have a central responsibility to create a learning environment that feels relaxed enough to allow children's attention to focus on the curriculum, and challenging enough to excite interest. Evaluation is one component of the educational milieu, and thus, all assessment situations need to avoid generating a perceived threat. Clearly, using a variety of methods for collecting data enhances the likelihood of matching an individual learner's ways of knowing, and provides a more complete picture of what is known and understood.

Emotions, learning, and memory are closely linked as different parts of the brain are activated in the learning process. It is crucial, especially during the first several years of the child's life, to provide a rich and safe environment that lays groundwork for this neurological network to develop. Early childhood programs ought to invite children to make choices about what and how they learn so that they are more willing to take risks and view their experiences as both relevant and positive. Children need to explore, play, and discover, in a safe and healthy environment, using all of their senses in making connections from one part of the curriculum to another.

CONCLUSION

Technological advancements during the past decade have seen the development of some sophisticated equipment that has helped to better understand the functions of the human brain. This technology and subsequent understanding of the brain, albeit overwhelming for most educators, supports many of the philosophical tenets of constructivism, rooted in the philosophy of Dewey (1964). He believed that children learn best when interacting in a rich environment. He also believed that children constructed meaning from real life applications, and further, he knew that when various senses were used simultaneously, the probability of learning would be greater. Our modern educational terminology—such as integrated curriculum, whole language, hands-on learning, authentic assessment, and developmentally appropriate practices—not only echoes brain research, but also, we believe, contains many of the underpinning beliefs, thoughts, and tenets of Dewey.

Brain research helps to explain further why constructivist educators such as Dewey (1964), Piaget and Inhelder (1969), and Vygotsky (1967) still prevail. It is hoped that with new understanding about how the brain works, combined with the tenets of Developmentally Appropriate Practice, our ability to educate future generations will be greatly enhanced. The neuroscientist's job is to better understand the workings of the mind and brain; it is our job, as educators, to carefully sift through their findings and connect them to what we know empirically about how children learn best.

REFERENCES

Adams, M. J. (1990). *Beginning to read: Thinking and learning about print.* Urbana-Champaign, IL: The Reading Research and Education Center.

Bredekamp, S., & Copple, C. (1997). *Developmentally appropriate practice in early childhood programs* (Rev. ed.). Washington, DC: National Association for the Education of Young Children.

Burts, D., Hart, C., Charlesworth, R., & Kirk, L. (1990). A comparison of frequencies of stress behaviors observed in kindergarten children in classrooms with developmentally appropriate versus developmentally inappropriate instructional practices. *Early Childhood Research Quarterly, 5,* 407–423.

Burts, D., Hart, C., Charlesworth, R., DeWolf, D., Ray, J., Manuel K., & Fleege, P. (1993). Developmental appropriateness of kindergarten programs and academic outcomes in first grade. *Journal of Research in Childhood Education, 8*(1), 23–31.

Caine, R. N., & Caine, G. (1997). *Education on the edge of possibility.* Alexandria, VA: ASCD.

Dewey, J. (1964). The relation of theory to practice in education. In R. Archamault (Ed.), *John Dewey on education: Selected writings* (pp. 313–338). New York: Random House.

Diamond, M., & Hopson, J. (1998). *Magic trees of the mind: How to nurture your child's intelligence, creativity, and healthy emotions from birth through adolescence.* New York: Penguin Putnam.

Dunn, L., Beach, S., & Kontos, S. (1994). Quality of the literacy environment in day care and children's development. *Journal of Research in Childhood Education, 9*(1), 24–34.

Elkind, D. (1981). *The hurried child.* Reading, MA: Addison-Wesley.

Erikson, E. H. (1963). *Childhood and society.* New York: Norton.

Fitzpatrick, S. (1995). Smart brains: Neuroscientists explain the mystery of what makes us human. *American School Board Journal.*

Frede, E., & Barnett, W. S. (1992). Developmentally appropriate public school preschool: A study of implementation of the High/Scope curriculum and its effects on disadvantaged children's skills at first grade. *Early Childhood Research Quarterly, 7,* 483–499.

Gardner, H. (1993). *Multiple intelligences: The theory in practice.* New York: Basic Books.

Graves, D. (1983). *Writing: Teachers and children at work.* Portsmouth, NH: Heinemann.

Hirsh-Pasek, K., Hyson, M., & Rescorla, L. (1990). Academic environments in preschool: Do they pressure or challenge young children? *Early Education and Development, 1,* 401–423.

Hyson, M., Hirsh-Pasek, K., & Rescorla, L. (1990). The classroom practices inventory: An observation instrument based on NAEYC's guidelines for developmentally appropriate practices for 4- and 5-year-old children. *Early Childhood Research Quarterly, 5,* 475–494.

Jensen, E. (1998). *Teaching with the brain in mind.* Alexandria, VA: Association for Supervision and Curriculum Development.

Kasten, W., & Clark, B. (1993). *The multi-age classroom: A family of learners.* New York: Richard C. Owen Publishers.

Kostelnik, M., Soderman, A., & Whiren, A. (1993). *Healthy young children: A manual for programs.* New York: Macmillan.

LaDoux, J. (1996). *The emotional brain: The mysterious underpinnings of emotional life.* New York: Simon & Schuster.

Piaget, J. (1952). *The origins of intelligence in children.* Toronto: George J. McLeod.

Piaget, J., & Inhelder, B. (1969). *The psychology of the child.,* New York: Basic Books.

Rushton, S. (in press). A developmentally appropriate and brain-based compatible learning environment. *Young Children.*

Sherman, C., & Mueller, D. (1996, June). *Developmentally appropriate practice and student achievement in inner-city elementary schools.* Paper presented at Head Start's Third National Research Conference, Washington, DC. (ED 401 354)

Sorgen, M. (1999, June). *Applying brain research to classroom practice.* Materials presented at the University of South Florida Brain/Mind Connections Conference, Sarasota, FL.

Spodek, B. (Ed.). (1993). *The handbook of research on the education of young children.* New York: Teachers College Press.

Snow, C. E., Tabors, P. O., & Nicholson, P. A. (1995, Fall/Winter). SHELL: Oral language and early literacy skills in kindergarten and first grade children. *Journal of Research in Childhood Education, 10,* 37–48.

Sroufe, L. A., Cooper, R. G., & DeHart, G. G. (1992). *Child development: Its nature and course* (2nd ed.). New York: Knopf.

Sylwester, R. (1997). The neurobiology of self-esteem and aggression. *Educational Leadership, 54*(5), 75–79.

Vygotsky, L. (1967). Play and its role in the mental development of the child. *Soviet Psychology, 12,* 62–76.

Weaver, C. (1990). *Understanding whole language: From principles to practice.* Portsmouth, NH: Heinemann.

Wolfe, J., & Brandt, R. (1998). What we know from brain research. *Educational Leadership, 56*(3), 8–14.

Stephen Rushton and Elizabeth Larkin are from the University of South Florida at Sarasota

Correspondence should be directed to Stephen Rushton, University of South Florida at Sarasota, 5700 N. Tamiami Trail, PMC 217, Sarasota, Florida 34243; e-mail: srushton@sar.usf.edu

---

From *Early Childhood Education Journal,* Volume 29, No. 1, 2001, pp. 25-33. Copyright © 2001 by Kluwer Academic Publishers. Reprinted with kind permission from Springer Science and Business Media.

For Parents Particularly—Mary Jane Blasi

To Be Successful—
Let Them Play!

Sally C. Hurwitz

Upon observing her son's class, a parent of a kindergarten child asked the principal, "These kids are just playing—when are they going to start learning something?"

All parents reach a point when they anxiously wait for their children to begin "real school." Up until that time, many parents view their children's activities as nothing more than mindless play. It is no surprise to parents that healthy young children devote much of their time and energy to play. After all, to adults play is just for fun; it's relaxing and recreational, not work. They perceive child's play as just that, play. And more important, many feel there is no learning value in their children's play.

Nothing could be further from the truth. Play for young children is creative, spontaneous, unpredictable, and absolutely fun. While play may seem like a frivolous activity, it is an important medium for young children's learning. It is a significant contributor to the child's cognitive, physical, emotional, and social development.

Play is the natural and best way for children to learn as they investigate for themselves and observe others at play and work. They are natural anthropologists who have a need and desire to investigate their world through real experiences and natural environments.

Take a moment to remember your own childhood. How did you spend your time? In play, of course! Outside or inside, quietly or loudly, with a big mess or no mess at all, play is the way children make sense out of the complicated and complex world in which we live. Play is the medium children use to take risks, to challenge themselves both physically and mentally, to create something new, to deal with fears, and to enjoy the moment as they construct new meanings.

For children, play is at the very heart of their learning and development. Five qualities distinguish play for young children from other activities:

- It is a process. The outcome is not as important as the process itself.
- Play is child-initiated. The activity is done for no other reason than the child wants to do it.
- In play, everything and anything can happen: a sheet over a table becomes a castle and the little girl inside is the princess. There is no question that the functions of objects are transformed during play—a process called nonliteral play.
- Play becomes the arena for testing rules, both logical and illogical. Rules freely appear and disappear in children's play; they may be simple or complex, and they are created from children's previous knowledge. An example of rules in play is the "rule" of roles. For example, when young children play in the housekeeping area, you will often hear one of the children assigning roles to each of the other children ("You be the baby").
- Play is very much an activity of the mind. Children may become deeply engrossed in their play and find it difficult to stop when asked. Engagement in play involves the mind in an active process as a child investigates, explores, and inquires during play.

Within a classroom setting, play and the curriculum should be deeply integrated; experienced teachers should be in a position to observe as children's cognitive, social, and physical learning takes place. A quality curriculum should rely heavily on play. Research supports the importance of play for young children, but it must be tempered with what we know about the individual child and what is age-appropriate for the child.

Children need multiple opportunities for meaningful play in a variety of settings and environments. Through many experiences, children begin to construct their knowledge and understanding of multiple skills, including creativity, cognitive competencies, social skills, and physical skills. These play experiences force children to constantly reexamine what they know to be true, and they challenge them to construct a new understanding based on new information. This "constructing" is repeated many times in a young child's life and helps him/her to construct a personal understanding of the world. It sounds simple enough, but the trick for parents, caregivers, and teachers is to provide multiple meaningful and appropriate experiences for the child within a safe environment.

When parents, caregivers, and teachers provide opportunities for children to play, they also are providing them with learning opportunities. During play, children may expand their expressive language proficiency; develop number sense as they build with blocks and other constructive materials; develop creativity through art activities and problem solving; and develop important social skills, such as taking turns and cooperating. They develop the eye-hand coordination necessary to hold a pencil and learn to read and write; develop a strong body through fine and gross motor activities; and develop early essential math skills, such as number concepts and classification skills. The dramatic arts area and the manipulatives area provide skills essential for an understanding of how things work, the library corner provides children a place for developing story sense and comprehension, and the ma-nipulative area offers opportunities to learn about the properties of a variety of objects. This list is not comprehensive, but it demonstrates that play is an essential for young children as they construct their own knowledge about the world in which they live.

Parents, caregivers, and teachers see children play in many ways. Learning to identify different types of play may give you further understanding of their importance. The many different play categories include:

- Practice Play—play that children do repeatedly, solely for pleasure, such as playing in sand and pouring it through their fingers.
- Constructive Play—play where children construct or create something, such as block building.
- Rough and Tumble Play—play that involves laughing and pretending; as the name implies, it can get a little rough (it is not aggressive play and, when done in a safe area, is an acceptable form of play).
- Dramatic Play—play that gives children the opportunity to take on the role of another person or of an object.
- Games With Rules—play governed by a set of rules, such as a game of "Duck, Duck, Goose."

Understanding these categories helps teachers plan appropriate play activities to meet the developmental needs of the whole child.

Many forms of learning are influenced in part by the belief that play is a beneficial component of young children's learning. A large body of research supports the value of play for a child's development. The research demonstrates that play promotes: cognitive development, problem solving, language development, creativity, discovery, reasoning and thought, group cooperation, social skills, and fine and gross motor skills. So the next time you see your children engaged in play, remember that they are practicing and developing the skills necessary to be successful students and members of the community. Let them have fun and play!

Sally C. Hurwitz is Coordinator of Field Experience, College of Education, Arizona State University West, Phoenix.

What Empathy Can Do

Students respond to us because we care—and because they like us.

By Ernest Mendes

With pursed lips and a furrowed brow, Julie strode into my second-period social studies class. She sat down, slammed her books on the desk, and said, "I hate this class!" I stood at my podium, reviewing my notes for the next period. On hearing her remark, I looked up and saw that Julie was not happy. I took a deep breath and walked slowly toward her. I squatted down next to her desk.

"Julie, you're really upset. What's wrong?" I asked.

"It's not fair. I hate this!" She paused. I waited. "We had a stupid pop quiz in math last period. I didn't have time to study last night because we had to pick my grandma up from the airport and got home late."

I acknowledged her frustration, took another deep breath, and said,

> Julie, just hang in there today. Do whatever you can. It's tough to have that happen first thing in the morning.

I walked back to my podium. By now, most of the sophomore students had arrived.

As class began, I noticed that Julie sat dazed at her desk. After about 15 minutes, she opened her notebook and began to participate in class. When the bell rang, she left without a word, which wasn't unusual for her; she rarely spoke when she entered my class and never made eye contact.

The next day, Julie was the first to arrive in class once again. As she passed by my podium, she smiled at me, her eyes bright, and said exuberantly, "Good morning, Mr. Mendes."

"Good morning, Julie," I replied.

"So, what are we going to do today?" she asked. I gave her a thumbnail sketch. When class began, she actively participated. When class was over, she passed by me and said enthusiastically, "Have a good day, Mr. Mendes." The next day—and every day thereafter—she greeted me, participated in class, and

left with a goodbye. She raised her grade from a C to an A that semester.

What happened here? Am I suggesting that my empathetic response during a brief conversation influenced her behavior that dramatically? Dozens of variables were present in Julie's life during that time. I know from my 23 years of teaching, however, that Julie's change was not an exception, but rather the rule. Every student with whom I consciously made an effort to establish a rapport or a caring relationship demonstrated dramatic changes in behavior, effort, and performance.

Positive responses create an emotional bank account that can absorb relational difficulties that occur along the way.

Students do respond just because we care—and because they like us. Some educators want students simply to respect rather than like their teachers. But earning the respect of students is not enough. Students must perceive that we care, and even that we like them deep down, as people. As it turns out, they will work harder for someone they like than for someone they simply respect. And in our professional adult capacity, we can maintain both friendship-like qualities and our leadership role.

Having rapport means that two people are alike physiologically, emotionally, or cognitively, even if the similarity is temporary. Knowing students' interests and concerns is one sure way to build rapport. Being physically on the same level when talking with students—matching their rate of speech and their tone when it is positive—can help build rapport. Using students' names during lectures and acknowledging all responses in some way during class discussions are also part of building rapport.

What does it take to build rapport? The teacher needs a genuine desire to build a connection with students and strategies for reframing experiences so that they elicit a student's interest rather than frustration.

Nurture and Structure

Moustakas (1994) asks student teachers to draw from personal experience to create a profile of an effective relationship with a caring adult and then work to replicate this relationship with their students. Students feel special, for example, when the teacher affirms their interests and needs and makes suggestions rather than impositions. Psychologist Carl Rogers (1951) described the ideal therapeutic relationship as one in which the therapist is genuine and nonjudgmental, providing unconditional positive regard. Teachers can develop these characteristics of a good therapist to create healthy teacher-student relationships.

Developing caring relationships does not negate the need for limits and structure in the classroom. Students need both structure and nurture, and the ways in which the teacher responds to these needs in the classroom are crucial. Caring teachers succeed in managing their classrooms effectively, including maintaining discipline, solving problems, and setting expectations, limits, and rewards (Gootman, 1997). Caring classrooms are home to warm, supportive, stable relationships and to the social and ethical dimensions of learning (Lewis, Schapps, & Watson, 1996).

Emotional Intelligence

Self-awareness and self-management are crucial elements of emotional intelligence. Self-awareness entails identifying your own emotional state—knowing when you feel frustrated, for example, and why. Self-awareness includes being able to distinguish between your own feelings and those of others.

Self-management is the ability to manage your emotions and use them to move toward a desired outcome. Self-managing behavior might include taking some deep breaths or calming yourself with internal suggestions, such as "Relax" or "I can handle this." Once you have achieved self-control, it is easier to listen and respond to others with *I-messages*, stating how the other person's statement is affecting you.

Earning the respect of students is not enough. Students must perceive that we care, and even that we like them deep down, as people.

When we are aware and in control of our own emotions, we also need to be aware of other people's emotions so that we can make appropriate choices about how and what we communicate. Training and coaching can help develop this skill in reading between the lines.

In a study that measured the emotional intelligence of 49 high school teachers, I found that a teacher's ability to accurately identify emotions was directly related to the number of years that the teacher had taught (Mendes, 2002). This finding is consistent with other research on emotional intelligence (Mayer, Caruso, & Salovey, 2000). Classroom teachers must possess these competencies if they are to succeed with students.

Choosing Empathy

Sometimes empathy can serve multiple purposes. For example, viewing a situation empathetically can lead to a calmer internal state, which can influence the response of the teacher. In the case of Julie, I thought about how awful it is to feel that angry and almost out of control. That insight influenced my behavior. In addition, my observation allowed me to perceive Julie's upset state. This ability to read and identify emotions works together with self-management and leads to the optimal timing of responses.

In the classroom, we might be excited about a great activity for our students. But if a student is having a bad day, how do we respond? Do we perceive the student as apathetic and as having a negative attitude? Do we stick to our behavioral management plan and give the student a warning, soon to be followed by a set of consequences?

How do we discern, in the moment, what state the student is in and what course of action would be best? It's not always an easy task. The observation skills required to make these quick daily decisions are part of empathy.

The Adolescent Brain

Every time I read about neuroscientists' findings about developmental stages, I am amazed that adolescents can function in a classroom at all. The adolescent's brain is undergoing a state of reorganization, and the frontal lobe region, which is crucial in controlling impulses and making healthy decisions, has not finished developing (Giedd et al., 1999). Further, uncontrollable temper outbursts and violence may be due to mini-seizures in the temporal lobes (Amen, 1998). When making important decisions, the amygdala, an emotional trigger, gets activated more frequently in an adolescent brain than in an adult brain. Hormones magnify the intensity of moods and behavior (Amen, 1998). A bad family situation, for example, may be wreaking havoc inside the student's head.

These difficulties are not excuses for student performance and behavior, but they represent some of the factors that play into the observable behavior you see every day. When I remember these mitigating factors, I feel more empathy.

How to Build Relationships

- Acknowledge all responses and questions.
- Mention students' names, skills, ideas, and knowledge in your presentations—without mentioning weaknesses or confidential information.
- Use self-disclosure when appropriate. Be a real person.
- Use responses beginning with "I agree," "I appreciate," and "I respect."
- Ask students about their interests. Collect an information card at the beginning of the year and have students update it regularly. Pay attention to students' nonverbal responses and make adjustments as you capture their interest or hit neutral ground.
- Build on what you hear from students by sharing stories, interests, and worries.
- Display empathy with individuals and with classes by communicating what you think their needs or feelings might be.
- Listen actively. Match students' expressions and conveyed moods. Paraphrase their message, when appropriate. Know your students' world and go there first to open the relationship door.

Opening the Relationship Door

Gottman describes people's attempts to make connections with others as *bidding* (Gottman & DeClaire, 2001). We make numerous attempts at interpersonal connections throughout the day, in all of our relationships, and people can respond to our bidding in one of three ways: toward the bid, away from it, or against it.

For example, if a person in your proximity commented on the warm weather, and you asked him to pass the newspaper, you would be moving *away* from response. If instead you agreed that a heat wave is in the making, you would be moving *toward* the attempted bid for connection. You would be making an *against* response if you replied, "What are you, the weather man?" Relationships that include many *toward* responses are more durable than those with many *away* and *against* responses. Positive responses create an emotional bank account that can absorb relational difficulties that occur along the way.

Bidding takes verbal and nonverbal forms. Depending on the relationship, a glance, a touch, or a verbal "hey" may be appropriate. When a student asks a question that is out of context and unrelated to the classroom discussion, we have choices: We can ignore it; acknowledge it and suggest another time to address it; or make a sarcastic response. Every response is either making a deposit to or a withdrawal from our relationship account. When an individual, either in a group or one-on-one, risks sharing an idea or thought with you, you have an opportunity to deposit or withdraw. Which will you choose?

Students need both structure and nurture, and the ways in which the teacher responds to these needs in the classroom are crucial.

We may need to practice making clear, recognizable bids to others. When we do not clearly communicate with students, they may misinterpret our intention. For example, an after-class conversation regarding a student's behavior may start out harshly and set the conversation on a downward spiral:

> Jessie, knock it off. I'm tired of your wisecracks in class. You're being a smart aleck, and you're going to be sorry if you don't stop.

Instead, the teacher should ask the student what's going on:

> You didn't seem your usual self today in class.

The student explains. The teacher uses self-control:

> When you said, "This class is stupid," I became defensive and felt angry because I thought you were attacking me in front of the class. I want to know where that comment came from.

The student explains. The teacher responds:

> In the future, if you're angry with me or at something else, I want you to take out a piece of paper and write me a note describing your feelings and why you feel that way. Then you can share it with me later. How does that sound?

The student comments. The teacher finishes:

> OK, I'll talk with you more tomorrow.

This dialogue is only one of the typical, ongoing bidding scenarios we face daily. How we bid and respond to bids has a cumulative effect.

To open the relationship door, teachers need to understand their students' world. To build relationships in the classroom, teachers need to know their students, their own strengths and limitations, and how to connect with students by demonstrating genuine interest in them.

References

Amen, D. G. (1998). *Change your brain, change your life*. New York: Random House.

Giedd, J. N., Blumenthal, J., Jeffries, N. O., Castellanos, F. X., Liu, H., Zijdenbos, A., Paus, T., Evans, A. C., & Rapoport, J. L. (1999). Brain development during childhood and adolescence. *Nature Neurosciences*, 2(10), 861-863.

Gootman, M. (1997). *The caring teacher's guide to discipline: Helping young students learn self-control, responsibility, and respect*. Thousand Oaks, CA: Corwin.

Gottman, J., & DeClaire, J. (2001). *The relationship cure*. New York: Crown Publishers.

Lewis, C., Schapps, E., & Watson, M. (1996). The caring classroom's academic edge. *Educational Leadership*, 54(1), 16-21.

Mayer, J., Caruso, D., & Salovey, P. (2000). Emotional intelligence meets traditional standards for an intelligence. *Intelligence, 27*(4), 267-298.

Mendes, E.J. (2002). *The relationship between emotional intelligence and occupational burnout in secondary school teachers*. Ann Arbor, MI: ProQuest Information and Learning Company.

Moustakas, C. (1994). *Phenomenological research methods*. Thousand Oaks, CA: Sage.

Rogers, C. (1951). *Client-centered therapy: Its current practice, implications, and theory*. Boston: Houghton Mifflin.

Ernest Mendes is an education consultant and President of Mendes Training and Consulting, 374 E. H St., Ste. A, PMB-314, Chula Vista, CA 91910; erniemendes@cox.net; www.erniemendes.com.

Differing Perspectives, Common Ground: The Middle School and Gifted Education Relationship

What Research Says

Middle school educators and advocates for the gifted share much common ground for addressing the needs of a wide variety of learners: flexible pacing, independent study, and teaching thinking skills.

By Hilda C. Rosselli & Judith L. Irvin

A curious relationship has evolved over the years between the fields of gifted education and middle grades education. On an initial glance, beliefs important to each field indicate an amazing overlap in philosophy and practices. However, when middle grades philosophy positioned heterogeneous grouping as one of the preeminent guideposts for policies and practices endorsed by the field, the common ground between the two fields lessened. Leaders in gifted education, unable to embrace a total abandonment of grouping, responded vehemently and expressed reservations regarding the ability of the middle school movement to meet the needs of high ability students (Gallagher, Coleman, & Nelson, 1995; Plucker & McIntire, 1996; Sicola, 1990; Tomlinson, 1992; 1994). The resulting differences reframed the relationship between experts from gifted education and middle grades education and fueled lively debates on the moral and efficacious nature of ability grouping. Others sought to re-examine the goodness of fit between the two movements by moving beyond the rhetoric of differences towards a healthier focus on programs and practices (Coleman, Gallagher, & Howard, 1993; Coleman & Gallagher, 1995; Mills & Durden, 1992; Rosselli, 1995). At the same time, with the advent of the National Research Center on the Gifted and Talented and federally funded Javits grants, a more defined research focus in gifted education provided a rich source for examining implications for middle level education. This article provides an overview of the literature that has historically framed the

debates between gifted education and middle grades education followed by discussion of research that seeks common ground between the two fields and implications relative to middle school education policies and practices that hold promise for considering the unique needs of high ability students.

Nature and definition of giftedness and intelligence

Although the field of gifted education has traditionally been grounded in the use of IQ scores for identification and definition purposes, the last twenty years has seen a growing interest in other views of intelligence and giftedness. On the heels of Howard Gardner's work (1983) has followed a redefining of gifted education by well-renowned experts (Gagne, 1995; Feldhusen, 1992; Renzulli, 1994; Treffinger, 1992) who are not convinced that traditional IQ measures are sufficient for identifying the unique and individual talents of capable youth. With the publication of National Excellence: A Case for Developing America's Talent (U.S. Department of Education, 1993), the term "talent" appeared liberally throughout the report and served as a cornerstone for encouraging more overlap between education reform and the development of individual gifts and talents. Furthermore, the 1990s saw growth in a researchable knowledge base regarding the diversity rather than the homogeneity within the gifted population (Betts & Neihart, 1988; Ford, 1993; Maker, 1996; Nielsen, Higgins, Hammond, & Williams, 1993). This work specifically focuses attention on the historically under-represented presence of students from culturally diverse backgrounds, from low socioeconomic environments, with limited English proficiency, and with two exceptionalities.

Characteristics and needs of gifted students

A number of developmental characteristics that apply to middle level adolescents apply to gifted adolescents as well, particularly: rapid physical growth, varying levels of cognitive operations, sporadic brain growth, affective ambivalence, and capacity of introspection. Like all adolescents, teens who are gifted must also cope with the achievement of independence, discovery of identity as a person, exploration and acceptance of sexuality, development of meaningful interpersonal relationships, and establishment of personal values and philosophy (Clark, 1988). Clearly, being gifted places some additional twists on the already difficult tasks of adolescent maturation. Wallace (1985) described the gifted adolescent as a doubly marginal individual. The obvious move is away from the family, which is part of the adolescent experience, as well as a move away from the system that perhaps supported and nurtured a specific gift or talent. This new autonomy may cause an additional burden or responsibility for the gifted adolescent, just at a time when he/she has few appropriate peer role models to emulate. Manaster and Powell (1983) reported that gifted adolescents may feel "out of stage" due to their perfectionism and focus on success, causing them to be out of touch with their immediate environment. In addition, alienation from their age-peer group may be influenced by gifted students' awareness of their unusual abilities or interests, causing them to feel "out of phase." Lastly, these students may feel "out of sync" as though they do not, should not, or cannot fit in. Buescher (1985) also found that ownership, or the simultaneous owning and questioning of the abilities of these youngsters, may compete with the beliefs that a debt is owed towards parents, teachers, and society.

To be gifted and to be under-challenged in school creates another undesirable combination. High ability students have reported school work being too easy (Tomlinson, 1995), spending little or no time studying, and group work leading to gifted students doing all the work (Clinkenbeard, 1991). In one study of high ability middle level students, Plucker and McIntire (1996) found that students exhibited a variety of nonconstructive behaviors such as interacting with peers, selected attention, and reduced effort when the level of stimulation or challenge was inappropriate. In addition, teachers in the study did not always recognize when high ability students were trying to stimulate themselves intellectually and sometimes even allowed the students to pursue nonconstructive behaviors rather than adapt or modify instruction.

Instructional implications

Middle school instruction is intended to respond to the recognized developmental needs of young adolescent students. Earlier research on brain periodicity fueled support for a movement away from abstract types of thinking. The resulting de-emphasis on academics also acknowledged that young adolescent students do not always prize school achievement and that over-challenging students at the middle school level could contribute to poor self-concept (National Association of Secondary School Principals, 1989). Tomlinson (1992) has questioned the implications of accepting findings that only 20% of 14 year-olds use even early formal operations. In her view, this finding still creates a need to explore viable options for these 20 percenters, many of whom might be identified as gifted students. In their study of talented teenagers, Csikszentmihalyi, Rathunde, & Whalen (1993) found that students seem to benefit more from a differentiated (more complex and even competitive) learning environment than an integrated (supportive and comfortable) environment. Beane and Lipka's (1986) finding that only 25% of an individual's academic school achievement is linked to IQ while 50% is related to self-concept has posed another dilemma. For gifted students, academic success plays an important role in maintaining self-esteem. This aspect of self-concept is supported by students' intellectual peers who act as "mental catalysts and who provide realistic perspective of their abilities" (Sicola, 1990). Furthermore, Bloom (1985) found in his study that "… exceptional levels of talent development require certain types of environmental support, special experiences, excellent teaching, and appropriate motivational encouragement at each stage of development" (p. 543).

To allow any student to underachieve continually can result in a negative impact on self-concept which, in turn, can impact future performance. Ironically, it was the middle school movement that reminded educators that lockstep-graded practices "force[s] many students to compromise the integrity of their individual readiness" (NASSP, 1989, p. 7). In 1988, Chapman and McAlpine conducted a study to examine the academic self-concepts of mainstreamed intellectually gifted and average students over a two-year period. They measured perceptions of ability in the areas of math, reading, spelling, general ability, penmanship, neatness, and confidence/satisfaction at the beginning and the end of the sixth grade year and then again at the end of the seventh year. These researchers found that, with the exception of penmanship, the students identified as gifted had overall higher perceptions of general ability as well as specific academic areas. However, the gifted students showed lower perceptions of school satisfaction than the average students. Chapman and McAlpine felt that lack of challenge in a mainstreamed environment may cause boredom which could explain the lower scores.

In a qualitative study conducted in a sixth grade gifted class, Clinkenbeard (1991) found that students who were identified gifted felt that their general classroom teachers and peers held sometimes unrealistic expectations of them. Teachers expected them to achieve and behave at a gifted level consistently, some days failing to acknowledge that the students' achievements were linked to effort as well as ability. Students who participated in the study also felt that they were graded harder than were other students and their age peers were sometimes jealous and insulting. Gifted adolescents appear to develop a variety of coping strategies to deal with these types of pressures, including the use of one's abilities to help others in classes, making friends with other bright students, selecting programs and classes designed for gifted/talented students, and achieving in areas outside of academics/school. In their study of gifted adolescents' adjustment, Buescher and Higharn (1989) found gender differences indicating girls to be more at risk for avoiding or walking away from their talents during early adolescence whereas boys more often select friends that provide support for their talent areas.

Equity and excellence

The greatest philosophical difference that separates advocates of gifted education and those of the middle school concept does not lend itself to traditional research methodology. As Plowman (1988) stated, "Education of the gifted and talented is consistent with the philosophical principles and basic tenets of our educational and political systems which include: concern for individuals, individualized instruction, equal opportunity, and equal access" (p. 60). Yet, services that address the needs of high ability learners are sometimes suspect and equated with social discrimination (Johnston & Markle, 1986; McKay, 1995). Helpful to this discussion is a closer look at what Salkind (1988) addressed as two other types of equity. Horizontal equity involves the equal treatment of individuals who have similar needs while vertical equity exists when children who have different needs are treated differently; otherwise referred to as the "unequal treatment of unequals." Both types of equity must guide policy and practices involving services for high ability adolescents.

Ability grouping

As mentioned previously, the main point of disagreement between the two fields often centers around the issue of ability grouping. Kulik and Kulik's

(1987) second meta-analysis coded 82 studies of between-class and 19 within-class programs and described the outcomes on a common scale. For inclusion in their analysis, the studies had to be quantitative, include both a control group and an experimental group with a similar aptitude, and involve a classroom rather than a lab setting. In 49 studies of comprehensive between-class grouping, the effect sizes were .12 for high, .04 for middle, and .00 for low groups with the difference between the high and low groups statistically significant at $p < .05$. In 25 studies dealing with special classrooms only for talented students, variation of effect size from -.27 to 1.25 led the Kuliks to believe that factors other than grouping played a role in the outcome. Two features showing significant relationships in an analysis of total class grouping within the classroom were instructor effects and flexibility/permanence of assignment. The Kuliks concluded that the strongest and clearest effects of grouping were in programs designed especially for talented students. They also concluded that programs designed for all students in a grade, rather than only for talented students, had significantly lower effects. The Kuliks noted that their results are, in some regards, similar to those of Slavin, particularly their findings that comprehensive grouping between classes has little or no effect, either positive or negative.

As the debates have ensued, Slavin (1990) has led a discussion on the practice of "regrouping" for select subject areas as an alternative to ability grouping. To be instructionally effective, Slavin believes that regrouping plans must meet two conditions: 1) instructional level and pace must be completely adapted to student performance level, and 2) regrouping should only be done for one or two subjects so that students remain in a heterogeneous setting most of the day. The National Association for Gifted Children believes that this type of flexible use of grouping will help match students' advanced abilities and knowledge while still maintaining the important social goals of the middle school movement (National Association for Gifted Children, 1994). However, many still question the practice of keeping high ability students in a heterogeneous setting for the majority of the day if their cognitive needs require more challenge.

Revisiting program organization

Over the years a wide variety of programs have been developed to meet the needs of gifted adolescents. Gifted education has rallied around options that move beyond the traditional pull-out and self-contained programs, such as early admission or acceleration options, special schools, mentorships, continuous progress, dual enrollment, and within-class individualization. As an alternative to formal grouping, Renzulli (1994) researched the use of Talent Pools which are composed of the top 15–20 percent of the general population using either general ability or one or more specific areas of ability. Students in these talent pools are then offered opportunities to learn subjects at a faster pace using "curriculum compacting"; thus, freeing up time for enrichment within the general education class. In addition, thousands of students now participate each year in Talent Searches during which seventh and eighth grade students take the SAT. The results of these talent searches can help districts identify able students who may be in need of more academic challenge. Allowing students to take Algebra as early as seventh grade permits them to be able to take more advanced math electives during high school such as: Differential Equations, Real Analysis, Linear Algebra, or Theory of Numbers.

Regardless of the delivery model employed, certain assumptions undergirding the philosophy of gifted services must be supported at the middle school level.

All children progress through challenging material at their own pace. Gifted students often reach mastery in significantly less time than other learners.

- Achieving success for all students is not equated with achieving the same results for all students.
- Most students gain self-esteem and self-confidence from mastering work that initially seems slightly beyond their grasp.
- In addition to sometimes serving as peer role models, high ability students also need to spend time learning new material and stretching to their full potential.
- Flexible grouping of gifted learners should be offered based on students' abilities and talents in these areas.
- Professionals working with gifted students require ongoing specialized training to support their ability to work with this population of students.
- Program strategies used with gifted students should address academic as well as social and personal needs.

In 1995, Coleman and Gallagher conducted a study to identify schools where the middle school movement was blended with quality program services for students who are gifted. Successful sites used instructional grouping to offer challenges to students as well as some form of enrichment. A variety of differentiation approaches were utilized, including mentoring, flexible pacing, independent studies, interdisciplinary units, and thinking skills. In addition, each site also had at least one person on staff who was knowledgeable about the needs of gifted students.

The call for more collaboration between the gifted and the middle school movements will be enhanced if schools first explore the common ground existing between the two fields (Coleman & Gallagher, 1992), namely, that both are committed to meeting the unique developmental needs of students during early adolescence. As programs for the middle school gifted student continue to evolve, the following touchstones can be useful in guiding program decisions:

1. Do the program services support excellence over mediocrity?
2. Will the program offerings help students see in themselves a strength, passion, or capability that can become a highly developed talent?
3. Do the program offerings support students' varying learning needs, e.g., pace, and style?
4. Do the program offerings eliminate an artificial ceiling for learning?
5. Do the program offerings promote depth of understanding rather than just access to quantity?
6. Do the program offerings promote the gifted student's capacities for creative and critical thinking skills?
7. Do the program offerings provide a balance of curricular and co-curricular offerings including appropriate exploratory activities?
8. Do the program offerings offer opportunities to develop an understanding for relationships within and between disciples?

References

Beane, J., & Lipka, R. (1986). *Self-concept, self-esteem, and the curriculum.* New York: Teachers College Press.

Betts, G., & Neihart, M. (1988). Profiles of the gifted. *Gifted Child Quarterly, 32*(2), 248–253.

Bloom, B. (1985). Generalizations about talent development. In B. Bloom (Ed.), *Developing talent in young people* (pp. 507–549). New York: Ballantine Books.

Buescher, T. M. (1985). A framework for understanding the social and emotional development of gifted and talented adolescents. *Roeper Review, 8*, 10–15.

Buescher, T. M., & Higham, S. J. (1989). A developmental study of adjustment among gifted adolescents. In J. Van Tassel-Baska & P. Olszcwski-Kubilius (Eds.), *Patterns of influence on gifted learners: The home, the self, and the school* (pp. 102–124). New York: Teachers College Press.

Chapman, J., & McAlpine, D. (1988). Students' perceptions of ability. *Gifted Child Quarterly, 32*(1), 222–225.

Clark, B. (1988). *Growing up gifted: Developing the potential of children at home and school* (3rd ed.). Columbus, OH: Charles E. Merrill.

Clinkenbeard, P. R. (1991). Unfair expectations: A pilot study of middle school students' comparisons of gifted and regular classes. *Journal for the Education of the Gifted, 15*(1), 56–63.

Coleman, M., & Gallagher, J. (1992). *Middle school survey report: Impact on gifted students.* Chapel Hill, NC: Gifted Education Policy Studies Program, University of North Carolina at Chapel Hill.

Coleman, M. R., & Gallagher, J. (1995). The successful blending of gifted education with middle schools and cooperative learning: Two studies. *Journal for the Education of the Gifted, 18*(4), 362–384.

Coleman, M. R., Gallagher, J., & Howard, J. (1993). *Middle school site visit report: Five schools in profile.* Chapel Hill, NC: Gifted Education Policy Studies Program, University of North Carolina at Chapel Hill.

Csikszentmihalyi, M., Rathunde, K., & Whalen, S. (1993). *Talented teenagers: The roots of success and failure*. Cambridge, UK: Cambridge University Press.

Feldhusen, J. (1992). *TIDE: Talent identification and development in education*. Sarasota, FL: Center for Creative Learning.

Ford, D. (1993). An investigation of the paradox of underachievement among gifted black students. *Roeper Review, 16*(2), 78–84.

Gagne, F. (1995). From giftedness to talent: A developmental model and its impact on the language of the field. *Roeper Review, 18*(2), 103–111.

Gallagher, J., Coleman, M. R., & Nelson, S. (1995). Perceptions of educational reform by educators representing middle schools, cooperative learning, and gifted education. *Gifted Child Quarterly, 39*(2), 66–76.

Gardner, H. (1983). *Frames of mind*. New York: Basic Books.

Johnston, J. H., & Markle, G. (1986). *What research says to the middle level practitioner*. Columbus, OH: National Middle School Association.

Kulik, J. A., & Kulik, C. L. C. (1987). Effects of ability grouping on student achievement. *Equity and excellence, 23* (1&2) 22–30.

Maker, C. L. (1996). Identification of gifted minority students: A national problem, needed changes, and a promising solution. *Gifted Child Quarterly, 40*(1), 41–50.

Manaster, G. J., & Powell, P. M. (1983). A framework for understanding gifted adolescents' psychological maladjustment. *Roeper Review, 6*(2), 70–73.

McKay, J. (1995). *Schools in the middle: Developing a middle-level orientation*. Thousand Oaks, CA: Corwin Press.

Mills, C. I., & Durden, W. G. (1992). Cooperative learning and ability grouping: An issue of choice. *Gifted Child Quarterly, 36*(1), 11–16.

National Association of Secondary School Principals. (1989). *Middle level education's responsibility for intellectual development*. Reston, VA: Author.

National Association for Gifted Children. (1994). *Position paper: Middle schools*. Washington, DC: Author.

Nielsen, E., Higgins, D., Harmmond, A., & Williams, R. (1993). Gifted children with disabilities. *Gifted Child Today, 15*(5), 9–12.

Plowman, P. (1988). Elitism. *Gifted Child Today, 56*(3), 60.

Plucker, J. A., & McIntire, J. (1996). Academic survivability in high-potential middle school students. *Gifted Child Quarterly, 40*(1), 7–14.

Renzulli, J. (1994). *Schools for talent development: A practical plan for total school improvement*. Mansfield Center, CT: Creative Learning Press.

Rosselli, H. (1995). Meeting gifted students halfway in the middle school. *Schools in the Middle, 5*(3), 12–17.

Salkind, N. (1988). *Equity and excellence: The case of mandating services for the gifted child*. Unpublished document. University of Kansas.

Sicola, P. K. (1990). Where do gifted students fit? An examination of middle school philosophy as it relates to ability grouping and the gifted learner. *Journal for the Education of the Gifted, 14*(1), 37–49.

Slavin, R. E. (1990). Achievement effects of ability grouping in secondary schools: A best evidence synthesis. *Review of Educational Research, 60*(3), 471–499.

Tomlinson, C. A. (1992). Gifted education and the middle school movement: Two voices on teaching the academically talented. *Journal for the Education of the Gifted, 15*(3), 206–238.

Tomlinson, C. A. (1994). Gifted learners: The boomerang kids of middle school? *Roeper Review, 16*(3), 177–182.

Tomlinson, C. A. (1995). Deciding to differentiate instruction in middle school: One school's journey. *Gifted Child Quarterly, 39*(2), 77–87.

Treffinger, D. (1992). Programming for giftedness: Needed directions. *INNOTECH Journal, 16*(1), 54–61.

U.S. Department of Education. (1993). *National excellence: A case for developing America's talent*. Washington, DC: Author.

Wallace, D. (1985). Giftedness and the construction of a creative life. In F. Horowitz (Ed.), *The gifted and talented: Development perspectives* (pp. 361–386). Washington, DC: American Psychological Association.

Hilda C. Rosselli is the Associate Dean for Undergraduate Programs in the College of Education at the University of South Florida, Tampa. E-mail: rosselli@tempest.coedu.usf.edu

Judith L. Irvin is a professor at Florida State University, Tallahassee. E-mail: irvin@coe.fsu.edu

Originally appeared in the January 2001 issue of *Middle School Journal*, pp. 57-62. Used with permission from National Middle School Association.

UNIT 3

Exceptional and Culturally Diverse Children

Unit Selections

Key Points to Consider

- What are some of the issues and concerns of including children in regular classrooms?

- Who are the gifted and talented? How can knowledge of their characteristics and learning needs help to provide them with an appropriate education?

- How will understanding the needs of culturally diverse and language minority students help them achieve success in school?

 Links: www.dushkin.com/online/
These sites are annotated in the World Wide Web pages.

The Council for Exceptional Children
http://www.cec.sped.org/index.html

Global SchoolNet Foundation
http://www.gsn.org

International Project: Multicultural Pavilion
http://curry.edschool.virginia.edu/curry/centers/multicultural/papers.html

Let 1000 Flowers Bloom/Kristen Nicholson-Nelson
http://teacher.scholastic.com/professional/assessment/100flowers.htm

Multicultural Publishing and Education Catalog
http://www.mpec.org

National Association for Multicultural Education
http://www.nameorg.org

National Attention Deficit Disorder Association
http://www.add.org

National MultiCultural Institute (NMCI)
http://www.nmci.org

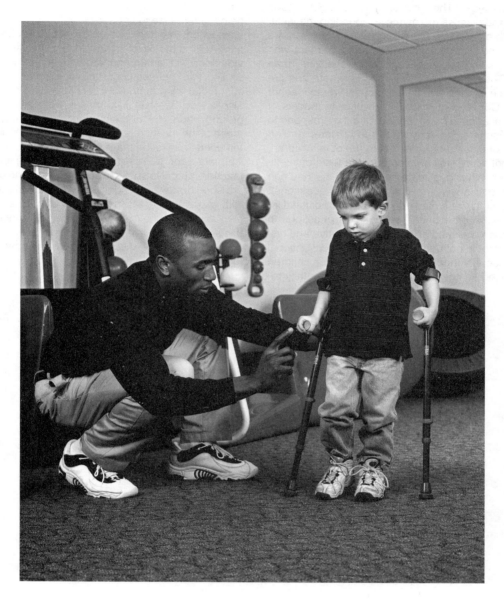

The Equal Educational Opportunity Act for All Handicapped Children (Public Law 94-142) gives disabled children the right to an education in the least-restrictive environment, due process, and an individualized educational program that is specifically designed to meet their needs. Professionals and parents of exceptional children are responsible for developing and implementing an appropriate educational program for each child. The application of these ideas to classrooms across the nation at first caused great concern among educators and parents. Classroom teachers whose training did not prepare them for working with the exceptional child expressed negative attitudes about mainstreaming. Special resource teachers also expressed concern that mainstreaming would mitigate the effectiveness of special programs for the disabled and would force cuts in services. Parents feared that their children would not receive the special services they required because of governmental red tape and delays in proper diagnosis and placement.

It has been more than two decades since the implementation of P.L. 94-142, which was amended by the Individuals with Disabilities Education Act (IDEA) in 1991 and introduced the term "inclusion." Inclusion tries to assure that disabled children will be fully integrated within the classroom. Many of the above concerns have been studied by psychologists and educators, and their findings have often influenced policy. For example, research has indicated that inclusion is more effective when regular classroom teachers and special resource teachers collaborate and work cooperatively with disabled children.

The articles concerning the educationally disabled confront some of these issues. Brent Hardin and Marie Hardin present "Into the Mainstream: Practical Strategies for Teaching in Inclusive Environments" while the authors of "Mom, Will Kaelie Always Have Possibilities?—The Realities of Early Childhood Inclusion" discuss and dismiss the myths surrounding the inclusion of children with disabilities. Other exceptional children are the gifted and talented. These children are rapid learners who can absorb, organize, and apply concepts more effectively than the average child. They often have IQs of 140 or more and are convergent thinkers (i.e., they give the correct answer to teacher or test questions). Convergent thinkers are usually models of good behavior and academic performance, and they respond to instruction easily; teachers generally value such children and often nominate them for gifted programs. There are other children, however, who do not score well on standardized tests of intelligence because their thinking is more divergent (i.e., they can imagine more than one answer to teacher or test questions). These gifted divergent thinkers may not respond to traditional instruction. They may become bored, respond to questions in unique and disturbing ways, and appear uncooperative and disruptive. Many teachers do not understand these unconventional thinkers and fail to identify them as gifted. In fact, such children are sometimes labeled as emotionally disturbed or mentally re-

tarded because of the negative impressions they make on their teachers. Because of the differences between these types of students, a great deal of controversy surrounds programs for the gifted. Such programs should enhance the self-esteem of all gifted and talented children, motivate and challenge them, and help them realize their creative potential. The two articles in the subsection on gifted children consider the characteristics of giftedness, and they explain how to identify gifted students and provide them with an appropriate education.

The third subsection of this unit concerns student diversity. Just as labeling may adversely affect the disabled child, it may also affect the child who comes from a minority ethnic background where the language and values are quite different from those of the mainstream culture. The term "disadvantaged" is often used to describe these children, but it is negative, stereotypical, and apt to result in a self-fulfilling prophecy whereby teachers perceive such children as incapable of learning. Teachers should provide academically and culturally diverse children with experiences that they might have missed in the restricted environment of their homes and neighborhoods. The articles in this section discuss strategies for positively influencing the self-concept of culturally diverse children and how to properly assess them in the classroom.

'Mom, Will Kaelie Always Have Possibilities?'

The Realities of Early Childhood Inclusion

Mary Frances Hanline and Steven Daley

LEIGHA, THE 5-year-old daughter of one of the authors, recently asked, "Mom, will Kaelie always have possibilities?" Since she was just a year old, Leigha has attended a child-care program that actively includes children with disabilities. And she was trying to understand her friend Kaelie's disabilities. While she confused "possibilities" and "disabilities," Leigha innocently identified the main reasons for creating inclusive early education programs: to create normalized expectations for children with disabilities and to foster an understanding of disabilities among the nondisabled.

However, while "best practices" in early childhood education and in early childhood special education support the inclusion of children with disabilities in early childhood programs,[1] about half of all young children with disabilities receive services in settings that serve only children with disabilities.[2] Thus many preschoolers with disabilities are isolated from the learning benefits that may occur when they have daily contact with their nondisabled peers. Children who do not have disabilities are also deprived of the positive outcomes that may occur when they interact with peers who have disabilities. Moreover, family members and teachers are unable to experience the potential advantages of inclusion if young children with disabilities are educated exclusively in segregated settings.

We wish to identify here some beliefs that work to prevent the implementation of inclusive programs. These beliefs focus on the perceived needs of young children with disabilities, on the potential reactions of nondisabled children, on the anticipated demands on teachers, and on parental concerns. We have become familiar with them through our reading of the literature on inclusion, as well as through our own experiences with inclusive programs.

Belief 1. The instructional needs of young children with disabilities can't be met in an early childhood education setting, because young children with disabilities need highly structured programs.

Reality 1. Best practice in early childhood education is based on developmental theories, such as those of Jean Piaget, Lev Vygotsky, and Erik Erikson, and on a philosophy of constructivism. The primary vehicle for promoting development in these programs is child-initiated, child-directed, teacher-supported play. In contrast, the field of early childhood special education is based primarily on the behavioral theories of John Watson, Edward Thorndike, and B. F. Skinner and on the educational psychology of mastery learning. The message from these theories is that the more time the child spends in direct instruction, the more the child will learn. A further assumption is that a child with disabilities will be unable to take advantage of environmental experiences that typically promote development. Thus special education programs for young children have traditionally been more teacher-directed than typical early education programs.

These philosophical differences between the two approaches have contributed to the belief that learning opportunities in early childhood programs may not be adequate to promote the development of children with disabilities. Recently, professionals have begun to realize that there is much in common in the practice of both approaches and that polarized thinking regarding best practice may prevent children from experiencing inclusion. For example, early childhood education in general has come to recognize that teacher-directed approaches have their place, and the best practice guidelines for early childhood special education programs increasingly recognize the importance of play-oriented approaches.

Research findings indicate that inclusive settings (compared to disabled-only environments) are more stimulating and responsive to young children with disabilities. More demands for appropriate social behaviors are placed on children in inclusive settings, there are opportunities for observational learning and interactions with nondisabled peers, and children with disabilities engage in higher levels of play when they are with nondisabled children.[3]

Belief 2. Young children with disabilities can't participate in the activities of an early childhood program. Their presence has the potential of disrupting the learning activities of the other children.

Reality 2. In order to be effective, education for children with disabilities must take place within a framework that recognizes that the majority of children with disabilities progress through the same developmental stages as nondisabled children. Responsiveness to the needs of the individual child within this framework allows typical early childhood activities to be modified to meet the needs of children with disabilities without disrupting the activities for nondisabled children. For example, children can sit side-by-side with crayons and paper, each involved in learning at an individually appropriate level. One child may scribble with the crayons, while another creates the face of his mother. Or children with and without disabilities can play within a sociodramatic center together. One child may be learning to engage in simple symbolic activities, such as feeding a baby doll with a bottle, while another child may be engrossed in more elaborate play involving a scenario of planning a party, writing invitations, and going to the post office to mail the invitations.

Because most activities in early childhood settings allow for a range of developmental levels and often require fewer adaptations than are needed for older children, the needs of young children with disabilities can usually be met within the context of developmentally appropriate activities. In this way, the learning of nondisabled peers is not interrupted. However, teachers must have time to plan these adaptations, possibly in consultation with other professionals, and to evaluate their effectiveness and appropriateness.

Belief 3. Nondisabled children will tease and make fun of their peers with disabilities. Nondisabled children don't want to be friends with young children with disabilities.

Reality 3. One reason to pursue inclusion is its potential impact on the attitudes of nondisabled children toward their peers with disabilities. It is believed that nondisabled children who grow up with the opportunity to interact with children with disabilities are more likely to show greater understanding of individuals with disabilities.

While research has demonstrated that preschool children recognize the presence of disabilities, studies assessing the reactions of nondisabled children to their peers with disabilities report few rejecting behaviors. Only two studies have reported negative outcomes of inclusion.[4] Both of these studies attributed the outcomes to lack of

support for the teachers, and both highlight the importance of the availability of specialists for consultation. Studies reporting positive outcomes have demonstrated increased understanding of and sensitivity to individual differences on the part of children without disabilities as a result of direct contact with peers who have disabilities.[5] In fact, nondisabled children tend to adapt their speech to the developmental level of a listener who is disabled, suggesting that nondisabled children are responsive to the needs of peers with disabilities.[6]

Although early studies of social interactions in inclusive preschools indicated that children with and without disabilities might not play together if interactions are left to chance, more recent studies have shown that positive behaviors develop with appropriate guidance, modeling, and direction from adults.[7] When adults answer children's questions about disabilities openly and honestly and model accepting behavior, children with and without disabilities form friendships, and nondisabled children willingly assist their peers with disabilities. In fact, it has been our experience that nondisabled children frequently must be reminded not to help their friends with disabilities too much!

Belief 4. Young children with disabilities require much more teacher time, thereby taking away from the time the teacher has to interact with and instruct all the children.

Reality 4. All children require teacher time. Although studies of teacher time required for the inclusion of young children have not been reported in the early childhood literature, studies evaluating the use of teacher time in elementary and high schools indicate that additional teacher time is not needed.[8]

However, the child with disabilities may need time to adjust to a new classroom. The teacher may also spend time with the nondisabled children, demonstrating how to accommodate the needs of their new peer. In addition, when children are making the transition from one activity to another, children who are not independently mobile may need one-to-one assistance to move to the new activity, and children may need more adult assistance during those activities that present the greatest challenges. For example, a child who gets easily frustrated during a group activity may need to sit close to the teacher leading the activity, and a child who has difficulty with fine motor tasks may need one-on-one assistance when building with blocks or playing with puzzles.

However, successful inclusion is not simply a matter of more teacher time for interactions with the child who has a disability. Time is needed to consult with specialists who may be coming to support the inclusion of the child with disabilities. Early childhood teachers have indicated a need for time to participate in inservice workshops, to discuss issues with instructional assistants, and to review curriculum materials.[9] To create time for accomplishing these tasks requires flexibility in scheduling and in assigning responsibility to teachers.

Belief 5. Preschool teachers aren't able to provide for the many and varied needs of young children with disabilities.

Reality 5. Early childhood teachers have a history of accommodating the individual learning styles of young children, and so they already possess the foundation knowledge they need to effectively teach preschoolers with disabilities. However, staff development is critical, as teacher attitudes, preparation, and ongoing support are factors that contribute to the success of inclusion. Such support is essential to counter misinformation, fear, and negative attitudes.

Staff support can take a variety of forms, including in-service workshops, on-site demonstrations, direct observation with supportive feedback, discussions during staff meetings, individual consultation, and written materials. To be most effective, the support should be responsive to the needs of individual programs. Time for teachers to engage in these activities should be provided, and participation in the activities must be considered a job responsibility of individuals involved in inclusion.

Belief 6. Young children with disabilities are a burden to the preschool teacher, as they upset the optimum adult/child ratio required by high-quality early childhood programs.

Reality 6. The guidelines of the National Association for the Education of Young Children (NAEYC) may be followed when including young children with disabilities in early childhood programs. The NAEYC-recommended adult/child ratio for 4- to 5-year-olds is two adults to 20 children. While the young child with disabilities may require the assistance of a specialist or a paraprofessional, as well as one-to-one interactions with a teacher at specific times of the day, the overall adult/child ratio does not need to be different because a child with disabilities has become part of the program. For example, a child could receive occupational therapy services during lunch to improve eating skills and physical therapy during outdoor time to improve gross motor skills.

Through interagency agreements with local school systems and private agencies, the ongoing participation of specialists from multiple disciplines can be ensured, thus meeting the needs of the young child with disabilities without adding full-time staff members. For example, the school system could provide a speech and language therapist to work with the children and consult with the teachers on a regularly scheduled basis. Furthermore, in many programs, teachers have incorporated assistants, cross-age tutors, volunteers, and parents into the program routines to help provide high-quality services to all children.

Belief 7. Parents of nondisabled children don't want their children to attend inclusive programs.

Reality 7. Parental attitudes about inclusion are a critical variable. The overwhelming majority of parents of nondisabled children support the inclusion of young children with disabilities in their children's programs, and they perceive drawbacks and benefits from inclusion that are similar to those noted by parents of children with disabilities. Both groups of parents believe that inclusion allows children with disabilities to experience the real world and to be accepted by others. In addition, parents of nondisabled children generally feel that their children's sensitivity to and acceptance of differences are increased through contact with children with disabilities. Parents whose children have had a positive inclusion experience are the most accepting of inclusion, as are parents who have been involved in planning for the inclusion process.[10]

Belief 8. Parents of children with disabilities fear that their child will not receive adequate services in inclusive settings.

Reality 8. When their child with disabilities attends an inclusive program, parents want the same services they perceive to be available in specialized settings. However, once they have experienced inclusion, parents express confidence that their children's needs are met. A growing body of research indicates that providing services in inclusive settings has become one indicator of high-quality programs.[11] In support of this idea, Phillip Strain stated, "Programs that are characterized by integrated service delivery tend to be state-of-the-art in a variety of other dimensions, including extensive parental involvement; highly structured scope, sequence, and method of instruction; and attention to repeated outcome assessments."[12] Professionals in inclusive settings, however, may want to ensure that the families also receive adequate support. Linking with community agencies and promoting interactions among families of children with and without disabilities may help the families of children with disabilities feel more supported.

Inclusion is one of the major challenges facing those who work to educate young children. With creative and flexible planning, caring attitudes on the part of adults, and the wise use of community resources to provide specialized services, children with disabilities can be included successfully in early childhood education programs. Everyone involved with the inclusion process has an opportunity to be involved with a program that supports equity and acceptance as a framework for providing services to young children and their families. In this way, Leigha's question can be answered with an emphatic, "Yes, Leigha, Kaelie will always have possibilities. And Kaelie's possibilities will be greater because you are her friend."

References

1. Sue Bredekamp and Carol Copple, eds., Developmentally Appropriate Practice in Early Childhood Programs (Washington, D.C.: National Association for the Education of Young Children, 1997); and DEC Task Force on Recommended Practices, DEC Recommended Practices: Indicators of Quality Programs for Infants and Young Children with Special Needs and Their Families (Reston, Va.: Council for Exceptional Children, 1993).

2. Twentieth Annual Report to Congress on the Implementation of the Individuals with Disabilities Education Act (Washington, D.C.: U.S. Department of Education, 1998).

3. Dorothy K. Lipsky and Alan Gartner, Inclusion and School Reform: Transforming America's Classrooms (Baltimore: Paul H. Brookes, 1997); and Michael J. Guralnick, "Early Childhood Mainstreaming," Topics in Early Childhood Special Education, Summer 1990, pp. 1–17.

4. Elaine P. Simon and Andrew E. Gilman, "Mainstreaming Visually Handicapped Children," Exceptional Children, vol. 45, 1983, pp. 463–64; and Pearl E. Tait and Charles Wolfgang, "Mainstreaming a Blind Child: Problems Perceived in a Preschool Day Care Program," Early Child Development and Care, vol. 13, 1984, pp. 155–67.

5. Susan Lamorey and Diane Bricker, "Integrated Programs: Effects on Young Children and Their Parents," in Charles A. Peck, Samuel A. Odom, and Diane D. Bricker, eds., Integrating Young Children with Disabilities into Community Programs (Baltimore: Paul H. Brookes, 1993).

6. Michael J. Guralnick and Diane Paul-Brown, "Functional and Discourse Analysis of Nonhandicapped Preschool Children's Speech to Handicapped Children," American Journal of Mental Deficiency, vol. 84, 1980, pp. 444–54.

7. Samuel L. Odom, Michelle DeKlyen, and Joseph R. Jenkins, "Integrating Handicapped and Nonhandicapped Preschoolers: Developmental Impact on the Nonhandicapped Children," Exceptional Children, vol. 51, 1984, pp. 41–49.

8. Margaret C. Wang, "Serving Students with Special Needs Through Inclusive Education Approaches," in Judy Lupart, Anne Marie McKeough, and Carolyn Yewchuck, eds., Schools in Transition: Rethinking Regular and Special Education (Toronto: Thomas Nelson Canada, 1996), pp. 143–63; and Debbie Straub and Charles A. Peck, "What Are the Outcomes for Nondisabled Students?," Educational Leadership, December 1994/January 1995, pp. 36–40.

9. William D. Eiserman, Lenore Shisler, and Suzanne Healey, "A Community Assessment of Preschool Providers: Attitudes Toward Inclusion," Journal of Early Intervention, vol. 19, 1992, pp. 149–67.

10. Kim Galant and Mary Frances Hanline, "Parental Attitudes Toward Mainstreaming Young Children with Disabilities," Childhood Education, vol. 69, 1993, pp. 293–99.

11. Ibid.

12. Phillip S. Strain, "LRE for Preschool Children with Handicaps: What We Know, What We Should be Doing," Journal of Early Intervention, vol. 14, 1990, p. 294.

MARY FRANCES HANLINE is an associate professor and chair of the Department of Special Education, Florida State University, Tallahassee. STEVEN DALEY is an associate professor in the Department of Special Education, Rehabilitation, and School Psychology, California State University, Sacramento.

Into the Mainstream: Practical Strategies for Teaching in Inclusive Environments

Brent Hardin and Marie Hardin

Christopher, thirty-two, teaches ninth-grade English at a high school on the outskirts of Atlanta, Georgia. Although he has been a teacher for eight years and has clearly moved beyond the induction phase of his career, some classroom challenges still seem overwhelming to him.

Christopher's average day begins before 7 a.m. After he arrives at his portable classroom behind the high school, he begins his first class at 7:30. He teaches six classes throughout the day—a mix of "Technical English" and college-preparatory courses. On top of his regular teaching load, Christopher often has to substitute teach during his one planning period during the day.

Christopher's job, however, involves far more than teaching about punctuation, active voice, and sentence structure to the 115 students who visit his trailer each day. He spends much of his energy on classroom management and administrative tasks, while he struggles to work with the many special-needs students who have been integrated into his courses. During first period, for instance, an aide joins Christopher to teach a group nearly half of whom have diagnosed emotional, behavioral, or learning problems. In another class later in the day, nine of fifteen students have some type of disability. Besides making accommodations for students during his lessons, Christopher is also required to remember other details, such as the times to send some students to the office to take medication. "I can put my kids into two different categories" he says, "They're completely bouncing off the walls or they're catatonic. It's a struggle. I try to keep my energy level up."

Christopher's situation is certainly not unique. Inclusion of students with a wide range of disabilities into regular classrooms can be a daunting prospect for teachers at any career stage. However, teachers at the induction or competency-building phases can find the task of teaching students with disabilities especially challenging because they lack sufficient training and support to work with these students (Werts et al. 1996).

Teachers can, however, use a number of strategies to cope with these demands and increase their effectiveness in an inclusive environment. Using peer tutors, implementing cooperative learning, and applying reverse-inclusion techniques in the classroom can be powerful strategies to provide successful learning for all students.

Changing Demographics

The need for teachers to cope with the demands of inclusive classrooms has increased during the past several years, as the numbers of students with disabilities in public education has climbed dramatically. The Nineteenth Annual Report to Congress on the Implementation of the Individuals with Disabilities Education Act revealed that during the 1994–1995 school year there were approximately 4.7 million schoolchildren with disabilities, or almost 10 percent of the student population. At least 48 percent of students requiring special education services attend inclusive classes for most or all of the school day, a 60 percent escalation from 1994 (McLeskey, Henry, and Hodges 1998). This trend is predicted to continue. All teachers, not just special educators, should be prepared to teach students with disabilities.

Teachers' Perceptions of Competence

Thousands of teachers, at all career stages, teach students with disabilities in inclusive classrooms every day, but many do not feel competent or confident in that role. Kelly, a third-year elementary teacher in north Florida, speaks of her confidence in teaching students with disabilities in an integrated classroom:

> Conceptually, I think inclusion is a great idea. But, at the same time, I don't think teachers are prepared. I know I am not. I really didn't get any experience or training teaching kids with disabilities mixed in with my regular classes. It's hard enough just handling a

regular class, but throw in students with special needs and it is really overwhelming if you don't have the training or the help.

Surveys of countless teachers echo Kelly's concerns. A recent synthesis of research (Scruggs and Mastropieri 1996), based on studies dating back to 1958, indicates that approximately two-thirds of the 10,560 general educators surveyed across the years agreed with the concept of inclusion, but their degree of enthusiasm decreased when asked, "Are you prepared to teach with disabilities in your classroom?" Confidence decreased even further when questions addressed teacher readiness to make curricular or instructional modifications for identified students. When Schultz (1982) surveyed teachers to determine what specific issues were of concern, teachers said that they felt a lack of expertise in accounting for individual differences when they designed and implemented their instructional strategies.

Research indicates that educators do not feel that they have been adequately trained for inclusive environments. Lyon, Vaasen, and Toomey (1989) surveyed 440 teachers concerning their perceptions of their undergraduate and graduate training programs, questioning how such programs prepared them to address individual differences within the classroom. Sadly, the majority of the respondents reported that the training programs that they completed did not prepare them to provide effective instruction for a diverse student population. Over 93 percent of the regular educators indicated that they did not receive any hands-on experience teaching students with disabilities in their training programs.

Gallagher, Malone, Cleghorne, and Helms (1997) interviewed 115 teachers concerning their perceived training needs related to children with disabilities. Although 64 percent of the respondents reported six or more years' experience teaching students with disabilities in inclusive classrooms, they reported low confidence in several areas of basic competency. Such challenges can be daunting for inexperienced teachers trying to learn basic classroom management skills, deal with failing students, and keep track of grades and paperwork.

Practical Classroom Strategies

Educators at any career stage can, however, implement a number of simple strategies to increase their effectiveness and grow more confident in inclusive environments. Subtle changes can accommodate students with special needs without obtrusively changing the class for other students.

Peer Tutoring

Students who serve as peer tutors have been trained to assist other students in the classroom. These tutors can work with special-needs students to provide the extra attention and feedback they need in order to learn, allowing the teacher to divide his or her attention more equally among the students. Also, students with and without disabilities can work together in tutoring pairs to positively affect each other.

Greenwood, Delquadri, and Garta (1997) maintain that teachers find peer tutoring valuable because it is adaptable to any teaching style and curriculum; easy to implement; cost effective; time efficient; and effective with all ability levels. Although students can learn from each other, the teacher should carefully select the peer tutors who will work with disabled students. Not all students will be ready or able to work in a partnership with special needs students. Ellery (1995) recommends that peer tutors be (a) slightly older than their disabled counterparts, (b) emotionally mature, (c) good communicators, (d) highly skilled, and (e) volunteers.

Peer tutors may need ongoing training to become skillful helpers. The teacher should allow time to make sure that tutors understand their responsibilities for the lesson. Also, the teacher should not overlook opportunities to offer students with disabilities the chance to tutor nondisabled students. For example, a student with spina bifida who is confined to a wheelchair is perfectly capable of providing instruction, encouragement, and feedback to another student. This arrangement extends the potential for a fully inclusive learning environment.

Cooperative Learning

This strategy brings students together in groups to accomplish shared goals. The goal of cooperative learning is to ensure that all members of the group master the information at their own levels. Oftentimes individuals in the group are given specific jobs or tasks that contribute to goal attainment. Students help each other and evaluate each member's progress toward individual and group goals. For cooperative learning to be effective, students must perceive that they are positively linked to other students in their group and that each member can and must contribute. In addition, each member must understand his or her role in the cooperative group. Less-skilled students, including students with disabilities, could be perceived to be the weak links if all members perceive that they must perform the same task. This will not happen if the group understands that each member has a unique task that maximizes his or her skills and contribution to the group goal.

One example of a cooperative learning activity is a literature circle (Zemelman, Daniels, and Hyde 1993). In a literature circle, groups of four or five students choose and read the same article or book. Each student then comes to the literature circle with an assigned discussion role that accommodates skill differences, allowing for different versions of the text, including tape, film, or Braille.

Kagan (1985) recommends a cooperative learning strategy called "numbered heads," designed to actively engage all students during teacher-led instruction and discussion. Students are organized into four-member heterogeneous learning teams. After the teacher directs a question to the entire class, students are asked to put their heads together to come up with their best answer. The teacher then calls for answers from one numbered member of a group, asking, for example, "Which number 1 can answer this question?"

A substantial body of research confirms the academic and social benefits of cooperative learning approaches to instruction for students of diverse abilities. Benefits have been noted in measures of student achievement (Slavin 1990), self-esteem (Johnson and Johnson 1989), and peer relationships and interactions (Johnson, Johnson, Warring, and Maruyama 1986).

Reverse Inclusion

One way to implement reverse inclusion is to integrate several students without disabilities into a class that has several students with disabilities (Block 1994). The students without disabilities participate in the class alongside students with disabilities. Another way is to have students without disabilities role-play the disabilities of their peers during certain lessons. Examples might include having students participate in a listening exercise while blindfolded or present a poem or speech using sign language. A teacher might also invite a guest speaker to teach the students about how to use and maneuver a wheelchair. The entire class may take part in a wheelchair basketball game as a culminating event for this instructional unit. This type of instruction promotes classwide understanding and respect for all students.

Planning to Mainstream

Although awareness of these strategies is advantageous, it is important that teachers focus on the particular needs of their individual students when designing classroom lessons. The goal is to allow all students the opportunity to participate and learn in a class that is challenging and that provides opportunities for success. Thus, it is important to evaluate the effect that any lesson strategy will have on the entire class. The following criteria, adapted from suggestions by Block (1994), can be used to evaluate classroom strategies:

1. Does the plan allow students with disabilities to participate successfully, yet still be challenged? For example, a teenage student with Down's syndrome should not be given reading material at a kindergarten level to present in a cooperative learning project. The student will probably be more challenged and comfortable working with age-related material that is developmentally appropriate.

2. Does the plan adversely affect students without disabilities? It might be wise from time to time to try alternative projects or activities that allow students without disabilities to experience what it is like to be in a wheelchair or have a visual impairment. However, such changes implemented on a regular basis might negatively affect the class for students without disabilities and promote resentment toward their disabled peers.

3. Does the application cause undue burden on the teacher? For example, a student with autism may need special assistance to complete many classroom tasks. It may not be feasible for the teacher to provide the individual attention needed while also teaching the other students in the class. A better adaptation might be assisting this student for part of the class and allowing a peer tutor or classroom aide to assist at other times.

Working with students in an inclusive classroom environment is a formidable prospect for teachers at all career stages; studies indicate that teachers feel neither confident nor competent about their training or ability to work with disabled students. For new teachers this challenge can be especially troublesome. Peer tutoring, cooperative learning, and reverse inclusion are three relatively simple techniques that inexperienced teachers can implement. Although no teaching strategy works in all situations and individual learner needs must be considered, such techniques have been demonstrated as effective in inclusive environments. The merits of such applications are clear. Teacher efficacy is enhanced and confidence is ensured while students' inclusive experiences are maximized.

Key words: special education, disabilities, inclusive classrooms, teacher competence, cooperative learning

REFERENCES

Block, M. E. 1994. A teacher's guide to including students with disabilities in regular physical education. Baltimore: Brookes.

Ellery, P. J. 1995. Peer tutors work. Strategies 5:12–14.

Gallagher P., M. Malone, M. Cleghorne, and A. Helms. 1997. Perceived in-service training needs for early intervention personnel. Exceptional Children 64:19–30.

Greenwood, C. R. J. G. Delquadri, and I. J. Carta. 1997. Together we can: Class-wide peer tutoring to improve basic academic skills. Longmont, GO: Sopris West.

Johnson, D. W., and R. T. Johnson. 1989. Cooperation and competition: Theory and research. Edina, MN: Interaction Books.

Johnson, D. W., R. T. Johnson, D. Warring, and G. Maruyama. 1986. Different cooperative learning procedures and cross-handicap relationships. Exceptional Children 53(3): 247–52.

Kagan, S. 1985. Cooperative learning. Mission Viejo, CA: Resources for Teachers.

Lyon, G., M. Vaasen, and F. Toomey. 1989. Teacher's perceptions of their undergraduate and graduate preparation. Teacher Education and Special Education 12(4): 164–69.

McLeskey, J., D. Henry, and D. Hodges. 1998. Inclusion: Where is it happening? Teaching Exceptional Children 31(1): 4–10.

Office of Special Education Programs. 1997. To assure the free appropriate public education of all children with disabilities. Nineteenth annual report to Congress on the implementation of the Individuals with Disabilities Education Act. Washington, DC: Office of Special Exceptional Children.

Schultz, L. 1982. Educating the special needs student in the regular classroom. Exceptional Children 48:366–67.

Scruggs, T. E., and M. A. Mastropieri. 1996. Teacher perceptions of mainstreaming/inclusion, 1958–1995: A research synthesis. Exceptional Children 63(1): 59–74.

Werts, M. G., M. Wolery, E. D. Snyder, N. K. Caldwell, and C. L. Salisbury. 1996. Supports and resources associated with inclusive schooling: Perceptions of elementary school teachers about need and availability. Journal of Special Education 30(2): 187–203.

Zemelman, S., H. Daniels, and A. Hyde. 1993. Best practice: New standards for teaching and learning in America's schools. Portsmouth, NH: Heinemann.

Brent Hardin is an assistant professor of physical education and Marie Hardin is an assistant professor of communications, both at State University of West Georgia, in Carollton.

Challenges of Identifying and Serving Gifted Children with ADHD

Lori J. Flint

How often have we, as parents and educators, watched a story about students labeled as one thing or another on the evening news and felt it was oversimplified? Those of us who regularly work with children know that we can't oversimplify like that because, like adults, children are not always what they appear to be. Children are complicated, with a variety of factors, both positive and negative, simultaneously affecting them. Many children are labeled as gifted or learning disabled or having attention-deficit hyperactivity disorder (ADHD) as though that label explains the child, when what it really does is provide appropriate educational services to that child. But what about children who bear one label and also display other tendencies?

Take, for example, the idea of gifted children. Many people probably think of children as being identified as gifted according to a single intelligence test and don't realize that giftedness today often is measured in other ways: high motivation, exceptional creativity, outstanding achievement, and fantastic products.

Whoever these children with exceptional gifts and talents are, and however their gifts are measured, they're all really good in school, and have it made in life, right? Not necessarily. Some students identified as being gifted have other exceptionalities, as well; some have exceptionalities that preclude them from ever being identified as gifted.

This article describes the special situations and needs of three children—Tony, Mikey, and Gina. As you read the first part of the article, think about your own suggestions for interventions—how you might help them in your home or classroom. Then read the rest of the article to see what others have to say about working with children who have both giftedness and attentional difficulties.

Three Children

Tony

Nine-year-old Tony is a charmer. He has an engaging smile and knows how to turn it on and off. Tony is also a challenge to have in the classroom. He blurts out answers constantly, never stops moving, and argues with the teacher and with his peers incessantly. He is of average intelligence, displays little creativity, earns low grades on both objective and project-based work, does not like school, and typically achieves at a below-average level. Tony is disorganized and distractible and is always either talking or making other noise. He is usually missing either his work or some vital component needed to do his work. He visits the office on a regular basis because he is removed from the classroom when he is so disruptive the teacher cannot continue teaching. Tony's teacher will be happy when this school year is over, but worries about where Tony will go next year and whether his new teacher will be able to handle him—he needs a teacher who is neither too permissive nor too authoritarian. Tony carries with him two labels: He has been diagnosed with ADHD and oppositional defiant disorder (ODD). Tony is one of four children in a family headed by a single parent.

Mikey

Six-year-old Mikey was referred to the schools' student support team (SST) by his classroom teacher. Why was he referred? Mikey was distractible, inattentive, fast-moving, and talkative, to the point of not functioning well in his first-grade classroom. He also displayed some aggressive behavior and poor social skills. One member of the SST was a perceptive administrator whose experience included a 14-year stint teaching gifted children. The recommendation from the team included referring the boy for testing for the gifted program.

Exercise caution in both the identification and treatment of ADHD in children identified as being gifted.

The gifted intervention specialist in the school began evaluating Mikey, first by observing him in his classroom on several occasions, then by administering a variety of mental ability, achievement, creativity, and motivation instruments; all designed to ascertain whether Mikey was gifted according to his state's multiple criteria identification law. As he sat to take a mental ability test in a one-on-one testing situation with his school's gifted specialist, the differences this child exhibited were quickly noted. Mikey was, indeed, exceptionally active; hanging off the chair, even standing, at times, during the testing. He vocalized and was impulsive in answering nearly all questions on the tests. During the administration of a mental ability test, he rushed through the verbal and quantitative sections, performing only at the 48th percentile, and slowing only when he came to something entirely new: the matrix section of the test. He barely listened to the instructions, then dove in. As soon as he was allowed to begin, he started solving the problems rapidly and accurately; thriving on the challenge. He missed none. Unfortunately, his score on this single subtest was not adequate to place him in the gifted program, so he required additional testing. Mikey's performance on the other evaluation measures was inconsistent, ranging from the 99th percentile on some instruments designed to evaluate creativity and mental ability to the 48th on others that measured achievement and motivation. The gifted intervention specialist worked with him, using movement to set the stage for optimal performance.

After several weeks of evaluation, Mikey qualified for the gifted program, identified as creatively and cognitively

gifted. Why did the gifted specialist work so hard to help this child qualify? Because she saw a child with immense potential, but who needed a great deal of help channeling that potential into constructive avenues. He was also identified, soon after this, by his family doctor as having ADHD, of both the inattentive and hyperactive types. Mikey comes from a blended family with economic difficulties. He was born when his mother was 14 years of age; his mother never finished high school, and is herself identified as having ADHD, like her mother before her.

Gina

Gina is a highly gifted fifth grader whose performance on mental ability, creativity, and achievement tests regularly place her in the 99th percentile, with scores at the ceiling of the tests. She is an award-winning artist and poet, and an academically high-achieving student who has been in gifted programs since kindergarten. Gina is easily frustrated by new tasks, cries with little or no provocation, and gloats when she figures out things the others have not. She takes great delight, outwardly at least, in all of her differences. She always wants to be first and best. Gina is in nearly constant motion: swooping into a room to announce her arrival; sitting like a frog on her chair, head hanging down and hair swinging around her face; always drawing, writing, or otherwise creating with her hands.

Most foods go untasted by her because she dislikes all but a few for various reasons: too strong, too slimy, wrong color, too disgusting. Gina will only wear clothing made of soft knits and whose tags have been removed, because everything else is either too constricting, or stiff, or makes her itch. She often has her nose turned up in distaste at environmental odors, whether they are caused by someone's lunch or the remnants of some cleaning solution.

Gina's social skills are not those of a typical fifth grader, either. Because of her emotional disability, she stands out in both her gifted and general classrooms. Her propensity toward arguing with adults amazes other students and frustrates the teachers, because she is not engaging in intellectual discourse, but rather, the sort of irrationality that comes of being opinionated and not listening to instructions, as well as an unwillingness to take academic risks. Gina comes from a family of highly gifted, highly educated people.

Attention Deficit or Overexcitability?

Though these three students display many similar behaviors, in each case the behaviors are attributable to different causes. In Tony's case, ADHD is considered the underlying problem; in Mikey's case, ADHD with psychological overintensities associated with giftedness; and in Gina's case, the psychological overintensities concomitant with giftedness alone. How can such similar behaviors be assigned such different attributions, and how can they be distinguished from one another so the correct diagnosis is made in each case?

Making a correct diagnosis is not simple; it requires that educators and other professionals make thorough evaluations for both giftedness and ADHD (Cramond, 1995; Lovecky, 1994; Ramirez-Smith, 1997). According to Webb and Latimer (1993), in recent years educators have increasingly referred gifted children for ADHD evaluation. Because characteristics and behaviors are the foundation of a diagnosis of ADHD, and they can be misleading in the case of gifted people, educators and other professionals must exercise great care when conducting such evaluation (Baum, Olenchak, & Owen, 1998), with parents and teachers working closely with the diagnosing physician.

Children with ADHD *can't* stop moving, whereas children with high psychomotor behavior *love* to move.

In children with average creative and cognitive intelligence, this diagnosis can be made by a physician well versed in the characteristics of children with attention-deficit disorder (ADD) or ADHD (see box, "What is Attention-Deficit Hyperactivity Disorder?") in a fairly straightforward manner by means of thorough psychological and physical examinations. In gifted children, however, the diagnosis may be complicated by other issues, such as psychological overexcitabilities (Dabrowski, 1972; Piechowski, 1986; Piechowski & Colangelo, 1984).

Dabrowski saw these "forms of psychic overexcitability" (OEs) as contributing to

What Is Attention-Deficit Hyperactivity Disorder?

Attention-deficit hyperactivity disorder is characterized by a particular set of behaviors that prevent a person from performing to his or her potential. These behaviors may include the following:

- Susceptibility to distraction with little provocation.
- Difficulty following instructions.
- Difficulty sustaining situation-appropriate attention (except when watching television or playing video games).
- Problems starting tasks.
- Constantly beginning new projects without finishing the existing ones.
- Hyperactivity.
- Impulsivity.
- Poor social skills.
- Rapid satiation to stimuli.
- Low frustration tolerance.
- Academic underachievement (American Psychiatric Association, 1994).

For professionals to make a diagnosis of ADHD, the behaviors must be pervasive and long lasting and interfere significantly with the discharge of daily responsibilities.

individuals' psychological development, so they were a measure of developmental potential. Overexcitabilities are so often present in creatively, academically, intellectually, or otherwise gifted people that some educators are searching for ways to measure overexcitabilities as a tool for identification of gifted people. Psychological intensities are such a part of people who are considered gifted that, for the purpose of this article, the behaviors should be considered to be present when giftedness is mentioned. Researchers have categorized *overexcitabilities* into five main areas: psychomotor, emotional, intellectual, imaginational, and sensual, as follows:

- Those with *psychomotor overexcitabilities* are easy to spot: They are nearly always moving. Their behavior has been characterized as feeling driven to move, a love of movement, restlessness, superenergy, and a need for a high level of activity. Rapid speech, impulsiveness, and a need to

act are also characteristic of those who possess this overintensity. All this sounds remarkably like the hyperactivity of ADHD (Barkley, 1990; Hallowell & Ratey, 1995), though the difference appears to be that children with ADHD *can't* stop moving, whereas children with high psychomotor behavior *love* to move.

- *Imaginational overexcitabilities* are characterized by a facility for invention and fantasy, an ability to engage in detailed visualization, a well-developed sense of humor, animistic and magical thinking, and elaborate application of truth and fiction. Children who possess imaginational OEs can have rich and fulfilling inner experiences during the pedestrian activities of a typical school day. What looks like inattention could be, instead, a rich imaginational scenario unfolding within the child's mind. A creatively gifted 4th-grade student described it like this: "Social studies can be really boring when we just read it aloud and take notes, so I like to pretend I'm in whatever situation we're learning about."

- *Emotional overintensity* is one of the more outwardly visible of the overexcitabilities. Characterized by an intensity of feeling, a marked ability to empathize with others, and somatic expression of feelings, these children are the ones who can see all sides of a situation, who can find it painfully difficult to make new friends, who cry at the smallest frustration. What appears to be the emotional overreactivity of ADHD could, instead, be the expression of emotional overintensity.

- *Sensual overexcitabilities* manifest themselves as extreme sensitivity to touch; delight with the aesthetic things in life, such as art, music, fabric, surroundings, or words; extreme dislike or love for certain foods due to specific textures or tastes; sensitivity to odors or chemicals in the environment; or any other sensory-related experiences. People who experience heightened pleasure when indulging in favorite foods or drinks are displaying this sort of sensual overexcitability. Stopping to feel the fabric of every item passed in a department store, noticing the particular blue of the sky, or admiring the shape of a flower could easily be con-

strued as distractibility, but it could also be illustrative of being tuned in to the beauty of one's surroundings.

Researchers have categorized *overexcitabilities* into five main areas: psychomotor, emotional, intellectual, imaginational, and sensual.

Look at a classroom full of students of any age. Some are simply there, doing as they are told, whereas others display an absolute thirst for learning. These individuals possess a drive to learn that knows no boundaries—**an intellectual overintensity.** What they learn does not seem to matter as long as it is new and interesting. These are the people who think and wonder, who ask the questions instead of knowing the answers, who exhibit sustained concentration, who have excessive curiosity, and who integrate intuition and concept. They are naturally metacognitive thinkers, are detailed planners, and express early concerns about values and morality. Many of these characteristics appear only in the child's mind, so may look, again, like inattention to the outside observer. At times, this overexcitability also may be seen as similar to the hyperfocusing in people with ADHD. Intellectual OEs may also be expressed as a hyperactivity seen by outsiders as distractibility, but which may be heightened mental arousal that never stops, even during sleep.

Who Are They?

With all these similarities, how can we tell the difference between a gifted child with overexcitabilities and one with ADHD? Both children possess exceptional mental faculties, but one has greater availability of resources, while the other founders in a quagmire of disorganization and distractibility. In such cases, parents and teachers find it difficult to distinguish between the child who *won't* do his or her work and the one who *can't*. Gifted children with ADHD are usually labeled as underachieving or lazy long before they are ever labeled as ADHD.

Studies have shown that gifted children identified as having ADHD are, generally, more gifted than their non-ADHD peers (Dorry, 1994; Zentall, 1997). Because the negative behavioral manifestations of ADHD may keep these children from performing well on group tests, many educators believe diagnostic tests uncover only the children who have extremely superlative talents or gifts. Though high intelligence can help the child overcome some of the challenges of ADHD over his or her lifetime (Barkley, 1990; Phelan, 1996), it does so only to the extent that it allows the child to compensate to the point of seeming average.

These children also tend not to be nominated for gifted testing or programs. Wolfle & French, in a presentation to the National Association for Gifted Children (1990), reported the following characteristics of a typical gifted child with ADHD excluded from gifted programs:

- Makes jokes or puns at inappropriate times.
- Is bored with routine tasks and refuses to do them.
- Is self-critical, impatient with failures.
- Tends to dominate others.
- Would rather stay by oneself.
- Has difficulty moving into another topic when engrossed.
- Often disagrees vocally with others in a loud, bossy manner.
- Is emotionally sensitive—may overreact.
- Is not interested in details, often hands in messy work.
- Refuses to accept authority, nonconforming, stubborn.

This is the portrait of a child who refuses to play the school game, has his or her own ideas about how to live, and will not compromise. Teachers do not particularly tend to like these children, thus they do not generally refer them for gifted programming because, in the teacher's mind, these students do not deserve to be there. Parents find them difficult to live with, and peers reject them, so life becomes a series of negative interactions with few opportunities for self-fulfillment. The worst part is that such children are intelligent enough to realize they are different, but may be helpless to change their behaviors at their own volition.

In his work with gifted children with ADHD, Mendaglio (1995) found that these children are painfully aware of their academic failures and misbehaviors. This awareness often manifests itself outwardly as nonspecific anger. On the positive side, he reported, when such children do qualify for and are placed into programs for gifted and talented children, they and their parents report immediate, lasting, positive increases in self-esteem and attitude.

The Creativity Link

Creativity and ADHD share many, many characteristics. Indeed, both creativity and ADHD are so difficult to define precisely and can look so much alike, one might be hard pressed to define certain characteristics as one or the other. In her study of 70 gifted children, Lovecky (1994) found that almost all of these children, even those with additional learning disabilities and exceptional hyperactivity, displayed creativity. The differences between them and their gifted/non-ADHD peers was, "organizing their creative ideas into products, and sustaining enough interest and motivation to finish a project once they had gotten past the novelty of the initial idea" (p. 3).

Hallowell and Ratey (1995) found certain characteristics of the ADHD mind beneficial to the development of creativity. These included a higher tolerance for chaos and ambiguity and no firm belief that there is one proper place for ideas or images. This can lead to unusual combinations of imagery and ideas and to new ways of seeing things.

Hyper-reactivity in the minds of people with ADHD is amazing to behold. The ideas come and come, changing from one topic to another with an awesome rapidity and proliferation. With this many ideas, new ones pop up with regularity, leading to people with creative/ADHD characteristics to think of themselves as "idea people."

Educators should place the child in classrooms where expectations are high and teaching is holistic, relevant, challenging, and meaningful.

The impulsivity of ADHD can lead to a need to create—anything. This impulse is an urge that demands satisfaction. Combined with the hyperfocusing of ADHD, this impulsivity can produce impressive results in a brief period of time. Of course, there will also be many times of distractibility to balance these periods of intense concentration and productivity.

Creative production also occurs when people spontaneously bring unlike items together in unusual ways. Creative people with ADHD do this often. They see and find amusing combinations others may never have thought of. This is a strategy others have to be taught to use, usually in expensive creativity-training workshops.

Cramond (1994), in a review paper, and Piirto (1992), in her book *Understanding Those Who Create*, noted that the defining characteristics of ADHD are also key descriptors in the biographies of highly creative people. Inattention, hyperactivity, and impulsivity were frequently mentioned as characteristic of many writers, artists, authors, inventors, and composers. These characteristics transferred across disciplines and were found in every area of creativity.

How Can You Tell Whether It Is Truly ADHD?

When we see ADHD-type behaviors, in combination with giftedness of either intellect or creativity, how can we tell if we need to take action to label and treat the ADHD? This is a question asked in nearly every article on the topic. The overwhelming primary response is this: Exercise caution in both the identification and treatment of ADHD in children identified as being gifted. Beyond that, research has identified several characteristics of gifted children with ADHD—characteristics that are not generally present in the child who is gifted but not identified as having ADHD.

The first is inconsistency in performance. Non-gifted ADHD children are known for inconsistency in school performance that occurs at any time in any subject (Barkley, 1990). Being gifted does not exempt children from these sorts of academic inconsistencies (Webb & Latimer, 1993). If children are functioning at a high level in a subject one day, then failing in the same subject days later, there may be reason to suspect a problem. A thorough history of the child's performance will reveal a pattern of variability of task performance over time. These children's performance may also be linked to the teacher's characteristics and teaching style; these students will not produce quality work for a teacher they do not like or respect.

There is a movement in the field now to find a means of measuring overexcitabilities as a tool for identification of gifted people.

A visit to a gifted resource classroom, otherwise known as a gifted "pullout" program, will generally reveal a higher than normal activity level, a great deal of talkativeness, and a high level of enthusiasm and task commitment for challenging, interesting tasks. The enthusiasm, movement, talkativeness, and high activity levels are desirable, though can be exhausting for the teachers involved, because these behaviors correspond to the ways gifted children are identified today. Gifted resource classrooms generally exist to serve gifted students in elementary schools, but sometimes can be found at higher grade levels. Wherever they are found, they are often the high point of a gifted students' day or week—time away from their general education classrooms to be spent with intellectual peers. While children with ADHD tend toward inattention, and distraction in nearly every situation, gifted children with ADHD will retain the hyperactivity and problems with sustained attention, except during certain highly stimulating, novel, motivating tasks, such as those to be found in the gifted resource classroom. Those gifted children who are unresponsive to even those tasks stand out among their peers and should be investigated.

Gifted children with ADHD, like all children, not only deserve, but *require* highly stimulating and mentally and psychologically challenging environments to be successful, something few schools provide. Many gifted children have problems with school environments that provide few opportunities for creativity, provide only concrete, linear-sequential instruction, teach only at the lower levels of the taxonomy, require excessively rote and repeti-

tive work, and do not allow learners to progress at their own rate (Baum et al., 1998; Cramond, 1995; Lovecky, 1994; Zentall & Zentall, 1983). This type of learning environment can be a disaster for any child, but you can virtually guarantee it will be for the child who has characteristics of both giftedness and ADHD. These children will frequently shut down when given repetitive tasks, even knowing that unfavorable consequences are certain to follow. When one 11-year-old gifted child with ADHD was asked about this, he responded, "It actually makes me feel sick to my stomach when they make me do the same thing over and over."

When the ADHD has gone undiagnosed for many years, the student may have developed problems with self-esteem and depression.

Whereas children with ADHD tend toward not liking school and gifted children usually do, gifted children with ADHD usually have a few subjects (particularly science) they really love and may not care about the rest (Zentall, 1997). This can lead to incredible power struggles in the home and school when parents and teachers see that the child can attend in some situations but won't (or can't) in others. In children like this, underachievement begins early, with the ADHD not generally identified until at least 6th grade (Lovecky, 1994). By then the child has set up a pattern of inconsistent performance and failure to complete work, leading to frequent negative feedback, leading in turn to diminished academic self-esteem and anger. This pattern of underachievement and the negative response it generates create a cycle within the school and the family that is difficult to break.

Though gifted children frequently display mental ages and social functioning well above those of their chronological peers, they still may exhibit some discrepancies within themselves between these developmental strands, while the gifted child with ADHD may exhibit a much wider and debilitating discrepancy between intellectual age and social and emotional ages. This can cause the child to be

out of sync with everyone (Lovecky, 1993). Social skills are usually underdeveloped in these children; as a result, they may have few friends, with those few generally being younger. Again, these children are aware of their differences and lack of friends, so may become depressed or oppositional in response.

How Do We Help These Paradoxical Children Become Achievers?

Research on underachievement in general, and in gifted people with ADHD specifically, has given us ideas on how to help these children become achievers. As far back as 1959, Passow and Goldberg provided insight in their landmark study on how to reverse underachievement. Their studies revealed that if teachers wish to reverse underachievement, they should place students in a stimulating, rich environment with a teacher who is kind and accepting, who values each of them as individuals, and who maintains high expectations. In addition, the researchers found that students needed further, intensive instruction in study and organizational skills; a characteristic shared by many underachievers, and nearly all children diagnosed with ADHD (Dorry, 1994; Maxwell, 1989). In today's world, gifted children with ADHD can be taught word processing and computer skills that will allow them to compensate for their inability to write quickly or neatly, or to keep their thoughts while writing (Ramirez-Smith, 1997).

Medication works most effectively when coupled with stable parental support at home.

Teachers who have successfully worked with gifted children with ADHD recognize that cognitive therapy is helpful. It is beneficial to talk openly with students about expectations and problems and include them in developing plans of action (Mendaglio, 1995). Contracts, with student-chosen rewards, are helpful in some cases. Because gifted children tend to be primarily intrinsically motivated, external rewards and punishments have little effect unless they are selected by the children themselves. Students need to be convinced that failure is not an option, that today's work will pay off in the future, and that hard work will benefit them personally. Goal setting is another useful strategy in this area, because it helps remove the child from the impulsivity of the moment and develop focus on the future.

What About Parents?

Parenting gifted children with ADHD can be an extremely frustrating experience. There is an awareness of the child's precocity and talents that leads to higher expectations, but that, when coupled with the ADHD behaviors, leads to frustration with the child's self-destructive behaviors. Parents need to deliberately educate themselves about how to deal appropriately with these children (see box, "Tried and True Strategies for Parents") and be advocates for them, while not being rescuers available to bail the children out of every jam (Zentall, 1997). Negativity and power struggles are common in families with gifted children with ADHD. On a more positive note, a child with ADHD who is gifted, who has a supportive family, and who is taught specific ways to compensate for his or her deficits has a much greater chance of becoming a productive adult (Phelan, 1996). Though the gifted child with ADHD may for many years demand an inordinate amount of the family's resources, it appears that early intervention and long-term support eventually pay off.

Home-school communication is essential for the success of gifted children with ADHD (Baum et al., 1998; Ramirez-Smith, 1997; Wolfle & French, 1990). Teachers need to be informed about these children's specific needs, and most are not. How could they be? In teacher education programs, there has traditionally been little room for teaching about gifted children at all, let alone those with additional exceptionalities. Parents can be useful in providing materials that inform educators about the characteristics and needs of a gifted child with ADHD. There should be ongoing, open communication between parent and teacher, with the child included as needed.

Tried & True Strategies for Parents of Gifted Children with ADHD or Overexcitability

- **Love your children for who they are**, not for what they do or don't do; obvious, but not always easy with these extremely challenging children.
- **Set standards and *insist* they be met**. Do what it takes to communicate that failure is *not* an option, and that every action has its consequences. If there are no natural consequences, design some specific to the situation.
- **Use humor to defuse stress and anger**. An advanced sense of humor is a characteristic many gifted children share. Take advantage of it.
- **There are no quick fixes**. Know that gifted children with ADHD require intensive, long-term, interventions. Be consistent over time.
- **Communicate regularly with your child's teachers** in a positive fashion, no matter what grade your child is in, and do so *before* problems surface. Remember, your mutual goal is to help the child be successful.
- **Impose organization on your children until they prove they can do it themselves**. Find a good system and teach and reteach it. Expect backsliding from time to time, all the way through school.
- **Provide opportunities for your child to express his or her creativity**. When things get really bad, this may be his or her lifesaver.
- **Nothing breeds success like success**. Find some way to show your child that he or she can be successful at something meaningful, if only he or she tries. Provide a choice of opportunities and insist he or she chooses one and sticks with it until successful completion.
- **Make sure your child is provided with appropriate curriculum and teachers from the start**. Positively but honestly present your child and his or her needs to school administrators *before* the end of this school year for next year's placement, then trust the school personnel to do the work of placing the child appropriately.

Because of the myriad needs generated by having a gifted child with ADHD in the classroom, administrators and teachers must hold discussions about classroom placements and include both current and former teachers, administrators, and parents. Educators should place the child in classrooms where expectations are high and teaching is holistic, relevant, challenging, and meaningful (DeLisle, 1995), and where teachers are willing to teach to the child's strengths while remediating the weaknesses. Multi-modal approaches allow the gifted child with ADHD to play to his or her strengths and express creativity (Lovecky, 1994). Several successful research projects have employed talent development and attention to students' specific intelligences, talents, or gifts as means to promote academic success for at-risk students (Baum, Owen, & Oreck, 1996; Baum, Renzulli, & Hebert, 1994; Olenchak, 1994). It is clear that proper curriculums, instruction, and pacing can make a great deal of difference in the school lives of gifted children with ADHD.

In some cases, physicians may prescribe medication for students to help control the ADD/ADHD symptoms, allowing the giftedness to emerge more fully. According to many researchers, doctors should not prescribe medication unless educators, parents, and other professionals have explored all other possible avenues because medication may have some detrimental effects on creativity, imagination, and intellectual curiosity (Baum et al., 1998; Cramond, 1995). That, of course, is a question to be decided by the doctors, parents, and children; and they should make such decisions on an individual basis. Wolfle & French (1990) stated that medication works most effectively when coupled with stable parental support at home. A review of literature on the effects of stimulant medication and children with ADHD has reinforced that medication alone provides only short-term effects; people should not expect it to improve long-term adjustment in either social or academic areas (Swanson et al., 1993).

Finally, researchers have suggested counseling for some of these children, especially when the ADHD has gone undiagnosed for many years, because the child may have developed problems with self-esteem and depression. When counseling is undertaken, however, educators, parents, and others must be careful to select counselors familiar with both the social and emotional needs of gifted children and children with ADD/ADHD (Webb & Latimer, 1993).

Now What?

The literature has little to say about children doubly blessed with giftedness and ADHD, even less of the literature is research based. In a search for materials on the subject, I found no information on this topic in traditional educational literature; I found some in the social sciences literature; and the rest in the gifted literature. Because most teachers have a hard enough time keeping up with information in their own area of expertise and seldom have the opportunity to examine the gifted literature, it seems logical that this information must be disseminated into mainstream education.

Educators need to do more to improve the quality of identification of these high-potential, though terribly at-risk children and to reduce the likelihood of misdiagnosis of children who are gifted and creative and overexcitable as having ADHD. On the other hand, writers and researchers can heighten our awareness of the existence of this segment of the population so that gifted children who actually *do* have ADHD are not missed in diagnosis. Misdiagnoses can cut some students off from services that they may need. Teachers who are educated on this topic can be of immense help when it comes time to work with doctors in diagnosing possible medical conditions such as ADHD.

Finally, we must learn to value these children; they have much to offer. Though the learning environments and teaching practices discussed earlier are desirable for all children, gifted or not, these doubly-blessed students possess the creative potential to produce great ideas and make wonderful contributions to our society. With appropriate curriculums; informed teachers and administrators; and educated, involved parents working together, we can reclaim a segment of our population who currently underachieve at a high rate. Most of all, we can teach these young people that in working to show their strengths and overcome their deficits, they make themselves even better. As educators, we need to help them learn who they are, what they are capable of, and how to reach their potential.

References

American Psychiatric Association (1994). *Diagnostic and statistical manual of mental disorders* (4th ed.: DSM IV). Washington, DC: Author.

Barkley, R. (1990). *Attention deficit hyperactivity disorder: A handbook for diagnosis and treatment*. New York: Guilford Press.

Baum, S., Olenchak, F., & Owen, S. (1998). Gifted students with attention deficits: Fact or fiction? Or, can we see the forest for the trees? *Gifted Child Quarterly, 42*(2), 96–104.

Baum, S., Owen, S., & Oreck, B. (1996). Talent beyond words: Identification of potential talent in dance and music in elementary students. *Gifted Child Quarterly, 40*(2), 93–102.

Baum, S., Renzulli, J., & Hebert, T. (1994). Reversing underachievement: Stories of success. *Educational Leadership, 52*(3), 48–53.

Cramond, B. (1994). Creativity and ADHD: What is the connection? *Journal of Creative Behavior, 28*(3), 193–210.

Cramond, B. (1995). The coincidence of attention deficit hyperactivity disorder and creativity. *Monograph of the National Research Center on the Gifted and Talented, RBDM 9508, United States Government: Connecticut.* (ERIC Document Reproduction Service No. 388 016)

Dabrowski, K. (1972). *Psychoneurosis is not an illness*. London: Gryf.

DeLisle, J. (1995). ADD gifted: How many labels can one child take? *Gifted Child Today, 18*(2), 42–43.

Dorry, G. (1994). The perplexed perfectionist. *Understanding Our Gifted, 6*(5), 3, 10–12.

Hallowell, E., & Ratey, J. (1995). *Driven to distraction*. New York: Simon & Schuster.

Lovecky, D. (1993). Out of sync with everyone. *Understanding Our Gifted, 5*(5A), 3.

Lovecky, D. (1994, July/August). The hidden gifted learner. *Understanding Our Gifted, 3 & 18.*

Maxwell, V. (1989). Diagnosis and treatment of the gifted student with attention deficit disorder: A structure of intellect approach. *Reading, Writing & Learning Disabilities, 5*, 247–252.

Mendaglio, S. (1995, July/August). Children who are Gifted/ADHD., *Gifted Child Today, 18*, 37–38.

Olenchak, F. (1994). Talent development: Accommodating the social and emotional needs of secondary gifted/learning disabled students. *Journal of Secondary Gifted Education, 5*(3), 40–52.

Passow, H., & Goldberg, M. (1959). Study of underachieving gifted. *Educational Leadership, 16,* 121–125.

Phelan, T. (1996). *All about attention deficit disorder.* Minneapolis, MN: Child Management Press.

Piechowski, M. (1986). The concept of developmental potential. *Roeper Review, 8*(3), 190–197.

Piechowski, M., & Colangelo, N. (1984). Developmental potential of the gifted. *Gifted Child Quarterly, 28,* 80–88.

Piirto, J. (1992). *Understanding those who create.* Dayton: Ohio Psychology Press.

Ramirez-Smith, C. (1997). *Mistaken identity: Gifted and ADHD.* Reston, VA: The Council for Exceptional Children. (ERIC Document Reproduction No. ED413690)

Swanson, J., McBurnett, K., Wigal, T., Pfiffner, L., Lerner, M., Williams, L., Christian, D., Tamm, L., Willcutt, E., Crowley, K., Clevenger, W., Khouzam, N., Woo, C., Crinella, F., & Fisher, T. (1993). Effect of stimulant medication on children with attention deficit disorder. A "review of reviews." *Exceptional Children, 60,* 154–162.

Webb, J., & Latimer, D. (1993). *ADHD and children who are gifted (ERIC Digest No. 522).* Reston, VA: The Council for Exceptional Children.

Wolfle, J., & French, M. (1990). *Surviving gifted attention deficit disorder children in the classroom.* Paper presented at the meeting of the National Association for Gifted Children, Little Rock, AR.

Zentall, S. (1997, March). *Learning characteristics of boys with attention deficit hyperactivity disorder and/or giftedness.* Paper presented at the annual meeting of the American Educational Research Association, Chicago, IL. (ERIC Document Reproduction No. 407791)

Zentall, S., & Zentall, T. (1983). Optimal stimulation: A model of disordered activity and performance in normal and deviant children. *Psychological Bulletin, 94,* 446–471.

Lori J. Flint, *Doctoral Candidate, Department of Educational Psychology, The University of Georgia, Athens.*

Address correspondence to the author at Department of Educational Psychology, The University of Georgia, 325 Aderhold Hall, Athens, GA 30602-7143, (e-mail: LJFSTAT@AOL.COM)

Raising Expectations for the Gifted

Five teaching strategies allow flexibility in meeting the needs of gifted students in inclusive classrooms.

By Colleen Willard-Holt

Most gifted students study in regular classrooms for most of their school careers and are taught using the same state standards intended for all students. Most state standards, however, do not provide sufficient intellectual challenge for gifted students.

Neuroscientific research has found that rats in unstimulating environments had thinner cortexes, the part of the brain where higher mental functions reside (Diamond & Hopson, 1998). This effect appeared after just four days!

Education research has shown that gifted students' motivation and performance also declined in the absence of mental stimulation, even leading to underachievement (Purcell, 1993; Whitmore, 1980), but that gifted students exposed to intellectually stimulating content at an accelerated pace outperformed gifted peers not in such programs (Cornell & Delcourt, 1990; Kulik, 1992). It is too great a risk to subject gifted students to a steady diet of unchallenging work.

Standards need not imply standardization of learning activities or expectations. Gifted students may need less time to master a given standard, or they may address the standard in greater depth. Classroom teachers might follow the principle of teaching all students at their optimal level of instruction—what Vygotsky would call their "zone of proximal development" (1978).

How can regular classroom teachers address the needs of their gifted students? The first step in differentiating a standards-based lesson or unit for gifted students is to identify the standards that the lesson will address. An efficient way to accomplish several tasks within one lesson is to combine content, skills, and arts standards. For example, making a poster for National Arbor Day can address science standards in environmental health, language arts standards in research and communication, and standards regarding the elements and principles of visual art.

Teachers can then assess students' grasp of content and skills. They might pretest the students, using an end-of-chapter test that integrates skills with content, or review students' achievement on content and skills that they have previously studied. Perusing student portfolios or assessing interests and multiple intelligences profiles can also provide insight into skills and content knowledge.

Once teachers have determined students' readiness levels, they can execute differentiation strategies. Curriculum compacting, flexible grouping, product choices, tiered assignments, and multilevel learning stations are excellent strategies for differentiating instruction for gifted students in regular classrooms (see Gregory & Chapman, 2002; Maker & Nielson, 1996; Reis, Burns, & Renzulli, 1992; Tomlinson, 1999; Willard-Holt, 1994). Some of these strategies also lend themselves well to meeting the needs of gifted students with disabilities.

Curriculum Compacting

Curriculum compacting is a powerful strategy for ensuring accountability for standards while acknowledging what students already know. Curriculum compacting means streamlining what is taught to students by first assessing their prior knowledge and then modifying or eliminating work that has been partially or fully mastered. After teachers assess student mastery of a particular standard, three groups often emerge: students with poor mastery, students with partial mastery, and students with full mastery who are ready for more advanced work.[1] The first group, usually the largest, proceeds with the planned sequence of instruction; the second group may accomplish the planned sequence more quickly and then proceed to a greater challenge; the third group may begin an independent project immediately.

Consider this math standard for grade 3: "Count, compare, and make change using a collection of coins and one-dollar bills" (PA Std. 2.1.3E).[2] The first group is ready to make several combinations of pennies, nickels, and dimes for given amounts. The second group is confident of these steps and can make change, but they need help using quarters. They will join the rest of the class when the teacher provides information and practice with quarters; the rest of the time they work together on a coin-related project that they will present to the class. The project might entail making a poster of U.S. coinage from colonial times to the present, using drawings, replicas, or actual coins when available. The third group's students, who tested 85 percent or above on the pretest, are making a chart that compares currency systems for different countries. They will defend their choice of the most efficient system at the end of the unit. Such higher-order thinking projects may also satisfy language arts standards, using a similar process for compacting skill standards in reading or writing.

In middle and high school grades, gifted students may not have the technical knowledge to meet a particular content standard and therefore may not show mastery on a pretest. They may be able to learn the content quickly by reading the text and completing application exercises on their own, however, and then successfully complete a criterion-referenced posttest. For example, a life sciences course might focus on the 10th grade standard, "Identify and characterize major life forms by kingdom, phylum, class, and order" (PA Std. 3.3.10A). The teacher invites students who have performed well in previous science units to read the text and work through a packet of exercises at their own pace. This packet consists of activities crucial to understanding the topic and differs from the step-by-step exercises given to the rest of the class. When ready, students take the posttest and, if they demonstrate mastery, undertake an in-depth project, such as creating a three-dimensional clay model of a dissected starfish (Miller & Willard-Holt, 2000). This project addresses skill and arts standards simultaneously.

Teachers can also use compacting with gifted students who have disabilities. If the goal is to master content quickly while circumventing the disability, the teacher can compact in areas of weakness as well as strength. For the standard, "Identify planets in our solar system and their general characteristics" (PA Std. 3.4.4D), the class assignment might be a written report on a planet. A gifted student with a writing disability who demonstrates mastery of the characteristics of the planets on a pretest might instead research current theories about the birth of galaxies and create a PowerPoint presentation.

It is not always necessary to focus on remediation. If the goal is to develop coping strategies for the disability, compacting can focus on the area of strength.

Flexible Grouping

Flexible grouping is particularly effective when students' achievement levels in content and skills differ, as is often the case for gifted students with disabilities. The teacher groups students according to strength, need, or interest, and groups change frequently, sometimes in the course of a single class session. As an illustration, an 11th grade English class might address the standards, "Analyze the relationships, uses, and effectiveness of literary elements used by one or more authors, including characterization, setting, plot, theme, point of view, tone, and style" (PA Std. 1.3.11B) and "Write short stories, poems, and plays" (PA Std. 1.4.11A). The class has read a scene from *Romeo and Juliet*, viewed the corresponding scene from *West Side Story*, and discussed similarities and differences. In groups, students write a contemporary scene in which young people are in love despite their families' differences. Drawing on their knowledge of current events, students research the conflict between the groups that the families represent, such as Israelis versus Palestinians, big business versus environmentalists, or Shiite versus Sunni Muslims. Students could also choose groups that are at odds in their immediate community.

Students initially come together around the specific conflict that most interests them, with groups changing later as needed. Each group has students with mixed levels of ability. The teacher provides mini-lessons to address specific skills—for example, how to research the conflict using print resources, Internet, and interviews of community leaders; write authentic dialogue; punctuate dialogue correctly; or write stage directions. Later, gifted students might meet together to choose a multi-layered conflict, the threads of which they must logically incorporate into the scene.

Product Choices

Another way to plan for gifted students is to allow them choices of what kind of product they will produce. In the *Romeo and Juliet* example, one group might complete a written script (verbal/linguistic intelligence); another, a videotaped dramatization of the scene (bodily/kinesthetic intelligence); and a third, a comic strip (visual/spatial intelligence). In this way, each group addresses the same content standard but uses a different skill or arts standard.

For the 6th grade standard, "Describe the human characteristics of places and regions by their cultural characteristics" (PA Std. 7.3.6B), students studying a unit on Central and South America might choose to create an authentic traditional costume, dance, food, artwork, or model of a home—developing a three-dimensional model, drawing, or verbal description. The projects appeal to different intelligences and address different skills and arts standards.

Product choices are important for gifted students with disabilities, allowing them to demonstrate their understanding of the content without their disability interfering. For example, a student with a learning disability in written expression may conduct research, make the necessary cognitive connections, and demonstrate understanding through art and oral expression, thereby circumventing writing. A blind student may conduct research by using text-to-speech interfaces on the Internet and create a three-dimensional model. In each case, the focus is on content mastery. Assignments in other areas would remediate or develop coping strategies for the disability.

Tiered Assignments

The advantage of this strategy is that the entire class studies the same content, but individual students choose assignments at different levels of complexity, with the teacher's assistance. For example, coupling a 4th grade science standard, "Know basic weather elements" (PA Std. 3.4.4C), with a math standard, "Organize and display data using pictures, tallies, tables, charts, bar graphs, and circle graphs" (PA Std. 2.6.5A), allows students to learn how to gather weather data from various sources and graph the data. Assignment choices might include

• Making a bar graph that shows the average monthly temperatures in two cities (basic level).

• Choosing two appropriate types of graphs to show the proportion of rainy days to sunny days, and the average rainfall by months in a city of your choice (average level).

• Generating two appropriate graphs on the computer to show the ratio of rain to snow, and monthly temperature and precipitation in a city of your choice (advanced level).

Students choose the assignment that sounds most interesting and best stimulates their learning. Gentle nudging might encourage students to accept the appropriate level of challenge.

Multilevel Learning Stations

Multilevel learning stations provide meaningful independent work that extends and enriches class discussions. For example, a learning station can assist 3rd grade students studying ancient civilizations by addressing history, geography, arts, and language arts standards, including the following:

• Compare similarities and differences between the earliest civilizations and life today (PA Std. 8.4.3C).

• Explain the historical, cultural, and social context of an individual work in the arts (PA Std. 9.2.3A).

• Relate works in the arts chronologically to historical events (PA Std. 9.2.3B) or geographic regions (PA Std. 9.2.3G).

Activity cards address such topics as leaders/famous people, arts, structures, ways of life, and location. In addition, the teacher codes the activity cards according to Bloom's thinking levels: red for knowledge/comprehension, blue for application, green for analysis, yellow for synthesis, and white for evaluation. On the basis of assessment data, each student receives an assignment sheet detailing the number of activities that he or she is to complete at each level. For example, Juan will do one of each color; Sarah will select five activities, all at green, yellow, or white levels; and Randy will choose five red or blue activities.

Product choices allow gifted students with disabilities to demonstrate their understanding of the content.

Teachers often assume that learning stations are appropriate only for the elementary grades, yet secondary students also seem to enjoy them. For example, U.S. history students addressing the Civil War might explore in depth topics relating to battles, leaders, military technology, camp life, civilian life, or the roles of women or African Americans in the war, according to their interests.

Inspiring Extraordinary Achievement

Some gifted students' capabilities and rates of learning are so far beyond their chronological ages that they would spend almost all of their time reviewing what they already knew if they followed the curriculum offered in a regular classroom. These students need a highly individualized program at an advanced level, perhaps through acceleration or mentoring. Other gifted students may be highly advanced in one subject and could benefit from acceleration or mentoring in that subject while remaining in the inclusive classroom for the remainder of the day.

Providing gifted students with instruction at the appropriate level also removes pressure that they might feel in cooperative learning situations within inclusive classrooms. It may be tempting to ask advanced students to tutor others—a strategy that is permissible on occasion, but inappropriate as a regular activity. Gifted students, like all students, come to school to encounter new learning challenges. Depending on gifted students as peer tutors also places them at risk for social isolation if other students come to view them as teacher's pets or know-it-alls (Robinson, 1990).

Teaching to standards need not mean standardization of learning activities or expectations. Simply meeting standards is not an adequate challenge for most gifted students, although that is all the law may require of them. As Tomlinson states in reference to the No Child Left Behind Act of 2001,

> There is no incentive for schools to attend to the growth of students once they attain proficiency…and certainly not to inspire those who far exceed proficiency. (2002, p. 36)

Don't we want more than minimal proficiency from our gifted students? By using strategies to challenge all students at their optimal levels of instruction, teachers can meet their responsibilities for accountability while inspiring extraordinary achievement.

Notes

13. A fourth group—those not yet ready to attempt the standard—is beyond the scope of this article.
14. I refer to Pennsylvania standards. The standards are available at www.pde.state.pa.us/stateboard_fed; click Academic Standards.

References

Cornell, D. G., & Delcourt, M. A. B. (1990). Achievement, attitudes, and adjustment. *Communicator, 20*(5), 28.

Diamond, M., & Hopson, J. (1998). *Magic trees of the mind.* New York: Plume Books.

Gregory, G. H., & Chapman, C. (2002). *Differentiated instructional strategies: One size doesn't fit all.* Thousand Oaks, CA: Corwin Press.

Kulik, J. A. (1992). *An analysis of the research on ability grouping* (RBDM 9204). Storrs, CT: University of Connecticut, The National Research Center on the Gifted and Talented.

Maker, C. J., & Nielson, A. B. (1996). *Curriculum development and teaching strategies for gifted learners* (2nd ed.). Austin, TX: Pro-Ed.

Miller, B., & Willard-Holt, C. (2000). *Dare to differentiate: Strategies for enrichment in middle school science.* Manassas, VA: Gifted Education Press.

Purcell, J. H. (1993). The effects of the elimination of gifted and talented programs on participating students and their parents. *Gifted Child Quarterly, 37*(4), 177-187.

Reis, S. M., Burns, D. E., & Renzulli, J. S. (1992). *Curriculum compacting.* Mansfield Center, CT: Creative Learning Press.

Robinson, A. (1990). Cooperation or exploitation? The argument against cooperative learning for talented students. *Journal for the Education of the Gifted*, 14(3), 9-27, 31-36.

Tomlinson, C. A. (1999). *The differentiated classroom: Responding to the needs of all learners*. Alexandria, VA: ASCD.

Tomlinson, C. A. (2002, Nov. 6). Proficiency is not enough. *Education Week*, 22(10), 36, 38.

Vygotsky, L. S. (1978). *Mind in society: The development of higher psychological processes*. Cambridge, MA: Harvard University Press.

Whitmore, J. R. (1980). *Giftedness, conflict, and underachievement*. Boston: Allyn and Bacon.

Willard-Holt, C. (1994). Strategies for individualizing instruction in regular classrooms. *Roeper Review*, 17(1), 43-45.

Colleen Willard-Holt is an associate professor of education in the School of Behavioral Sciences and Education at Penn State—Capital College; cxw20@psu.edu.

Celebrating Diverse Minds

Many faltering students have specialized minds—brains exquisitely wired to perform certain kinds of tasks masterfully.

Mel Levine

A distraught mother recently sent me this e-mail: *Every morning when I send Michael off to school, I feel as if I'm sending him to jail. He can't spell, he forgets his math facts even after we study them together, his handwriting is hard to decipher, and he is hopelessly absent-minded. The other kids see his papers and say that he "writes like a mental case." All day, he faces nonstop criticism from his teacher. She scolds him in front of his classmates for not trying. And you know, his teacher's right. He's not trying—he's scared to try. He's decided that if you're going to fail, it's better to fail without trying.*

He can fix absolutely anything that's broken and he is brilliant when he plays with his Legos. I can't believe the complicated things he makes. He is convinced that he is hopelessly dumb, and he worries about school all the time. A lot of nights, Michael cries himself to sleep. We are losing this darling boy and he is such a beautiful child, such a decent kid. Please help us.

We have all heard the success stories of Albert Einstein, Thomas Edison, Steve Jobs, and Charles Schwab—accomplished adults whose minds failed to fit in school. But what becomes of those whom we never hear about—students like Michael, who give up on themselves because they lack the kinds of minds needed to satisfy existing criteria for school success?

For more than 30 years, my work as a pediatrician has been dedicated to such out-of-step children and adolescents. Although some of them have officially acknowledged collisions with word decoding or attention, many contend with more elusive differences in learning. These students may have trouble organizing time and prioritizing activities, communicating effectively, grasping verbal or nonverbal concepts, retrieving data precisely and quickly from long-term memory, recognizing and responding to recurring patterns, or assimilating fine detail.

Such insidious dysfunctions can constitute daunting barriers, especially when they are not recognized and managed. Most important, these breakdowns can mislead us into undervaluing, unfairly accusing, and even undereducating students, thereby stifling their chances for success in school and life.

The Challenge of Disappointing School Performance

Many faltering students have specialized minds—brains exquisitely wired to perform certain kinds of tasks masterfully, but decidedly miswired when it comes to meeting other expectations. A student may be brilliant at visualizing, but embarrassingly inept at verbalizing. Her classmate may reveal a remarkable understanding of people, but exhibit no insight about sentence structure.

Within every student contending with learning differences, an area invariably exists in which her or his mind has been amply equipped to thrive. In the e-mail from Michael's mother, the clue to his mind's early specialization practically jumps out at you: "He can fix absolutely anything that's broken." Michael's mechanical brilliance gets eclipsed by our focus on what he can't do.

I love to spend time explaining his strengths and their possibilities to a student like Michael who feels depleted and diminished (and perhaps even demolished) by the experience of school. I talk to him about the different careers in which he could readily succeed given the abilities he already possesses. I feel as if I have stepped inside a shadowy passageway suddenly illuminated, as revealed by a newly radiant facial expression. I can't help but conclude that the real challenge for schools rests more with identifying and fortifying individuals' strengths than with caulking academic crevices.

My long-term experience working at the interface between pediatrics and education has allowed me to synthesize the body of research on neurodevelopmental function and variation (Levine & Reed, 1999) and to construct a framework for understanding the enigma of disappointing school performance. Three factors play major roles:

• The traditional paradigms for understanding learning differences focus on exposing and fixing deficits, often neglecting the latent or blatant talents within struggling learners.

• Instructional practices and curricular choices fail to provide educational opportunities for diverse learners and to prepare them for a successful life.

• Because knowledge about learning emanating from the explosion of insights from brain research is not yet part of teacher preparation and professional development, most educators lack the expertise to understand and support their students' diverse minds.

To stem the tide of needless and wasteful failure facing thousands of kids, we need to take robust action on three fronts: broadened student assessment, curriculum reexamination, and professional development for educators.

Broadened Student Assessment

The methods that schools typically deploy to assess students with learning problems are not up to the task. The discrepancy formulas used to determine eligibility for specialized assistance have been shown repeatedly to have serious flaws (Kavale & Forness, 2000).

Moreover, testing that merely generates a label, such as LD or ADD, accomplishes little. These vague labels do not suggest specific approaches to remediation; instead, they pessimistically imply a relatively permanent pathological condition. What a colossal self-fulfilling prophecy! Most important, diagnosis spawned from a deficit model fails to take into account the most important feature of a student—his strengths.

Smokescreen Labels

Phillip's parents reported that he seemed to generate about two highly original and unorthodox ideas per minute. His teacher described this irrepressible 4th grader as a brilliant conceptualizer, always coming up with creative analogies. When the class studied terrorism, Phillip compared suicide bombers to strep germs that make you sick and then die in your throat.

But Phillip's day-to-day performance in school was disappointing. When he listened or read, Phillip missed or forgot much of the information he was expected to absorb. He would tune out and become fidgety during extended explanations or directions. His parents sought help from their son's pediatrician, who diagnosed ADD and prescribed a stimulant medication. This treatment helped, but not much.

It turns out that Phillip owned the kind of mind that becomes enthralled with the big picture and rejects fine detail. Consequently, in math he mastered the concepts readily but couldn't be bothered to notice the difference between a plus sign and a minus sign (a mere detail). His writing was creative and amusing but sparse on specific information. In subject after subject, Phillip's overall understanding far exceeded his handling of the details.

Like Phillip, many kids with problems don't ooze easily into categories. Students with his kind of detail intolerance often get diagnosed with ADD or accused of not really trying. In Phillip's case, the label ADD was a smokescreen that obscured people's view of his remarkable strengths and stopped them short of managing his specific weakness in detail assimilation. Phillip improved markedly after his teacher began encouraging him to make detail thinking a separate step in any activity he undertook—scan first, get the big picture, have some great ideas, and then revisit the material to vacuum up the important details.

Incidentally, society desperately needs big-picture people who can collaborate meaningfully with administrators who thrive on detail. So let's take care not to disparage or discourage the flourishing of Phillip's kind of mind.

Assessment for Diverse Minds

In addition to rethinking the assessments used to diagnose learning problems, schools need to design regular tests and quizzes so that different kinds of minds can show what they know in different ways. Teachers should be careful not to tap exclusively rote memory or straight regurgitation of skills and knowledge. They should often allow students to use notes and encourage them to take as much time as they need to respond to questions. It makes more sense to limit space than time—for instance, telling students, "You can't write more than two pages, but you can take as long as you want to do so."

High-stakes testing can pulverize many mismatched students. How commonly does end-of-grade testing discriminate against certain kinds of minds? Frequently. As a clinician, I encounter many students who have difficulty performing on multiple-choice tests or operating under timed conditions. These students' dysfunctions in certain skill areas are more than out-weighed by their assets in other domains, but standardized testing never gives them the opportunity to exhibit their strengths.

> ## I look forward to the day when our schools offer every student the opportunity to become a leading expert on a chosen topic.

On entering the medical profession, we take an oath that in our practice we will first of all "do no harm." I offer five suggestions (see "Do No Harm" Testing Practices, p. 17) to my professional colleagues in education so that they may strive for testing practices that do no harm to students with different kinds of minds. We need to advocate for the elimination of testing practices that inflict needless damage and unfair humiliation on so many students.

Curriculum Reexamination

It's ironic that at the same time that neuroscience is telling us so much about differences in learning, we are imposing curriculum standards that offer our students fewer learning alternatives than ever before. If we aspire to meet the challenge of leaving no child behind, we must provide diverse learners with diverging pathways that lead to their success. Such roads should maintain rigorous performance standards, while permitting innovation and creativity in curricular choices and allowing early, highly specialized minds to envision and prepare for productive adulthood.

For example, children like Michael, with his impressive mechanical aptitude, should not be sentenced to wait until adulthood to experience success. We should encourage, not constrain, the development of magnet schools and vocational education opportunities. I look forward to the day when thousands of students pursue a vocationally oriented curriculum that does not put a ceiling on their aspirations.

> If we aspire to meet the challenge of leaving no child behind, we must provide diverse learners with diverging pathways that lead to their success.

While studying auto mechanics (and the physics that is a part of it), a teenager should learn the ins and outs of various related careers. She or he should see the possibility of someday climbing the corporate ladder at Ford Motor Company, owning a repair business franchise, designing solar-powered engines, or managing the service department of a dealership. In this way, no one gets written off or limited because of the nature of his passions or the specialized apparatus of her mind.

Many schools have worked against odds to provide educational experiences that involve all students in conducting independent study projects in their area of personal affinity and ability. One school, for example, asked all 3rd grade students to pick a country and become the school's leading expert on that nation. The projects carried over from 3rd through 5th grade, and the students traversed content areas as they studied their country's culture, history, language, animal life, government, and music. They did art projects and wrote reports on their country.

Students learned how it feels to know more about something than anyone around, including their teachers and parents. They became valued consultants on particular countries; when the newspaper reported a current event in their country, they were asked to provide some commentary in class—a great vitamin for intellectual self-esteem!

Another school pursued a similar strategy during students' three years in middle school. Students selected any topic from a list for long-term pursuit across disciplines. They found experts in the community to assist them with their topics. Any student who did not want to claim one of the listed topics could submit one of his or her own choosing.

I look forward to the day when our schools offer every student the opportunity to become a leading expert on a chosen topic—one that harmonizes with his or her kind of mind—and to share that expertise with the community through Web sites, community-based projects, and other venues. Such a practice would give students a powerful experience of success, as well as cultivate their appetite for systematic research and focused, in-depth knowledge.

While advocating ardently for flexibility in achieving the educational aims of schooling, we can still preserve student accountability. No student should be permitted to work, study, or produce less than his or her peers. But we should never insist that everyone put forth identical output.

Professional Development for Educators

In medical practice, highly specific knowledge of the individual needs of a patient is indispensable when selecting the best treatment. This holds true in all "helping" professions—especially in education.

Teachers are in an excellent position to observe, interpret, and celebrate all kinds of minds on a daily basis. Newly acquired knowledge emanating from neuroscientific and education research can empower educators to observe and understand students' minds. Most of the phenomena that determine a student's individual strengths, shortcomings, and preferred ways of learning and producing cannot be found on any test that a clinician gives. Classroom teachers enjoy exclusive screenings—if they pay attention and know what to look for.

Becky

Eight-year-old Becky is an accomplished origami creator, a deft modern dancer, and a gifted mathematician. She thrives on science and computers. Yet in school, this girl appears shy, passive, and eternally anguished. Becky has accurate spelling, but she dislikes writing and avoids it. Becky's teacher, Mrs. Sorenson, having been educated to observe neurodevelopmental phenomena, has noticed that Becky seems to struggle and falter when called on in class. Recently, the teacher led a discussion on whether animals have feelings as people do. She called on Becky and the following dialogue ensued:

Becky: My puppy feels, uh, things like happy and, um, sad.

Mrs. Sorenson: Becky, what makes her happy or sad?

Becky (after a long pause): Different things.

Mrs. Sorenson: Such as?

Becky: Like a dog, uh, basket.

Mrs. Sorenson: Do you mean a dog biscuit?

Becky: Yeah, like that.

Becky's reading comprehension is more than a year above grade level. Yet she has trouble with word finding, shows pronounced verbal hesitancy, puts forth only simple or incomplete sentences, and fails to use verbal elaboration. The same phenomena are conspicuous in her

"Do No Harm" Testing Practices

1. Testing can help elevate education standards, but not if it creates larger numbers of students who are written off as unsuccessful. When a student does poorly, determine which link in the learning chain is uncoupled. Always have constructive, nonpunitive contingency plans for students who perform poorly on a test. Testing should not be an end in itself, but rather a call to action.

2. Not all students can demonstrate their strengths in the same manner. Allow different students to demonstrate their learning differently, using the means of their choice (portfolios, expert papers, oral presentations, and projects, as well as multiple-choice tests).

3. Never use testing as justification for retaining a student in a grade. Retention is ineffective and seriously damaging to students. How can you retain a child while claiming you are not leaving anyone behind?

4. Some students who excel on tests might develop a false sense of security and confidence, failing to realize that adult careers tap many abilities that no test can elicit. Take care to nurture vital capacities that are not testable.

5. Avoid the hazard of teachers' teaching to the tests because your work or school is being judged solely on the basis of examination scores. Teachers should never have their students rehearse or explicitly prepare for tests. Testing should be unannounced. Good results on such tests should be the product of the regular, undisturbed curriculum.

—Mel Levine

writing. Becky has strong receptive language but markedly weak expressive language—she understands better than she talks. No wonder she's so shy, self-conscious, and passive! Language output plays a vital role in school success. Verbal communication affects writing, class participation, social success, and the control of emotions and behavior.

Becky could fall through the cracks because we do not have valid tests of language production. For example, the WISC (the commonly used IQ test in her age group) does little to capture expressive language fluency. In fact, by far the best test of expressive language is a classroom teacher who knows what to listen for in gauging the adequacy of a student's verbal output, and who understands the everyday classroom phenomena associated with breakdowns in language production.

Bruce

Here's another example of the role that teachers can play in detecting learning differences. Bruce was disruptive in most of his 7th grade classes. He fashioned himself as an entertainer and often disengaged from classroom activities. Mr. Jackson, a social studies teacher knowledgeable about early adolescent development and learning, made the astute observation that Bruce often appeared confused about dates and about the sequences of events in the various historical periods that they studied. Mr. Jackson also noted that Bruce often looked distressed when given directions.

On one occasion, Mr. Jackson told the class:

> This morning I want you all to open your books to page 47, read the first three paragraphs, and study the diagram at the top of the page. And when you're finished doing that, read and think about the first two questions at the end of the chapter. I'm going to give you 10 minutes, and then I'll be calling on you to discuss the questions.

Bruce seemed to hear only something about page 47 (or was it 57?). His teacher suspected rightly that this boy was having problems processing sequences—sequential directions, chains of events in history, and multi-step explanations. His weak temporal-sequential ordering accounted for his problems in social studies and in math. This insight enabled teachers to give Bruce strategies to manage his sequencing problems: taking notes, whispering sequences under his breath, and picturing sequences in his mind. His behavior and demeanor in class improved dramatically.

Although continuing education programs abound to help teachers stay abreast of their content, we have found few comprehensive programs devoted to helping educators deepen their expertise in the science of learning. Our not-for-profit institute, All Kinds of Minds, has developed a professional development and school service model called Schools Attuned to help experienced classroom educators become knowledgeable about neurodevelopmental function and variation.[1] Participating teachers learn to analyze how their own instructional delivery and content taps specific aspects of memory, attention, motor function, language, and other areas of brain function. They are guided to observe everyday classroom phenomena that open windows on relevant learning processes (Levine, 1994).

Equipped with their Schools Attuned training, teachers lead a coalition involving the student, parents, and other adults in the school to unmask the specific learning profile of a struggling student. With help from professionals trained as neurodevelopmental consultants, whom we call profile advisors (usually school psychologists or special educators), teachers become the primary detectors of student strengths, weaknesses, and content affinities. The teachers then infuse their insights into their daily group instructional strategies and lesson designs. Frequently, a strategy that they develop to help a particular struggling student benefits the entire class. It's called excellent pedagogy.

Testing that merely generates a label, such as LD or ADD, accomplishes little.

Schools Attuned teachers are also committed to making sure that all of their students learn about learning while they are learning. Through a process called demystification, they help students whose neurodevelopmental profiles do not currently mesh with expectations to learn about their own strengths and weaknesses and acquire the terms for the specific processes that they need to work on. With profile advisors as their consultants, regular classroom teachers take the lead in formulating management plans for these students.

Where We Need to Go

The core theme of K-12 education in this century should be straightforward: high standards with an unwavering commitment to individuality. In proposing that educators reexamine assessment, curriculum, and the role of teachers, I am advocating neurodevelopmental pluralism in our schools—the celebration of all kinds of minds. Such an ethos will be the most effective and humane way of realizing our commitment to leave no child behind.

Note

1. More information about the Schools Attuned program and All Kinds of Minds is available online at www.allkindsofminds.org.

References

Kavale, K. A., & Forness, S. R. (2000). What definitions of learning disability say and don't say: A critical analysis. *Journal of Learning Disabilities, 33,* 239-256.

Levine, M. (1994). *Educational care* (2nd ed.). Cambridge, MA: Educators Publishing Service.

Levine, M., & Reed, M. (1999). *Developmental variation and learning disorders* (2nd ed.). Cambridge, MA: Educators Publishing Service.

Author's note: Mary Dean Barringer, Stacy Parker-Fisher, Chris Osmond, and Tamara Nimkoff contributed to this article.

Mel Levine, M.D., is a professor of pediatrics at the University of North Carolina Medical School in Chapel Hill, North Carolina; Director of the University's Clinical Center for the Study of Development and Learning; and the founder of All Kinds of Minds. His most recent books are *A Mind at a Time* (Simon and Schuster, 2002) and *The Myth of Laziness* (Simon and Schuster, 2003).

When Should Bilingual Students Be in Special Education?

How can we avoid the inappropriate provision of special education services to culturally and linguistically diverse students?

Janette K. Klingner and Alfredo J. Artiles

In recent years, schools have made progress in meeting the needs of culturally and linguistically diverse students with special education needs. Even so, a number of long-standing issues still plague this field. Researchers and practitioners today express concern that culturally and linguistically diverse students are disproportionately represented in special education (Baca & Cervantes, 1998). Research offers some helpful insights into the inappropriate assessment and placement practices that lead to these discrepancies.

Our discussion here of some of the current challenges in special education for culturally and linguistically diverse students takes place within the larger context of increasing minority[1] enrollment. In schools across the United States, the percentage of students of diverse cultures is growing. The U.S. Department of Education (2003) estimates that more than 3.5 million students in U.S. schools have limited English proficiency. In 2000, 42.6 percent of the school-age population in California and 32.4 percent in Texas spoke a home language other than English. The figure was more than 20 percent in Arizona, Florida, Nevada, New Jersey, New Mexico, New York, and Rhode Island, and more than 10 percent in 12 additional states (U.S. Census Bureau, 2003). Hispanics are the fastest-growing ethnic group in

U.S. schools, having passed African Americans as the largest minority group in the United States (U.S. Census Bureau, 2003).

Many cultural minority groups—Hispanic students in particular—continue to underachieve at alarming rates. Hispanic students have higher dropout rates than non-Hispanics (National Center for Education Statistics, 2000). In 1998, only 63 percent of 18- to 24-year-old Hispanics had finished high school or earned a GED, compared with 85 percent of the total population (U.S. Department of Education, 2003). Although the achievement gap between Hispanics and whites narrowed in the 1970s and 1980s, it widened in the late 1980s and 1990s and remains large today (Lee, 2002).

Disproportionate Representation

The Challenge

Educators have been concerned for more than three decades about the overrepresentation of culturally and linguistically diverse students in certain special education categories (learning disabilities, mental retardation, and emotional disturbance) and their under-representation in programs for the gifted and talented (Artiles, Trent, & Palmer, in press). The phenomenon has recently come under closer scrutiny, however, with the publication of reports by the National Re-

search Council (Donovan & Cross, 2002) and the Harvard Civil Rights Project (Losen & Orfield, 2002).

Although nationally, Hispanic students are only slightly overrepresented in the learning disabilities category and not at all in the mental retardation or emotional disturbance categories (Donovan & Cross, 2002), national data do not reflect the wide variability at the level of individual states and school districts. As Donovan and Cross explain,

The nationally aggregated data have been interpreted to suggest no overrepresentation of either black or Hispanic students in LD [learning disabled]. But state-level data tell a more complex story. For black students, for example, the risk index[2] ranges from 2.33 percent in Georgia to 12.19 percent in Delaware. For Hispanic students, the risk index ranges from 2.43 in Georgia to 8.93 in Delaware. Clearly, there is overrepresentation for these two minorities in the LD category in some states. (2002, p. 67)

This extensive variation in placement rates across states (Artiles & Trent, 2000) and within school districts (Losen & Orfield, 2002) occurs chiefly in the three "judgmental" categories of special education: learning disabilities, mental retardation, and emotional disturbance.

These conditions are usually identified after a child starts school and are diagnosed by school personnel rather than by medical professionals. School clinicians typically exercise wide latitude in determining whether a student is eligible for services in one of these categories (Gottlieb, Alter, Gottlieb, & Wishner, 1994). In contrast, Hispanics and African Americans are not overrepresented in low-incidence, nonjudgmental disability categories, such as visual, auditory, or orthopedic impairment (Donovan & Cross, 2002).

We know little about the representation of English-language learners in special education programs.

Although state departments of education collect data about the ethnicity of students in special education, they typically do not accumulate information about students' language proficiency. Thus, we know little about the representation of English-language learners (students not fully proficient in English) in special education programs. Emerging evidence from urban districts in California, however, suggests that this population is overrepresented in high-incidence disability categories, and that those English-language learners classified as lacking proficiency in both their first language and in English are heavily overrepresented (Artiles, Rueda, Salazar, & Higareda, 2003).

Prospective Solutions
Professional groups and the U.S. federal government have given more attention and invested more resources in recent years to understand and address disproportionate representation. For example, the U.S. Department of Education recently funded a technical assistance center to address disproportionate representation: the National Center for Culturally Responsive Educational Systems (see www.nccrest.org). New tools and resources for practitioners have been published (for example, see National As-

sociation for Bilingual Education & IL-IAD Project, 2002). In addition, recent amendments to the Individuals with Disabilities Education Act (IDEA) have strengthened nondiscriminatory mandates and regulations in the prevention, identification, assessment, and treatment of disabilities (Hehir, 2002).

The LD Definition and the Exclusionary Clause

The Challenge
IDEA's definition of learning disabilities contains an exclusionary clause stipulating that before a school determines that a student has a learning disability, it must ascertain that the student has had sufficient opportunity to learn—including adequate instruction in a language that the student can understand. Yet school personnel involved in placement decisions tend to disregard this exclusionary clause, paying insufficient attention to the influence of a student's native language, ignoring the ecology of the student's regular education classroom, and only sporadically implementing prereferral strategies (Klingner, Harry, Sturges, Artiles, & Wimes, 2003).

Without classroom observations, evaluation teams cannot know whether a student has had adequate opportunity to learn in a culturally responsive environment.

Ochoa, Rivera, and Powell (1997) surveyed 859 school psychologists who had conducted psychoeducational assessments of bilingual students. These psychologists indicated that they considered a variety of factors in their efforts to ascertain that students had had sufficient opportunity to learn, but frequently omitted consideration of the student's native language and the number of years of English instruction that the student had received—two crucial factors. Only 6 percent of psychologists reported asking about the student's home

language, and only 1 percent attempted to determine whether a learning problem occurred in both English and the student's home language. The researchers called these findings "especially disheartening" (1997, p. 165). Disregard for the potential influence of language and culture on students' school performance can increase the incidence of false positive diagnoses, with devastating consequences for culturally and linguistically diverse students.

In an ethnographic study of the referral processes in 12 schools, we found that members of child study teams and Individualized Education Program (IEP) committees gave little weight to factors related to language acquisition when making decisions about special education eligibility and placement. Even for students who were not yet considered fully proficient in English and who had been tested bilingually, only English test results were typically included in psychologists evaluation reports or discussed at IEP team meetings. The teams did not address the possible influence of second-language acquisition on the students' performance (Klingner et al., 2003).

We also found that the teams paid almost no attention to the ecology of the classrooms from which students were referred. Although many students were referred by teachers with weak instructional and classroom management skills, frequently neither the evaluating psychologist nor anyone else on the IEP team conducted classroom observations. From the start, team members seemed to assume that the student must have an internal deficit of some kind and that classroom observations were unnecessary. When asked whether she observed students whom she assessed in their classrooms, one psychologist said that she rarely did, noting,

> The whole morning with them [spent testing] gives you a good idea; you know it does. And you rely on the teacher's comments.

Some psychologists did indicate that they would like to conduct classroom observations but had insufficient time in their busy schedules. Without classroom observations, evaluation teams cannot know whether a student has had adequate opportunity to learn in an appropriate, culturally responsive environment.

In addition, we found that school personnel were inconsistent in their use of prereferral interventions designed to provide students with additional assistance before evaluating them for special education. Generally, this step in the referral process was not taken seriously by teachers, many of whom felt that these strategies were "just what we do anyway," or "something checked on a form to meet referral requirements." Similarly, in an investigation of the schooling characteristics of 46 Hispanic elementary students with limited English proficiency referred to or participating in bilingual special education in New York City, Carrasquillo and Rodriguez (1997) found that few prereferral interventions had been tried with students prior to their placement.

Prospective Solutions
We recommend a three-pronged approach for addressing this problem. First, schools should provide professional development to enhance professionals' understanding of the exclusionary clause, the factors that school personnel must consider in determining whether a student has received adequate opportunity to learn, and how to implement meaningful prereferral strategies.

Second, a professional with expertise in English-language acquisition should be present when IEP committees meet and when child study teams discuss prereferral interventions and eligibility evaluations (Klingner et al., 2003; Ortiz, 1997). This person should be knowledgeable about language and cultural issues and able to point out when language could be contributing to a student's difficulties.

Third, the child study team and IEP team members should consider classroom context when discussing students' behavior and learning (Harry, Klingner, Sturges, & Moore, 2002). To ensure that the student is receiving an adequate opportunity to learn, evaluators should conduct observations in the student's regular classroom and other settings. Someone other than the classroom teacher should complete these observations to ascertain whether the student's difficulties are being exacer-

bated by ineffective or culturally insensitive instruction.

Inappropriate Testing Practices

The Challenge
The assessment of culturally and linguistically diverse students is fraught with theoretical misunderstandings and flawed practices. Schools that use the same few tests with most students and fail to take language proficiency into account are setting up diverse students for assessment failure.

The test performance of culturally and linguistically diverse students may be affected by their differential interpretation of questions, lack of familiarity with vocabulary, limited English language proficiency, and issues of language dominance (Garcia & Pearson, 1994). Even students who have demonstrated English fluency on oral language measures may not be ready to demonstrate their achievement on tests at higher cognitive levels in English.

When is an English language learner ready to be tested only in English? We have not yet developed a test of language proficiency that can adequately answer this question (Ortiz, 1997). Even students who demonstrate English proficiency on language assessment measures typically demonstrate a low verbal IQ/high performance IQ profile (Figueroa, 1990).

If a school transitions a student prematurely from a bilingual or ESOL program to a regular classroom, the student's achievement and scores on tests of intelligence will likely suffer. English-language learners are often moved to English-only programs after one or two years, when they have attained basic interpersonal communication skills but have not yet developed the cognitive academic language proficiency required for demanding learning tasks, which often takes from four to seven years (Cummins, 1984; see MacSwan, 2000, for a critique of Cummins's distinction between cognitive and interpersonal skills).

Many standardized tests (for example, intelligence, oral language proficiency, and achievement tests) yield valid scores for most students but tend to underestimate the potential of culturally and linguistically diverse students

(Abedi, 2002). This limitation was documented in a longitudinal study that compared students' grade point averages, standardized reading scores, and standardized math scores in 1982 with their 1972 scores on the Full-Scale WISC-R, an IQ test (Valdez & Figueroa, 1994). Students who achieved at higher levels than predicted by their IQ scores were considered to be "overachievers"; those who achieved at lower levels than predicted were considered to be "underachievers." Hispanic students who in 1972 had scored at or below the mean on the WISC-R were more likely than their Anglo counterparts to show above-expected school grades and achievement, thus placing them in the "overachiever" category, especially if they lived in homes where Spanish was spoken. Valdez and Figueroa (1994) concluded that decisions based on IQ tests can lead to inaccuracies in decision making for Hispanic pupils.

Prospective Solutions
Moll (1990) recommends looking for the cultural, linguistic, and social resources—funds of knowledge—that students and their families bring to the school setting and viewing these as strengths on which to build problem-solving abilities. Harry and colleagues (2002) suggest acknowledging the arbitrariness of assessment and placement decisions, which would pave the way for more useful, less expensive, and less stigmatizing ways of helping students with learning and behavioral difficulties.

One prospective solution that the reauthorization of IDEA may promote is to stop using IQ tests and discrepancy formulas to determine who qualifies for special education services (Fletcher et al., 2002). Instead, students would be found eligible using a *response to intervention* model that provides students with increasingly intensive levels, or *tiers,* of support (Fuchs, Fuchs, & Speece, 2002; Gresham, 2002).

In three-tiered models, the first tier consists of high-quality instruction in a general education classroom. Students who do not reach expected curriculum benchmarks then receive intensive second-tier assistance, either through tutoring or in small groups, still as part of a general education support system. Students who continue to struggle are provided with a third tier of assistance, which many would consider to be special education. Linan-Thompson and colleagues (2003) are investigating the three-tiered model with English-language learners, with promising results.

The assessment of culturally and linguistically diverse students is fraught with misunderstandings and flawed practices.

This approach may solve some of the problems associated with the biased testing of culturally and linguistically diverse students, but only if we ensure that the interventions offered to students are culturally and linguistically appropriate. Like previous eligibility criteria, this model seems to assume that if a student does not make adequate progress, he or she must have an internal deficit. As with earlier identification criteria, this model must be based on students having received an adequate opportunity to learn.

Schools should also find alternative procedures for conducting linguistically and culturally sensitive assessments, such as portfolios (for example, Brown, Campione, Webber, & McGilly, 1992; Gonzalez, Brusca-Vega, & Yawkey, 1997; Rueda, 1997).

The Challenges Ahead

The special education referral process for culturally and linguistically diverse students remains a complex and challenging task. The field has not yet adequately determined how to distinguish between disabilities and normal second-language learning development, nor have we discovered how to assess students' true learning potential rather than knowledge acquired through previous home and school experiences.

The special education profession needs to overcome the widespread tendency to view culturally and linguistically diverse children from a deficit perspective. This shift holds the key to building a knowledge base and a professional culture that account for the role of culture in learning and for the complex historical contexts within which educators, students, and families live and labor.

Notes

1. We use the term *minority* interchangeably with *culturally and linguistically diverse*. We recognize, however, that some U.S. ethnic or linguistic groups have become the numerical majority in some regions. The term *minority* signals the continued marginalized status of these groups.
2. The risk index is calculated "by dividing the number of students in a given racial or ethnic category served in a given disability category by the total enrollment for that racial or ethnic group in the school population" (Donovan & Cross, 2002, pp. 42-43).

References

Abedi, J. (2002). Standardized achievement tests and English language learners: Psychometric issues. *Educational Assessment, 8*, 231-257.

Artiles, A. J., Rueda, R., Salazar, J., & Higareda, I. (2003). *Within-group diversity in minority overrepresentation: English language learners in urban school districts*. Manuscript submitted for publication.

Artiles, A. J., & Trent, S. C. (2000). Representation of culturally/linguistically diverse students. In C. R. Reynolds & E. Fletcher-Jantzen (Eds.), *Encyclopedia of special education* (2nd ed., Vol. 1, pp. 513-517). New York: Wiley.

Artiles, A. J., Trent, S. C., & Palmer, J. (in press). Culturally diverse students in special education. In J. A. Banks & C. M. Banks (Eds.), *Handbook of research on multicultural education* (2nd ed.). San Francisco: Jossey-Bass.

Baca, L. M., & Cervantes, H. T. (Eds.). (1998). *The bilingual special education interface*. New Jersey: Merrill/Prentice Hall.

Brown, A. L., Campione, J. C., Webber, L. S., & McGilly, K. (1992). Interactive learning environments: A new look at assessment and instruction. In B. R. Gifford & M. C. O'Connor (Eds.), *Changing assessments: Alternative views of aptitude, achievement, and instruction* (pp. 121-211). Boston: Kluwer.

Carrasquillo, A. L., & Rodriguez, J. (1997). Hispanic limited English-proficient students with disabilities. *Learning Disabilities: A Multidisciplinary Journal 8*(3), 167-174.

Cummins, J. (1984). *Bilingualism and special education: Issues in assessment and pedagogy*. San Diego, CA: College Hill.

Donovan, M. S., & Cross, C. T. (2002). *Minority students in special and gifted education*. Washington, DC: National Research Council.

Figueroa, R. A. (1990). Assessment of linguistic minority group children. In C. R. Reynolds & R. W. Kamphaus (Eds.), *Handbook of psychological and educational assessment of children* (Vol. 1). New York: Guilford.

Fletcher, J. M., Lyon, G. R., Barnes, M., Stuebing, K. K., Francis, D. J., Olson, R. K., et al. (2002). Classification of learning disabilities: An evidence-based evaluation. In R. Bradley, L. Danielson, & D. P. Hallahan (Eds.), *Identification of learning disabilities: Research to practice* (pp. 185-250). Mahwah, NJ: Erlbaum.

Fuchs, L. S., Fuchs, D., & Speece, D. L. (2002). Treatment validity as a unifying construct for identifying learning disabilities. *Learning Disability Quarterly, 25*, 33-45.

Garcia, G. E., & Pearson, P. D. (1994). Assessment and diversity. In L. Darling-Hammond (Ed.), *Review of research in education, 20* (pp. 337-391). Washington, DC: American Educational Research Association.

Gonzalez, V., Brusca-Vega, R., & Yawkey, T. (1997). *Assessment and instruction of culturally and linguistically diverse students*. Needham Heights, MA: Allyn and Bacon.

Gottlieb, J., Alter, M., Gottlieb, B. W., & Wishner, J. (1994). Special education in urban America: It's not justifiable for many. *The Journal of Special Education, 27*, 453-465.

Gresham, F. (2002). Responsiveness to intervention: An alternative approach to the identification of learning disabilities. In R. Bradley, L. Danielson, & D. P. Hallahan (Eds.), *Identification of learning disabilities* (pp. 467-519). Mahwah, NJ: Erlbaum.

Harry, B., Klingner, J. K., Sturges, K., & Moore, R. (2002). Of rocks and soft places: Using qualitative methods to investigate the processes that result in disproportionality. In D. J. Losen & G. Orfield (Eds.), *Racial inequality in special education*. Boston: Harvard Education Press.

Hehir, T. (2002). IDEA and disproportionality: Federal enforcement, effective advocacy, and strategies for change. In D.J. Losen & G. Orfield (Eds.), *Racial inequity in special education* (pp. 219-238). Cambridge, MA: Harvard Education Press.

Klingner, J. K., Harry, B., Sturges, K. M., Artiles, A. J., & Wimes, C. (2003, April). *The role of child study and multidisciplinary team meetings in the overrepresentation of culturally and linguistically diverse students in special education*. Paper presented at the annual meeting of the

American Educational Research Association, Chicago, IL.

Lee, J. (2002). Racial and ethnic achievement gap trends: Reversing the progress toward equity. *Educational Researcher, 31*, 3-12.

Linan-Thompson, W., Vaughn, S., Hickman-Davis, P., & Kouzekanani, K. (2003). Effectiveness of supplemental reading instruction for 2nd grade English language learners with reading difficulties. *Elementary School Journal, 103*, 221-238.

Losen, D. J., & Orfield, G. (Eds.). (2002). *Racial inequity in special education*. Cambridge, MA: Harvard Education Press.

MacSwan, J. (2000). The Threshold Hypothesis, semilingualism, and other contributions to a deficit view of linguistic minorities. *Hispanic Journal of Behavioral Sciences, 22*, 3-45.

Moll, L. C. (Ed.). (1990). *Vygotsky and education*. Cambridge, MA: Cambridge University Press.

National Association for Bilingual Education (NABE), & ILIAD Project. (2002). *Determining appropriate referrals of English language learners to special education: A self-assessment guide for principals*. Washington, DC: National Association for Bilingual Education.

National Center for Education Statistics. (2000). *High school dropouts, by race/ethnicity and recency of migration* (NCES 2000-009). Washington, DC: Author.

Ochoa, S. H., Rivera, B. D., & Powell, M. P. (1997). Factors used to comply with the exclusionary clause with bilingual and limited-English-proficient pupils: Initial guidelines. *Learning Disabilities Research & Practice, 12*, 161-167.

Ortiz, A. A. (1997). Learning disabilities occurring concomitantly with linguistic differences. *Journal of Learning Disabilities, 30*, 321-332.

Rueda, R. (1997). Changing the context of assessment: The move to portfolios and authentic assessment. In A. J. Artiles & G. Zamora-Duran (Eds.), *Reducing the disproportionate representation of culturally diverse students in special and gifted education* (pp. 7-25). Reston, VA: Council for Exceptional Children.

U.S. Census Bureau. (2003, Feb. 25). U.S. Census Bureau, Population Division. Available: www.ed.gov/population/www/cen2000/phc-t20.html

U.S. Department of Education. (2003, June). *Key indicators of Hispanic student achievement: National goals and benchmarks for the next decade*. Washington, DC: Author. Available: www.ed.gov/pub/hispanicindicators

Valdez, G., & Figueroa, R. A. (1994). *Bilingualism and testing: A special case of bias*. Norwood, NJ: Ablex.

Authors' note: The writing of this article was supported by the National Center for Culturally Responsive Educational Systems awarded by the U.S. Department of Education Office of Special Education Programs.

Janette K. Klingner is an associate professor in the School of Education, University of Colorado at Boulder, 249 UCB, Boulder, CO 80309; janette.klingner@colorado.edu.

Alfredo J. Artiles is an associate professor in the Departments of Special Education and Teaching and Learning, Peabody College, Vanderbilt University, Box 328, Nashville, TN 37203; aj.artiles@vanderbilt.edu.

Cultural Influences on the Development of Self-Concept:

Updating Our Thinking

Hermine H. Marshall

Why is it that some children try new things with enthusiasm and approach peers and adults with confidence, whereas other children seem to believe that they are incapable of succeeding in many situations?... What can we learn from research that will allow us to help children approach new situations and other people with confidence?

—H. H. Marshall,
"Research in Review. The
Development of Self-Concept"

Twelve years ago I assumed along with many early childhood educators that approaching new situations with confidence indicated a child's strong self-concept; hesitation and hanging back could indicate lack of self-esteem. In my review of research on the development of self-concept written at that time, the notion that children's behavior is influenced by their cultural background had only begun to enter the research literature and thinking of early childhood educators. I pointed out briefly that cultural values can affect self-esteem and different cultures may value and encourage different behaviors. For instance, taking personal control, important in dominant American culture, might not be valued in other cultures. Yet I indicated that autonomy and initiative are behaviors to look for as reflecting positive self-concept. I implied that children who lacked these traits might have low self-esteem.

We need to increase our awareness that our perceptions, actions, and interactions and those of children derive their meanings from the cultures in which they are embedded.

The last decade has seen an increase in research on child development in different cultures. Awareness of this research has enhanced early childhood educators' sensitivity to how perspectives may vary in cultures that are different from the culture of individual educators as well as the dominant culture. Culture impacts not just which behaviors are valued and displayed but also our interpretations of these behaviors. As a result of this decade of research, it has become clear that what many of us have taken for evidence of self-esteem is influenced by our cultural perceptions. It is important, therefore, to revisit some of the issues related to self-concept development in light of a more sophisticated understanding of cultural influences. To this end, as educators we need to increase our awareness that our perceptions, actions, and interactions and those of children derive their meanings from the cultures in which they are embedded.

Constructing a view of self: independent/interdependent

Children construct their views of self "by participating in interactions that caregivers structure according to cultural values about the nature of human existence" (Raeff 1997). In Western cultures, striving toward *independence* and individuality and asserting oneself are seen as important accomplishments (Markus & Kitayama 1991). As a consequence, Westerners perceive children who are outgoing and eagerly explore new situations as demonstrating competence and having a positive self-concept, especially compared to children who do not appear to seek out and actively participate in these situations.

In contrast, Eastern cultures place greater emphasis on maintaining harmonious, *interdependent* relationships. Markus and Kitayama (1991) note that interdependent views are also characteristic of many African, Latin American, and southern European cultures. (See also Greenfield 1994.) In cultures influenced by Confucian and Taoist philosophies, self-restraint and control of emotional expressiveness is considered an indication of social maturity (Chen et al. 1998). Asserting oneself may be seen as a sign of immaturity (Markus & Kitayama 1991). Children who are shy, reticent, and quiet are likely to be considered competent and well behaved by parents and teachers in the People's Republic of China (Chen et al. 1998; Rubin 1998). These children—whom North American teachers from the dominant culture might see as inhibited and lacking in self-confidence—have a positive view of themselves and of their social relationships.

Similarly, in other cultures where interdependence or "relative enmeshment" (Garcia Coll 1990) are seen as ideal mature relationships, interdependency and interpersonal dependency are likely to be fostered between young children and their mothers. When asked about desirable child behavior, mothers from Latino cultures, such as Spanish-speaking Puerto Rican mothers, are likely to focus on respectfulness (*respecto*), a concept which assumes appropriate interrelatedness. In contrast the Anglo mothers in one study focused on autonomy and active exploration, reflecting more independent values (Harwood 1992). Moreover, some cultures such as traditional Navajo cultures expect children to observe before attempting to try things (Bacon & Carter 1991). For these children too, standing back and observing rather than exploring should not be taken as an indication of low self-esteem.

Nevertheless, although Chinese parents tend to value interdependence and cohesion and may minimize the development of individuality within the family. Taiwanese and immigrant Chinese parents seem to encourage independence so that children will be able to succeed in the larger society (Lin & Fu 1990). Likewise, some Mexican immigrant families may begin to approve of their children's independent thinking related to school topics as they become more acculturated (Delgado-Gaitan 1994).

In addition, in Eastern cultures (Markus & Kitayama 1991) and Latino cultures (Parke & Buriel 1998), primary concern centers on other people and the self-in-relationship-to-other rather than self alone. Most people in these cultures value developing empathetic understanding and attention to the needs of others. These behaviors serve to maintain harmonious relationships more than would attending to meeting one's own needs.

These contrasts should not be taken to mean that independence and interdependence are mutually exclusive (Raeff 1997). Both independent and interdependent tendencies are common to human experience. People in Western cultures value relationships and cooperation as well as independence. "Every group selects a point on the independence/ interdependence continuum as its cultural ideal" (Greenfield 1994, 4).

The impact on socialization and development

Varieties of both independence and interdependence affect socialization and development. Consequently we should be aware that how children see themselves in relationship to others is also a part of their self-concept. Educators need to expand their views of what is considered important to self-concept beyond the typical notions of autonomy, self-assertion, self-enhancement, and uniqueness and include characteristics such as empathy, sensitivity to others, modesty, cooperation, and caring as well.

We must be careful not to assume that just because children or families are from a specific ethnic or racial group that they necessarily share a common cultural experience. There are differences within cultures and within families.

Although it is important to be aware that our perceptions and interpretations of behavior are influenced by the culture(s) in which we were raised and in which we reside and that the meaning of behavior may vary for different cultures, we must be careful not to assume that just because children or families are from a specific ethnic or racial group they necessarily share a common cultural experience. There are differences within cultures and within families. Other factors impinge on how children are raised and the meanings accorded to behavior, such as the family's countries of origin, the length of time immigrant families have been in the United States, the degree of acculturation the family has experienced, educational background, and social status (Delgado-Gaitan 1994; Killen 1997; McLloyd 1999).

Some children and families experience the influence of multiple cultures. This is particularly true when parents are from different ethnic, racial, or cultural groups. In these families parents may bring values from two or more cultures to their views and practices in raising children. Regardless of children's apparent ethnic or cultural background, it is important for teachers to be sensitive to *individual* children and family members and to how a family's beliefs, attitudes, and values may affect children's behavior.

Children who are able to maintain comfort with behaviors that are valued in their home as well as those valued in the wider society may be most likely to have positive views of themselves in both cultural contexts.

Attempting to understand what each family values as important behaviors and watching for these behaviors may provide clues to the meaning of children's actions for that family and child. It is important to recognize and affirm behaviors valued by the home culture. It is also essential to provide opportunities for children to learn behaviors that are valued by the Western culture (Delpit 1988). Children who are able to maintain comfort with behaviors that are valued in their home as well as those valued in the wider society

may be most likely to have positive views of themselves in both cultural contexts.

What does this mean in practice?

My earlier research on self-concept development describes a number of ways to influence self-concept. These include helping children (1) feel they are of value, (2) believe they are competent, (3) have some control over tasks and actions, (4) learn interpersonal skills. Also noted as important is becoming aware of your expectations for children. The particular techniques for each of these recommendations remain valid today (see Marshall 1989).

Beyond these fundamentals, the following steps are based on a more sophisticated awareness of cultural and individual variations in values and behaviors. Using them as a guide will increase your sensitivity to the values and practices of the families whose children are in your care and enable you to support the development of positive self-concepts.

1. Be aware of the ways your own culture influences your expectations of children. Think about how you were raised, your family values. What behaviors were encouraged? How did your family make you feel proud? Talk to friends or other teachers about their upbringing. Within your own community, there are likely variations in what families value and in the bases for positive self-concept. This reflection and knowledge may help you begin to expand your awareness of the indications of positive self-concept.

2. Consider the cultural backgrounds of the children in your setting and their community. Observe how children approach new tasks, relate to other people, and react to praise. This may raise some questions. Be a good listener. If you teach at the primary level, chat with the children before and after school or at lunchtime. Be careful that surface appearances

do not influence your perceptions or interactions. Gather more information about the cultural and ethnic groups represented in your class (as noted below).

3. Learn about the cultures from which the children in your program or school may come. Read about the values and child rearing practices of these cultures. (See the "For further reading" list.) Talk to community leaders or people you know who have greater knowledge of these cultures.

Contact community-based organizations, such as the National Council of La Raza (NCLR). Inviting representatives of such organizations to talk to teachers in your setting may be helpful. Still, do not assume that this general information is sufficient. Further understanding of the cultural background of *particular* children in your class will be necessary since, in every cultural and ethnic group, individual and generational differences are likely.

4. Use your basic knowledge of the culture to talk with each family about its values and practices. Learn what families think is important to consider for their children. You might share with them what you have been learning about their culture or cultures. Explain that you recognize that every family is different and that you would like to know what they think and what they value as important. Asking about the families' methods for teaching and learning may be useful. Discuss what happens if children raise questions or explore on their own and how children and adults show respect. It is important to accept what family members say as valuable information to consider and avoid letting your own values and methods stifle communication.

5. Build on what you have learned from each family. Provide opportunities for children to learn in a variety of ways. For example, children might learn by observing first, trying things out on their own, or by doing tasks with a partner or group of peers. Children need opportunities to demonstrate caring and cooperating.

All children will benefit from enhanced opportunities to learn and interact in a variety of ways. Enlarge your repertoire of responses; some children will find more comfort in nonverbal acceptance—a smile or nod—than praise. In all cases, showing respect for ways of interacting that derive from the home culture is critical to the support and development of a child's self-concept. Practices that are clearly harmful to the child, of course, should not be supported. In such a case, being able to discuss with the family why the practice is detrimental is important (see Gonzalez-Mena & Bhavnagri 2000).

6. Infuse the curriculum and classroom environment with a rich variety of materials from the cultures of your children as well as other cultures. Parents may be able to share songs or stories or bring in something special representing their home culture. Find books and posters that represent the children in your class. Introduce as snacks special treats from the children's cultures. Seeing their ethnic groups and cultures of origin valued will enhance children's self-concepts.

Conclusion

It is not enough to assume that affirming young children's assertiveness, confidence, and independence suffices to support self-concept development. Such qualities as show-

ing respect for and being sensitive to others, learning by observing, and exhibiting humility may also evidence positive self-concept and should be nourished. Acknowledging the contributions and values of all the families whose children are in our care while also supporting children's development of necessary skills to succeed in mainstream America is most likely to enhance the development of children's self-esteem.

Hermine H. Marshall, Ph.D., is emerita professor at San Francisco State University, at which she was coordinator of the early childhood and master's degree programs. She has conducted research on self-concept, self-evaluation, and classroom processes. She thanks Elsie Gee for critical comments on an earlier version of this article.

UNIT 4
Learning and Instruction

Unit Selections

Key Points to Consider

- Compare and contrast the different approaches to learning. What approach do you think is best, and why? What factors are important to your answer (for example, objectives, types of students, setting, personality of the teacher)?

- What are some principles for effective teaching that derive directly from brain research and different conceptualizations of intelligence?

- What teaching strategies could you use to promote greater student retention of material? What are good ways to attract and keep students' attention? Must a teacher be an "entertainer"? Why or why not?

- How can a teacher promote positive self-esteem, values, character, caring, and attitudes? How are they related to cognitive learning? How much emphasis should be put on cultivating character or positive student interactions? How would you create a "caring" classroom? Discuss whether or not this would interfere with achievement of cognitive learning targets.

- If you wanted to create a constructivist classroom in the subject area and/or grade in which you want to teach, what would the classroom look like? What would you emphasize, and how would your actions reflect constructivist principles and research on intelligence? How would technology be used in an effective manner with constructivist approaches?

- What are some of the advantages and disadvantages to differentiated instruction? What skills should the teacher have to be able to organize learning experiences that are matched to student abilities, achievement, and interests?

 Links: www.dushkin.com/online/
These sites are annotated in the World Wide Web pages.

Education Week on the Web
http://www.edweek.org
Online Internet Institute
http://www.oii.org
Teachers Helping Teachers
http://www.pacificnet.net/~mandel/
The Teachers' Network
http://www.teachers.net/

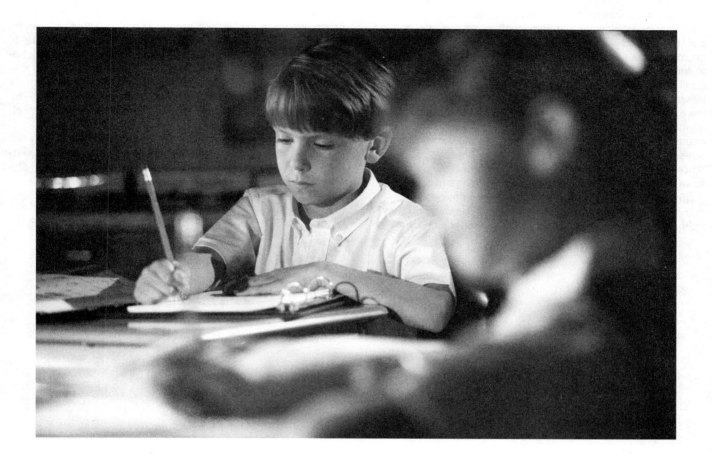

Learning can be broadly defined as a relatively permanent change in behavior or thinking due to experience. Learning is not a result of change due to maturation or temporary influences. Changes in behavior and thinking of students result from complex interactions between their individual characteristics and environmental factors. A continuing challenge in education is understanding these interactions so that learning can be enhanced. This unit focuses on approaches within educational psychology that represent different ways of viewing the learning process and related instructional strategies. Each approach to learning emphasizes a different set of personal and environmental factors that influence certain behaviors. While no one approach can fully explain learning, each is a valuable contribution to our knowledge about the process and the improvement of student performance.

The discussion of each learning approach includes suggestions for specific techniques and methods of teaching to guide teachers in understanding student behavior and in making decisions about how to teach. The articles in this section reflect a recent emphasis on applied research conducted in schools, research on the brain, and on constructivist theories.

Researchers have recently made significant advances in understanding the way our brain works. Information processing re-

fers to the way that the mind receives sensory information, stores it as memory, and recalls it for later use. This procedure is basic to all learning, no matter what teaching approach is taken, and we know that the method used in processing information determines to some extent how much and what we remember. The first two articles in this subsection present some of the fundamental principles of brain functioning, information processing and cognition. The third and fourth articles focus on human intelligences and show how more recent conceptualizations of intelligence can promote student achievement.

In the past, behaviorism was the best-known theory of learning. Most practicing and prospective teachers are familiar with concepts such as classical conditioning, reinforcement, and punishment, and there is no question that behaviorism has made significant contributions to understanding learning. But behaviorism has also been subject to much misinterpretation, in part because it seems so simple. In fact, the effective use of behavioristic principles is complex and demanding, as the fifth article on praise points out.

Constructivist learning theory is currently the predominant theory of learning that is recognized by educational psychologists. According to constructivists, it is important for students to actively create and reorganize knowledge. There is a need for students to interpret within meaningful contexts so that what is learned is well connected with existing knowledge. Constructivism is illustrated with the use of cognitive maps called webs of skills in one article in this section and is also emphasized in two articles in the section on Instructional Strategies.

Social psychological learning emphasizes the affective, social, moral, and personal development of students. Social psychology is the study of the nature of interpersonal relationships in social situations. In education, this approach looks at teacher-pupil relationships and group processes to derive principles of interaction that affect learning. Two articles in this section examine the application of social psychological principles to learning. In the first, the importance of recognizing and inviting such needs as affirmation, contribution, purpose, and power is stressed. In the second article, the authors argue for the importance of social and emotional learning and positive relationships as needed characteristics of a positive learning environment.

Instructional strategies are the teacher behaviors and methods of conveying information that affect learning. Teaching methods or techniques can vary greatly, depending on objectives, group size, types of students, and personality of the teacher. For example, discussion classes are generally more effective for enhancing thinking skills than are individualized sessions or lectures. For the final subsection, five articles have been selected that show how teachers can use principles of cognitive psychology and intelligence in their teaching within the current standards-based environment. In the first article, implications of using a constructivist approach are summarized, with an emphasis on collaboration and cooperative inquiry. In the second article the principles of constructivism are used as a foundation for using block scheduling to promote deep understanding. The third article summarizes several evidence-based principles of effective teaching.

Technology is also becoming a pervasive opportunity for teaching and learning. The fourth article in this section summarizes effective applications of technology in the classroom. Differentiated instruction is addressed in the last chapter as a teaching method that can accommodate learning for all students.

ASK THE COGNITIVE SCIENTIST

Students Remember...
What They Think About

How does the mind work—and especially how does it learn? Teachers make assumptions all day long about how students best comprehend, remember, and create. These assumptions—and the teaching decisions that result—are based on a mix of theories learned in teacher education, trial and error, craft knowledge, and gut instinct. Such gut knowledge often serves us well. But is there anything sturdier to rely on?

Cognitive science is an interdisciplinary field of researchers from psychology, neuroscience, linguistics, philosophy, computer science, and anthropology who seek to understand the mind. In this regular American Educator *column, we will consider findings from this field that are strong and clear enough to merit classroom application.*

By Daniel T. Willingham

Issue: The teacher presents a strong, coherent lesson in which a set of significant facts is clearly connected to a reasonable conclusion. But, at test time, the students show no understanding of the connections. Some students parrot back the conclusion, but no facts. Others spit back memorized facts, but don't see how they fit together. Though the lesson wasn't taught in a rote way, it seems like rote knowledge is what the students took in. Why do well-integrated, coherent lessons often come back to us in a less meaningful, fragmented form? Can cognitive science help explain why this result is so common—and offer ideas about how to avoid it?

Response: Rote knowledge is devoid of all meaning (as discussed in my last column, Winter 2002). The knowledge that these students appear to be regurgitating is probably not rote knowledge. It is probably "shallow" knowledge: The students' knowledge has meaning (unlike rote knowledge), in that the students understand each isolated part, but their knowledge lacks the deeper meaning that comes from understanding the relationship among the parts. For reasons noted below, this is a common problem in the early stages of learning about a new topic. But it also has another remediable source, which is the focus of this column.

Cognitive science has shown that what ends up in a learner's memory is not simply the material presented—it is the product of what the learner thought about when he or she encountered the material. This principle illuminates one important origin of shallow knowledge and also suggests how to help students develop deep and interconnected knowledge.

Let's start with an example of shallow knowledge. Suppose that you are teaching a high school class unit on World War II and develop a lesson on the Japanese attack on Pearl Harbor. Many facts might be included in such a lesson: (a) Japan had aspirations to be a regional power; (b) Japan was engaged in a protracted war with China; (c) because they were at war, European countries could not protect their colonies in the South Pacific; and (d) the attack on Pearl Harbor resulted in a declaration of war on Japan by the United States. The overarching point of this lesson might be to show that the attack on Pearl Harbor was a strategic mistake for the Japanese, given their war aims. (See Figure 1 for a diagram of the lesson.)

We can see two ways that this meaningful lesson might end up as shallow knowledge in the student's mind. The student might commit to memory some or all of these four facts. But knowing these facts without understanding how they relate to one another and can be integrated to support the conclusion leaves the facts isolated; they are not without meaning, but neither are they as rich as they might be. The student has the trees, but no view of the forest.

Alternatively, the student might commit to memory the conclusion, "The attack on Pearl Harbor, although militarily a successful battle for Japan, was ultimately detrimental to its long-range war plans." But memorizing this conclusion without understanding the reasoning behind it and knowing the supporting facts is empty. It isn't rote—the student knows Japan initiated and won a battle at the place called Pearl Harbor. But the knowledge certainly is "shallow"—it has no connections.*

We have all had students memorize phrases from class or a textbook more or less word-for-word, and although what the student says is accurate, we can't help but wonder whether he or she really understands the ideas those words represent. Let's dig deeper.

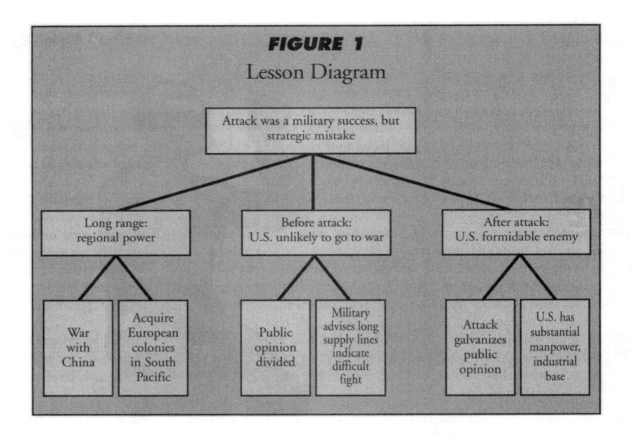

FIGURE 1

Lesson Diagram

Attack was a military success, but strategic mistake

Long range: regional power

Before attack: U.S. unlikely to go to war

After attack: U.S. formidable enemy

War with China

Acquire European colonies in South Pacific

Public opinion divided

Military advises long supply lines indicate difficult fight

Attack galvanizes public opinion

U.S. has substantial manpower, industrial base

Memory Is as Thinking Does

When students parrot back a teacher's or the textbook's words, they are, of course, drawing on memory. Thus, the question of why students end up with shallow knowledge is really a question about the workings of memory. Needless to say, determining what ends up in memory and in what form is a complex question, but *there is one factor that trumps most others in determining what is remembered: what you think about when you encounter the material*. The fact that the material you are dealing with has meaning does not guarantee that the meaning *will* be remembered. If you think about that meaning, the meaning will reside in memory. If you don't, it won't. For example, if I teach about Pearl Harbor, some sailing enthusiasts may start thinking about the ships of the era and pay minimal attention to the rest of the class—just a few minutes after the bell rings they won't remember much about the causes and consequences of Pearl Harbor. Memory is as thinking does.

A classic experiment illustrating this principle was conducted by Thomas Hyde and James Jenkins in 1969. It examined how one thinks about material and the effect of that thinking on memory. Subjects in their experiment listened to a list of words at a rate of one word every two seconds. Different groups of subjects were to perform different tasks upon hearing each word. Some were to rate each word as to whether it made them think of pleasant or unpleasant things, whereas others were asked to count the number of times the letter *E* appeared in the word. Rating the pleasantness forces the subject to think about the word's meaning; the word *garbage* is unpleasant because of what it means—what it is associated

with in one's memory. Counting *E*s, on the other hand, forces one to think about the spelling of the word, but not its meaning. Thus, the experimenters manipulated what subjects thought about when they encountered each word. Subjects were not told that their memory for the words would later be tested; they thought they were merely to make the pleasantness or the *E*-counting judgment.

One other detail of the experiment is especially important. The word list actually consisted of 12 pairs of very highly associated words, such as *doctor–nurse*, although this fact was not pointed out to any of the subjects. The order in which the words were read was random (except that related words were not allowed to be next to one another in the list).

The results are shown in Figure 2. First look at the left side of the chart, which shows the mean number of words recalled. Memory was much better when subjects made the pleasantness ratings. Thinking about the meaning of material is especially helpful to memory. This finding is consistent across hundreds of other experiments.

The right side of the figure shows a measure of clustering— the extent to which subjects paired the associated words as they tried to remember them. When a subject recalled a word (e.g., *doctor*), what percentage of the time was the next word recalled the highly associated one (*nurse*)? As the figure shows, subjects who thought about the word's meaning (i.e., rated pleasantness) not only remembered more words, they tended to remember the related words together, even though the related words did not appear together in the list. The subjects who counted *E*s did not tend to remember related words together.

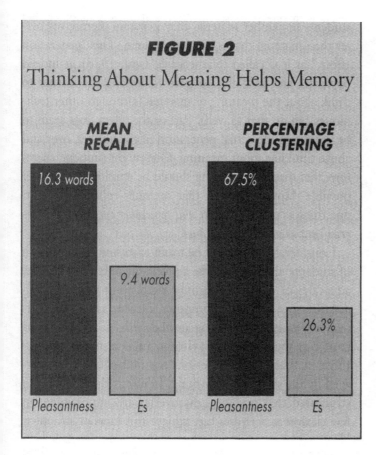

FIGURE 2

Thinking About Meaning Helps Memory

MEAN RECALL

16.3 words — Pleasantness

9.4 words — Es

PERCENTAGE CLUSTERING

67.5% — Pleasantness

26.3% — Es

These results forcefully make the point that meaningful structure that is in the environment may or may not end up being stored in memory. In the Hyde and Jenkins experiment, the fact that some of the words were related in meaning was largely lost on the subjects who counted *E*s because thinking about *E*s did not encourage the subjects to process meaning. Subjects who made the pleasantness ratings tended to group the words together by meaning as they recalled them. Whatever subjects thought about when they heard the words (which, teachers will note, depends on what they were *asked* to think about) was what ended up in memory.

In the Hyde and Jenkins experiment, the "what they think about" principle is divided into thinking about meaning versus not thinking about meaning. Other experiments show that even if one thinks about meaning, the particular *aspect* of the meaning that one considers will be stored in memory, and other aspects of meaning will not. For example, in one experiment (Barclay et al., 1974), subjects were presented with words to remember in the context of a sentence. The sentence biased subjects to think of one or another feature of the to-be-remembered word: For example, some subjects read "The man lifted the *piano*," which encouraged thinking about the fact that pianos are heavy. Other subjects read "The man tuned the *piano*," which encouraged considering that pianos produce music. In the next phase of the experiment subjects were told that their memory for some of the nouns in the sentences would be tested and that for each sentence they would get a hint. For *piano*,

some subjects were given the hint, "something heavy." If they had read the sentence about lifting the piano, this hint matched the feature they had thought about, but if they read the sentence about tuning the piano, the hint didn't match. (Other subjects saw a hint that matched the piano tuning sentence; that hint was "something with a nice sound.")

The results showed that subjects remembered about three times as many words when the hint for the test matched what subjects had thought about when they first read the word. Again, the point is that what is stored in memory is quite specific to what you think about when you encounter the material. It is not the case that if you think about *piano*, then *piano* and all of its features are stored in memory. You might think about its music-producing qualities, its weight, its cost, and so on. Or you might not focus on the referent at all, but rather on the physical properties of the word itself, as when Hyde and Jenkins asked subjects to count *E*s. In each case, what you think about is what you remember.

So what does this have to do with shallow knowledge? It shows where shallow knowledge might come from. Meaning that is in the environment won't end up in memory if students don't think about it. Students with shallow knowledge have apparently thought about the material in a shallow way. This conclusion reframes the question we might ask: Why would students think about the material in a shallow way, given that we didn't present it to them that way? Obviously, a student would learn only isolated facts or unsupported conclusions if that is what the teacher taught, but I find it difficult to believe that this is a common practice. The notion that education should emphasize meaning is deeply ingrained in our system and has been for a generation or more. There cannot be many teachers who ask their students to learn facts without concern for a larger picture. So how do students end up with shallow knowledge? There are several possible answers.

1. As noted at the beginning of this article, in one form, shallow knowledge is simply a step on the way to deep knowledge. Consider again the hierarchical diagram shown in Figure 1. I argued that shallow knowledge could either be memorization of the conclusion (top of the hierarchy) without knowing the facts that back it up (bottom of the hierarchy), or memorization of the facts without integrating them into a conclusion. Clearly the sort of deep knowledge we want our students to have is objectively harder to obtain than shallow knowledge, because knowledge of the facts *and* knowledge of the conclusion *and* knowledge of their interrelationships are prerequisite to it. We want students to know how the different levels of hierarchy relate to one another; it's not enough to have memorized each level in isolation of the others. That connected knowledge will inevitably be the last thing that the student acquires. Thus, some students' knowledge will be shallow simply because they are not far enough along yet.

2. Other students may effectively quit learning before they reach the deep understanding that is our goal for them. A student may learn the facts about Pearl Harbor and think

"All right, I've learned a lot about this stuff." The student is correct (so far as it goes) and simply doesn't realize that there is yet more to do.

3. Students' perception of what they are supposed to learn—and what it means to learn—may contribute to shallow knowledge. A student may seek to memorize definitions and pat phrases word-for-word from the book because the student *knows* that this information is correct and cannot be contested. When I was in eighth grade, we were given a list of vocabulary terms that we were to define and then study in preparation for a weekly test. A friend defined "cherub" as "an angel of the second order." My friends and I teased him because his definition missed what we thought was the key aspect of the word—that a cherub is small, chubby, and rosy-cheeked. He was unmoved and kept repeating "that's what the dictionary said." He liked the fact that his answer was uncontestable. Students may memorize exactly what the teacher or textbook says in order to be certain that they are *correct*, and worry less about the extent to which they understand.

4. Despite what was offered to students in the teacher's lesson, the students attended to (thought about) something different—and that's what they remembered.

What Does This Mean for Teachers?

This fundamental principle of memory—memory is as thinking does—yields a clear strategy to encourage deep, meaningful knowledge. If students think about the meaning of material, meaning will end up in memory. How can teachers be sure that students are thinking about meaning?

Obviously there is no one way to ensure that students think about the meaning of material. A compelling story may be appropriate for one lesson, whereas a carefully designed laboratory project works for a second, and a well-structured group discussion for a third. One possible common misconception is that learners can only understand meaning if they themselves construct the meaning in a physically active way. A moment's reflection should tell us that "listening" does not imply passivity or shallowness. We have all been to "active, participatory" workshops that felt like a waste of time, and we have been to lectures where we "just listened" that were gripping and informative. Constructing meaning is a matter of being *mentally* engaged; being physically engaged might help at times, but it is not necessary.

How can we ensure that students are mentally engaged? While there is still more to learn about applying this research on thinking and memory to teaching, several key principles have emerged to guide teachers in developing assignments, classroom activities, and assessments.

• **Anticipate what your lesson will lead students to think about**. The direct relationship between thought and memory is so important that it could be used as a self-check for a teacher preparing virtually any assignment: *Always try to anticipate what students will be thinking when they are doing the assignment*. Doing so may make it clear that some assignments de-

signed with one purpose in mind will achieve another. For example, a teacher once told me that, as part of a unit on the Underground Railroad, he had his students bake biscuits so that they would appreciate what escaped slaves ate most nights. He asked what I thought of the assignment and my reply was that his students will remember baking biscuits. In other words, his students probably thought for 30 seconds about the relation of the baking to the course material, and then spent 30 minutes thinking about measuring flour, mixing dough, and so on.

Another example comes from my recent observation of my nephew as he completed a book report. The teacher asked the students to draw a poster that depicted all of the events of the book. The purpose of the assignment was to have students think of the book as a whole, and to consider how the separate events related to one another. This purpose got lost in the execution. My nephew spent a lot more time thinking about how to draw a good castle than he did about the plot of the book.

• **Use discovery learning carefully**. The principle above—anticipate the students' thoughts—also illuminates the use and misuse of discovery learning. There is little doubt that students remember material they generate themselves better than material that is handed to them. This "generation effect," as it is called (Slamecka & Graf, 1978), is indeed powerful, and it is due, in part, to forcing the learner to think about the meaning of material (although other techniques can do that as well). Part of the effect does seem to be unique to the actual generation of the answer, over and above thinking about meaning. One might suppose, therefore, that discovery learning should be employed whenever possible. However, given that memory follows thought, one thing is clear: *Students will remember incorrect "discoveries" just as well as correct ones.*

Considerable care must be taken to ensure that the path of students' thoughts will be a profitable one. For example, advocates of discovery learning often point out that children learn to use some computer software rapidly and effectively merely by "playing around with it." That may be true, but that learning environment is also quite structured in that profitless actions are immediately discouraged by the system not working. In effect, the system is so structured that profitless discoveries are impossible; but few classroom activities can achieve this kind of structure. How much anatomy will students learn by "playing around" with frog dissection? Can one anticipate the thoughts of students who dissect frogs with little direction? Although discovery learning may be powerful in highly structured contexts that make the correct discovery virtually inevitable, in others it is likely to prove unproductive.

Constructing meaning is a matter of being mentally engaged.

• **Design reading assignments that require students to actively process the text**. Many concrete strategies have been suggested for helping students to get more out of reading that likely have some or all of their effect by making readers think about the meaning of what they are reading. *Techniques such as writing outlines, self-examination during learning, review* *questions, and previews can encourage or require students to integrate the material and to thereby process (i.e., think about) the meaning.* These different techniques are more or less effective in different situations, perhaps due to the specific materials being studied (e.g., McDaniel & Einstein, 1989); general principles guiding when each technique should be used have not been forthcoming. Nevertheless, although one technique or another may be more effective for a given lesson or group of students, using any strategy that encourages the processing of meaning is almost always better than not using one.

• **Design lessons so that students can't avoid thinking about the lesson's goal.** On a more positive note, the "memory is as thinking does" principle can yield steps teachers can take to help students develop deep, interconnected knowledge: *Lessons should be directed so that students are very likely to think (or can't help but think) about the goal of the lesson.* The goal of the Underground Railroad lesson was not really about biscuits—it was to encourage students to consider the experience of escaped slaves. Therefore, a more effective starting point for that lesson would be to ask students leading questions that encourage consideration of what escaped slaves' experiences would be like, which might include questions of how they would obtain food, and what the constraints were on the food they could get (inexpensive, cooked rapidly, etc.). My nephew would have gotten more out of his book report project if it had emphasized what the teacher was really interested in (the connection among the book's events), perhaps by having the students label the events and connections among them (e.g., this event moves the character towards his goal; this event causes that event) and de-emphasizing the students' artistic contribution by having them use clip art or simply writing the events in words.

• **Design tests that lead students to think about and integrate the most important material.** The "memory is as thinking does" principle may also be applied to methods of assessing student knowledge: *Like lessons, study guides for texts should be developed that force students to think about the goals of the lessons being assessed.* For better or worse, some students expend their greatest effort to understand material as they prepare for an examination. Even if you would rather see such students motivated by a passion to learn, you can use the students' motivation to earn a good grade to ensure that they are getting the most out of your lessons. Announcing the general topics to be covered on an exam leaves the specifics of what to learn up to the student. Even if the teacher emphasizes that deep understanding will be tested, the student may misconstrue what is deep or, as noted earlier, the student may quit once some facts have been memorized, believing that he or she has already done quite a bit of studying. Suppose, however, that the teacher provides a list of integrative questions for the students to study from, such as "Describe why the attack on Pearl Harbor was a strategic mistake by Japan, given its war aims." Suppose further that the students know that the examination will consist of five questions from the 30-question list that they have been given, with an essay to be written on each of the five questions. Students will very likely restrict their studying to the 30 question list, but that might be just fine with the teacher if he or she feels that any student who can answer those 30 questions has mastered the material. This method of testing has the advantage of ensuring that while students are highly motivated, they think about the deepest meaning of the material that the teacher intended.

In summary, in the early stages of learning, students may display "shallow" learning. These students have acquired bits of knowledge that aren't well-integrated into a larger picture. Research tells us that deep, connected knowledge can be encouraged by getting students to think about the interrelation of the various pieces of knowledge that they have acquired. Cognitive science has not progressed to the point that it can issue prescriptions of exactly how that can be achieved—that job is very much in the hands of experienced teachers. But in considering how to encourage students to acquire meaningful knowledge, teachers will do well to keep the "memory is as thinking does" principle in mind.

References

Barclay, J. R., Bransford, J. D., Franks, J. J., McCarrel, N. S., & Nitsch, K. (1974). Comprehension and semantic flexibility. *Journal of Verbal Learning & Verbal Behavior, 13,* 471–481.

Hyde, T. S. & Jenkins, J. J. (1969). Differential effects of incidental tasks on the organization of recall of a list of highly associated words. *Journal of Experimental Psychology, 82,* 472–481.

McDaniel, M. A. & Einstein, G. O. (1989). Material-appropriate processing: A contextualist approach to reading and studying strategies. *Educational Psychology Review, 1,* 113–145.

Slamecka, N. J. & Graf, P. (1978). The generation effect: Delineation of a phenomenon. *Journal of Experimental Psychology: Human Learning & Memory, 4,* 592–604.

Readers can pose specific questions to "Ask the Cognitive Scientist," American Educator, 555 New Jersey Ave. N.W., Washington, DC 20001 or to amerend@aft.org

*My last column (Winter 2002, available at **www.aft.org/ american_educator/winter2002/CogSci.html**) discussed another common problem for students: inflexible knowledge. Like shallow knowledge, inflexible knowledge is meaningful—the catch is that it doesn't translate well to other relevant situations. To extend our World War II example, a student with inflexible knowledge may learn the conclusion and an adequate number of supporting facts, developing a real understanding of Japan's mistake. But, when the history class moved on to study another war, the student may not recognize an analogous strategic mistake. Developing flexible knowledge, such as being able to track strategic mistakes as a theme throughout military history (or to generalize, for example, to corporate history) requires much further study.

Daniel T. Willingham is associate professor of cognitive psychology and neuroscience at the University of Virginia and author of Cognition: The Thinking Animal. *His research focuses on the role of consciousness in learning.*

Beyond Learning By Doing:
The Brain Compatible Approach

The current position of the field of experiential education within mainstream education places at a premium attempts to significantly broaden and deepen experiential pedagogy beyond mere "learning by doing." This article will explore one such attempt—the Brain Compatible Approach—and its potential linkages with experiential education. An overview of the Brain Compatible Approach will be outlined, followed by a discussion of several key principles. Linkages between these principles and experiential education will be discussed, as well as several "Quick Tips" on possible practical applications of the research. Finally, the benefits of aligning experiential education with the Brain Compatible Approach will be explored.

Keywords: Education, Brain Compatible, Pedagogy

Jay W. Roberts

Over the last ten years, experiential education has made many in-roads with the mainstream educational establishment. The success of programs such as Project Adventure and Outward Bound working within schools has been well documented. Additionally, ropes course, environmental, and outdoor education programs have become prevalent in many school districts across the country. Yet, with all these advances, there are still many barriers between our pedagogy and traditional schooling. We remain literally, and figuratively, "outside" the educational establishment. Recent initiatives toward accountability and standards have placed experiential education in the crosshairs of reform-minded politicians and school consultants. "Learning by doing" is often described as "process heavy," devoid of content, and a hold-out from 1960s progressivists' approaches. One researcher has gone so far as to say "recent history of American education and controlled observations have shown that learning by doing and its adaptations are among the least effective pedagogies available to the teacher" (Hirsch, 1996, p. 257).

The current position of the field within mainstream education places at a premium attempts to significantly broaden and deepen experiential pedagogy beyond mere "learning by doing." This paper will explore one such attempt—the Brain Compatible Approach—and its potential linkages with experiential education. An overview of the Brain Compatible Approach will be outlined, followed by a discussion of several key principles. Linkages between these principles and experiential education will be discussed as well as several "Quick Tips" on possible practical applications of the research. Finally, the benefits of aligning experiential education with the Brain Compatible Approach will be explored.

The Brain Compatible Approach

In July of 1989, President George Bush declared the 1990s the "Decade of the Brain." What followed was a revolution in research, articles, books, and television specials on what we know about how the brain functions and learns. The medical advances in particular have been many and remarkable. We have learned more about the brain in the past five years than the previous one hundred. Additionally, nearly 90 percent of all neuroscientists who have ever lived are alive today (Brandt & Wolfe, 1998).

While still relatively new as a field of inquiry, the Brain Compatible Approach has yielded several intriguing findings:

- *Neuroplasticity:* The brain changes physiologically as a result of experience and it happens much quicker than originally thought. The environment in which the brain operates determines to a large degree the functioning ability of the brain (Brandt & Wolfe, 1998).

- *The brain is complex and interconnected:* Just as a city or jazz quartet has many levels of interaction and connectedness, the brain has an infinite number of possible interconnections. In essence, there are no isolated, specialized areas but rather the brain is simultaneously processing a wide variety of information all at once (Caine & Caine, 1994).

- *Every brain is unique:* Our brains are far more individualized in terms of physiology, neural wiring, bio-chemical balance, and developmental stage than previously thought (Jensen, 2000).

Each of these findings suggests re-consideration of the way we currently educate. Caution must also be practiced. Much of the current research is new, and steps from research to application are inherently complex and difficult. Already, several researchers have questioned the validity of educational applications of brain research (Bruer, 1997). If nothing else, the sheer volume of new information about how the brain functions and learns forces us to question what we truly "know" about learning and educational practice.

Principles of Brain Based Learning

Drawing from the findings above, several intriguing principles and practical implications have emerged. The following principles are of particular interest to experiential educators as they support some long-standing practices within experiential education and also push the envelope of what may be possible in the future.

Principle #1: Pattern and Meaning Making

Research supports the claim that the search for meaning is innate and occurs through patterning (Caine & Caine, 1994). Patterning refers to the meaningful organization and categorization of information (Nummela & Rosengren, 1986). The brain is designed to search for and integrate new information into existing structures and actively resists "meaningless" patterns (Caine & Caine). The process is constant and does not stop—regardless of whether or not we have stopped teaching! This principle reinforces many of the practices we attribute to experiential learning including emphasis on context and framing, learner involvement in the teaching of the material, alternating between details and big picture (whole/part), reflection components, and relevancy (i.e., relating information to students' previous experience and learning).

Quick Tip #1: Chunking can be an effective tool for presenting the learner with information in an organized, meaningful way. Look at the following list of letters: IBFVTNOJBLKFJ. Try to memorize them as presented. Now look at the next list of letters: JFK, LBJ, ON, TV, FBI. The second list is much easier to memorize even though they are the same letters. They have simply been chunked and arranged in a meaningful way that draws on previous experience and information. Consider how you might chunk small activities (lessons or even directions) and large, multi-day experiences. How can you arrange the information in a more meaningful, patterned way?

Quick Tip #2: Use a "Big Picture." Remember that your students do not have the same view of the course, lesson, or program that you do. Provide them with a big picture as soon as possible at the beginning of the experience. Rather than an exhaustive outline or itinerary, the big picture gives your students a taste of what's coming and allows them to begin making patterns, connections, and frames for the experience. Revisit the big picture a few times throughout the experience to further solidify the link. In this regard, it is helpful to have it on a flip chart or other visual aid. Try using a "you are here" map with a movable arrow.

Principle #2: The Brain as a Parallel Processor

The human brain is the ultimate, multi-tasking machine, constantly doing many things at once. This is because the brain is geared toward survival and is, in actuality, poorly designed for linear, lock-step instruction (Jensen, 2000). Consider how you learned to ride a bicycle. Did you learn through reading a book or hearing a lecture on the separate topics of bike parts, safety, and operation? No. It is more likely you learned through a more dynamic and complex series of experiences. Current research supports the notion that the brain learns best through rich, complex, and multi-sensory environments (Jensen). In this sense, the teacher is seen more as an *orchestrator* of learning environments rather than an instructor of linear lesson plans or even a facilitator of experiences (Deporter, Reardon, & Singer-Nourie, 1999). Practical applications for parallel processing include the use of multi-modal instructional techniques (visual, auditory, kinesthetic) and multiple intelligence activities (Gardner, 1985). Simulations and role-plays mimic our natural learning environment and encourage complex processing. Lastly, enriched learning environments can be orchestrated through the components of challenge, novelty, choice, high feedback, social interaction, and active participation (Diamond & Hopson, 1998). If the benefits of enriched, multi-sensory, complex learning environments continue to be supported by the research, experiential theory and practice can and must play a larger role in the classroom of the future.

Quick Tip #3: Use the EELDRC (Enroll, Experience, Label, Demonstrate, Review, Celebrate) design frame (Deporter et al., 1999) to create a dynamic, complex, multi-sensory lesson plan. In the *Enroll* segment, seek to engage students in the material through intrigue and answering the learner question "What's In It For Me?" Give them a brief *Experience* to immerse students in the new information. Use the *Label* segment to punctuate the most salient points with a "lecturette" or debrief. Provide an opportunity for the participants to *Demonstrate* with the new information to encourage connections and personalization of the material. *Review* the material to cement the big picture and, finally, find a way to *Celebrate* the experience to reinforce positive associations with the learning.

Principle #3: Stress and Threat

Learning is enhanced by challenge and inhibited by threat (Jensen, 2000). Paul MacLean offers a model for considering this principle through his Triune Brain theory (1978). MacLean categorizes the brain into three main regions or separate brains—the Reptilian (or R-complex), the Mammalian (or Limbic), and the Neo-Mammalian (or Neo-Cortex). The reptilian brain controls physical survival and basic needs (flight or fight responses). This is our most primitive "brain." The second brain—the Mammalian—houses both the hippocampus and amygdala—the primary centers for emotion and memory. Lastly, the most advanced part of our brains, according to MacLean, is our Neo-Cortex. It is here where we use higher order thinking skills—synthesizing, logical and operational thinking, speech, and planning for the future (Caine & Caine, 1994).

In this model, the brain has the capacity to "shift" up or down depending on perception of the immediate environment. Perceived threat an force the brain to "downshift" to lower order thinking (Hart, 1983). Yet, heightened challenge and stress, referred to as eustress, can invite an up-shift response into higher order thinking skills in the neo-cortex. Recent research has suggested that the chemical and physiological responses to stress and threat are radically different (Caine & Caine, 1994). Psychological models also support a difference between perceived challenge and threat (Csikszentmihalyi, 1991). This idea is expressed in experiential pedagogy through the concepts of adaptive dissonance and the "comfort zone." In both cases, the felicitator or teacher intentionally places the learner in stressful situations to encourage and invite new adaptive behaviors and mental models that may be more successful or effective for the learner.

Caine and Caine (1994), suggest that specific learning conditions can create situations of up-shifting or downshifting. Downshifting can occur when "pre-specified 'correct' outcomes have been established by an external agent; personal meaning is limited; rewards and punishments are externally controlled; restrictive time lines are given; and the work to be done is relatively unfamiliar with little support available" (Caine & Caine, p. 84). By contrast, to create up-shifting conditions "outcomes should be relatively open ended; personal meaning should be maximized; emphasis should be on intrinsic motivation; tasks should have relatively open-ended time lines; and should be manageable and supported" (Caine & Caine, p. 85). Emotions also play a critical role in both memory encoding and threat perception (LeDoux, 1996). Too little emotion and the brain has a difficult time "tagging" the material for long term memory. Too much emotion and the situation may be perceived as threatening, causing a downshift in mental functions (Brandt & Wolfe, 1998).

Practical applications of the stress/threat principle are numerous and exciting for the experiential field. Experiential pedagogy, with its emphasis on novelty, interpersonal interaction, challenge by choice, and the use of emotions such as play, fear, and humor, is uniquely suited to address stress/threat balances. Understanding how these brain compatible principles can be strengthened by experiential learning opens the possibility for meaningful dialogue with mainstream education.

Quick Tip #4: To lower threat levels early in your program, make a strong emphasis on relationship building both peer-peer and teacher-student. Work the group from the "inside-out" by making a conscious effort to spend personal time with as many students as possible, either on the trail or at water breaks. Work the group "outside-in" by facilitating highly interactive experiences like paired shares, new games, or trust activities.

Quick Tip #5: Use the 60/40 rule for planning your lesson plans. Sixty percent of your experiences should be ritual based activities that are repetitive (like morning check-ins, skill progressions, warm-ups, or post-activity debriefs) to allow your participants to experience known activities in an unknown environment. But be sure to make approximately 40 percent of activities novel. The introduction of elements of suspense, surprise, and disorder keep learners engaged and can be an effective way to manage attention spans. Instead of circling up every time, "rhombus-up" with your group every so often. Mix-up de-briefs by using paired shares, group reports, or silent journaling instead of large group discussion. Introduce skill sections playfully with characters and costumes (knots with Ivana Climbalot, or baking with Chef Boyarentyouhungry).

Conclusion

Evidence and theories from the Brain Compatible Approach support much of what we do. Understanding the human brain's tendency toward pattern and "meaning-making" reinforces the intentional use of reflection and synthesis in experiential education. Viewing the brain as a parallel processor encourages the creation of enriched environments for learners. Experiential methodology facilitates such enriched environments through challenge, social interaction, feedback, and active participation. Finally, the differences between stress and threat responses support our pedagogical approach including the effective use of emotion and the importance of novelty and choice. Recent developments in brain research should also push us toward new questions and research queries. What is the role of emotion in experiential education? How do we define, operationally, the differences between stressful and threatening experiences and responses? How is the mind-body connection supported in current brain research? What part can experiential methodology play in the creation of enriched classroom environments?

We must move beyond mere "learning by doing" for our fields' philosophical underpinnings and practical approaches to become more influential in mainstream education. Using only the learning by doing definition, experiential education becomes nothing more than activities and events with little to no significance beyond the initial experience. One educator recently told me she calls this the "Inoculation Effect" (shoot 'em up; hope it takes). This was not John Dewey's vision and it cannot be our lasting legacy. Many of us entered this field after becoming disenchanted or burned-out on mainstream educational practice. We have also seen the remarkable changes and results that can occur through experiential learning. We believe very strongly that it works. Yet, as a field, we remain long on practice and short on theory and research. The Brain Compatible Approach is one avenue for helping experiential educators articulate how and why the methodology is effective.

How can we achieve more legitimacy while holding fast to our principles? Moves toward identifying the philosophical approaches of experiential education should be encouraged (Itin, 1999). Efforts must be made to increase both qualitative and quantitative research that cross into mainstream education. As educators, we also have a responsibility to learn about our field. At a recent AEE conference, I was surprised to learn how few experiential education practitioners knew of E.D. Hirsch—one of the strongest critics of progressive approaches and a major figure in the standards-based movement. Hirsch defines learning by doing as "a phrase once used to characterize the progressivist movement but little used today, possibly because the formulation has been the object of much criticism and even ridicule" (Hirsch, 1996, p. 256). With critics like this and few legitimate platforms from which to respond, it is not surprising that experiential education remains largely locked out of our schools. Knowing some of the latest trends and movements within the fields of education, psychology, and sociology will strengthen our voice and message.

While there is value in experiential education's subversive, outside-the-mainstream persona, we must also seek ways to come in from the "outside," invite dialogue, and encourage interaction across disciplines. The Brain Compatible Approach, as a promising new area of research and study, offers an excellent opportunity to do just that. In the next 20 years, will experiential education be a program (like field trips, ropes courses, and character education) to be implemented in schools or, will it be a broader, pedagogical foundation from which to work? The future depends on how we live that question.

References

Brandt, R., & Wolfe, P. (1998). What do we know from brain research? *Educational Leadership, 56*(3), 8–13.

Bruer, J. T. (1997). Education and the brain: A bridge too far. *Educational Researcher, 26*(8), 4–16.

Caine, G., & Caine, R. (1994). *Making connections: Teaching and the human brain.* New York: Addison Wesley.

Csikszentmihalyi, M. (1991). *Flow: The psychology of optimal experience.* New York: Harper Perrenial.

Deporter, B., Reardon, M., & Singer-Nourie, S. (1999). *Quantum teaching.* Needham Heights, MA: Allyn & Bacon.

Diamond, M., & Hopson, J. (1998). *Magic trees of the mind.* New York: Penguin Putnum.

Gardner, H. (1985). *Frames of mind: The theory of multiple intelligences.* New York: Basic Books.

Hart, L. (1983). *Human brain, human learning.* New York: Longman.

Hirsch, E. G. (1996). *The schools we need and why we don't have them.* New York: Doubleday.

Itin, C. (1999). Reasserting the philosophy of experiential education as a vehicle for change in the 21st century. *Journal of Experiential Education, 229*(2), 91–98.

Jensen, E. (2000). *Brain-based learning.* San Diego, CA: The Brain Store.

LeDoux, J. (1996). *The emotional brain: The mysterious underpinnings of emotional life.* New York: Simon & Schuster.

MacLean, P. D. (1978). A mind of three Minds: Educating the triune brain. In J. Chall, & A. Mirsky (Eds.), *Education and the brain* (pp. 308–342). Chicago: University of Chicago Press.

Nummela, R., & Rosengren, T. (1986). What's happening in students' brains may redefine teaching. *Educational Leadership 43*(8), 49–53.

Jay Roberts, M.Ed., is the Director of Wilderness Programs at Earlham College in Richmond, Indiana and teaches in the Education program. He also spent seven years working as a facilitator for Learning Forum Supercamp, an internationally recognized brain compatible learning program. He can be reached at roberja@earlham.edu

ABILITY AND EXPERTISE

It's Time to Replace the Current Model of Intelligence

BY ROBERT J. STERNBERG

BILLY HAS an IQ of 121 on a standardized individual intelligence test, and Jimmy has an IQ of 94 on the same test. What do these scores, and the difference between them, mean? The conventional answer to this question is that they represent a kind of intellectual predestination: The two children possess inborn gifts that are relatively fixed and will, to a large extent, predict their future achievement. So no one will be surprised if Billy goes on to do well in high school and gets into a good college—or if Jimmy barely gets through school and ends up with a minimum-wage job—because that's what this familiar and widely accepted model of human intelligence would lead us to expect.

But a scientific model is just a way of fitting together pieces of information and things we have observed into a pattern that makes sense. It does not represent the certain or only way of arranging the pieces, and models can be and often are modified or even discarded when we make new discoveries or look at what we know in new ways. This happened, for example, in the early seventeenth century, when the Ptolemaic model of the solar system, in which all the heavenly bodies were said to revolve around the earth, was replaced by the Copernican, sun-centered, model of the solar system.

Many psychologists now question the simple identification of IQ with ability, which the old model of human intelligence posits. They believe that abilities are too broad and too complex to be measured by the kind of IQ test that Billy and Jimmy took. They also believe that environment and genetics play a part and, furthermore, that abilities are not a fixed quantity: They can be modified by education and experience. I'd like to propose a further, and important, building block for this new model of human intelligence—namely that the difference in Billy's

and Jimmy's IQ scores simply means that the two children are at a different stage in developing the expertise measured by the IQ test. Furthermore, I suggest that people who study abilities and those who study expertise are really talking about the same thing. What we are measuring when we administer a Wechsler Intelligence Scale for Children (WISC) or an Iowa Test of Basic Skills (ITBS) or an SAT are the same. They are not different in kind but only in the point at which we are measuring them.

In the Eye of the Beholder

When we give an achievement test, we accept the idea that we are testing a form of expertise, but this is equally true when we administer an IQ test. What differs is the level of expertise we measure and, probably more important, the way we perceive what we are measuring. The familiar IQ/ability model creates a certain expectation: that one kind of accomplishment (IQ test scores) will predict—and, in fact, lead to—another kind of accomplishment (grades or scores on achievement tests). And of course we also use different words to describe the two kinds of accomplishment.

But this way of looking at the two kinds of test scores is a familiar convenience rather than a psychological reality. Solving problems on a verbal-analogies test or a test of mathematical problem solving, which are supposed to test a child's abilities, calls for expertise just the way so-called achievement tests do: You can't do well on these so-called tests of ability without knowing the vocabulary or having some familiarity with problem-solving techniques. The chief difference between ability and achievement tests is not what they measure but the point at which they measure it. IQ and other tests of ability are, typically, administered early in a child's school career, whereas various indications about school performance, such as grades or achievement test scores, are collected later. However, all of the various kinds of assessments are of the same kind, psychologically. They all test—to some extent—what you know and how well you can use it. What distinguishes ability tests from the other kinds of assessments is how the ability tests are used (usually, predictively), rather than what they measure. There is no qualitative distinction.

But if the distinction between what these tests measure does not exist, how do we come to make it? The answer is a complicated story, but the principal reason is historical accident. Briefly, the two kinds of testing were developed separately and used on different groups of people. IQ/ability testing, which originated in Alfred Binet's testing of young children, focused on exceptionally low levels of performance and came to be viewed primarily as predictive. Early studies of expertise were done with adults. They focused on exceptionally high levels of performance and came to be viewed as measures of achievement.

The Traditional Model

According to the traditional model of fixed individual differences, the capabilities that a child inherits interact with the child's environment to produce, at an early age, a relatively fixed potential for achievement. Children fulfill this potential to a greater or lesser degree. Thus, if a child who scores well on ability tests does well in school, we say he is living up to his potential. If, as sometimes happens, his achievement does not match his test scores, we call him an *underachiever*—or if the kid confounds expectations by working hard and doing well, he gets the label of *overachiever*. Ironically, ability test scores are considered a better indicator of what a child can achieve (or should achieve) than what the child actually does. A test of verbal analogies, in this view, might actually tell us more about a person's verbal abilities than the person's comprehension of the reading he or she does in everyday life; or a test of mathematical problem-solving skills might be viewed as more informative than the mathematical problem solving the person does on the job.

According to this model, the more intelligent students (that is, the ones with higher IQs) do better in school. As a result, they are likely to attend selective colleges, go on to professional schools, and eventually get well-paying jobs and enjoy other forms of success. The less intelligent do worse in school and may drop out. At best, they probably have to be satisfied with low-status credentials that reflect hard work rather than ability, and their role in the labor market is to fill the jobs that the more intelligent people don't want to do.

This is the view Richard Herrnstein and Charles Murray present in *The Bell Curve* (1994), and as people who have read the book will remember, it assigns African Americans as a group to the status of an underclass, based on the average "potential" of group members displayed in IQ and other ability tests. Herrnstein and Murray's use of the traditional model has occasioned a great deal of controversy. However, the view of IQ as fixed and determinant is, unfortunately, consistent with many current educational practices and common views about intellectual competence.

Developing Expertise

The idea that abilities are a form of developing expertise offers a more flexible and optimistic view of human capabilities, and one that is more in line with what we are discovering about human intelligence. Children become experts in the skills needed for success on ability tests in much the same ways that they become experts in doing anything else—through a combination of genetic endowment and experience (Ericsson, 1996). To do well on a test, a child needs to acquire, store, and learn how to use at least two kinds of knowledge: explicit knowledge of a domain and implicit or tacit knowledge of a field. Knowledge of a domain is subject-matter knowledge: In American history, for example, it would be the facts, trends, and major ideas about the political, economic, and social development of our country. Implicit knowledge is the kind of knowledge one needs to be successful in a field but which is not part of the subject matter and often is not even talked about. For example, in American history, the role of the Federalist Papers in the shaping of the U.S. Constitution would be explicit knowledge; how to use the library or Internet to research an essay about the Federalist Papers and how to take and organize notes and carry the paper through successive drafts to completion would be implicit knowledge.

Tests measure both explicit and implicit knowledge: knowledge of the subject matter and knowledge about how to take a test. This is as true of ability tests as it is of achievement tests. A verbal-analogies test, for example, measures explicit knowledge of vocabulary and a student's ability to reason with this knowledge, but the test also measures implicit knowledge of how to take a test. Thus, the student has to work within certain time limits and choose the best answer from a list of answers no one of which is exactly right.

To translate the gaining of expertise on test-taking into procedural terms, students need

- direct instruction in how to solve test-like problems—usually this takes place in school;
- practice in solving such problems, again usually in academic contexts;
- an opportunity to watch others, such as teachers or other students, solve test-like problems;

- practice thinking about such problems, some-times mentally simulating what to do when confronting them;
- rewards for successful solutions (good grades, praise from teachers, other kinds of recognition), thereby reinforcing such behavior.

The difference between Billy's score of 121 and Jimmy's 94 also reflects a number of personal and cultural factors, and they do not all pertain to what we usually consider expertise. For example, the two boys may possess different degrees of "test-wiseness," that is, understanding the tricks of taking tests (Millman, Bishop, and Ebel, 1965; Bond and Harman, 1994). They may feel differing levels of anxiety and/or alertness on the day they are tested, and this would probably show itself in their scores. Cultural differences between them may lead to different attitudes about the importance of doing well on a test, particularly one that clearly does not "count." Most important of all, the boys may be at different levels of developing expertise in the skills that the test measures.

Individual Differences

But saying that IQ tests and other assessments of ability are testing the same thing as achievement tests and that the expertise revealed is not fixed should not be taken to mean that everybody has the same intellectual capacity. The difference in expertise that Billy and Jimmy reveal on their IQ tests may indicate an underlying difference in their capacities. However, IQ tests do not directly measure these differences and neither do any of the other ways in which we currently seek to measure ability (see, for example, Vygotsky, 1978). Individual differences in developing expertise result in much the same way as in most kinds of learning: from (a) the rate of learning (which can be caused by the amount of direct instruction received, the amount of problem solving done, the amount of time and effort spent in thinking about problems, and so on); and from (b) the asymptote of learning—that is, the limit set by ability to what a student can ultimately achieve, given unlimited training. This limit, or asymptote, can be caused by differences in numbers of schemas—the networks of information on various subjects stored in our memories—the organization of schemas, efficiency in using schemas, and so on (see Atkinson, Bower, and Crothers, 1965). For example, children can learn how to solve the various kinds of mathematical problems found in tests of mathematical abilities, whether through regular schooling, a special course, or through assimilation of everyday experience. When they learn, they will learn at different rates, and reach different asymptotes. Ultimately the differences represent genetic and environmental factors that are interacting in ways that we cannot now measure.

Various Kinds of Expertise

As I've already noted, the so-called ability tests typically come earlier in a student's school career than the various types of achievement tests, but what IQ tests measure is not psychologically prior. Achievement tests might just as well be used to predict scores on ability tests—and sometimes they are, as for instance, when school officials try to predict a student's college admissions test scores on the basis of the student's grades. When we look at the test of abilities as though they are psychologically prior, we are confusing the order in which students usually take these tests with some kind of psychological ordering. But in fact, our temporal ordering implies no psychological ordering at all. The recent change in the meaning of the acronym *SAT* (from Scholastic Aptitude Test to Scholastic Assessment Test) reflects the recognition that what was called an aptitude test measures more than just "aptitude"—indeed, it hints at the interchangeability of the two kinds of tests. Nevertheless, the SAT is still widely used as an ability test, and the SAT-II, which more directly measures subject-matter knowledge, as a set of achievement tests.

Tests that claim to measure ability through questions employing vocabulary, reading comprehension, verbal analogies, arithmetic problem solving, and the like are all, in part, tests of achievement. Even abstract-reasoning tests measure achievement in dealing with geometric symbols, which is a skill taught in Western schools (Laboratory of Comparative Human Cognition, 1982). Indeed, if we examine the content of ability tests, it is clear that they measure achievement that the students taking the test should have accomplished several years back. We could just as well use academic performance to predict ability-test scores. The problem with the traditional model is not that it proposes a correlation between ability tests and other forms of achievement. That undoubtedly exists. It is rather the traditional model's proposing that the capacities measured by the tests *cause* later success—or failure—instead of merely preceding it.

An Illusion of Causality

The notion that success on ability tests predicts success in many other areas gains credibility from the fact that some of the skills or qualities that make people more expert at taking tests are also likely to make them successful in other aspects of life in our culture. Taking a test, say, of verbal or figural analogies, or of mathematical problem solving, typically requires skills such as (a) puzzling out what someone else wants (here, the person who wrote the test), (b) command of English vocabulary, (c) reading comprehension, (d) allocation of limited time, (e) sustained concentration, (f) abstract reasoning, (g) quick thinking, (h) symbol manipulation, and (i) suppression of anxiety and other emotions that can interfere with test performance. These skills are also part of what is required for successful performance in school and in many kinds of job performance. Thus, an expert test-taker is likely also to have skills that will be involved in other kinds of expertise as well, such as expertise in getting high grades in school.

To the extent that the expertise required for one kind of performance overlaps with the expertise required for another kind of performance, there will be a correlation between performances. However, the expertise that ability tests measure is not the cause of school or job expertise; it is itself an expertise that overlaps with school or job expertise. Differences in test scores, academic performance, and job performance are all effects of different levels of expertise.

The New Model

The notion of *developing* expertise means that people are constantly in the process of developing expertise when they work within a given domain. Individuals can differ in rate and asymptote of development. However, the main constraint in achieving expertise is not some fixed prior level of capacity, of the kind measured by IQ tests. It is the degree to which students are purposefully engaged in working and teachers in helping them. This involves direct instruction, active participation, role modeling, and reward.

The model of developing expertise has five key elements: metacognitive skills, learning skills, thinking skills, knowledge, and motivation. The elements all influence one another, both directly and indirectly. For example, learning leads to knowledge, but knowledge facilitates further learning.

1. Metacognitive skills. Metacognitive skills refer to students' understanding and control of their own learning. These skills would include what a student knows about writing papers or solving arithmetic word problems, both in regard to the steps that are involved and how these steps can be executed effectively (Sternberg 1985, 1986, 1988; Sternberg and Swerling, 1996).

2. Learning skills. Learning skills are sometimes divided into explicit learning, which occurs when we make an effort to learn, and implicit learning, which occurs when we simply pick up information without any particular effort. Examples of learning skills are distinguishing relevant from irrelevant information; putting together the relevant information; and relating new information to information already stored in memory (Sternberg, 1985, 1986).

3. Thinking skills. There are three main sets of thinking skills. Critical (analytical) thinking skills include analyzing, critiquing, judging, evaluating, comparing and contrasting, and assessing. Creative thinking skills include

creating, discovering, inventing, imagining, supposing, and hypothesizing. Practical thinking skills include applying, using, and practicing (Sternberg, 1985, 1986, 1994, 1997). They are the first step in translating thought into real-world action.

4. Knowledge. There are two main kinds of knowledge that are relevant in academic learning. Declarative knowledge is of facts, concepts, principles, laws, and the like. It is "knowing that." Procedure knowledge is of procedures and strategies. It is "knowing how." Of particular importance is procedural tacit knowledge, which involves knowing how the system in which one is operating functions (Sternberg, Wagner, Williams & Horvath, 1995).

5. Motivation. There are a number of different kinds of motivation, and in one or another of its forms, motivation is probably indispensable for school success. Without it, the student never even tries to learn (McClelland, 1985; McClelland, Atkinson, Clark, and Lowell, 1976; Bandura, 1977, 1996; Amabile, 1996; Sternberg and Lubart, 1996).

6. Context. All of the elements discussed above are characteristics of the learner. However, it is a mistake to assume, as conventional tests usually do, that factors external to the student's mastery of the material play no part in how well the student does on a test. Such contextual factors include whether the student is taking the test in his or her native language, whether the test emphasizes speedy performance, the importance to the student of success on the test, and the student's familiarity with the kinds of material on the test.

Novices—beginning learners—work toward expertise through deliberate practice. But this practice requires an interaction of all five of the key elements in the model. At the center, driving the elements, is motivation. Without it, nothing happens. Motivation drives metacognitive skills, which in turn activate learning and thinking skills, which then provide feedback to the metacognitive skills, enabling the student's level of expertise to increase (see also Sternberg, 1985). The declarative and procedural knowledge acquired through the extension of the thinking and learning skills also results in these skills being used more effectively in the future.

All of these processes are affected by, and can in turn affect, the context in which they operate. For example, if a learning experience is in English but the learner has only limited English proficiency, his or her learning will be inferior to that of someone with more advanced English language skills. Or if material is presented orally to someone who is a better visual learner, that individual's performance will be reduced.

Eventually, as the five elements influence one another, the student reaches a kind of expertise at which he or she becomes a reflective practitioner who is able to consciously use a certain set of skills. But expertise occurs at many levels. The expert first-year graduate or law student, for example, is still a far cry from the expert professional. People thus cycle through many times, on the way to successively higher levels of expertise.

Implications for the Classroom

The model of abilities as a form of developing expertise has a number of immediate implications for education, in general, and classroom practice, in particular.

First, teachers and all who use ability and achievement tests should stop distinguishing between what the two kinds of tests assess. The measurements are not different in kind but only in the point at which they are being made.

Second, tests measure *achieved* levels of developing expertise. No test—of abilities or anything else—can specify the highest level a student can achieve.

Third, different kinds of assessments—multiple-choice, short answer, performance-based, portfolio—complement one another in assessing multiple aspects of developing expertise. There is no one "right" kind of assessment.

Fourth, instruction should be geared not just toward imparting a knowledge base, but toward developing reflective analytical, creative, and practical thinking with a knowledge base. Students learn better when they think to learn, even when their learning is assessed with straightforward multiple-choice memory assessments (Sternberg, Torff, and Grigorenko, 1998).

The model I've proposed here views students as novices who are capable of becoming experts in a variety of areas. The traditional model, which posits fixed individual differences—and typically bases the kind of instruction a student gets on these differences—holds many students back from attaining the expertise they are capable of. It is true that for various reasons (including, perhaps, genetic as well as environmentally based differences), not all individuals will reach the same ultimate level of expertise. But they should all be given the opportunity to reach new levels of competence well beyond what they, and in some cases, others may think possible. The fact that Billy and Jimmy have different IQs tells us something about differences in what they now do. It does not tell us anything about what ultimately they will be able to achieve.

References

Amabile, T. M. (1996). *Creativity in context*. Boulder, CO: Westview.

Atkinson, R. C., Bower, G. H., & Crothers, E. J. (1965). *An introduction to mathematical learning theory*. New York: John Wiley & Sons.

Bandura, A. (1977). Self-efficacy: Toward a unifying theory of behavioral change. *Psychological Review*, 84, 181–215.

Bandura, A. (1996). *Self-efficacy: The exercise of control*. New York: Freeman.

Bond, L., & Harman, A. E. (1994). Test-taking strategies. In R. J. Sternberg (Ed.), *Encyclopedia of human intelligence* (Vol. 2, pp. 1073–1077). New York: Macmillan.

Ericsson, A. (Ed.) (1996). *The road to excellence*. Mahwah, NJ: Erlbaum.

Herrnstein, R. J., & Murray, C. (1994). *The bell curve*. New York: Free Press.

Laboratory of Comparative Human Cognition (1982). Culture and intelligence. In R. J. Sternberg (Ed.), *Handbook of human intelligence* (pp. 642–719). New York: Cambridge University Press.

McClelland, D. C. (1985). *Human motivation*. New York: Scott Foresman.

McClelland, D. C., Atkinson, J. W., Clark, R. A., & Lowell, E. L. (1976). *The achievement motive*. New York: Irvington.

Millman, J., Bishop, H., & Ebel, R. (1965). An analysis of test-wiseness. *Educational and Psychological Measurement*, 25, 707–726.

Sternberg, R. J. (1985). *Beyond IQ: A triarchic theory of human intelligence*. New York: Cambridge University Press.

Sternberg, R. J. (1986). *Intelligence applied*. Orlando, FL: Harcourt Brace College Publishers.

Sternberg, R. J. (1988). *The triarchic mind: A new theory of human intelligence*. New York: Viking-Penguin.

Sternberg, R. J. (1994). Diversifying instruction and assessment. *The Educational Forum*, 59(1), 47–53.

Sternberg, R. J. (1997). *Successful intelligence*. New York: Plume.

Sternberg, R. J., & Lubart, T. I. (1995). *Defying the crowd: Cultivating creativity in a culture of conformity*. New York: Free Press.

Sternberg, R. J., & Lubart, T. I. (1996). Investing in creativity. *American Psychologist*, 51, 677–688.

Sternberg, R. J., & Spear-Swerling, L. (1996). *Teaching for thinking*. Washington, DC: APA Books.

Sternberg, R. J., Torff, B., & Grigorenko, E. L. (1998). Teaching triarchically improves school achievement. *Journal of Educational Psychology*, 90, 374–384.

Sternberg, R. J., Wagner, R. K., Williams, W. M., & Horvath, J. (1995). Testing common sense. *American Psychologist*, 50, 912–927.

Vygotsky, L. S. (1978). *Mind in society: The development of higher psychological processes*. Cambridge, MA: Harvard University Press.

This work was supported by the U.S. Office of Educational Research and Improvement (Grant R206R50001), but this support does not imply endorsement of positions taken or conclusions reached.

Robert J. Sternberg is IBM Professor of Psychology in the Department of Psychology at Yale University. His areas of specialization are human abilities and cognition. A long version of this article appeared in Educational Researcher, April 1998.

From the Spring 1999 issue of the *American Educator*, pp. 10-13, 50-51. Reprinted by permission of the *American Educator*, the quarterly journal of the American Federation of Teachers, and Robert J. Sternberg.

It's No Fad: Fifteen Years of Implementing Multiple Intelligences

by Thomas R. Hoerr

Educators do a great job of identifying winners and losers in the classroom. Regardless of how sensitively academic hierarchies are designed, everyone recognizes the pecking order they create. Is it any wonder, then, that students who aren't considered smart often lose interest in school? How many of us, after all, continue to engage in activities at which we repeatedly fail?

Granted, not all children are equally smart, and failure can sometimes be even more enlightening than the smooth road of success. What makes the theory of multiple intelligences (MI) significant is its acknowledgment that children demonstrate intelligence in many different ways. The job of an educator, then, becomes identifying the ways in which children exhibit intelligence and using their particular strengths to help them learn.

In *Frames of Mind* (1983), Howard Gardner challenged the general perception of intelligence by suggesting that there are eight different ways to learn (see Table 1). Gardner was speaking mainly to an audience of psychologists, but the realization that there are many ways to demonstrate intelligence resonated with educators. MI revealed a way to help more students learn and to help students learn more.

Table 1
THE THEORY OF MULTIPLE INTELLIGENCES

Intelligence	Definition	Examples of persons who evidence this intelligence
LINGUISTIC	sensitivity to the meaning and order of words	Winston Churchill Mario Cuomo Barbara Jordan
LOGICAL-MATHEMATICAL	the ability to handle chains of reasoning and to recognize patterns and order	Benjamin Banneker Bill Gates Stephen Jay Gould
MUSICAL	sensitivity to pitch, melody, rhythm, and tone	Louis Armstrong George Gershwin Yo Yo Ma
BODILY-KINESTHETIC	ability to use the body skillfully and handle objects adroitly	Mia Hamm Harry Houdini Michael Jordan
SPATIAL	ability to perceive the world accurately and to re-create or transform aspects of that world	Maya Lin Peter Max Frank Lloyd Wright
NATURALIST	ability to recognize and classify numerous flora and fauna of an environment	Charles Darwin Jane Goodall John Muir
INTERPERSONAL	ability to understand people and relationships	Martin Luther King, Jr. Ronald Reagan Oprah Winfrey
INTRAPERSONAL	access to one's emotional life for understanding oneself and others	Bill Cosby Anne Frank Eleanor Roosevelt

The faculty of New City School has been implementing MI since 1988. Before 1988, New City was considered a creative and diverse school, but there was no organizing framework, no intellectual or pedagogical model that guided our efforts. *Frames of Mind* seemed to support our faculty's extant beliefs: All children have strengths; the arts are important; and who you are is more important than what you know. I convened a voluntary faculty committee at New City, and we spent several months discussing the practicalities of implementing MI.

MI gave us a model and a vocabulary to talk about how curriculum, instruction, and assessment could be designed to enable more students to succeed. Not only did MI expand our conception of academics; it changed how we communicate with parents. For us, MI has become a philosophy of education that affects our relationships with students, administrators, parents, and each other.

Despite our grounding in MI, New City still administers standardized tests each spring (Hoerr 2000). Our students' scores on these tests, consistently several years above grade level, illustrate that high test scores can be achieved through non-traditional teaching techniques.

MI has made our curriculum and instruction far more inclusive of varied learning styles. Rather than simply relying on the linguistic approach to teaching, we have found ways to incorporate other intelligences into our instruction. One first-grade teacher introduces the *th* sound by having her students *th*read yarn into a piece of fabric. A third-grade teacher at New City demonstrates ratios by having her students lie on the floor inside a full-size shape of a buffalo made with masking tape so they can compare the length of their limbs to the buffalo's. A fifth-grade teacher has his students explore the American Civil War period through visual art. Students learn that through clothing, facial expressions, jewelry, and even calluses on hands, they can make inferences about how people lived and what they believed.

At New City, solid assessment is intertwined with curriculum and instruction; here, too, MI provides the foundation. In one class, kindergartners demonstrate how the systems of the human body function using everyday objects to create a model. The children then explain the life-size bodies they have created: a juice box serves as the heart and, as it contracts, forces air into plastic bags that serve as lungs. There is a spine of popsicle sticks and a brain of pasta. Veins and arteries, made of yarn, are respectively red and blue. Second-graders show their understanding of the challenges that faced Lewis and Clark by creating frontier stores to sell the provisions needed for the journey across the uncharted West. Fourth-graders dress as famous figures they have studied to demonstrate an understanding of the concept of biography. As Rosa Parks or Albert Einstein, the students are encouraged to embrace the characteristics that made the individual famous. Sixth-graders reflect on identity and the future by creating multi-volume biographies that include writings, drawings, family photos, survey results, charts, graphs, and information obtained from interviews with relatives.

These examples capture only part of what happens at New City School each day. Rather than fitting kids to curriculum, predetermining scholastic winners and losers, MI allows educators to help develop kids' strengths. Some of the core differences between traditional teaching and teaching in an MI school are shown in Table 2.

Educators at New City believe that who you are is more important than what you know. Success in most of life's endeavors is dependent upon knowing oneself, capitalizing on personal strengths, and working well with others. As a result, we explicitly teach the interpersonal and intrapersonal intelligences. Our report card, for example, begins with *Intrapersonal Intelligence* and addresses areas such as motivation, confidence, problem-solving, responsibility, effort, and work habits. *Interpersonal Intelligence* follows and focuses on appreciation for diversity and teamwork. At each parent-teacher conference, we begin by talking about the qualities—the intelligences—that we feel are most important.

Table 2

DIFFERENCES BETWEEN TRADITIONAL AND MI CLASSROOMS

In a traditional classroom	In an MI classroom
The kids with strong scholastic intelligences are smart and the other kids are not.	Everyone has a different profile of intelligences; we are all smart in different ways.
Teachers create a hierarchy of intellect.	Teachers use all students' intelligences to help them learn.
The classroom is curriculum-centered.	The classroom is child centered.
Teachers help students acquire information and facts.	Teachers help students create meaning in a constructivist way.
The focus is on the scholastic intelligences, the 3 R's.	The Personal Intelligences are valued: Who you are is more important than what you know.
Teachers work from texts.	Teachers create curriculum—lessons, units, themes.
Teachers assess students by paper and pencil "objective" measures.	Teachers create assessment tools—Projects, Exhibitions, Portfolios (PEPs)—which incorporate MI.
Teachers close the door and work in isolation.	Teachers work with colleagues in using MI, developing collegiality.

Our pursuit of MI has transformed our faculty relations as well. Roland Barth's notion of "collegiality" (1990)—adults learning with and from one another—has become the norm. Our faculty committees, framed around our professional growth, examine various aspects of MI implementation, from the garden committee for exploring the naturalist intelligence, to the assessment committee incorporating MI in determining what students know, to the diversity committee for helping us better appreciate one another. Our frequent educator visitors and our MI conferences have helped us become reflective practitioners, aware of what we are doing and why we are doing it.

Implementing MI requires a creative and energetic faculty willing to work together to find strategies that help kids grow. Rather than just presenting information in a test-retest format, teachers develop curriculum and design assessment tools. Both students and teachers flourish in this kind of setting. Clearly, based on the fifteen-year experiment with multiple intelligences at New City School, MI is no fad, but a proven approach to education for the twenty-first century.

References

Barth, R. 1990. *Improving Schools from Within*. Jossey-Bass: San Francisco.

Gardner, H. 1983. *Frames of Mind: The Theory of Multiple Intelligences*. New York: Basic Books.

Hoerr, T. 2002. *Becoming a Multiple Intelligences School*. Alexandria, Va.: ASCD Press.

Thomas R. Hoerr is the head of the New City School in St. Louis

CAUTION—PRAISE CAN BE DANGEROUS

By Carol S. Dweck

THE SELF-ESTEEM movement, which was flourishing just a few years ago, is in a state of decline. Although many educators believed that boosting students' self-esteem would boost their academic achievement, this did not happen. But the failure of the self-esteem movement does not mean that we should stop being concerned with what students think of themselves and just concentrate on improving their achievement. Every time teachers give feedback to students, they convey messages that affect students' opinion of themselves, their motivation, and their achievement. And I believe that teachers can and should help students become high achievers who also feel good about themselves. But how, exactly, should teachers go about doing this?

In fact, the self-esteem people were on to something extremely important. Praise, the chief weapon in their armory, is a powerful tool. Used correctly it can help students become adults who delight in intellectual challenge, understand the value of effort, and are able to deal with setbacks. Praise can help students make the most of the gifts they have. But if praise is not handled properly, it can become a negative force, a kind of drug that, rather than strengthening students, makes them passive and dependent on the opinion of others. What teachers—and parents—need is a framework that enables them to use praise wisely and well.

Where Did Things Go Wrong?

I believe the self-esteem movement faltered because of the way in which educators tried to instill self-esteem. Many people held an intuitively appealing theory of self-esteem, which went something like this: Giving students many opportunities to experience success and then prais-

ing them for their successes will indicate to them that they are intelligent. If they feel good about their intelligence, they will achieve. They will love learning and be confident and successful learners.

Much research now shows that this idea is wrong. Giving students easy tasks and praising their success tells students that you think they're dumb.[1] It's not hard to see why. Imagine being lavishly praised for something you think is pretty Mickey Mouse. Wouldn't you feel that the person thought you weren't capable of more and was trying to make you feel good about your limited ability?

But what about praising students' ability when they perform well on challenging tasks? In such cases, there would be no question of students' thinking you were just trying to make them feel good. Melissa Kamins, Claudia Mueller, and I decided to put this idea to the test.

Mueller and I had already found, in a study of the relationship between parents' beliefs and their children's expectations, that 85 percent of parents thought they needed to praise their children's intelligence in order to assure them that they were smart.[2] We also knew that many educators and psychologists thought that praising children for being intelligent was of great benefit. Yet in almost 30 years of research, I had seen over and over that children who had maladaptive achievement patterns were already obsessed with their intelligence—and with proving it to others. The children worried about how smart they looked and feared that failing at some task—even a relatively unimportant one—meant they were dumb. They also worried that having to work hard in order to succeed at a task showed they were dumb. Intelligence seemed to be a label to these kids, a feather in their caps, rather than a tool that, with effort, they could become more skillful in using.

In contrast, the more adaptive students focused on the process of learning and achieving. They weren't worried about their intelligence and didn't consider every task a measure of it. Instead, these students were more likely to concern themselves with the effort and strategies they needed in order to master the task. We wondered if praising children for being intelligent, though it seemed like a positive thing to do, could hook them into becoming dependent on praise.

Praise for Intelligence

Claudia Mueller and I conducted six studies, with more than 400 fifth-grade students, to examine the effects of praising children for being intelligent.[3] The students were from different parts of the country (a Midwestern town and a large Eastern city) and came from varied ethnic, racial, and socioeconomic backgrounds. Each of the studies involved several tasks, and all began with the students working, one at a time, on a puzzle task that was challenging but easy enough for all of them to do quite well. After this first set, we praised one-third of the children for their *intelligence*. They were told: "Wow, you got *x* number correct. That's a really good score. You must be smart at this." One-third of the children were also told that they got a very good score, but they were praised for their *effort*: "You must have worked really hard." The final third were simply praised for their *performance*, with no comment on why they were successful. Then, we looked to see the effects of these different types of praise across all six studies.

We found that after the first trial (in which all of the students were successful) the three groups responded similarly to questions we asked them. They enjoyed the task equally, were equally eager to take the problems home to practice, and were equally confident about their future performance.

In several of the studies, as a followup to the first trial, we gave students a choice of different tasks to work on next. We asked whether they wanted to try a challenging task from which they could learn a lot (but at which they might not succeed) or an easier task (on which they were sure to do well and look smart).

The majority of the students who had received praise for being intelligent the first time around went for the task that would allow them to keep on looking smart. Most of the students who had received praise for their effort (in some studies, as many as 90 percent) wanted the challenging learning task. (The third group, the students who had not been praised for intelligence or effort, were right in the middle and I will not focus on them.)

These findings suggest that when we praise children for their intelligence, we are telling them that this is the name of the game: Look smart; don't risk making mistakes. On the other hand, when we praise children for the effort and hard work that leads to achievement, they want to keep engaging in that process. They are not diverted from the task of learning by a concern with how smart they might—or might not—look.

The Impact of Difficulty

Next, we gave students a set of problems that were harder and on which they didn't do as well. Afterwards, we repeated the questions we had asked after the first task: How much had they enjoyed the task? Did they want to take the problems home to practice? And how smart did they feel? We found that the students who had been praised for being intelligent did not like this second task and were no longer interested in taking the problems home to practice. What's more, their difficulties led them to question their intelligence. In other words, the same students who had been told they were smart when they succeeded now felt dumb because they had encountered a setback. They had learned to measure themselves from what people said about their performance, and they were dependent on continuing praise in order to maintain their confidence.

In contrast, the students who had received praise for their effort on the easier task liked the more difficult task just as much even though they missed some of the problems. In fact, many of them said they liked the harder problems even more than the easier ones, and they were even more eager to take them home to practice. It was wonderful to see.

Moreover, these youngsters did not think that the difficulty of the task (and their relative lack of success) reflected on their intelligence. They thought, simply, that they had to make a greater effort in order to succeed. Their interest in taking problems home with them to practice on presumably reflected one way they planned to do this.

Thus, the students praised for effort were able to keep their intellectual self-esteem in the face of setbacks. They still thought they were smart; they still enjoyed the challenge; and they planned to work toward future success. The students who had been praised for their intelligence received an initial boost to their egos, but their view of themselves was quickly shaken when the going got rough. As a final test, we gave students a third set of problems that were equal in difficulty to the first set—the one on which all the students had been successful. The results were striking. Although all three groups had performed equally well on the first trial, the students who had received praise for their intelligence (and who had been discouraged by their poor showing on the second trial) now registered the worst performance of the three groups. Indeed, they did significantly worse than they had on the first trial. In contrast, students who were praised for working hard performed the best of the three groups and significantly better than they had originally. So the different kinds of praise apparently affected not just what students thought and felt, but also how well they were able to perform.

Given what we had already seen, we reasoned that when students see their performance as a measure of their intelligence, they are likely to feel stigmatized when they perform poorly and may even try to hide the fact. If, however, students consider a poor performance a temporary setback, which merely reflects how much effort they have put in or their current level of skill, then it will not be a stigma. To test this idea, we gave students the opportunity to tell a student at another school about the task they had just completed by writing a brief description on a prepared form. The form also asked them to report their score on the second, more difficult trial.

More than 40 percent of the students who had been praised for their intelligence lied about their score (to improve it, of course). They did this even though they were reporting their performance to an anonymous peer whom they would never meet. Very few of the students in the other groups exaggerated their performance. This suggests that when we praise students for their intelligence, failure becomes more personal and therefore more of a disgrace. As a result, students become less able to face and therefore deal with their setbacks.

The Messages We Send

Finally, we found that following their experiences with the different kinds of praise, the students believed different things about their intelligence. Students who had received praise for being intelligent told us they thought of intelligence as something innate—a capacity that you just had or didn't have. Students who had been praised for effort told us they thought of intelligence more in terms of their skills, knowledge, and motivation—things over which they had some control and might be able to enhance.

And these negative effects of praising for intelligence were just as strong (and sometimes stronger) for the high-achieving students as for their less successful peers. Perhaps it is even easier to get these youngsters invested in looking smart to others. Maybe they are even more attuned to messages from us that tell them we value them for their intellects.

How can one sentence of praise have such powerful and pervasive effects? In my research, I have been amazed over and over again at how quickly students of all ages pick up on messages about themselves—at how sensitive they are to suggestions about their personal qualities or about the meaning of their actions and experiences. The kinds of praise (and criticism) students receive from their teachers and parents tell them how to think about what they do—and what they are.

This is why we cannot simply forget about students' feelings, their ideas about themselves and their motivation, and just teach them the "facts." No matter how objective we try to be, our feedback conveys messages about what we think is important, what we think of them, and how they should think of themselves. These messages, as

we have seen, can have powerful effects on many things including performance. And it should surprise no one that this susceptibility starts very early.

Melissa Kamins and I found it in kindergarten children.[4] Praise or criticism that focused on children's personal traits (like being smart or good) created a real vulnerability when children hit setbacks. They saw setbacks as showing that they were bad or incompetent—and they were unable to respond constructively. In contrast, praise or criticism that focused on children's strategies or the efforts they made to succeed left them hardy, confident, and in control when they confronted setbacks. A setback did not mean anything bad about them or their personal qualities. It simply meant that something needed to be done, and they set about doing it. Again, a focus on process allowed these young children to maintain their self-esteem and to respond constructively when things went wrong.

Ways of Praising

There are many groups whose achievement is of particular interest to us: minorities, females, the gifted, the underachieving, to name a few. The findings of these studies will tell you why I am so concerned that we not try to encourage the achievement of our students by praising their intelligence. When we worry about low-achieving or vulnerable students, we may want to reassure them they're smart. When we want to motivate high-achieving students, we may want to spur them on by telling them they're gifted. Our research says: Don't do that. Don't get students so invested in these labels that they care more about keeping the label than about learning. Instead of empowering students, praise is likely to render students passive and dependent on something they believe they can't control. And it can hook them into a system in which setbacks signify incompetence and effort is recognized as a sign of weakness rather than a key to success.

This is not to say that we shouldn't praise students. We can praise as much as we please when they learn or do well, but should wax enthusiastic about their strategies, not about how their performance reveals an attribute they are likely to view as innate and beyond their control. We can rave about their effort, their concentration, the effectiveness of their study strategies, the interesting ideas they came up with, the way they followed through. We can ask them questions that show an intelligent appreciation of their work and what they put into it. We can enthusiastically discuss with them what they learned. This, of course, requires more from us than simply telling them that they are smart, but it is much more appreciative of their work, much more constructive, and it does not carry with it the dangers I've been describing.

What about the times a student really impresses us by doing something quickly, easily—and perfectly? Isn't it appropriate to show our admiration for the child's ability? My honest opinion is that we should not. We should not be giving students the impression that we place a high value on their doing perfect work on tasks that are easy for them. A better approach would be to apologize for wasting their time with something that was too easy, and move them to something that is more challenging. When students make progress in or master that more challenging work, that's when our admiration—for their efforts—should come through.

A Challenging Academic Transition

The studies I have been talking about were carried out in a research setting. Two other studies[5] tracked students with these different viewpoints in a real-life situation, as they were making the transition to junior high school and during their first two years of junior high. This is a point at which academic work generally becomes more demanding than it was in elementary school, and many students stumble. The studies compared the attitudes and achievement of students who believed that intelligence is a fixed quantity with students who believed that they could develop their intellectual potential. We were especially interested in any changes in the degree of success students experienced in junior high school and how they dealt with these changes. For the sake of simplicity, I will combine the results from the two studies, for they showed basically the same thing.

First, the students who believed that intelligence is fixed did indeed feel that poor performance meant they were dumb. Furthermore, they reported, in significantly greater numbers than their peers, that if they did badly on a test, they would seriously consider cheating the next time. This was true even for students who were highly skilled and who had a past record of high achievement.

Perhaps even worse, these students believed that having to make an effort meant they were dumb—hardly an attitude to foster good work habits. In fact, these students reported that even though school achievement was very important to them, one of their prime goals in school was to exert as little effort as possible.

In contrast to the hopelessly counterproductive attitude of the first group, the second group of students, those who believed that intellectual potential can be developed, felt that poor performance was often due to a lack of effort, and it called for more studying. They saw effort as worthwhile and important—something necessary even for geniuses if they are to realize their potential.

So once again, for those who are focused on their fixed intelligence and its adequacy, setbacks and even effort bring a loss of face and self-esteem. But challenges, setbacks, and effort are not threatening to the self-esteem of those who are concerned with developing their potential; they represent opportunities to learn. In fact, many of these students told us that they felt smartest when things were difficult; they gained self-esteem when they applied themselves to meeting challenges.

What about the academic achievement of the two groups making the transition to junior high school? In both studies, we saw that students who believed that intelligence was fixed and was manifest in their performance did more poorly than they had in elementary school. Even many who had been high achievers did much less well. Included among them were many students who entered junior high with high intellectual self-esteem. On the other hand, the students who believed that intellectual potential could be developed showed, as a group, clear gains in their class standing, and many blossomed intellectually. The demands of their new environment, instead of causing them to wilt because they doubted themselves, encouraged them to roll up their sleeves and get to work.

These patterns seem to continue with students entering college. Research with students at highly selective universities found that, although they may enter a situation with equal self-esteem, optimism, and past achievement, students respond to the challenge of college differently: Students in one group by measuring themselves and losing confidence; the others by figuring out what it takes and doing it.[6]

Believing and Achieving

Some of the research my colleagues and I have carried out suggests that it is relatively easy to modify the views of young children in regard to intelligence and effort in a research setting. But is it possible to influence student attitudes in a real-life setting? And do students become set in their beliefs as they grow older? Some exciting new research shows that even college students' views about intelligence and effort can be modified—and that these changes will affect their level of academic achievement.[7] In their study, Aronson and Fried taught minority students at a prestigious university to view their intelligence as a potentiality that could be developed through hard work. For example, they created and showed a film that explained the neural changes that took place in the brain every time students confronted difficulty by exerting effort. The students who were instructed about the relationship between intelligence and effort went on to earn significantly higher grades than their peers who were not. This study, like our intelligence praise studies, shows that (1) students' ideas about their intelligence can be influenced by the messages they receive, and (2) when these ideas change, changes in performance can follow.

But simply getting back to basics and enforcing rigorous standards—which some students will meet and some will not—won't eliminate the pitfalls I have been describing. This approach may convey, even more forcefully, the idea that intelligence is a gift only certain students possess. And it will not, in itself, teach students to value learning and focus on the *process* of achievement or how to deal with obstacles. These students may, more than ever, fear failure because it takes the measure of their intelligence.

A Different Framework

Our research suggests another approach. Instead of trying to convince our students that they are smart or simply enforcing rigorous standards in the hopes that doing so will create high motivation and achievement, teachers should take the following steps: first, get students to focus on their potential to learn; second, teach them to value challenge and learning over looking smart; and third, teach them to concentrate on effort and learning processes in the face of obstacles.

This can be done while holding students to rigorous standards. Within the framework I have outlined, tasks are challenging and effort is highly valued, required, and rewarded. Moreover, we can (and must) give students frank evaluations of their work and their level of skill, but we must make clear that these are evaluations of their current level of performance and skill, not an assessment of their intelligence or their innate ability. In this framework, we do not arrange easy work or constant successes, thinking that we are doing students a favor. We do not lie to students who are doing poorly so they will feel smart: That would rob them of the information they need to work harder and improve. Nor do we just give students hard work that many can't do, thus making them into casualties of the system.

I am not encouraging high-effort situations in which students stay up studying until all hours every night, fearing they will displease their parents or disgrace themselves if they don't get the top test scores. Pushing students to do that is not about valuing learning or about orienting students toward developing their potential. It is about pressuring students to prove their worth through their test scores.

It is also not sufficient to give students piles of homework and say we are teaching them about the importance of effort. We are not talking about quantity here but about teaching students to seek challenging tasks and to engage in an active learning process.

However, we as educators must then be prepared to do our share. We must help students acquire the skills they need for learning, and we must be available as constant resources for learning. It is not enough to keep harping on and praising effort, for this may soon wear thin. And it will not be effective if students don't know *how* to apply their effort appropriately. It is necessary that we as educators understand and teach students how to engage in processes that foster learning, things like task analysis and study skills.[8]

When we focus students on their potential to learn and give them the message that effort is the key to learning, we give them responsibility for and control over their achievement—and over their self-esteem. We acknowledge that learning is not something that someone gives students; nor can they expect to feel good about themselves because teachers tell them they are smart. Both learning and self-esteem are things that students achieve as they tackle challenges and work to master new material.

Students who value learning and effort know how to make and sustain a commitment to valued goals. Unlike some of their peers, they are not afraid to work hard; they know that meaningful tasks involve setbacks; and they know how to bounce back from failure. These are lessons that cannot help but serve them well in life as well as in school.

These are lessons I have learned from my research on students' motivation and achievement, and they are things I wish I had known as a student. There is no reason that every student can't know them now.

Endnotes

1. Meyer, W. U. (1982). Indirect communications about perceived ability estimates. *Journal of Educational Psychology, 74,* 888–897.
2. Mueller, C. M., & Dweck, C. S. (1996). Implicit theories of intelligence: Relation of parental beliefs to children's expectations. Paper presented at the Third National Research Convention of Head Start, Washington, D.C.
3. Mueller, C. M., & Dweck, C. S. (1998). Intelligence praise can undermine motivation and performance. *Journal of Personality and Social Psychology; 75,* 33–52.
4. Kamins, M., & Dweck, C. S. (1999). Person vs. process praise and criticism: Implications for contingent self-worth and coping. *Developmental Psychology.*
5. Henderson, V., & Dweck, C. S. (1990). Achievement and motivation in adolescence: A new model and data. In S. Feldman and G. Elliott (Eds.), *At the threshold: The developing adolescent.* Cambridge, MA: Harvard University Press; *and* Dweck, C. S., & Sorich, L. (1999). Mastery-oriented thinking. In C. R. Snyder (Ed.). *Coping.* New York: Oxford University Press.
6. Robins, R. W. & Pals, J. (1998). Implicit self-theories of ability in the academic domain: A test of Dweck's model. Unpublished manuscript, University of California at Davis; *and* Zhao, W., Dweck, C. S., & Mueller, C. (1998). Implicit theories and depression-like responses to failure. Unpublished manuscript, Columbia University.
7. Aronson, J., & Fried, C. (1998). Reducing stereotype threat and boosting academic achievement of African Americans: The role of conceptions of intelligence. Unpublished manuscript, University of Texas.
8. Brown, A. L. (1997). Transforming schools into communities of thinking and learning about serious matters. *American Psychologist, 52,* 399–413.

Carol S. Dweck is a professor of psychology at Columbia University, who has carried out research on self-esteem, motivation, and academic achievement for thirty years. Her new book, Self-Theories: Their Role in Motivation, Personality, and Development, *was just published by The Psychology Press.*

Webs of Skill:
How Students Learn

Identifying the complex and variable ways that students learn and develop can help educators provide differentiated instruction.

Kurt W. Fischer and L. Todd Rose

Two bright, energetic 7-year-olds, Clara and Scott, want to read well, but they differ greatly in their patterns of skills. Clara can read the words "dog," "black," and "waffle" (as well as many others), and she can make rhymes with them and sound out the letters to pronounce the word. Scott can read those words, too, but he struggles with the rhyming and sounding out, especially for "black" and "waffle." Scott's performance changes dramatically when his teacher helps him. She provides a choice of words that rhyme with "black" or shows Scott how to sound out the word, and he performs perfectly for a while. Then, after a few minutes without her support, he again struggles with the rhyming and sounding out.

To understand and explain these variations in learning and development, we must detect the patterns behind Clara's and Scott's actions. When faced with the task of explaining such complexity, scientists and educators have typically retreated into oversimplifications. Most focus on a single factor to explain variation—typically, intelligence, developmental stage, or developmental norm. "Clara is smarter than Scott," or "Clara is at a higher stage than Scott," or "Scott is below grade norm, and Clara is at norm." But why can Scott perform the tasks correctly with his teacher? There is more to the differences than can be explained by a one-factor ladder of increasing competence, knowledge, or intelligence.

As researchers, educators, and parents, we are keenly aware, and often painfully reminded, that students do not all climb the same ladder. Their individual academic and social skills do not develop at the same time or in the same manner but in much more interesting and complex ways. A dynamic analysis of how students construct their skills offers a richer understanding of their learning dif-

ferences—both the diverse pathways of different children, such as Clara and Scott, and the large variations in skills of an individual child that occur as a function of context and emotional state, as in Scott's activities with his teacher.

Each student constructs distinct pathways in every important learning domain, including reading, mathematics, and social interaction. At the same time, each student possesses a different level of skill in the learning domains; these variations in performance are a function of the student's emotional state and how much immediate support the student receives.

Constructive Webs of Development

An alternative framework for understanding learning and development is a dynamic approach that moves beyond the static one-dimensional ladder and builds on the concept of a constructive web of skills (Fischer & Bidell, 1998). Seeing learning as a dynamic construction of webs facilitates understanding the complex patterns of development and learning. Figure 1 depicts a small-scale version of this web; the strands represent potential skills that are developing in a domain, and the points of connection among the strands represent the integration of these skills. To read words, for example, the student needs to develop two different learning domains: visual-graphic skills, such as reading written letters and words; and sound analysis, such as rhyming and sounding out words. The idea of constructive webs explains how students can vary yet remain stable in development and leads to a recognition of patterns of variability that have eluded the classical models in the ladder framework.

Students continually construct multiple strands in their webs, such as sight and sound strands for reading words, with each skill contributing to the emergence of more complex skills along a strand. For example, identifying the letters of the alphabet helps students build the skills of reading and spelling individual words. A strand considered by itself is like a ladder of skills in a domain; however, it branches and connects with other strands—and there are many strands, not just one. In reading an alphabetic language such as English, the reader connects strands for visual-graphic and sound analysis to read effectively.

Students do not all learn in the same cookie-cutter fashion, and a dynamic analysis of learning and development provides powerful new tools for understanding their variations.

The development of a given skill involves diverse strands, branches, and connections, with one student showing a web like that in Figure 1 for reading and another student showing a different web. Unlike the rigid steps of a ladder, the sequence and order of the strands in a constructive web are not predetermined, nor is there one universal sequence.

FIGURE 1

A Constructive Web of Development

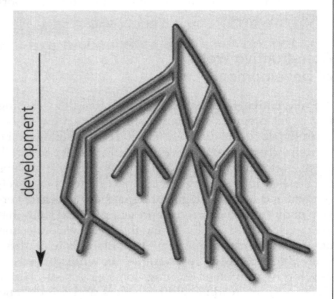

The strands represent potential skills that are developing in a learning domain, and the points of connection among the strands represent the intergration of these skills.

FIGURE 2

Pathway A: A Common Web for Reading Words

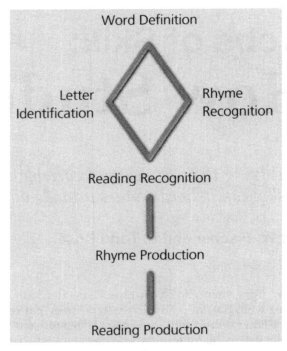

In this illustration of the constructive web for the standard theory of reading alphabetic languages, the sight (letter indentification) and sound (rhyme recognition) domains are at first independent but then come together as students integrate sight and sound skills to read words.

At the same time, webs often demonstrate a great deal of order. Students commonly show similar strands, branches, and connections, as well as similar start and end points. These components are completely lost in the one-dimensional image of a ladder, which forces all students into one rigid model. Uncovering the orderly patterns through dynamic analysis of constructive webs creates powerful tools to help educators move beyond normative approaches and build effective individualized instruction. Two students in the same classroom may look similar in test performance, but their strengths and problems can be different because they are progressing through distinct developmental webs.

Early development of reading illustrates this type of ordered variability. In one study by our research group, the Dynamic Development Research Group at Harvard University (Knight & Fischer, 1992), 120 students in 1st, 2nd, and 3rd grades, ages 6-8, performed a series of six tasks with familiar words from their scholastic reading series in school. The six tasks all related to reading individual words: word definition, letter identification, rhyme recognition, rhyme production, reading recognition, and reading production. Examining these tasks allowed us to identify for each individual student the webs of skill development for learning to read single words (Fischer, Knight, & Van Parys, 1993). The webs from the study are far simpler than the one in Figure 1 because of the small number of tasks that we included in the study. With more tasks, the webs would show more strands and connections.

Individual students perform and understand differently depending on context, especially whether they receive high or low support from their teachers or others.

According to the standard theory of reading development, proficient reading comes from the integration of visual-graphic skills, such as letter identification, with sound-analysis skills, such as rhyme recognition (LaBerge & Samuels, 1974; Snow, Burns, & Griffin, 1998; Torgesen, Wagner, & Rashotte, 1994). The constructive web that illustrates this standard theory, shown as Pathway A in Figure 2, starts with word definition because students must know the word before they can use it appropriately. Initially, the sight and sound domains are independent and not integrated, forming separate branches for the early tasks: letter identification and rhyme recognition. Later, the two branches come together as students integrate sight and sound skills to read words and become proficient readers.

In our study, most normal readers, like Clara, demonstrated this developmental pathway and fit the standard theory. Clara's rhyming and reading tasks connected closely for each word that she read, so the sight and sound tasks in her constructive web integrated to form reading skills.

At the same time, a number of students performed the tasks differently and constructed two distinctive alternative webs that did not indicate integration (see fig. 3). Scott had difficulty with rhyming and sounding out words such as "black" and "waffle," even though he could read them. He was developing along one of the alternative webs, in which sight and sound tasks were not integrated. In Pathway B, the two strands remain separate and unintegrated. The web begins like the others, with word definition and then letter identification, but the remaining tasks develop along independent branches for reading and rhyming and do not achieve full integration. Rhyming tasks typically develop later than reading tasks, as with Scott.

The third web, Pathway C, shows even less integration, with three separate branches for letter identification, rhyming, and reading, as well as slow development of both reading and rhyming skills. The students who produced Pathway C all showed serious reading problems, and some of those developing along Pathway B had prob-

lems, too. These alternative webs illustrate the difficulty that poor readers have in integrating skills across strands.

Focusing only on deficits in the alternative webs is a mistake, however. The students producing these webs could read many of the words in the study, and some performed normally on standardized reading tests. They were developing along alternative pathways, learning to read without integrating the sights and sounds of words in the "normal" way. Learning to read is more difficult for most students following alternative pathways, but eventually many students with severe reading problems become skilled readers and writers by developing along distinctive pathways. In a study of highly successful adults who were dyslexic as students, Rosalie Fink (1995) found that they had become powerfully literate readers and writers, even though they still retained their difficulties with reading individual words, especially integrating the sights and sounds of novel words. These successful adults had found their own independent pathways to literacy.

Developmental Range

Although a student develops along an individual web for reading, no individual acts consistently at a specific level on a strand; instead, he or she acts within a range of levels. Initially, Scott could not rhyme or sound out the words, but when his teacher provided support, he moved temporarily to a higher level, rhyming and sounding out successfully for several minutes. All students show similar variations in developmental range. They never remain fixed at one stage, even for a specific domain, such as reading words in the class curriculum, but instead vary across several stages or levels. Teachers know intuitively about this variation and are wary of claims that students operate at a fixed level of ability.

At first glance, this kind of variability may appear random or chaotic, especially when viewed through the lens of classic developmental theory. Like the differences in developmental pathways, however, there is order in what looks like chaos. An especially powerful influence on variation is contextual support for complex performance. Scott showed his ability to rhyme and sound out the harder words when his teacher provided support by prompting rhyming and sounding out, but this high-level ability disappeared in a few minutes after her support stopped.

The same variation occurs in all skills. A youth's competence at chess improves greatly in response to support from a mentor, and it varies with other factors: new situations, different challengers, and varying emotional states. Adults show this variation, too, especially when they are learning new material. For example, a member of our research group took a course about neural networks. In class, he demonstrated good use of network concepts with the support of the teacher's instruction, but when he went home and tried to explain neural networks to his

FIGURE 3

Two Alternative Webs for Reading Words

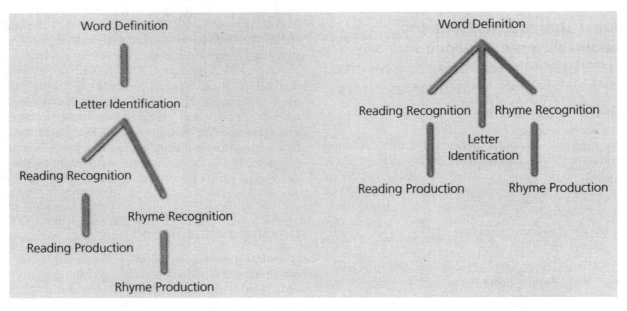

All pathways of reading development begin with word definition skills (see figure 2), but these alternate pathways to reading show different skills developing independently. Learning to read is more difficult for most students following alternative pathways, but eventually many become skilled readers.

wife, his level of understanding plummeted to much simpler, less sophisticated concepts.

Extensive research has shown that each learner's range of development is defined by two upper limits of performance—the functional and optimal levels (Fischer & Bidell, 1998; Fischer, Knight, & Van Parys, 1993). Under low-support conditions, students function less skillfully, and their highest competence is their functional level, which is their best performance in most everyday functioning. When they receive high support, their highest competence is their optimal level, their best performance when a person or the context prompts the key components of the task for them. The optimal level develops in spurts during certain age periods, which are related to growth in neural networks in the brain (Fischer & Rose, 1998), but the functional level develops more slowly and continuously and varies greatly across domains.

Jill, 15, illustrates optimal and functional levels as she learns the mathematical relation between addition and multiplication for positive whole numbers. Addition and multiplication both involve combining numbers to get bigger numbers, with addition combining single numbers and multiplication combining groups of numbers (Fischer, Hand, & Russell, 1984). Explaining this conceptual relation between addition and multiplication eludes most adoles-

cents, but when they turn 15 or 16, they can explain it with high contextual support. When Jill's teacher or friend prompts her with key ideas, Jill can explain this relation coherently for several specific arithmetic problems (such as 8 + 8 + 8 + 8 + 8 = 40 and 5 x 8 = 40) and exhibit competence at her optimal level. Within a few minutes after the prompting ends, however, her level of performance drops abruptly, and she cannot successfully explain the same relation that she dealt with cogently with support. Her level of performance on a test will depend similarly on whether the test question prompts the key components or not. In the classroom, students demonstrate this kind of fluctuation in understanding every day.

A primary goal of education is to improve the functional-level performance of students so that they can then produce the skill on their own.

The range between optimal and functional levels is large, as shown in the graph for skill growth in Figure 4. The graph shows only the levels that emerge during the

FIGURE 4

Developmental Range: Optimal and Functional Levels

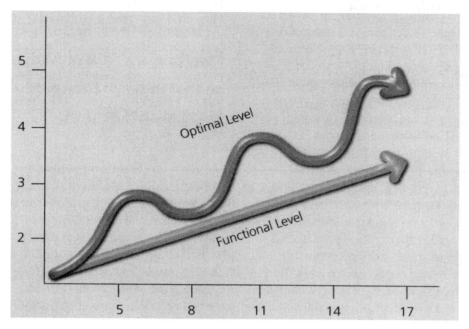

The optimal level of skill is the level that a student can reach when he or she receives support. The functional level of skill is the level the student demonstrates independently, without help from context or teachers.

school years; 13 developmental levels emerge between birth and age 30. Jill is in the midst of the spurt in optimal understanding that occurs at about age 15, but several years will pass before she can sustain the same understanding in ordinary performance and without high support. Variation of this kind occurs in almost all types of skills—not only reading, mathematics, and science, but also sports, social interaction, planning, and self-organization.

Dynamic Development

Students do not all learn in the same cookie-cutter fashion, and a dynamic analysis of learning and development provides powerful new tools for understanding their variations. The multiple webs of development capture the natural variability among students, and developmental range demonstrates how the variability occurs within each student.

Identifying common alternative webs provides a useful tool for educators because the webs illuminate the different ways that students learn important skills and show that students learn in multiple ways. Even individual students perform and understand differently depending on context, especially whether they receive high or low support. A primary goal of education is to improve the func-

tional-level performance of students so that they can then produce the skill on their own. At the same time, an optimal-level skill is a target that students experience as realistic because they can achieve it if given high support.

When educational assessments distinguish alternative developmental webs for learning and note the differences between functional and optional levels of skill, educators can teach better, write more effective curricular materials, and improve the quality of their students' learning.

References

Fink, R. (1995). Successful dyslexics: A constructivist study of passionate-interest reading. *Journal of Adolescent and Adult Literacy, 39,* 268–280.

Fischer, K. W., & Bidell, T. R. (1998). Dynamic development of psychological structures in action and thought. In R. M. Lerner (Ed.), *Handbook of child psychology: Vol. 1. Theoretical models of human development* (5th ed., pp. 467-561). New York: Wiley.

Fischer, K. W., Hand, H. H., & Russell, S. L. (1984). The development of abstractions in adolescence and adulthood. In M. Commons, F. A. Richards, & C. Armon (Eds.), *Beyond formal operations* (pp. 43–73). New York: Praeger.

Fischer, K. W., Knight, C. C., & Van Parys, M. (1993). Analyzing diversity in developmental pathways: Methods and concepts. In R. Case & W. Edelstein (Eds.), *Contributions to human development: Vol. 23. The new structuralism in cognitive development: Theory and research on individual pathways* (pp. 33–56). Basel, Switzerland: Karger.

Fischer, K. W., & Rose, S. P. (1998). Growth cycles of brain and mind. *Educational Leadership, 56*(3), 56–60.

Knight, C. C., & Fischer, K. W. (1992). Learning to read words: Individual differences in developmental sequences. *Journal of Applied Developmental Psychology, 13,* 377–404.

LaBerge, D., & Samuels, S. J. (1974). Toward a theory of automatic information processing in reading. *Cognitive Psychology, 6,* 293–323.

Snow, C. E., Burns, M. S., & Griffin, P. (Eds.). (1998). *Preventing reading difficulties in young children.* Washington, DC: National Academy Press.

Torgesen, J., Wagner, R., & Rashotte, C. (1994). Longitudinal studies of phonological processes of reading. *Journal of Learning Disabilities, 27,* 276–286.

Authors' note: Thomas Bidell, Jeanne Chall, Rosalie Fink, Jane Haltiwanger, Catherine Knight, Samuel P. Rose, and Robert Thatcher contributed to the arguments and evidence in this paper. Preparation of this article was supported by grants from Mr. and Mrs. Frederick P. Rose, Harvard University, and NICHD grant #HD32371.

Kurt W. Fischer is Charles Bigelow Professor and Director of the Mind, Brain, and Education Concentration, Harvard Graduate School of Education, Larsen Hall 702, Appian Way, Cambridge, MA 02138; kurt_fischer@email.msn.com. **L. Todd Rose** is a doctoral student, Harvard Graduate School of Education, Human Development and Psychology, Larsen Hall 103, Appian Way, Cambridge, MA 02138; rosela @gse.harvard.edu.

Invitations to Learn

*Students care deeply about learning when their teachers meet their need for
affirmation, contribution, purpose, power, and challenge.*

Carol Ann Tomlinson

Do students care about learning? The answer is, of course, that "it depends." At 4 years old, David asked his teacher a question as a lesson began: "Is this going to be a 'learning experience'? Because if it is, I don't want to do it." That same 4-year-old had the patience of Job in trying to figure out how to navigate a new computer program at home.

In 10th grade, Kenisha did what she had to do to pass her classes. By 11th grade, she was part of an AVID group[1] and was proud of the high grades she was making in advanced classes.

Josh was often reduced to tears by homework. Yet, the best part of his day was the discussions and debates on such topics as ethics and philosophy that he shared with his family over dinner each evening.

Until this year, Bethany was convinced that students who did well in class were either smarter than she was, or luckier, or just better liked by the teacher. She drifted through school and the principal's office, alternating between anger and resignation. Now she loves parent-teacher conference days, when she can share with her mother her learning goals and evidence of her growth.

The students in Ms. Larrick's 6th period English class began the year by skipping class whenever they could. They hated English. By the end of the year, they refused to miss class discussions of *Antigone*.

Early in the year, Jana was skeptical about math. Her teacher told the students that he expected them to work like mathematicians. They would learn math as a language—a way of thinking. They would have to decide which tools to use to be effective with a range of problems that would crop up in school, in town, or in the news. Jana wasn't sure that she could do math that way. It seemed less predictable than math had always been in the past. In June, she wrote her teacher a note saying that she thought that she might like to be a math teacher, or maybe an engineer.

Javier was angry last year that his family had moved to a place where he knew no one and no one understood him when he spoke. This year, he works hard at spelling and math. His teacher asked him to tutor a Spanish-speaking boy three years younger than he is. The boy looks forward to sessions with Javier, and Javier can't let him down. Javier's teacher also helps him find books about Mexican culture and Mexican Americans that he can share with his young friend as they work together on reading.

Jessica and Dane had always found history boring. Ms. Brittle asked them to go on a personal odyssey in their community as they read Homer's *Odyssey* and studied the history of ancient Greece and Rome. They found possibilities in themselves and their town that they had never considered. They also saw a purpose in history that they hadn't seen before.

Do students care about learning? Absolutely—when they are invited to learn.

What Is Invitational Learning?

Few students are drawn to lists of facts. Not many find computations, theorems, and proofs inherently interesting. Worksheets evoke little satisfaction in the young.

The impetus to learn generally does not come first from content itself, but rather because a teacher has learned to make the content inviting.

Although there are students who dutifully learn the facts, perform the computations, and complete the worksheets, it would be hard to argue that such activities lead even these students to be eager learners. At best, such tasks promote intellectual compliance and a hunger for stars and *A*s—not an insatiable desire to learn. The impetus to learn generally does not come first from content itself, but rather because a teacher has learned to make the content inviting.

What invites students to learn? Because students vary, what is inviting will vary as well. In general, however, students have at least five needs that teachers can address to make learning irresistible: affirmation, contribution, purpose, power, and challenge. Sometimes, teachers find that the learning environment is key to meeting student needs. Sometimes the mode of instruction is key. Generally, environment and instruction work in tandem to invite, inspire, and sustain student learning. Together, they make the content important.

Affirmation

Many young people seek first an affirmation that they are significant in the classroom. Perhaps more and more young people are uncertain of their significance in the world at large, or perhaps the young have always been on a quest for significance. Whatever the reason, students come to school needing to know that

- I am accepted and acceptable here just as I am.
- I am safe here—physically, emotionally, and intellectually.
- People here care about me.
- People here listen to me.
- People know how I'm doing, and it matters to them that I do well.
- People acknowledge my interests and perspectives and act upon them.

Initially, Javier did not feel accepted and acceptable in his class as he was. The class did not feel safe, either emotionally or academically. Javier felt as though his lack of English was an inconvenience for his teacher. He did not feel listened to. No one seemed to know his interests or perspectives.

Kenisha also lacked a sense of affirmation in her 10th grade classes. She was often the only African American student in advanced classes. No links existed between her community and the content of her classes. When she didn't complete her work, teachers generally "let it slide."

Josh does not feel affirmed in his class. He has a learning disability, and despite his best efforts, he cannot keep up with the written tasks.

Homework is especially problematic because there is so much of it and he is already exhausted from the effort of the day. He believes that he is a poor student and that he is not smart. The work that his teacher assigns is not designed for him; it makes him feel like a misfit.

Teachers issue a crucial invitation to learning when young learners feel an abiding sense of affirmation from teacher and peers in a class. When that sense of affirmation is lacking, learning is at risk.

Contribution

To make a difference in any sort of community, one must contribute. Many students come to school looking for a way to contribute to their world. They need to feel that

- I make a difference in this place.
- I bring unique and valuable perspectives and abilities to this place.
- I help other students and the entire class to succeed.
- I am connected to others through mutual work on common goals.

Javier's new teacher understood the power of contribution to promote learning. Even when Javier's language skills were at their most tentative, she found someone to whom Javier's contribution was crucial. Because Javier knew someone else was counting on him, he was able to accept the inevitable frustrations that stem from acclimating to a new language and culture.

Twelve-year-old Toby awoke one Monday feeling ill. When Toby's mother realized that he wasn't feeling well, she suggested that he stay in bed. Toby's response surprised her: "I can't stay home, Mom," he said with conviction. "What would Mrs. Lind do if I weren't in class today? And how could my writing group get its work done?" This would be a remarkable story in any case. It's more potent perhaps because Toby has Down's syndrome. In his mixed-ability English class, his role was clear and important to him. He made a difference there, and he needed to be there.

The child who can remain mute in class discussions for days, weeks, and months does not feel like a contributor. The student who is always "the taught" during group work—and never "the teacher"—does not feel like a contributor. By contrast, teachers invite students to learn when students feel that their presence makes a positive, tangible difference in the work of the class.

Purpose

Students come to school in search of purpose. They need to know that

- I understand what we do here.
- I see significance in what we do.
- What we do reflects me and my world.
- The work we do makes a difference in the world.
- The work absorbs me.

At 4, David saw no purpose in most of his kindergarten "learning experiences." But the computer was another story: The programs gave him access to things he cared about—ideas and activities that seemed important to him.

Ms. Larrick's 6th period students had a long history of seeing literature as unrelated to their lives. The language in their books seemed so unlike the language they spoke. They were uninterested in dissecting plot, setting, protagonist, antagonist, and conflict. Ms. Larrick changed all that when she asked them, "Have you ever felt like a victim?" They talked about what it meant to be a victim, whether people have to be victims, what people can change in their lives, and what they can do when they can't change circumstances. Hand-waving discussions ensued. Then she asked the students, "Want to read a book about a victim and see if your ideas hold up?" *Antigone* became their favorite book—at least until they discovered themselves in the next book.

For Javier, decoding words, writing, and spelling remain arduous. His work feels more purposeful to him when he reads and writes about the country he left behind and about other young people who learned to make a new life in a new place.

Teachers invite their students to learn when they demonstrate that student learning has purpose—when students discover meaning and relevance implicit in books, ideas, and tasks. Without meaning, schoolwork is purposeless for students.

Power

From infancy, the young seek increasing dominion over their world. Turning over in the crib, learning to open the refrigerator door, crossing the street, deciding what to wear to school, and spending the night at a friend's house are important milestones, in part because they signal growing independence and power. Teachers who purposefully assist young learners to develop a sense of power invite their students to learn. To feel powerful in the classroom, students need to believe that

- What I learn here is useful to me now.
- I make choices that contribute to my success.
- I know what quality looks like and how to create quality work here.
- Dependable support for my journey exists in this classroom.

Jessica and Dane saw history as a parade of data to be memorized to satisfy adults—until this year. This year, the teacher showed them how to find themselves in the past and how to use history as a tool for thinking. As one student explained, "Other teachers told us *what* to think. This one is different because she showed us *how* to think and that we *can* think."

Kenisha found AVID to be an important part of her life because the program empowered her to achieve academic success. Through AVID, she learned how to take notes, use her time wisely, select crucial courses, study with peers, prepare for exams, apply to college, and more. The program also placed her in the company of peers and teachers who overtly supported her journey as a student.

Bethany is also having a better year because she has found a sort of power in the classroom. This year, her teacher works with students to set learning goals for each topic and skills area. Some goals are common to the class; others indicate an individual's need for continued growth. Students keep records of their progress on the goals. Rubrics and work samples help students understand the hallmarks of quality work. For the first time, the route to success is not a mystery to Bethany. She feels in control of her fate as she participates in parent-teacher conferences, presenting to her mother both her goals and evidence of her growth during the marking period.

A teacher invites students to learn when the classroom is a place that consistently builds students' capacity to be at the helm of their fate. By contrast, when students feel powerless in the classroom, learning loses its appeal.

Challenge

Something deep inside humans seeks challenge despite fears. Students feel challenged in the classroom when they perceive that

- The work here complements my ability.
- The work stretches me.
- I work hard in this classroom.
- When I work hard, I generally succeed.
- I am accountable for my own growth, and I contribute to the growth of others.
- I accomplish things here that I didn't believe were possible.

Josh did not feel challenged by the work in his class—he felt defeated. Rather than complementing his abilities, the work ran counter to his strengths. No matter how much effort he expended, he experienced little success—just the promise of more work. In his classroom, he didn't accomplish the impossible. Instead, he became more convinced that school was impossible for him.

Jana had been successful in past math classes. This year, she wasn't so sure of herself. The teacher abandoned math as solely algorithmic and instead challenged students to be math thinkers. At first, the new approach was frightening to Jana. In the end, she found herself stretched. Not only was she successful, but she had a new sense of herself as a mathematician.

What constitutes a challenge for one student may feel like defeat to another. When teachers design routes to learning that push individual students into a bit of discomfort—and when they then support student success at that new level—they invite students to learn.

Issuing Invitations to Learn

Teachers extend learning invitations in many ways. Such invitations exist in the way that a teacher addresses students, in the learning environment, in classroom procedures, and in student work that provokes both engagement and understanding.

The message of learning invitations may take a variety of forms: I want to know you. I have time for you. I try to see things through your eyes. This classroom is ours, not mine.

The message of such invitations may take many forms: I have respect for who you are and who you can become. I want to know you. I have time for you. I try to see things through your eyes. This classroom is ours, not mine. There is room for what you care about in what we learn. Your peers and I need you here as a partner in learning. I will help you understand yourself and your world through what we learn. What we do here today will open up all sorts of possibilities for you. You have essential roles here that help us all be more effective and efficient. I enjoy thinking about what we do here. Your success is central in this classroom. There is a clear roadmap to success here, and I will share it with you. When one route to learning doesn't work, we'll find another. I am your partner in growth. We are on a mission to learn. There is great support for you here but no room for excuses. I watch you and listen to you carefully. I make sure that I use what I learn to help you learn better. You're growing, but you're not finished growing. There is no finish line in learning.

In fact, what teachers actually say to students is less important to invitational learning than are students' collective experiences in the classroom. Excellent teachers may speak the invitations to learn, but students respond because the actions of those excellent teachers consistently convey invitation.

Do students care about learning? One of the most satisfying discoveries in the teacher's life is that when teaching is genuinely invitational, there exists no "off switch" to student engagement in learning.

Note

1. AVID (Advancement Via Individual Determination) provides academic and social support to ensure that students—particularly the least-served students with desire and academic potential—will succeed in the most rigorous curriculum and enroll in 4-year colleges.

AVID serves more than 65,000 middle and high school students at 1,275 schools in 21 states and 15 countries.

Carol Ann Tomlinson is Professor of Educational Leadership, Foundations, and Policy at the University of Virginia, Charlottesville, VA 22903; cat3y@virginia.edu. She is author of *How to Differentiate Instruction in Mixed-Ability Classrooms* (ASCD, 2001).

Promoting Academic Achievement through Social and Emotional Learning

by Katharine Ragozzino, Hank Resnik, Mary Utne-O'Brien, and Roger P Weissberg

In this day of high-stakes testing, educators are eager and even anxious to find new policies, instructional methods, and educational practices to improve academic performance. In their search they have reexamined such policies as teacher certification, school choice, grade retention, summer school, and the latest pedagogies for teaching particular academic subjects. Increasingly, however, educators and policymakers are also discovering the importance of social and emotional variables for academic performance and achievement. Consequently, they are turning their attention to methods and practices that foster students' social and emotional development.

Acknowledging the importance of social and emotional variables is one thing. Really understanding their critical role and developing social and emotional skills among students are different matters. What teacher has not felt the frustration of working with a capable student who has neither the motivation nor the perseverance to perform to capacity? What teacher has not felt that he or she could teach better, and his or her students learn better, in caring, supportive school and classroom environments? Teachers have long recognized, and a body of research now corroborates, that facilitating student achievement means addressing barriers to learning. Many of these barriers are social and emotional.

Social and Emotional Learning (SEL) Defined

Social and emotional competence refers to the capacity to recognize and manage emotions, solve problems effectively, and establish and maintain positive relationships with others (see sidebar, next page). Social and emotional competence and the learning environments that support their development have been shown to enhance academic performance in various direct and indirect ways (Zins et al. in press). SEL programming in schools, when carried out systematically and comprehensively, supports caring classroom environments and helps develop positive relationships. SEL programming also provides students with varied skills that positively affect academic achievement. They include:

- managing emotions that interfere with learning and concentration

- developing motivation and the ability to persevere even in the face of academic setbacks and challenges

- working cooperatively and effectively in the classroom and in peer learning groups

- setting and working toward academic goals

For example, learning in a history class improves markedly when students are taught to use problem solving to understand and analyze a historic event. Teaching students social and emotional skills also makes them less likely to behave in ways that interfere with learning.

What the Research Says

A substantial body of research supports the notion that social and emotional variables are integral rather than incidental to learning (Wang, Haertel, and Walberg 1997). Wilson, Gottfredson, and Najaka's meta-analysis (2001) of 165 studies examined the effectiveness of various school-based prevention activities. Their study revealed that social and emotional learning programs increased attendance and decreased the dropout rate. Zins et al. (in press) found that SEL programs improved student attitudes, behaviors, and academic performance.

Rather than diverting schools from their primary academic mission, improving students' social and emotional competence advances the academic mission of schools, while also ensuring that they meet their broader mission to produce caring, responsible, and knowledgeable students. Social and emotional learning provides students with basic skills for success not just in school but ultimately in their personal, professional, and civic lives.

What teacher has not felt the frustration of working with a capable student who has neither the motivation nor the perseverance to perform to capacity?

Such findings should not be surprising. The nature of learning, certainly in school settings, is fundamentally social. In the classroom the most successful children are likely to be actively and prosocially engaged with their peers and teachers Feshbach and Feshbach 1987; Chen, Rubin, and Li 1997). Such students communicate ideas effectively; listen to, evaluate, and integrate the ideas of others; elicit ideas and input from others; and ask teachers and peers for help when necessary.

Students emotionally connected to peers and teachers who value learning and high academic performance often adopt similar values (Hawkins et al. 2001). Student perceptions of teacher warmth and supportiveness can accurately predict student engagement (Ryan and

Patrick 2001). Similarly, students who benefit from positive relationships and interactions tend to achieve above the average academically (Osterman 2000).

In short, educators who want children to care about learning must first ensure they feel supported and offer them frequent opportunities to use SEL skills in meaningful ways (Hawkins 1997).

From Research to Reality

The Collaborative for Academic, Social, and Emotional Learning (CASEL), an organization working to establish SEL as an essential part of P–12 education, has identified specific ways in which SEL, programs positively affect academic performance. These approaches are documented in more detail at <www.CASEL.org>, CASEL's Web site.

Encourage students to apply SEL skills to classroom behaviors that enhance learning. For instance, a teacher can encourage active listening by asking students to identify specific academic goals for themselves. Such goals could be grade-based ("to receive better than C's in all my courses") or related to academic behaviors ("to turn in all my assignments on time"). Students can then anticipate barriers to reaching their goals ("I hate math") and identify ways to overcome those barriers ("I can stay after school and receive tutoring").

Encourage students to apply SEL skills directly to subject matter. Students can apply SEL skills not just to situations in their own lives but to circumstances facing characters in novels or to actual events, past or present. For a class discussion of the Israeli-Palestinian conflict, students can analyze how each party would define the problem. Questions might include:

"What are the perspectives of each party?"

"What are some possible solutions that would reduce the tension between the parties?"

"What are the possible consequences of each proposed solution?"

Such activities both promote deeper understanding of academic material and help students gain familiarity and ease with SEL skills.

Use instructional practices that promote SEL and academic learning. Specific SEL-focused classroom-management techniques—cooperative learning groups, academic choice periods, peer tutoring, and service-learning—can improve students' social-emotional competence and academic performance. Such techniques help establish a respectful classroom environment and minimize disruptions. Instruction in interpersonal skills, followed by opportunities to use the skills in cooperative learning groups, teaches students to collaborate on group goals. Service-learning can enhance students' social awareness and commitment to others.

CORE SEL COMPETENCIES

Self-Awareness: Knowing what we are feeling in the moment; having a realistic assessment of our own abilities and a well-grounded sense of self-confidence

Social Awareness: Sensing what others are feeling; being able to take their perspective; appreciating and interacting positively with diverse groups

Self-Management: Handling our emotions so they facilitate rather than interfere with the task at hand; being conscientious and delaying gratification to pursue goals; persevering in the face of setbacks and frustrations

Relationship Skills: Handling emotions in relationships effectively; establishing and maintaining healthy and rewarding relationships based on cooperation; resistance to inappropriate social pressure; negotiating solutions to conflict; seeking help when needed

Responsible Decision-Making: Accurately assessing risks; making decisions based on a consideration of all relevant factors and the likely consequences of alternative courses of action; respecting others; taking personal responsibility for one's decisions

(From Safe and Sound: An Educational Leader's Guide to Social and Emotional Learning Programs, 2003.)

Remember that learning is relationship-centered. Teachers should make sure they know their students by name, take time to talk with students individually, show concern for their academic progress, and create a caring classroom environment.

Many teachers and administrators contend that effort devoted to SEL may harm academic performance. However, addressing SEL helps schools provide students with a learning context in which students are less likely to behave in ways that harm their health, academic performance, and ability to stay in school. All educators want to create knowledgeable, responsible, and caring

students. SEL is an approach to learning that helps students achieve success in school and life.

References

Chen, X., K. Rubin, and D. Li. 1997. "Relation between Academic Achievement and Social Adjustment: Evidence from Chinese Children." *Developmental Psychology* 33: 518-525.

Collaborative for Academic, Social, and Emotional Learning (CASEL). 2003. *Safe and Sound: An Educational Leader's Guide to Social and Emotional Learning Programs.* Available at <www.casel.org>.

Feshbach, N., and S. Feshbach. 1987. "Affective Processes and Academic Achievement." *Child Development* 51: 1149-1156.

Hawkins, J. D. 1997. "Academic Performance and School Success: Sources and Consequences." Pp. 278-305 in *Enhancing Children's Wellness*, eds. R. P Weissberg, T. R Gullotta, R. L. Hampton, B. A. Ryan, and G. R. Adams. Thousand Oaks, Calif.: Sage.

Hawkins, J. D., J. Guo, K. G. Hill, S. Batfin-Pearson, and R. D. Abbott. 2001. "Long-term Effects of the Seattle Social Development Intervention on School Bonding Trajectories." *Applied Developmental Science* 5(4): 225-236.

Osterman, K. E. 2000. "Students' Need for Belonging in the School Community." *Review of Educational Research* 70:323-367.

Ryan, A., and H. Patrick. 2001. "The Classroom Social Environment and Changes in Adolescents' Motivation and Engagement during Middle School." *American Educational Research Journal* 38(2): 437-60.

Stevahn, L., D. W. Johnson, R. T. Johnson, and D. Real. 1996. "The Impact of a Cooperative or Individualistic Context on the Effectiveness of Conflict Resolution Training." *American Educational Research Journal* 33(3): 801-823.

Wang, M. C., G. D. Haertel, and H. J. Walberg. 1997. "Learning Influences." Pp. 199-211 in *Psychology and Educational Practice*, eds. H. J. Walberg and G. D. Haertel. Berkeley, Calif.: McCutchan.

Wilson, D. B., D. C. Gottfredson, and S. S. Najaka. 2001. "School-based Prevention of Problem Behaviors: A Meta-analysis." *Journal of Quantitative Criminology* 17:247-272.

Zins, J. E., R. P. Weissberg, M. L. Wang, and H. J. Walberg, eds. In press. *Building School Success through Social and Emotional Learning: Implications for Practice and Research.* New York: Teachers College.

The authors acknowledge and appreciate the support of the Academic Development Institute, the Ford Foundation, the Mid-Atlantic Regional Educational Laboratory for Student Success at Temple University, the Surdna Foundation, the U.S. Department of Education, and the William T. Grant Foundation.

Katharine Ragozzino is a projects coordinator at the Collaborative for Academic, Social, and Emotional Learning (CASEL). Hank Resnik is the Director of Communications at CASEL. Mary Utne-O'Brien is the associate director of CASEL. Roger P Weissberg is Professor of Psychology and Education at the University of Illinois at Chicago and the executive director of CASEL.

Reprinted with permission of *educational HORIZONS,* quarterly journal of Pi Lambda Theta Inc., International Honor Society and Professional Association in Education, P O Box 6626, Bloomington, IN 47401, Summer 2003, pp. 169-171.

Teachers Bridge to Constructivism

Kathryn Alesandrini and Linda Larson

People learn while doing," says the constructivist update of an old adage. Teachers, however, often learn without doing when it comes to learning about constructivism and related teaching methods. Many teachers have not participated in a constructivist-type classroom or even seen it modeled, so they tend to teach as they were taught. Until teachers experience constructivism themselves, they may not be equipped to plan and facilitate constructivist activities by their students. In this article, we discuss and illustrate the value of using a constructivist bridge-building activity to help teachers make the transition to constructivist classrooms.

What Teachers Need to Know about Constructivism

Constructivism has become a popular term that can refer to many things, including the way teachers teach and the way students learn. Some have dubbed the constructivist approach that we describe "radical constructivism" (Spiro et al. 1991), but we refer to it simply as "constructivism." Indeed, the constructivist approach posits a radical departure from traditional teaching practices (Brooks and Brooks 1993; Jonassen, Peck, and Wilson 1999; Kafai and Resnick 1996; Lambert 1995) as the following basic tenets of constructivism illustrate:

Learning results from exploration and discovery. Constructivists see learning as a process of actively exploring new information and constructing meaning from the new information by linking it to previous knowledge and experience. Throughout the learning experience, meaning is constructed and reconstructed based on the previous experiences of the learner. In the constructivist paradigm, the teacher's role is not to lecture or provide structured activities that guide students, step by step, to mastery of some teacher-imposed goal. Instead, teachers in a con-

structivist classroom are called to function as facilitators who coach learners as they blaze their own paths toward personally meaningful goals.

Learning is a community activity facilitated by shared inquiry. Collaboration and cooperative inquiry have proved to be effective educational strategies, yet conventional methods often limit interactivity to cooperative discussion groups. Constructivism favors collaborative work groups that actually work together interactively to accomplish shared goals. Collaboration goes beyond cooperation, because it requires learners to reflect upon and share their insights with the group (cf. Henderson 1996; Driscoll 1994). Collaboration facilitates each member's ability to see problems from multiple perspectives or different points of view. Group members constantly "negotiate meaning" during the constructivist activity to adjust to the developing solution of the problem. The product evolves and changes as a result of the interaction between group members.

Learning occurs during the constructivist process. Rather than requiring an understanding *before* applying that understanding to the construction of something, students in a constructivist classroom learn concepts *while* exploring their application. During this application process, students explore various solutions and learn through discovery. Learners play an ongoing, active, and critical role in assessment. Teachers evaluate end products in traditional assessment, but the constructivist approach to evaluation emphasizes self-assessment. In constructivist classrooms, learners articulate what they have learned as it relates to their prior knowledge. In fact, it is through the self-assessment activities of reflection and verbalization that learners actually realize the meaning of what they have experienced.

Another major difference from the traditional approach is that assessment is done throughout the entire learning process, not just at the end. Formative evaluation (assessment that occurs throughout the learning process) therefore plays a key role in helping learners as they experiment during the constructivist activity. To the constructivist, the process of evaluation is as important, if not more important, than the outcomes of evaluation.

Learning results from participation in authentic activities. Constructivists believe that learning should be based on activities and problems that students might encounter in the "real world." In traditional classrooms, however, activities often are decontexualized to the point that they bear little resemblance to meaningful, authentic activities.

Outcomes of constructivist activities are unique and varied. A traditional hands-on activity that is teacher guided often results in student products that essentially "all look alike." In contrast, constructivism posits that learners create knowledge from new information in light of their previous experiences. Since each learner brings a distinct background of experience, results of constructivist projects will differ. Typically, no two products from a constructivist activity look anything alike.

Constructivism clearly represents a fundamental change in all aspects of the teaching and learning process. Teachers cannot be expected to embrace these changes without adequate preparation involving hands-on experience and modeling in the adoption of these new methods.

Why Bridge Building for Teachers?

Based on the premise that the best way to learn about constructivism is to experience it firsthand, we devised a simple constructivist activity—building a paper bridge—that teachers could experience to learn the basics about constructivism. A follow-up authentic activity allowed the teachers to take the next step and develop a constructivist activity for their own classrooms.

In the bridge-building activity, teachers work in small groups to plan, construct, and reflect on building a paper bridge (figures 1-3). The challenge is for each group to create, using only newspaper, tape, and rubber bands, a unique structure strong enough to hold at least a 16-ounce bottle of water. Prior to actually building the bridge, each group specifies several additional objectives and develops a scoring rubric.

The bridge-building activity consists of a 10-step "constructivist activity" process closely related to the design technology process (Dunn and Larson 1998). The constructivist activity process entails five major components: investigation, invention, implementation, evaluation, and celebration. Investigation includes the development of context, clarification of the task, and inquiry through questioning and research. Invention consists of planning and realizing or building a model. Implementation sometimes overlaps with invention and occurs through the process of realizing or building a model and later modifying it as needed. Evaluation refers to the activities of testing, interpreting, and reflecting on the experience. The last major component, celebration, is described below along with the preceding nine steps illustrated with comments from several teams of teachers.

1. *Contextualizing.* Working in small groups, teachers draw on their past experiences in deciding how the team will proceed. "Bridges are normally sturdy; they have support poles. We integrated multiculturalism in our design by designing human figures as the support base" (Team A).

2. *Clarifying.* Teams determine what they needed to know to build the bridge. "We need to know how bridges are structured, how weight is held by a bridge" (Team A).

3. *Inquiring.* Teachers conduct research by posing relevant questions and searching credible sources for answers. "One member of our group found a Web site that outlined all components and typical designs of bridges. From our research we have concluded that our bridge will consist of vertical and horizontal beams" (Team B).

4. *Planning.* Teachers sketch their plans on paper and may even build a test-case model. "Since we decided to create the bridge using beams, we used pencils, pens, and tape to create our premodel. Our premodel proved that our bridge would be easy to construct, functional, and sturdy" (Team B).

Team A

5. *Realizing.* Using only newspaper, tape, and rubber bands, teachers construct bridges to achieve their objectives. No two bridges look alike since groups are not following a cookbook-type recipe for the project. Each group produces a unique creation to achieve its own objectives. "Once we knew how to assemble the bridge from our premodel, we started the construction process" (Team B).

6. *Testing.* Teachers test the model bridge and record observations. "We tested our model by placing a 20-ounce water bottle on top, and it held up fine as long as the dolls' legs were in the right position. But there was not enough diagonal support" (Team A). "Our bridge did not hold the bottle of water. We decided to create a frame for our bridge" (Team C).

7. *Modifying.* Teachers make necessary modifications to achieve stated objectives. "We repositioned the two center supports to face a different direction and better support the bridge" (Team A). "We added the frame which worked" (Team C).

8. *Interpreting.* Teachers interpret the results of their tests. "This is a great model for building a bridge out of newspaper. This bridge was easy to construct, sturdy, and structurally sound, fast to construct, and looked very much like a bridge" (Team B).

9. *Reflecting.* Teachers evaluate their bridges by applying the rubrics they created earlier. "I felt our bridge represented our group, because we had a Latina, an Asian, a Caucasian, and an African American. We used newspapers in English, Spanish, Japanese, and Chinese. I really felt passionate and proud of our bridge. I felt that its main purpose, which was to represent different cultures coming together, was clear" (Team A).

Team C

10. *Celebration.* Teachers in the small groups share their accomplishments by presenting results to the larger group. "We shared our rubric with the group, explaining our criteria for a [top] score of 4. The group agreed that we earned a 4" (Team A). Another teacher wrote, "Celebration and sharing was the best! It gave us a sense of pride and accomplishment."

Most teachers who participate in this 10-step bridge-building activity report that it helps them learn about

Team B

constructivism. Of the four teams cited here, 82 percent found the activity "very or extremely useful." Over 90 percent of the participants say they enjoyed the social interaction of the activity.

Assessment within a Constructivist Framework

Teachers actively engage in the assessment process from the beginning, when they specify objectives and write rubrics to score the results of the constructivist activity. As stated, the only imposed requirement is that the bridges be strong enough to hold at least a 16-ounce bottle of water. In addition to the strength criterion, each group specifies three other objectives and related criteria for their rubrics. Often the criteria reflect the values, experiences, and backgrounds of group members. For example, Team A selected multiculturalism as one of their criteria to reflect the cultural diversity of the group. Their bridge looked like a parade float, with an arch supported by human figures from different cultures. Other criteria have included design creativity, design simplicity, bridge span, conservation of resources, and a host of other factors. Each group of teachers uses the rubric they initially create to score their final product. Not surprisingly, each group generally achieves a perfect or near-perfect score. After scoring their own team's bridge, teams participate in a "gallery walk" in which each team uses both their own and the other teams' rubrics to score the bridges produced by others. Teachers realize that their "excellent" work would likely receive a poor or failing grade when held to a different standard. For example, Team B's more traditional bridge structure with beams did not adhere to the multicultural or creativity criteria of Team A and would therefore be graded down if Team A's rubric were used to score it. The experience helps teachers appreciate the limitations of traditional grading practices in a constructivist classroom.

Taking the Next Step: Constructivism in the Classroom

In the follow-up activity to bridge building, teachers prepare an authentic constructivist activity for their own students on any topic of their choosing. The only requirements are that the activity be authentic and that it address one or more skills in the subject matter frameworks. Teachers work individually to structure an activity according to the same 10-step process they used to build the paper bridge. They begin by setting objectives and creating a scoring rubric that both they and their students may use to assess the final products. They then plan the activity, create a model, and reflect upon their respective projects. Finally, they try out the activity with their own students.

Prior to the bridge-building activity, a common misconception among teachers is that a hands-on activity is synonymous with a constructivist activity. Many hands-on activities, of course, don't allow for multiple solutions and outcomes—students are expected to follow the teacher's directions and create a copy-cat product rather than generating their own unique productions. While less than one-third of teachers surveyed felt confident that they could create constructivist activities for their students prior to the bridge-building activity, over 90 percent successfully created a true constructivist activity on the first try after it. We believe that this success results from the modeling they experienced during the bridge-building activity.

The benefits of constructivism are reinforced as teachers observe the impact of their authentic constructivist projects on their students. A high school math teacher, for example, devised a geometry activity that requires students to construct 3-D scenes or objects from three-dimensional polygons. The teacher's model consisted of a small paper-flower garden. Students used paper pyramids, cubes, decahedrons, and more to construct a wide array of unique characters: a dinosaur, clown, rat, puppy, flower, turtle, and so forth. In another project, a sixth grade teacher created a phonogram chart to help students understand hieroglyphics used by the ancient Egyptians. Her students worked in teams to create unique charts, which they used to code their own names and common words. These teachers reported that their students enjoyed the constructivist project, just as they had, and gained a sense of accomplishment in what they created.

Most teachers find it difficult to create a truly constructivist activity for their students. As one participant explained, "The activity that we created was very difficult. It really makes you examine your subject thoroughly and understand how difficult these concepts are for students to master. The inclusion of constructivist activities greatly increases a student's involvement in the topic."

The bridge-building activity helps teachers literally see the unique productions that result when team members bring their own background and experience to bear on the creative process. They witness that constructivism goes beyond the typical hands-on activity. They also learn that assessment is relative—grades result from applying a rubric that relates to specified criteria or objectives. Perhaps most important, teachers appreciate the pure enjoyment joined with a sense of pride and accomplishment that result from constructivist activities.

Key words: constructivism, classroom activities, assessment, teaching process, facilitation

REFERENCES

Brooks, J. G., and M. C. Brooks. 1993. *The case for constructivist classrooms.* Alexandria, VA: Association for Supervision and Curriculum Development.

Driscoll, M. P. 1994. *Psychology of learning for instruction.* Boston, MA: Allyn & Bacon.

Dunn, S., and R. Larson. 1998. *Design technology: Children's engineering.* Philadelphia: The Palmer Press.

Henderson, J. G. 1996. *Reflective teaching.* 2nd ed. Englewood Cliffs, NJ: Merrill.

Jonassen, D. H., K. L. Peck, and B. G. Wilson. 1999. *Learning with technology: A constructivist approach.* Columbus, OH: Prentice Hall.

Kafai, Y. B., and M. Resnick. 1996. *Constructionism in practice: Designing, thinking and learning in a digital world.* Mahwah, NJ: Lawrence Erlbaum Associates.

Lambert, L. 1995. *The constructivist leader.* New York: Teachers College Press.

Spiro, R., P. Feltovich, M. Jacobson, and R. Coulson. 1991. Knowledge representation, content specification, and the development of skill in situation-specific knowledge assembly: Some constructivist issues as they relate to cognitive flexibility and hypertext. *Educational Technology* 31 (9): 22–25.

Kathryn Alesandrini is a professor of instructional design and technology at California State University, Los Angeles. Linda Larson is a full-time lecturer in the Department of Educational Psychology at California State University, in Long Beach.

From *The Clearing House*, January/February 2002, pp. 118-121. Reprinted with permission of the Helen Dwight Reid Educational Foundation. Published by Heldref Publications, 1319 Eighteenth St., NW, Washington, DC 20036-1802. © 2002.

Constructivism and Block Scheduling:

Making the Connection

The student-centered learning practices associated with constructivism could benefit from the increased class time that block scheduling offers. But, Mr. Hackmann observes, too often block scheduling is adopted as an end in itself, not as a tool to facilitate a specific pedagogical approach.

BY DONALD G. HACKMANN

THROUGHOUT much of the 20th century, classroom instructional practices tended to follow behaviorist learning theory, which regards teaching as a highly diagnostic and prescriptive process. The behaviorist approach typically advocates the presentation of curriculum content in small increments followed immediately by student practice. Behaviorism continues to play a significant role in today's classrooms, where many teachers rely primarily on direct instruction methods.[1]

In the past few decades, a growing body of research on cognitive processing has made inroads into classroom practices. Whereas behaviorism primarily focuses on the teacher's role as transmitter of knowledge, a different view of learning has emerged—constructivism—that emphasizes the student's role in the learning process. Building upon the work of Jean Piaget, Lev Vygotsky, and others, constructivist theory is based on the premise that individuals must be socially engaged in learning—actively creating knowledge from their existing knowledge base, beliefs, and personal experiences.[2] Constructivists advocate learners' participation in context-bound, real-world problem solving and call upon students to engage in meta-cognition.

Although constructivism appears to be attracting a growing following, it has not been readily embraced at the secondary school level. Arguably, constructivist practices may be implemented more easily in self-contained elementary classrooms or through the interdisciplinary teaming approach commonly used in middle schools. High schools tend to be departmentalized and more concerned with curriculum, and secondary teachers may be less willing to employ methods perceived as reducing the emphasis on content.

An additional factor limiting attention to the constructivist movement at the secondary level could be the involvement of many faculties in another restructuring initiative—block scheduling. Much of the recent literature on high school education has addressed alternative scheduling, which may have overshadowed other educational trends. In the 1980s and 1990s, national task forces denounced the excessive rigidity of the traditional high school schedule—uniform 45- to 55-minute periods—and its stifling effect on classroom practices.[3] In response, many faculties created block models that divide the instructional day into 80- to 110-minute class sessions, roughly double the length of traditional daily-period classes.

Block scheduling has become established practice in high schools, but many educators are unable to explain why it is superior to traditional daily-period formats and what results it is intended to produce. Currently, there is no solid theoretical foundation for block scheduling, and there also is limited research documenting its effectiveness in improving student achievement.[4] Many teachers have struggled to make effective use of the longer time blocks because they lack a conceptual understanding of the purpose for these extended time frames and of how they may facilitate learning.

Constructivism and block scheduling appear to have occurred in parallel, yet independent, movements. However, there are many points of convergence between these two concepts. Here I present the commonalities between the two movements and demonstrate that block scheduling should logically be considered as a vehicle to promote constructivist practices.

CONSTRUCTIVIST DIALOGUE AT THE SECONDARY SCHOOL LEVEL

In contrast to the well-developed teaching models based on behaviorism, constructivism is an emerging theory that is currently descriptive, not prescriptive, in nature.[5] To promote greater comprehension and mastery of content, constructivists emphasize depth of understanding rather than a superficial treatment of subject matter. Educators are encouraged to refashion their roles to become learning facilitators—acting as a "guide on the side" instead of a "sage on the stage." As teachers strive to create constructivist environments, they initially may find it difficult to grasp how specific instructional methods align with constructivist principles. However, as this theory evolves, it seems likely that more refined constructivist models will emerge.

When describing the shift from teaching to learning, educators sometimes revert to catch phrases—such as "hands-on learning," "active engagement of the learner," and "depth over breadth"—without explaining how these concepts can be applied in the classroom and without attributing them to constructivism. For example, two principles of the Coalition of Essential Schools—"less is more" and "student as worker,"[6]—promote constructivist beliefs, and the National Association of Secondary School Principals recommends that teachers act "as coaches and as facilitators of learning to promote more active involvement of students in their own learning."[7] Neither organization, however, suggests strategies that educators can use to implement these concepts or cites constructivist theory as the pedagogical foundation for these practices.

Some writers warn that constructivists are overzealous in promoting learner-centered practices, arguing that behaviorist models are necessary in certain instructional situations and that hands-on approaches are not easily developed in every discipline.[8] The key is to strike an appropriate balance so that teacher-directed and student-centered learning activities complement one another. However, secondary teachers may find it difficult to maintain this equilibrium, especially when addressing the content standards now mandated in 49 states. A complicating factor is the excessive number of standards identified by various professional organizations. Although the standards movement, ironically, was heavily influenced by constructivism,[9] teachers may fall back on direct instruction as an efficient means to effect at least a superficial treatment of an immense amount of subject content.

Although the topic of scheduling does not appear frequently in the constructivist literature, a few writers have expressed the desirability of increased time to facilitate constructivist practices. For example, observing that structure frequently drives practice, Richard Elmore notes that teachers find it difficult to implement constructivist strategies within rigid, discrete time frames.[10] Elmore and Mark Windschitl advocate for larger blocks to facilitate the use of constructivist instructional strategies.[11]

HISTORICAL OVERVIEW AND EMERGENCE OF BLOCK SCHEDULING

Prior to the 1900s, American high schools and academies were characterized by significant flexibility. Subjects were offered in varied formats—each course differing in the number of days each week in which instruction was delivered.[12] In 1909, in an effort to eliminate inconsistencies among institutions, the College Entrance Examination Board adopted the Carnegie unit, which mandated a total of 120 hours of classroom instruction to be delivered in 40- to 60- minute classes during an academic year of 36 to 40 weeks.[13] This drive toward standardization was influenced by the scientific management era, which emphasized efficiency, mass production, and work uniformity. The daily-period schedule was created during this time as an organizational solution to the problem of efficiently educating large numbers of students.

Much of the published literature on block scheduling tends to focus primarily on issues having to do with school climate or implementation—pedagogy typically receives only cursory treatment.

Scheduling models remained relatively unchanged until the introduction of modular scheduling in the late 1950s. Instructional responsiveness was the hallmark of this model, since class sessions could be structured according to the number of modules (10, 15, or 20 minutes in length) needed to teach a concept.[14] The model afforded varied course formats, with classes meeting daily or scattered throughout the week in differing lengths. Modular scheduling peaked in the early 1970s, when approximately 15% of the nation's high schools used this approach.[15] However, variations in class sessions meant that many students were unscheduled and unsupervised at various times throughout the school day, leading to potential disciplinary problems. Consequently, although it is still used in a small number of schools today, flexible modular scheduling faded from the secondary scene in the late 1970s, and most schools returned to daily-period scheduling.

In the late 1980s, critics began challenging the wisdom of daily-period models, arguing that they reinforce the use of lecturing, contribute to excessive fragmentation of the instructional day, discourage in-depth exploration, and inhibit curriculum integration. Block scheduling emerged partly in response to these criticisms, although charting the birth and development of the block-scheduling movement is a difficult task. Shared through such administrative venues as conference presentations, educational publications, and professional networking, block scheduling was rapidly proliferating by the mid-1990s. In Virginia, for example, the percentage of blocked high schools leaped from 2% to 33% in only two years' time.[16]

In the past 20 years, various block formats have been piloted in secondary schools, including hybrids that incorporate both block and daily-period features. Two approaches have emerged as the most common: the 4x4 semester plan, in which students complete four classes each semester for a total of eight courses per year, and the eight-block alternating-day model, in which students receive instruction in one-half of their courses on alternate days and continue in these courses throughout the year. The most recent estimates indicate that approximately 30% of the nation's high schools now use some form of block scheduling,[17] although implementation levels vary regionally.

Faculties implement block scheduling for numerous reasons, which include providing course flexibility, enhancing the quality of students' educational experiences, improving instructional strategies, providing enhanced time for learning, improving the school climate, stimulating curriculum reform, and addressing staffing needs.[18] Surveys indicate that blocks improve teacher morale, increase student satisfaction, and enhance the quality of teacher/student relationships.[19] Much of the published literature on block scheduling, however, tends to focus primarily on issues having to do with school climate or implementation—pedagogy typically receives only cursory treatment.

WHERE BLOCK SCHEDULING AND CONSTRUCTIVISM CONVERGE

In many schools, the decision to adopt a block schedule is made after extensive study and dialogue, from which the faculty develops a comprehensive understanding of the reasons for initiating the change. However, as they go about restructuring, many educators do not seem to have fully interconnected the dimensions of teaching, the process of learning, and the organization of the school day. For example, principals of blocked schools often express a desire to increase opportunities for hands-on learning, yet they do not cite constructivism to support this aim.[20] In fact, many secondary principals and teachers are unaware of constructivist theory, and they frequently are at a loss to explain how scheduling adjustments are intended to promote improved student learning.

In other schools, the change may result from a unilateral administrative decree, possibly because block scheduling appears to be the latest fad, or because it is intended to spearhead a dramatic transformation in the school, or because principals "just want to shake things up."[21] There may have been relatively little discussion among the faculty and administration concerning why block scheduling may be desirable or what problem the change is intended to resolve.

The adoption of block scheduling has significant instructional implications, but some teachers may resist changing their classroom practices because they do not fully understand how longer time frames can facilitate learning. Furthermore, without adequate professional development, even supportive and well-intentioned teachers may incorporate ineffective methods. As Linda Wyatt warns, "block scheduling without fundamental changes in instruction is merely longer blocks of the same old stuff."[22] Even when faculties implement block scheduling simply to improve their school climate, they cannot ignore the instructional ramifications of their decision. Regardless of the factors prompting it, once the decision is made to adopt block scheduling, teachers are immediately confronted with the hard reality of figuring out how to use the blocks effectively.

Absent a solid theoretical framework, secondary school faculties cannot fully grasp the purpose of these longer instructional units and are likely to view block scheduling as the end itself rather than a means to an end.

It is on this point of instructional practices that the block-scheduling literature begins to show striking similarities to constructivist principles, even though constructivist theory is rarely mentioned. Various reports related to changing instructional strategies in blocked classrooms discuss an increased emphasis on depth of understanding and a "less is more" approach to curriculum content.[23] Two leading block-scheduling proponents, Robert Lynn Canady and Michael Rettig, note that one of the goals of the high school scheduling reform movement—although it is far down on their list—is to "allow and encourage the use of active teaching strategies and greater student involvement."[24] Yet they fail to mention constructivist theory in any of their published works on the topic of scheduling, including their edited text devoted to instructional strategies in a block.

A variety of instructional approaches and models of teaching are mentioned in both the block-scheduling and constructivist literature, including cooperative learning, problem-based learning, curriculum integration, teaming, and performance assessments. These techniques, however, are presented in significantly different frameworks. In constructivist writings, instructional strategies are explained as vehicles for creating and sustaining a classroom culture that promotes "deep and elaborate understandings of subject matter."[25] In contrast, block-scheduling proponents typically use a very limited frame of reference, describing how blocks can be subdivided "for purposes of survival of both teachers and students."[26] In the block-scheduling dialogue, the emphasis is frequently placed on reducing reliance on the lecture method and eliminating boredom rather than on structuring a culture that promotes student learning.

WHICH COMES FIRST?

One segment of the block-scheduling debate focuses on a perennial "chicken or egg" issue: Should a scheduling change initiate new instructional practices, or should pedagogical beliefs dictate the scheduling model to be implemented? Canady and Rettig appear to support the former position, asserting, "We strongly believe that scheduling is an untapped resource which can serve as a catalyst for school improvement."[27] Michael Wronkovich argues the latter position:

> Often, schools start with the concept of changing to blocking, then try to assess what outcomes are being observed from the change. It would be preferable to ask first what changes the school is seeking to make collectively, then to assess if alternative scheduling is one means for accomplishing these goals.[28]

Kurt Lewin once said, "There is nothing so practical as good theory."[29] One also may argue a corollary to Lewin's statement: there is nothing so impractical as the absence of theory. In examining the block-scheduling phenomenon, it is apparent that this movement was conceived without a clear theoretical foundation. Absent a solid theoretical framework, secondary school faculties cannot fully grasp the purpose of these longer instructional units and are likely to view block scheduling as the end itself rather than a means to an end.

Lacking in theory, many blocked schools may fall victim to the same problem that has besieged schools using the traditional model: the schedule's rigid format does not provide the flexibility to promote varied teaching/learning activities. Uniform blocks force all disciplines into larger time frames, even though some subjects actually may benefit from shorter instructional times.[30] For some disciplines, several spaced and evenly distributed practices may be far more effective in facilitating student learning than a few massed practice sessions.[31] Time allocations are arbitrary, regardless of whether they are 50- or 100-minute intervals. When the schedule is chosen without a pedagogical foundation, teachers may continue to focus on the *act* of teaching—simply "filling up" the blocks—instead of concentrating on the *process* of learning, as promoted by constructivist principles.

In this era of school accountability, educators would be remiss if they adopted reforms without considering the potential effects on student performance. To date, the research base related to block scheduling and student achievement is relatively sparse and inconclusive. Ann Pliska, Matt Harmston, and I found no differences in mean composite ACT scores between students in eight-period, eight-block, alternating-day schools and 4x4 block schools.[32] In a study conducted by the College Board, students enrolled in semester-blocked schools generally scored lower on Advanced Placement (AP) examinations than did students in yearlong classes.[33] While blocked schools in Virginia demonstrated greater percentile gains in the subjects of reading and math than did traditionally scheduled schools,[34] students in blocked schools in Canada scored lower on the Third Provincial Assessment of Science than did their peers in traditional schools.[35]

One limitation of these studies is that they were unable to control for variations in teaching strategies in individual classrooms. The Texas Education Agency acknowledged this problem in its investigation of the impact of scheduling on student achievement, which used a variety of standardized metrics, including the SAT, ACT, AP examinations, and the Texas Assessment of Academic Skills. After controlling for numerous variables—including school size, student demographics, staff characteristics, and attendance—the report concluded that

> available data on high school schedules used in Texas public education do *not* systematically explain or account for variation in overall high school performance. When school context is taken into account, other factors, including *how effectively* students engage in the teaching-learning process , appear to matter more than the particular length of the class periods.[36]

Theoretical principles must drive practice, and, as Elmore strongly advocates, "principles of practice should drive structure."[37] It seems reasonable to conclude that faculties should first reach consensus on theories of the teaching/learning process and then create a scheduling structure that allows them to put their theories into practice.

MAPPING BLOCK SCHEDULING ONTO CONSTRUCTIVIST THEORY

Block-scheduling discussions are currently on the periphery of constructivist dialogue, but the two movements should become more closely aligned. The rationale is simple: when educators' pedagogical beliefs are too far removed from the primary theoretical source, the result is often the adoption of distorted tertiary-source practices that are not an adequate match for school purposes.[38] Such is the case with block scheduling. Secondary educators who lack a comprehensive theoretical foundation may mistakenly assume that the catch phrases and slogans, created as metaphors to illustrate the theory, are the actual theory. Consequently, teachers may implement a host of relatively minor and disconnected instructional strategies simply to fill time, without considering their appropriateness as learning tools or fully comprehending how they connect in the "big picture" to promote student learning.

Constructivism has been described as "a culture—a set of beliefs, norms, and practices that constitute the fabric of school life."[39] Once the connection between block scheduling and constructivism becomes firmly rooted in the consciousness of teachers and part of ongoing professional dialogue, block scheduling can be considered as part of a comprehensive model that is intended to help transform the classroom. The emphasis will shift from the *event* of implementing a block schedule to the *process* of creating a constructivist school culture.

In such a culture, teachers purposefully select strategies during lesson preparation, not because they are "hands-on" and use up time, but because they are designed to help students construct meaning from the curriculum. Instructional techniques—such as interdisciplinary teaming, curriculum integration, direct instruction, problem-based learning, cooperative learning, Socratic seminars, and inquiry learning—and assessment strategies are viewed collectively through a constructivist lens and are employed when they support learning in the constructivist culture that is being created within the school.

My aim here has not been to retrofit the block-scheduling movement to constructivist theory. Rather, my purpose has been to demonstrate that block scheduling, as a stand-alone initiative, has no theoretical foundation and does not constitute a school reform. It should simply be considered as one component of a comprehensive and concurrent package of reforms. Constructivist theory helps faculties to understand the interrelationships of teaching and learning and to recognize how the schedule can be an essential tool in creating a culture that promotes improved student achievement.

Practice should drive structure. Constructivist principles should be the driving force behind any decision to implement block scheduling.

Notes

1. Allan C. Ornstein and Francis P. Hunkins, *Curriculum: Foundations, Principles, and Issues*, 3rd ed. (Needham Heights, Mass.: Allyn and Bacon, 1998).
2. Jacqueline G. Brooks and Martin D. Rettig, *In Search of Understanding: The Case for Constructivist Classrooms* (Alexandria, Va.: Association for Supervision and Curriculum Development, 1993).
3. *Prisoners of Time: Report of the National Educational Commission on Time and Learning* (Washington, D.C.: National Educational Commission on Time and Learning, 1994).
4. Richard F. Bowman, "If Block Scheduling Is the Answer, What Is the Question?," *Clearing House*, vol. 71, 1998, pp. 242-44.
5. Peter W. Airasian and Mary E. Walsh, "Constructivist Cautions," *Phi Delta Kappan*, February 1997, pp. 444-49.
6. Coalition of Essential Schools, "Ten Common Principles," www.essentialschools.org/aboutus/phil/10cps/10cps.html.
7. *Breaking Ranks: Changing an American Institution* (Reston, Va.: National Association of Secondary School Principals, 1996), p. 21.
8. Airasian and Walsh, op. cit.; and Karen R. Harris and Steve S. Graham, "Memo to Constructivists: Skills Count, Too," *Educational Leadership*, February 1996, pp. 26-29.
9. William G. Cunningham and Paula A. Cordeiro, *Educational Administration: A Problem-Based Approach* (Needham Heights, Mass.: Allyn and Bacon, 2000).
10. Richard F. Elmore, "Teaching, Learning, and School Organization: Principles of Practice and the Regularities of Schooling," *Educational Administration Quarterly*, vol. 31, 1995, pp. 355-74.
11. Ibid.; and Mark Windschitl, "The Challenges of Sustaining a Constructivist Classroom Culture," *Phi Delta Kappan*, June 1999, pp. 751-55.
12. Burton W. Gorman, *Secondary Education: The High School America Needs* (New York: Random House, 1971).
13. John D. McNeil, *Curriculum: A Comprehensive Introduction*, 5th ed. (New York: Harper-Collins, 1996); and Ornstein and Hunkins, op. cit.
14. J. Lloyd Trump and Dorsey Baynham, *Focus on Change: Guide to Better Schools* (Chicago: Rand McNally, 1961).
15. Jeri Goldman, "Flexible Modular Scheduling: Results of Evaluations in Its Second Decade," *Urban Education*, vol. 18, 1983, pp. 191-228.
16. Robert L. Canady and Michael D. Rettig, *'Block Scheduling': A Catalyst for Change in High Schools* (Princeton, N.J.: Eye on Education, 1995).
17. Michael D. Rettig and Robert L. Canady, "The Effects of Block Scheduling," *School Administrator*, March 1999, pp. 14-16, 18-20.
18. Donald G. Hackmann, "The Status of High School Scheduling in Illinois," *Mid-Western Educational Researcher*, Spring 1999, pp. 25-31.
19. Daniel C. Buckman, B. B. King, and S. Ryan, "Block Scheduling: A Means to Improve School Climate," *NASSP Bulletin*, May 1995, pp. 9-18.
20. Hackmann, op. cit.
21. Tony Wagner, "Change as Collaborative Inquiry: A 'Constructivist' Methodology for Reinventing Schools," *Phi Delta Kappan*, March 1998, p. 515.
22. Linda D. Wyatt, "More Time, More Training: What Staff Development Do Teachers Need for Effective Instruction in Block Scheduling?," *School Administrator*, September 1996, pp. 16-18.
23. Jodi Benton-Kupper, "Can Less Be More? The Quantity Versus Quality Issue of Curriculum in a Block Schedule," *Journal of Research and Development in Education*, vol. 32, 1999, pp. 168-77; and Wyatt, op. cit.
24. Canady and Rettig, p. 12.
25. Windschitl, p. 754.
26. Canady and Rettig, p. 210.
27. Ibid., p. 29.
28. Michael Wronkovich, "Block Scheduling: Real Reform or Another Flawed Educational Fad?," *American Secondary Education*, June 1998, pp. 1-2.
29. Kurt Lewin, *Field Theory in Social Science: Selected Theoretical Papers* (New York: Harper and Row, 1951), p. 169.
30. Wronkovich, pp. 1-6.
31. Lorin W. Anderson and Herbert J. Walberg, *Timepiece: Extending and Enhancing Learning Time* (Reston, Va.: National Association of Secondary School Principals, 1993); and Wronkovich, op. cit.
32. Ann-Maureen Pliska, Matt T. Harmston, and Donald G. Hackmann, "The Relationship Between Secondary School Scheduling Models and ACT Assessment Scores," *NASSP Bulletin*, May 2001, pp. 42-55.

33. *Block Schedules and Student Performance on AP Examinations: Research Notes, RN-03* (New York: Office of Research and Development, The College Board, 1998).
34. Yvonne V. Thayer and Thomas L. Shortt, "Block Scheduling Can Enhance School Climate," *Educational Leadership*, December 1998-January 1999, pp. 76-81.
35. David J. Bateson, "Science Achievement in Semester and All-Year Courses," *Journal of Research and Science Teaching*, vol. 27, 1990, pp. 233-40.
36. *Block Scheduling in Texas Public High Schools* (Austin: Office of Policy Planning and Research , Division of Research and Evaluation, Texas Education Agency, 1999), p. 24.
37. Elmore, p. 370.
38. Thomas J. Sergiovanni, *Leadership for the Schoolhouse* (San Francisco: Jossey-Bass, 1996).
39. Windschitl, p. 752.

DONALD G. HACKMANN is an associate professor in the Department of Educational Leadership and Policy Studies, Iowa State University, Ames.

What Is High-Quality Instruction?

According to a study of 364 lessons,
few students receive exemplary instruction.

By Iris R. Weiss and Joan D. Pasley

In an effort to assess the quality of mathematics and science instruction in U.S. classrooms, our Horizon Research team spent 18 months observing more than 350 representative lessons and conducting follow-up interviews with teachers to explore their instructional decision making. The assertion by Burstein and colleagues (1995) that educators cannot measure some aspects of instruction without observing teacher-student interactions expresses the need that inspired our *Inside the Classroom* study (Weiss, Pasley, Smith, Banilower, & Heck, 2003). We documented, analyzed, and assessed lessons according to specific indicators in several areas: the quality of the mathematics and science content, the quality of implementation, and the extent to which the classroom culture facilitated learning (see Sample Indicators, p. 27).

The observers rated individual indicators in each area on a 1-5 scale, with 1 designating poor and 5 designating excellent, and then looked across these indicators to categorize the lesson's overall quality as low (1, 2), medium (low 3, solid 3), or high (high 3, 4, 5). Low-quality lessons were unlikely to enhance students' understanding of important mathematics or science content or their ability to engage successfully in the processes of science or mathematics. At the other end of the scale, high-quality lessons were structured and implemented in a manner that engaged students with important mathematics or science concepts; such lessons were very likely to enhance student understanding of these concepts and to develop their capacity to do mathematics or science successfully.

> One of the most important aspects of effective mathematics and science lessons is significant, worthwhile content.

Lack of Rigor and Excellence

The findings of our study suggest that U.S. schools fall very short of the ideal of providing high-quality mathematics and science education for all students. Observers classified only 15 percent of K-12 mathematics and science lessons as high in quality; 27 percent were medium, and 59 percent were low.

On the plus side, most mathematics and science lessons included accurate, significant, and worthwhile content, and teachers generally appeared confident in their ability to teach mathematics and science. Fewer than one in five lessons, however, were intellectually rigorous, included effective teacher questioning, or guided students appropriately in making sense of the lesson's content.

Our analyses indicated that the quality of lessons did not depend on whether the teacher used a "reform-oriented" approach or a traditional approach. Some lessons judged to be effective were traditional in nature, using lectures and worksheets; others were reform-oriented, involving students in open inquiries. We also saw both traditional and reform-oriented lessons that were far lower in quality.

We also observed a troubling pattern of differential quality of instruction across types of communities, in classes with varying proportions of minority students, and in classes of varying ability levels. Compared with lessons taught in suburban and urban schools, those taught in rural schools tended to be lower in quality on such key indicators as intellectual rigor and sense making. Similarly, lessons in classes with high percentages of minority students tended to be lower in quality than lessons in other classes. Finally, lessons in classes composed of students considered "low ability" or "middle ability" tended to be lower in quality than those in heterogeneous and high-ability classes.

Features of High-Quality Classrooms

To determine which characteristics were most important in determining quality, we conducted an in-depth analysis of lessons rated very *effective* and very *ineffective*. The following factors distinguished the most effective lessons from the least effective ones.

Student Engagement with the Content

One of the most important aspects of effective mathematics and science lessons is significant, worthwhile content. The majority of lessons in the study did, in fact, include such content: observers rated 89 percent of lessons at 3 or above on this indicator.

But important content is not enough. High-quality lessons also invite students to interact purposefully with the content. Effective mathematics and science lessons use various strategies to involve students and to build on their previous knowledge, often using real-world examples or engaging students in firsthand experiences with the concepts or phenomena. For example, in a lesson on fractions and as an introduction to percentages, one teacher in a 7th grade mathematics class asked three students to come to the front of the class for a demonstration. One student measured the height and arm spread of a second student while the third student wrote the measurements on the board. The students used these numbers to express the relationships both as a ratio and as a percentage.

Lessons also need to be at the appropriate level for students, taking into account what students already know and challenging them to learn more.

Some lessons go further than simply providing content at an appropriate level for students. Many lessons judged to be highly effective include a variety of experiences that enable students to tap into multiple pathways in developing or reinforcing a concept.

Culture Conducive to Learning

High-quality classrooms are both respectful and rigorous. Students feel free to contribute their ideas and questions, but they are also challenged to engage deeply with the content. Findings from the study suggest that teachers have difficulty combining these two elements: 45 percent of lessons received high ratings for respect, but only 13 percent of lessons were both respectful and rigorous.

> Students in high-quality classrooms are challenged to engage deeply with the content.

Of course, the development of a respectful and rigorous culture does not occur in a single lesson. The teacher must foster this climate over the course of the school year. In observing individual lessons, observers noted evidence of a culture conducive to learning when teachers asked questions that challenged and broadened students' thinking, when students felt free to contribute new ideas and to question the ideas of their peers, and when students exchanged constructive criticism about the findings of an investigation. For example, students in a 5th grade science class worked well in pairs. One student concluded that a rubber band conducted electricity, but her teammate pointed out that she had accidentally touched the wire to one of the clips, completing the circuit. The pair of students then tried the experiment again, taking care to touch only the rubber band, and found that the rubber band was not a conductor. The observer wrote,

> The teacher eagerly answered questions and encouraged exploration. There was—pardon the pun—an air of electricity and excitement in the room, and the students had to be shooed away from their activities for recess. It would be hard to imagine a classroom more conducive to learning.

Equal Access for All Students

A crucial aspect of the teacher's role is ensuring that no students slip between the cracks. When observers rated the extent to which lessons encouraged active participation of all students, they found that approximately half of the lessons did provide access for all students, but 29 percent of lessons were rated low in this area. Observers described cases in which some students were left out of the lesson as well as cases in which the teacher succeeded particularly well at engaging learners with differing needs.

A 3rd grade lesson provides an example of a teacher ensuring access for all students by altering her lesson plan to accommodate the varying levels of her students. She required all students to depict their observations of the experiment that they had conducted during the class. The more able students completed a six part, step-by-step description, with pictures, of the experiment. Other students, who had more difficulty with writing, were allowed to express their understanding through a drawing.

Effective Questioning

Teachers' questions are crucial in helping students make connections and learn important mathematics and science concepts. Effective questioning—the kind that monitors students' understanding of new ideas and encourages students to think more deeply—was relatively rare in the mathematics and science classes we observed. One 8th grade mathematics class illustrates a teacher's question that led students to examine and deepen their understanding:

> When searching for examples of tessellations around the room, one student proposed the border of the bulletin board, which was made of circles.
>
> Student: "How about the border?"
>
> Students: "No . . . that won't work." (Several students talk at the same time and reject this contribution.)
>
> Teacher: "Why won't it work? Can the circle ever work?"
>
> The discussion became focused on why the circle did not create a pattern that fit the definition of a tessellation. Although the student who suggested the border had been focusing more on patterns, the disagreement helped him redirect his analysis back to the definition of tessellations presented earlier in the lesson.

Unfortunately, teachers more often used low-level, "fill in the blank" questions asked in rapid-fire fashion with an emphasis on getting the right answer and moving on rather than helping students make sense of the concepts, as in this 1st grade mathematics lesson:

> The teacher distributed crayons and worksheets and began the lesson by noting, "Today, we're going to find differences for facts of five. When we say difference, does that mean add or subtract?" (Calls on a student.)
>
> Student: "Add?"
>
> Teacher repeats what she said.
>
> Another student says: "Subtract?"
>
> Teacher: "That's right. Before we start, I want to pass out these mats and counters. Take five counters out of the bag. Place them on the top line of the mat. Now put three white counters on the bottom.
>
> If I tell you 5 + 3, are you going to add everything or take something away?"
>
> Students: "Take away."
>
> Finally a student says: "Add."
>
> Teacher: "If I say 9 - 5, how many are you going to take away?"
>
> Students call out every number except five.

Sample Indicators from *Inside the Classroom* Study

- The mathematics/science content was significant and worthwhile.
- The mathematics/science content was appropriate for the developmental levels of the students in this class.
- Content information provided by the teacher was accurate.
- Students were intellectually engaged with important ideas relevant to the focus of the lesson.
- The degree of "sense making" of mathematics/science content within this lesson was appropriate for the developmental levels/needs of the students and the purposes of the lesson.
- The pace of the lesson was appropriate for the developmental levels/needs of the students and the purposes of the lesson.
- The teacher was able to "read" the students' level of understanding and adjusted instruction accordingly.
- The teacher's questioning strategies were likely to enhance the development of student conceptual understanding/problem solving (the teacher, for example, emphasized higher-order questions, used wait time appropriately, and identified prior conceptions and misconceptions).
- The teacher encouraged and valued active participation of all.
- There was a climate of respect for students' ideas, questions, and contributions.
- The climate of the lesson encouraged students to generate ideas, questions, conjectures, and/or propositions.
- Intellectual rigor, constructive criticism, and the challenging of ideas were evident.

Teacher (getting impatient): "You're not listening."

Assistance in Making Sense of the Content

Teacher questioning is not the only way to help students understand mathematics or science content. A teacher's ability to provide clear explanations at appropriate junctures as the lesson unfolds often determines students' opportunities to learn. Effective lessons engage students in doing intellectual work, with the teacher helping to ensure that students are making sense of the key mathematics and science concepts.

Most of the lessons that we observed lacked an adequate emphasis on sense making. Only 16 percent of lessons observed received high ratings in this area. In some lessons, however, teachers did help students make sense of the content and see connections among ideas. The teacher in a high school human anatomy and physiology class, for example, began a lecture by drawing a diagram of a nerve receptor connected by a nerve fiber to the brain. He explained the concept of the threshold for a receptor, noting that stimuli could be either sub-threshold, threshold, or super-threshold; he stressed that the receptor responds to the stimulus and sends a signal to the brain only after the threshold is reached. He spent most of the remainder of the lesson explaining that receptors vary in threshold, emphasizing that "your brain recognizes the highest threshold receptor stimulated." The teacher summarized the lecture by reiterating the threshold principle and the differentiation of nerve receptors by threshold. The observer commented,

> This lecture was extremely engaging, accessible, and focused on worthwhile content. The teacher emphasized sense making throughout the lesson, using examples familiar to the students and connecting the content to their lives.

Instructional Decisions of Teachers

In planning lessons, teachers are influenced by a multitude of factors that determine what content they teach, how they teach it, and what materials they use to engage students with the content. We need to understand these instructional influences as a precursor to improving curriculum and instruction.

Following our observations, we conducted extensive interviews with the teachers to determine what factors influenced their instructional design decisions. Our findings indicated that someone other than the teacher usually made the decisions about the content of mathematics and science lessons. Teachers cited state- or district-level curriculum standards, textbooks and curriculum programs selected at the district level, and accountability systems related to student achievement as influences on their decisions about what to teach. For many teachers, pressure for their students to do well on high-stakes testing drove their selection of topics.

These external policy instruments appeared to have a smaller influence, however, on the selection of instructional strategies in lessons. Although most teachers relied to some extent on the textbook or curriculum program in their school or district, for the most part teachers reported designing their instruction with little external guidance. They used resources and strategies grounded in their beliefs about mathematics and science, about effective pedagogy, and about the students they taught.

Preparing and Supporting Teachers

The findings of the *Inside the Classroom* study have implications for the continuing education of the mathematics and science teaching force and for the support provided to teachers.

Teachers need a vision of effective instruction to guide the design and implementation of their lessons. Findings from this study suggest that rather than advocating one type of pedagogy over another, the vision of high-quality instruction should emphasize the need for important and developmentally appropriate mathematics or science learning goals, instructional activities that engage students with the mathematics or science content, a learning environment that simultaneously supports and challenges students, and attention to appropriate questioning and sense making. A number of interventions would help teachers understand this vision and improve instructional practice in their specific contexts.

First, teachers need opportunities to analyze a variety of lessons in relation to these key elements of high-quality instruction. Lesson study conducted with skilled, knowledgeable facilitators would provide teachers with helpful learning opportunities.

> **The teacher's content knowledge does not guarantee high-quality instruction.**

Second, the support materials accompanying textbooks and other instructional materials should provide more targeted assistance for teachers—clearly identifying the key learning goals for each suggested activity, sharing the research on students' cognitive development in each content area, suggesting questions and tasks that teachers can use to monitor student understanding, and outlining the key points that the teacher should emphasize to help students make sense of the mathematics or science concepts.

Third, workshops and other teacher professional development activities should reflect the elements of high-quality instruction with clear, explicit learning goals, a supportive but challenging learning environment, and ways to ensure that teachers are developing their understanding. Without question, teachers need to have sufficient knowledge of the mathematics and science content they teach. The teacher's content knowledge, however, does not guarantee high-quality instruction. The *Inside the Classroom* observations indicate that teachers also need expertise in helping students develop an understanding of that content. Teachers need to know how students typically think about particular concepts, how to determine what a particular student or group of students thinks about those ideas, and how to help students deepen their understanding.

Fourth, policymakers need to explore the apparent inequities in quality of instruction and, if these inequities are confirmed, take steps to resolve them. All students must receive high-quality instruction, regardless of the location of their schools or the demographic composition of their classes.

Finally, administrators and policymakers need to ensure that teachers receive a coherent set of messages.

Only when preservice preparation, curriculum, student assessment, professional development, and teacher evaluation policies at the state, district, and school levels are aligned with one another, and in support of the same vision of high-quality instruction, can we expect to achieve the goal of excellence and equity for all students.

Authors' note: This study was funded by the National Science Foundation. The authors' writings do not necessarily reflect the views of the National Science Foundation.

References

Burstein, L., McDonnell, L. M., Van Winkle, J., Ormseth, T., Mirocha, J., & Guitton, G. (1995). *Validating national curriculum indicators.* (Report No. DRU-1086-NSF). Santa Monica, CA: Rand.

Weiss, I. R., Pasley, J. D., Smith, P. S., Banilower, E. R., & Heck, D.J. (2003). *Looking inside the classroom: A study of K-12 mathematics and science education in the United States.* Chapel Hill, NC: Horizon Research. Available: www.horizon-research.com/insidetheclassroom/reports/highlights/highlights.pdf

Iris R. Weiss (iweiss@horizon-research.com) is President and **Joan D. Pasley** (jpasley@horizon-research.com) is Senior Research Associate, Horizon Research, 326 Cloister Ct., Chapel Hill, NC 27514.

The Integration of Instructional Technology into Public Education: Promises and Challenges

Rodney S. Earle
Contributing Editor

Introduction

Will instructional technology (IT) ever be integrated into public schools? An interesting question—or rather a series of related questions of interest to educators and parents: What do we mean by "instructional technology"? What is integration? What is the current status of IT in classrooms? Are there constraints or barriers to integration? What are the effects of preservice teacher preparation and inservice professional development? How does one proceed with technology integration? How do we apply the lessons learned from "older" technologies to the "newer" technologies of the last two decades?

This article will address each of these questions in order to help us to grasp the prospects for the integration of instructional technology into public education as well as to consider the promises and challenges of such a venture.

Instructional Technology Defined

What is "instructional technology"? Is it merely a synonym for computers, or does its meaning transcend hardware and software to include both physical and intellectual facets in its domain?

Let us start with trying to understand the concept of technology. Although *Webster's New Collegiate Dictionary* takes a sociological perspective in its definition of technology as "… the totality of the means employed to provide objects necessary for human sustenance and comfort" and "a technical method of achieving a practical purpose," the prevailing public definition based on current usage is "technology equals machinery." This limited focus on machinery at the expense of process ignores the true sense of technology as "the systematic application of scientific and other organized knowledge to practical tasks" (Galbraith, 1967, p. 12) and thus as a problem-solving process using human and other resources to seek solutions to human problems.

Within this broader sociological framework of technology, we find the terms "educational technology" and "instructional technology." Often used interchangeably, both share a common interest in the processes of human learning and teaching, with some variations in definitions and levels of complexity, depending upon one's personal viewpoint. For convenience and consistency, we will most likely blend elements of the two terms, but use "instructional technology" as our primary focus in this article.

Instructional technology may best be understood by reviewing several definitions culled from the writings of several scholars in the field:

[Instructional technology] is concerned with improving the effectiveness and efficiency of learning in educational contexts, regardless of the nature or substance of that learning.... Solutions to instructional problems might entail social as well as machine technologies. (Cassidy, 1982, p. 1)

The systemic and systematic application of strategies and techniques derived from behavioral and physical sciences concepts and other knowledge to the solution of instructional problems. (Gentry, 1995, p. 7)

... the media born of the communications revolution which can be used for instructional purposes along side the teacher, textbook, and blackboard... [as well as]... a systematic way of designing, carrying out, and evaluating the total process of learning and teaching in terms of specific objectives, based on research in human learning and communications, and employing a combination of human and nonhuman resources to bring about more effective instructions. (Commission on Instructional Technology, 1970, p. 19)

... the application of our scientific knowledge about human learning to the practical tasks of teaching and learning. (Heinich *et al.*, 1993, p. 16)

... a complex, integrated process involving people, procedures, ideas, devices, and organizations for analyzing problems, and devising, implementing, evaluating, and managing solutions to those problems involved in all aspects of human learning. (AECT, 1977, p. 1)

Instructional technology is the theory and practice of design, development, utilization, management, and evaluation processes and resources for learning. (Seels & Richey, 1994, p. 9)

Despite these more comprehensive viewpoints from the literature that instructional technology encompasses the broader processes of teaching and learning, the prevailing public perspective incorporates instructional technology as a synonym for computer technology. In other words, as noted above, technology means computers in the minds of many. That myopic view has generated some of the problems related to integration, in particular, the focus on access to hardware at the expense of effective pedagogy, as if one particular medium is the panacea for the challenges facing education. Isn't this a *déjà vu* experience for the field of educational technology? Haven't most technological innovations in our past concentrated on hardware rather than the process? Think back forty years, if, like me, you've been involved in the field that long. Remember instructional television? Federal and state funding loaded schools with television sets, with very little attention to pedagogical processes and professional development for teachers. We

cannot assume that, just because adequate resources have been obtained, integration would naturally follow.

However, since the challenges of integrating instructional design and other *technological processes* into teacher practices have been addressed adequately elsewhere (Branch, 1994; Driscoll, Klein, & Sherman, 1994; Earle, 1994, 1998; Reiser, 1994), the focus of our discussion here will be on aspects of the integration of new computer and communications technologies into schools.

The Current Status of Classroom Technology

A nationwide survey of teachers and superintendents commissioned by Jostens Learning Corporation (1997) indicated that the computer revolution has had a tremendous impact in the classroom. Surprisingly, however, the emphasis was on student access to information outside the classroom and improved student motivation, not on specific academic achievement. In fact, fewer than half of the teachers used computers for instructional purposes, rather than word-processing, spreadsheets, or graphics for personal productivity only. Differing priorities showed that teachers would rather see additional funding used to increase the number of computers in classrooms, while superintendents felt that teacher training would best improve computer effectiveness. A variety of other surveys (Bosch, 1993; Niess, 1991; Trotter, 1997), while reporting strong computer usage by teachers, actually indicated a lack of integrated use with the curriculum. In many instances, it has been a case of fitting the curriculum to the computer rather than the computer to the curriculum.

Let us begin with a comprehensive look at school technology in a series of articles by *Education Week* (1997), which shared several interesting facts about the state of computer technology in public education:

- "The dividends that educators can expect from this... unprecedented support for school technology... are not yet clear.... There is no guarantee that technology improves student achievement." (Trotter, 1997, p. 6)
- 43% of respondents in a survey felt that the introduction of computers into public schools was not happening fast enough. (Trotter, 1997, p. 7)
- Despite the lack of research evidence, 74% of the public and 93% of educators agreed that computers had indeed improved the quality of education, teaching, and learning. (Trotter, 1997, p. 8)
- Research on the effects of technology on student achievement offers mixed results. (Viadero, 1997, p. 12)
- Placing computers and software in classrooms is not enough. Discovering whether technology "works" is not the point. The real issue is when and under what circumstances. Like any other tool, teachers have to

come up with a strategy or pedagogy to make it work. (Viadero, 1997, p. 16)

- Wise use of technology takes adequate training time, planning, support, and teacher ownership (Viadero, 1997, p. 16)
- Money spent on school technology is wasted without an equal effort to help teachers with its use and integration into the curriculum. (Zero, 1997, p. 24)

Is it possible that blasphemies are beginning to be heard outside the church of technology? Bronner (1997) posed this question and, in describing an "intellectual backlash" and feelings of skepticism about technology use, cited several educational sources to criticize the use of "glitzy toys" and "bogus stuff" in the middle of an "educational catastrophe" where children cannot read or write. Such a backlash will be productive if it makes us re-examine how we use technology in the classroom (Pool, 1997). Bronner's comment that "schools may be overwired and children undertaught" is cause for reflection for those who feel that "new media tools offer a great promise for a new model of learning—one based on discovery, participation…, learning partnerships, and learning cultures" (p. 4).

The promise is indeed real—as illustrated by recent studies showing that new technologies have indeed transformed classrooms for K–12 students and teachers. "Around the nation teachers are using technology to create exciting and creative learning environments where students teach and learn from each other, solve problems, and collaborate on projects that put learning in a real-world context" (*GLEF Blast Newsletter,* 2001, p. 1). In a meta-analysis of the value and use of technology in K–12 education (Valdez *et al.,* 2000), the North Central Regional Laboratory found that "technology innovations are increasing the demand for reforms in teaching and learning approaches that, in turn, are having a significant impact on technology use expectations" (p. iii). The report also found a very strong connection between appropriate teacher use of technology and increased student achievement.

Technology offers opportunities for learner-control, increased motivation, connections to the real world, and data-driven assessments tied to content standards that, when implemented systematically, enhance student achievement as measured in a variety of ways, including but not limited to standardized achievement tests. (p. iii)

Working in an appropriately designed technology-rich environment has the potential of producing a variety of positive outcomes (Tiene & Luft, 2001): improved patterns of social interaction, changes in teaching styles, more effective teaching, increased student (and perhaps, teacher) motivation, and enhanced student learning. Achieving this potential, however, is the challenge, and it requires the correct vision of technology and its integration.

A Closer Look at Technology Integration

Definitions of both terms (technology and integration), whether broad or limited, drive the problem. Computer technology is merely *one* possibility in the selection of media and the delivery mode—part of the instructional design process—not *the* end but merely one of several means to the end. Integration does not just mean placement of hardware in classrooms. If computers are merely add-on activities or fancy work sheets, where is the value (Hadley & Sheingold, 1993)? Technologies must be pedagogically sound. They must go beyond information retrieval to problem solving; allow new instructional and learning experiences not possible without them; promote deep processing of ideas; increase student interaction with subject matter; promote faculty and student enthusiasm for teaching and learning; and free up time for quality classroom interaction—in sum, improve the pedagogy. Wager (1992) argued that "the educational technology that can make the biggest difference to schools and students is not the hardware, but the process of designing effective instruction" (p. 454), which incorporates computer technology and other media appropriately.

Integrating technology is not about technology—it is primarily about content and effective instructional practices. Technology involves the tools with which we deliver content and implement practices in better ways. Its focus must be on curriculum and learning. Integration is defined not by the amount or type of technology used, but by how and why it is used.

Successful technology adoption/integration requires concerted focus on the mission of improving education for all students. It grows from the mission. As an add-on or fad, it soon withers. It must be seen as an ongoing innovative process designed to meet instructional/learning needs (Robey, 1992). Bernauer (1995) captured a significant insight when he stated that "it is not technology *per se* that has resulted in improved student outcomes, but rather how the technology was used and integrated into instructional processes" (p. 1). While noting increased student proficiency in using technology for learning rather than as technology for its own sake, he also attributed such achievements to teacher planning and expertise, recognizing that true success must be measured in terms of improvement in teaching and learning, not merely in the placement of computers in classrooms. Munoz (1993), who described herself as a technophile, emphasized the prudent, ethical use of technology and warned us to "resist the seductive force of technology to replace rather than enhance" (p. 49). She stressed that very human elements such as intuition, judgment, imagination, and creativity cannot be replaced and that technology may fail if it is viewed as change for the sake of change.

Dede (1997) reinforced this perspective by stressing that "unless other simultaneous innovations occur in pedagogy, curriculum, assessment, and school organization, the time and effort expended on instructional technology produce few improvements in educational outcomes—a result that reinforces many educators' cynicism about fads based on magical machines" (p. 13).

Fullan (2000), in a review of educational reform, reminds us that, since technology is ubiquitous, the issue is not whether, but *how* we contend with it. He stresses that as technology becomes more powerful, good teachers become more indispensable.

> Technology generates a glut of information, but it has no particular pedagogical wisdom—especially regarding new breakthroughs in cognitive science about how learners must construct their own meaning for deep understanding to occur. This means that teachers must become experts in pedagogical design. It also means that teachers must use the powers of technology, both in the classroom and in sharing with other teachers what they are learning. (p. 582)

Initially, the real power of technology probably lies in the way its use causes teachers to develop different perspectives through rethinking teaching and learning (Riedl, 1995; Ritchie & Wilburg, 1994). Teaching with technology causes teachers to confront their established beliefs about instruction and their traditional roles as classroom teachers.

Forces of Change

Kurt Lewin's (1951) force field analysis theory illustrates the dynamics at work in the change process. Movement from the present level of performance to a desired level is facilitated by driving or encouraging forces, while at the same time, it is hindered by restraining (or resisting, discouraging) forces. The present situation usually represents a state of equilibrium or balance between these driving and restraining forces.

Driving forces for technology integration might include the power and potential of new developments, rapid availability, creativity, Internet access, ease of communication, or the promise of impact on learning. Restraining forces might include barriers and constraints such as technical support, teacher expertise, time for planning, or pedagogical applications.

So, how do we make changes? Do we increase the driving forces or decrease the restraining forces? The former, by far the easiest because of our control over such forces, proves to be the less effective, since all that results is an increase in tension with a quick return to the status quo. Senge (1990) has stressed that when innovators change one part of a system, the system almost always works to change itself back again unless those solutions move from a symptomatic to a fundamental change in the system. For technology to become an integral aspect of classrooms and curricula, the changes in teacher and student behaviors must, of necessity, be fundamental to the

system rather than quick fix or Bandaid solutions which merely focus on the surface symptoms. Reiser and Salisbury (1995) have referred to this phenomenon as "straighten[ing] the deck chairs [while] the structure of the ship we are traveling on remains the same" (p. 232).

Covey's (1990) analogy provides a useful strategy for addressing change through the responses to driving and restraining forces:

> The question of whether to increase driving or decrease restraining forces is analogous to the question, "If I'm driving a car and see the emergency brake is partly on, should I release the brake or put on more gas?" Accelerating may increase the speed, but it may also burn up the engine. Releasing the brake, on the other hand, would allow you to attain high speeds more efficiently. (p. 223)

Hence, focusing on reducing restraining forces would appear to be a more productive use of our energy. So let us attempt to identify these forces and consider their nature.

Constraints and Barriers: Identification of Restraining Forces

Despite the general sense that the computer revolution of the last decade has had a major impact in schools, the nature of this impact seems to be limited to access and information retrieval rather than improved teaching methods or revitalized school and classroom structures (Hativa & Lesgold, 1996). Did we over-promise and fail to deliver? Was it a matter of unfulfilled expectations? Were there unexpected outcomes, constraints, barriers, or contextual considerations which were overlooked or underestimated?

What are the restraining, resisting, or discouraging forces that affect change efforts in teacher practices, especially related to technology? The following constraints and barriers have been acknowledged by a number of scholars (Pelgrum, 2001). What would it take to convert these barriers to facilitating factors in technology integration? Often it seems to be a fine line between the two perspectives. It is in this arena that we should expend the bulk of our energy.

- Access to hardware and software as well as funding (Hope, 1997; Lan, 2000; Leggett & Persichitte, 1998; Lumley & Bailey, 1993).
- Time for planning, personal exploration, online access, and skill development (Duffield, 1997; Hope, 1997; Lan, 2000; Leggett & Persichitte, 1998; Sheingold & Hadley, 1990).
- Technical and administrative support and resources (Leggett & Persichitte, 1998; Schrum, 1995).
- Training and expertise (Cafolla & Knee, 1995; Hope, 1997; Shelton & Jones, 1996).

- Resistance, passivity, school cultures, and traditions of teaching (Beacham, 1994; Cafolla & Knee, 1995; Cohen, 1987; Cuban, 1986; Ertmer, 1999; Hope, 1997; Lumley & Bailey, 1993).
- Vision and leadership (Cafolla & Knee, 1995; Ely, 1995; Hope, 1997; Lan, 2000; Lumley & Bailey, 1993).
- Support for integration of technologies into instruction and the curriculum (Cuban, 1986; Hancock & Betts, 1994).

Ertmer (1999) grouped these barriers into two categories: first-order barriers extrinsic to teachers (access, time, support, resources, training) and second-order barriers intrinsic to teachers (attitudes, beliefs, practices, resistance). She asserted that "even if every first-order barrier were removed, teachers would not automatically use technology" (p. 51) and in fact, rather than being eliminated completely, such barriers will "continue to ebb and flow throughout the evolutionary integration process" (p. 52).

Teachers and Technology

Tucker (1992) advocated "unleashing the full potential of technology" by "letting the genie out of the bottle" (p. 50)—as if, by allowing this powerful force to roam into schools, something magical will automatically happen and all our wishes will be granted. Although many of us strongly believe in the great promise that technology holds for both learners and teachers, we also need to remember that, first and foremost, technology is a communication tool. "It is not the silver bullet that will solve all of our education problems, but it is certainly a useful tool that enables us to link various learning communities together in new and different ways" (Taylor, 2000, p. 4). It is not about what technology by itself can do, but what teachers and learners may be able to accomplish using these tools.

In labeling technology as the "great siren song of education," Kearsley (1998) argued that "educational technology [has become] primarily, if ironically, a distraction (on a grand scale) from what matters most—effective learning and good teaching" (p. 47). By focusing merely on how to use computers, technology training has failed and has caused us to miss the forest for the trees by not addressing how to teach students more effectively using a variety of technological tools. Kearsley further lamented the lack of technology preparation for teachers (too little and too late), stressing the realistic need for extensive and sustained practice over years, not one-day workshops (p. 49). What teachers need to know most is how to teach content more effectively. Because of our quick fix mindset in education, we myopically "teach people how to use specific types of technology [rather than] how to solve educational problems using technology when needed and appropriate" (p. 50). A recent survey by Jostens Learning Corporation (1997) and the American Association of School Administrators reported that teacher training, while readily available, focuses merely on basic computer operation and fails to address helping teachers use technology to teach more effectively.

Even though Gardner (1991) has expressed the view that "a well-trained and effective teacher is still preferable to the most advanced technology, and that even excellent hardware and software are to little avail in the absence of appropriate curricula, pedagogy, and assessment" (p. 223), he nevertheless admitted that "immersing oneself in a problem using the latest technology… can make a significant contribution to student learning" (p. 223). For him, the most important question is "whether such technological prosthetics actually improve classroom performance and lead to deeper understandings" (p. 223) and become "helpful handmaidens in the [learning] process" (p. 233).

Postman (1992) has warned us that new technologies alter "the things we think about…, the things we think with…, and the arena in which thoughts develop" (p. 20). Hence, technology has become a serious arena for academic work (Mollgaard & Sides-Gonzales, 1995). This is the promise and the potential. It is also the challenge. The questions to be addressed are: "Who is in charge? Who is the driving force?" The answer should be the teachers who use the technology well. It cannot be the technology in and of itself.

A review of research studies and reports compiled in the early years of the past decade (Sivin-Kachala & Bialo, 1995) demonstrated the value of technology in enhancing student achievement, improving students' attitudes about themselves and about learning, and changing the learning environment. However, these authors emphasized that "the decisions made by well-trained educators [necessarily] determine the computer's ultimate instructional effectiveness" (p. 17) and that "the most important determinant of student attitudes when using technology is the teacher" (p. 24).

Lessons from Our Technological Past

The future belongs to those who respect the past, acknowledge the present, and grasp the future (Gustafson, 1993, p. 31).

In our past attempts at educational reform we have always looked for *new* solutions to old problems, equating "change" with "newness," and "ineffective" with "old." People just like the idea of newness. That's what grabs their attention. New for old. Not effective for ineffective. Not efficient for inefficient (Earle, 1992).

Focusing exclusively upon the newness of computer technology alone, independent of teaching and learning processes, may cause us to repeat technological history without reaping the potential benefits of this remarkable technology. We may unintentionally succumb to the malady of "data, data everywhere, but not a thought to think" (Theodore Roszak, in Rhee, 2000).

Our infatuation with the promises and possibilities of technology as hardware at the expense of technology as a process has overshadowed key lessons which we have learned from prior experiences in the field of educational technology: There is no one best medium; the medium is the means, not the ends; and the medium is not the message. Snider (1992) reminds us that focusing exclusively on technology as a panacea for improving schools has been somewhat fruitless across decades of technological innovations. "From lantern slides to language labs, from closed-circuit television to microcomputers, attempts to improve American schools with modern machines have been something less than a resounding success. Beginning with the magic lantern and the stereoscope of 1900, machines in the classroom have generated some promise, a fair amount of controversy, and a great deal of hype. During these 90-plus years, however, the basic acts of classroom teaching have changed very little despite sporadic efforts at research and reform—with and without machines" (p. 316).

Callister (1992) has added his own historical insights to our current dilemma in order to remind us of yet another lesson from the past: the power of the teacher in technology integration.

Inventions from Edison's phonograph and the blackboard to audiotape and instructional television have all been pressed into service to make up for the perceived deficiencies of the ordinary classroom teacher. But efforts to replace teachers with technology have uniformly failed. Inventions intended to take over teaching come and (mostly) go; what happens in classrooms looks pretty much the same.

Why? Because technology enthusiasts continue to forget a basic fact: Machines are tools, valuable only when a human intelligence organizes their use in a productive way. In the classroom, that human is the teacher, who controls the nature of the environment and what happens there. Good classroom tools extend the teacher's power to create a rich learning environment. If the teacher does not know what to make of the tool, or fears it, or misconstrues its uses, it will be used badly or not at all. If the teacher perceives the machine as a master, not as a servant, its potential will never be realized. (pp. 324–325)

Principles of Integration

Instructional technology does, indeed, hold a remarkable promise for changing the quality of teaching and learning in our schools. It is the catalyst for transformation—but this does not mean that we merely need more computers in our classrooms. Technology also involves *process*. Too often our efforts to improve education have resulted in our unrealistic isolation of technological processes. Remember my earlier reference to our experiences with educational television? We expended our resources on installing equipment, which soon began to gather dust because we neglected the process components—learning, teaching practices, and curricula. Technologies are valuable resources, but only when used in a systematic process for developing human competence (Earle, 1992).

Questions about technology integration often center around schools and classrooms. Such questions fall short of the target. It is relatively easy to "place" technology in physical locations. The real question must focus on integration into teaching practices, learning experiences, and the curriculum. Integration (from the Latin *integrare,* to make whole) includes a sense of completeness or wholeness and incorporates the need to overcome artificial separations by bringing together all essential elements in the teaching and learning process—including technology (as *one* of the elements, not the sole element).

Change starts with the individual teacher, who, upon catching the vision, is willing to take risks, to experience Christopherian confrontations or encounters (Gardner, 1991) in rethinking teaching and learning, and to model for and be a mentor to peers. Just as Christopher Columbus confronted the intuitive impression that the earth is flat with the conception of a spherical earth, so teachers must grasp the opportunity to reconsider established practices and rethink teaching and learning. Conversion to a theory, practice, process, or approach, such as technology integration, is a very personal process. It involves *preparation* of the teacher (building relationships of trust, helping teachers feel and recognize the power of teaching with technology, personalizing training, and finding out teacher needs, interests, and concerns), *commitment* by the teacher, *following-up* on that commitment by the support team, and *resolving teacher concerns* arising during the change process. Teachers move through at least three levels—confidence, competence, and creativity. It is a process of gradualness as they progress from learner to adopter to leader. At first they utilize existing practices, then adapt to their own needs, and finally design their own integrated experiences. Such teachers "face their own fears and struggles with technology and change by taking the time to reflect on their own role and professional practice in this process of integration" (Norum *et al.,* 1999, p. 202).

It is important to remember that technology is not a subject (Duffield, 1997). The focus of integration is on pedagogy—effective practices for teaching and learning. Teachers need to be able to make choices about technology integration without becoming technocentric by placing undue emphasis on the technology for its own sake without connections to learning and the curriculum. For both preservice preparation and inservice professional development, this means providing experiences, primarily in instructional design, media selection, modeling exemplary technology practices, clinical activities, resource sharing, and extensive and sustained training and practice. Ertmer (1999) explains that "teachers need opportunities to observe *models* of integrated technology use, to *reflect* on and discuss their evolving ideas with mentors and peers, and to *collaborate* with others on meaningful projects as they try out their new ideas about teaching and learning with technology" (p. 54).

The curriculum must be the vehicle for technology integration. Just as reading is content-free (i.e., incorporates all subject areas), so is technology. We must weave technology into the fabric of learning, or as Cuban (1986) admonished: Fit the computer to the curriculum, not the curriculum to the computer.

Exemplary practices reported in professional journals such as *Educational Technology, Tech Trends, Technology and Learning, Educational Leadership,* and *Learning and Leading with Technology* have showcased individuals, programs, and schools that have successfully taken on the restraining forces listed above. Such efforts show us that reducing these forces is the key to overcoming the obstacles and breaking down the barriers to the meaningful integration of technology into teaching and learning. Converting these restraining forces to facilitating factors is essential. Take any of the restraining forces listed above—access, time, support, training, leadership, or resistance—and one can see that it is much easier to remove the barrier by resolving and reducing concerns than to attempt to use additional force to plow through the barrier—the former approach is facilitative and constructive while the latter is divisive and destructive. The solutions are many and varied depending on local conditions (Leggett & Persichitte, 1998; Lumley & Bailey, 1993).

Final Reflections

Any innovation is fraught with promises and challenges. Involving key stakeholders is often the way to achieve the potential promises while addressing and overcoming the related challenges (Waddoups *et al.,* 2001). Hence the need to focus on the teacher and the learner and not the technology—through the curricula and practices which bring teachers and learners together. Contrary to critical comments about the sparseness and poor quality of technology research, Margaret Honey at the Education Development Center recently testified before the U.S. Senate that one can find ample empirical evidence that technology does have a positive impact *when the right conditions are in place* (Honey, 2001). She concluded that, if technologies are to be used to support real gains in educational outcomes, six factors must be in place: leadership, solid educational objectives, professional development, adequate technology resources, time, and evaluation (Honey, Culp, & Carrigg, 2000). Additionally, Norris, Smolka, and Soloway (2000), in a convergent analysis of technology studies, have identified their set of critical conditions as access to technology and time on task, adequate teacher preparation, effective curriculum,

supportive school/district administration, and supportive family. In other words, establish appropriate conditions by converting restraining forces to facilitating factors.

Such remarkable interactive technologies deserve the opportunity to deliver on their promises and meet (or even exceed) their potential. Let us truly learn from our technological past and grasp the future by addressing today's realities so that we can reap tomorrow's possibilities.

References

Association for Educational Communications and Technology (1977). *The definition of educational technology.* Washington, DC: AECT.

Beacham, B. (1994). Making connections: Transforming ivory towers and little red school houses. In J. Willis, B. Robin, & D. A. Willis (Eds.). *Technology and Teacher Education Annual 1994* (pp. 742–744). Charlottesville, VA: Association for Advancement of Computing in Education.

Bernauer, J. A. (1995). *Integrating technology into the curriculum: First year evaluation.* A paper presented at the annual meeting of the American Educational Research Association, San Francisco, CA, (ED 385-224).

Bosch, K. A. (1993). Is there a computer crisis in the classroom? *Schools in the Middle, 2*(4), 7–9.

Branch, R. M. (1994). Common instructional design practices employed by secondary school teachers. *Educational Technology, 34*(3), 25–33.

Bronner, E. (November 10, 1997). High-tech teaching is losing its gloss. *New York Times,* p. 4.

Cafolla, R., & Knee, R. (1995). Factors limiting technology integration in education: The leadership gap. *Technology and Teacher Education Annual 1995* (pp. 556–559). Charlottesville, VA: Association for Advancement of Computing in Education.

Callister, T. A. (1992). The computer as doorstep: Technology as disempowerment. *Phi Delta Kappan, 74*(4), 324–329.

Cassidy, M. F. (1982). Toward integration: Education, instructional technology, and semiotics. *Educational Communications and Technology Journal, 20*(2), 75–89.

Cohen, D. (1987). Educational technology, policy, and practice. *Educational Evaluation and Policy Analysis, 9,* 153–170.

Commission on Instructional Technology. (1970). *To improve learning: A report to the President and the Congress of the United States.* Washington, DC: Commission on Instructional Technology.

Covey, S. R. (1990). *Principle-centered leadership.* New York: Simon & Schuster.

Cuban, L. (1986). *Teachers and machines: The classroom use of technology since 1920.* New York: Teachers College Press.

Dede, C. (1997). Rethinking how to invest in technology. *Educational Leadership, 55*(3), 12–16.

Driscoll, M. P., Klein, J. D., & Sherman, G. P. (1994). Perspectives on instructional planning: How do teachers and instructional designers conceive of ISD planning practices? *Educational Technology, 34*(3), 34–42.

Duffield, J. A. (1997). Trials, tribulations, and minor successes: Integrating technology into a preservice preparation program. *Tech Trends, 42*(4), 22–26.

Earle, R. S. (1992). Talk about teaching: New lamps for old. *Educational Technology, 32*(3), 35–37.

Earle, R. S. (1994). Instructional design and the classroom teacher: Looking back and moving ahead. *Educational Technology, 34*(3), 610.

Earle, R. S. (1998). Instructional design and teacher planning: Reflections and perspectives. In R. M. Branch & M. A. Fitzgerald (Eds.), *Educational Media and Technology Yearbook* (Volume 23, pp. 29–41). Englewood, CO: Libraries Unlimited.

Education Week (1999, Nov. 10). Schools and reform in the information age, *17*(11).

Ely, D. (1995). *Technology is the answer! But what was the question?* Capstone College of Education Society, University of Alabama, (ERIC Document Reproduction Service No. ED 381 152).

Ertmer, P. (1999). Addressing first- and second-order barriers to change: Strategies for technology implementation. *Educational Technology Research and Development, 47*(4), 47–61.

Fullan, M. (2000). The three stories of education reform. *Phi Delta Kappan, 81*(8), 581–584.

Galbraith, J. K. (1967). *The new industrial state.* Boston, MA: Houghton Mifflin.

Gardner, H. K. (1991). *The unschooled mind: How children think and how schools should teach.* New York: Basic Books.

Gentry, C. G. (1995). Educational technology: A question of meaning. In G. Anglin (Ed.), *Instructional technology: Past, present, and future.* Englewood, CO: Libraries Unlimited.

GLEF Blast Newsletter. (2001, August 2), San Francisco CA: The George Lucas Educational Foundation.

Gustafson, K. L. (1993). Instructional design fundamentals: Clouds on the horizon. *Educational Technology, 33*(2), 27–32.

Hadley, M., & Sheingold, K. (1993). Commonalities and distinctive patterns in teachers' integration of computers. *American Journal of Education, 101,* 261–315.

Hancock, V., & Betts, J. (1994). From the lagging to the leading edge. *Educational Leadership, 51*(7), 24–29.

Hativa, N., & Lesgold, A. (1996). Situational effects in classroom technology implementations: Unfulfilled expectations and unexpected outcomes. In S. J. Kerr (Ed.), *Technology and the future of schooling: Ninety-fifth yearbook of the National Society for the Study of Education,* part 2 (pp. 131–171). Chicago: University of Chicago Press.

Heinich, R., Molenda, M., & Russell, J. D. (1993). *Instructional media and the new technologies of instruction.* New York: Macmillan.

Honey, M. (2001, July 25). Technology's effectiveness as a teaching and learning tool. Testimony and statement for the record before the Labor, HHS, and Education Appropriations Subcommittee of the U.S. Senate. Education Development Center, Inc. Available: http://www.edc.org/spotlight/Tech/mhtestimony.htm

Honey, M., Culp, K. M., & Carrigg, F. (2000). Perspectives on technology and education research: Lessons from the past and present. *Educational Computing Research, 23*(1), 5–14.

Hope, W. C. (1997). Why technology has not realized its potential in schools. *American Secondary Education, 25*(4), 29.

Jostens Learning Corporation. (1997, April 7). Survey analysis by Global Strategy Group. San Diego: Jostens Learning Corporation.

Kearsley, G. (1998). Educational technology: A critique. *Educational Technology, 38*(2), 47–51.

Lan, J. (2000). Leading teacher educators to a new paradigm: Observations on technology integration. *AACTE Briefs 21*(10), 4–6.

Leggett, W. P., & Persichitte, K. A. (1998). Blood, sweat, and TEARS: 50 years of technology implementation obstacles. *Tech Trends, 43*(3), 33–36.

Lewin, K. (1951). *Field theory in social science.* New York: Harper.

Lumley, D., & Bailey, G. D. (1993). *Planning for technology: A guidebook for school administrators.* New York: Scholastic.

Mollgaard, T., & Sides-Gonzales, K. (1995). Stockbroker of the technological curriculum: Leadership and technology. *Tech Trends, 40*(5), 28–30.

Munoz, Z. C. (1993). A technophile looks at technology, education, and art. *Art Education, 46*(6), 48–49.

Niess, N. L. (1991). Computer-using teachers in a new decade. *Education and Computing, 7,* (3–4), 151–156.

Norris, C., Smolka, J., & Soloway, E. (2000). Extracting value from research: A guide for the perplexed. *Technology & Learning, 20*(11), 45–48.

Norum, K. E., Grabinger, R. S., & Duffield, J. A. (1999). Healing the universe is an inside job: Teachers' views on integrating technology. *Journal of Technology and Teacher Education, 7*(3), 187–203.

Pelgrum, W. J. (2001). Obstacles to the integration of ICT in education: Results from a worldwide educational assessment. *Computers and Education, 37*(2), 163–178.

Pool, C. R. (1997). A new digital literacy: A conversation with Paul Gilster. *Educational Leadership, 55*(3), 6–11.

Postman, N. (1992). *Technopoly: The surrender of culture to technology* New York: Vintage Books.

Reiser, R. A. (1994). Examining the planning practices of teachers: Reflections on three years of research. *Educational Technology, 34*(3), 11–16.

Reiser, R., & Salisbury, D. (1995). Instructional technology and public education in the United States: The next decade. In G. Anglin (Ed.), *Instructional technology: Past, present, and future* (pp. 227–235). Englewood, CO: Libraries Unlimited.

Rhee, R. (2,000, July 8). Quantity vs. quality. *Korea Herald,* p. 1.

Riedl, J. (1995). *The integrated technology classroom: Building self-reliant learners.* Boston: Allyn and Bacon.

Ritchie, D., & Wilburg, K. (1994). Educational variables influencing technology integration *Journal of Technology and Teacher Education, 2*(2), 143–153.

Robey, E. (Ed.) (1992). *Opening the doors: Using technology to improve education for students with disabilities.* Macro International Inc.

Schrum, L. M. (1995). *Telecommunications for personal and professional uses: A case study.* Paper presented at the annual meeting of the American Educational Research Association, San Francisco, CA (ERIC Document Reproduction Service No. ED 385 230).

Seels, B. B., & Richey, R. C. (1994). *Instructional technology: The definition and domains of the field.* Washington, DC. AECT.

Senge, P. M. (1990). *The fifth discipline: The art & practice of the learning organization.* New York: Doubleday/Currency.

Sheingold, K. & Hadley, M. (1990). *Accomplished teachers: Integrating computers into classroom practice.* New York: Bank Street College of Education, Center for Technology in Education.

Shelton, M., & Jones, M. (1996). Staff development that works! A tale of four t's. *NAASP Bulletin, 80*(582), 99–105.

Sivin-Kachala, J., & Bialo, E. R. (1995). *Report on the effectiveness of technology in schools 1990–1994.* Washington, DC: Software Publishers Association.

Snider, R. C. (1992). The machine in the classroom. *Phi Delta Kappan, 74*(4), 316–323.

Taylor, D. R. (2000). Developing powerful learning communities using technology. *AACTE Briefs, 21*(14), 4–5.

Tiene, D., & Luft, P. (2001). Teaching in a technology-rich classroom. *Educational Technology, 41*(4), 23–31.

Trotter, A. (1997). Taking technology's measure. In *Technology counts: Schools and reform in the information age.* (Vol. 17, Issue 11, pp. 6–11), *Education Week.*

Tucker, M. (1992). The genie in the bottle. *Electronic Learning, 12*(3), 50.

Valdez, G., McNabb, M., Foertsch, M., Anderson, M., Hawkes, M., & Raack, L. (2000). *Computer-based technology and learning: Evolving uses and expectations.* Oak Brook, IL: North Central Regional Laboratory.

Viadero, D. (1997). A tool for learning. In *Technology Counts: Schools and reform in the information age* (Vol. 17, Issue 11, pp. 12–18), *Education Week.*

Waddoups, G. L., Wentworth, N. M., & Earle, R. S. (2001, in press). Faculty learning to use technology: PT3 supported systemic reform initiatives in teacher education. *Tech Trends.*

Wager, W. (1992). Educational technology: A broader vision. *Educational and Urban Society, 24*(4), 454–465.

Zehr, M. A. (1997). Teaching the teachers. In *Technology Counts: Schools and reform in the information age* (Vol. 17, Issue 11, pp. 24–29). *Education Week.*

Rodney S. Earle is Professor of Teacher Education at Brigham Young University, Provo, Utah (e-mail: rodney_earle@byu.edu).

Using Data to Differentiate Instruction

In an age of standards, using assessment data to differentiate instruction is essential.

Kay Brimijoin, Ede Marquissee, and Carol Ann Tomlinson

At Redlands Elementary School, Ms. Martez's 5th graders are studying the math concept of greatest common factor.[1] Following an interactive lesson, students participate in a self-assessment procedure that Ms. Martez has created. Using a car windshield metaphor, she asks,

> How many [of you] are clear as glass about how greatest common factor works? How many have bugs on your windshield? How many have windshields covered with mud? (Brimijoin, 2002)

On the basis of their spontaneous self-assessment of "glass, bugs, and mud" and their earlier work on greatest common factor, Ms. Martez assigns students to three follow-up activities. With only a few exceptions, the students' self-assessment matches what Ms. Martez had determined from her pre-assessment.

Because the group of students who are as "clear as glass" understands and can apply greatest common factor at both the conceptual and skill levels, she has these students use a Euclidean algorithm to find the greatest common factor in a series of exercises. A group of "buggy" students—who understand the basic concept of greatest common factor, but still need to build their confidence through application—play a greatest common factor game that Ms. Martez has created. And she sends the "muddy" group to sort factors in a giant Venn diagram constructed of two hula-hoops. This oversized graphic organizer provides a kinesthetic and interpersonal learning experience for those who need additional practice to master the basic concept and skills.

During this time, Ms. Martez offers support and answers questions using a red-yellow-green cup system to prioritize student requests for assistance. A student sets a red cup on his or her desk to say "I can't go on without help." A yellow cup means that the student has questions but isn't completely blocked, and a green cup means that the student understands what he or she is doing. Two students tell Ms. Martez they are "really buggy *and* muddy," and she immediately announces the opening of a "math clinic" where she works on intensive, explicit instruction.

Because Ms. Martez had devoted time at the beginning of the year to talk with her students about the importance of gathering assessment data directly from them, students engage in their tasks smoothly and do not question groupings or complain about assignments. She had modeled the windshield strategy and together she and her class had created a generic rubric for each degree of understanding. Teaching students this self-assessment technique helped accustom them to instruction differentiated by readiness and structures that support student-centered learning (Tomlinson, 1999).

Three-Dimensional Data Collection

For Ms. Martez, informal and formal data about student learning not only shape instruction but also determine its effectiveness. She uses multiple methods of data collection and views the process as dynamic and continuous. She sees her role as data collector in three dimensions: to determine students' prior understanding and achievement, to track their responses to moderate challenges, and to measure their outcomes against expected performance goals (Brimijoin, 2002; Bruner, 1963; Tomlinson, 1995).

Pre-Assessment

Ms. Martez uses a wide array of pre-assessments when teaching new content. During a math lesson introducing basic algebra concepts, for instance, she asks students,

> What do you suppose it means to think algebraically? Take out your math logs and write, even if you write that you don't know.

Oral questioning, written journal prompts, objective tests, webbing, K-W-L (What do you *know*? What do you still *want* to know? What did you *learn*?) charts, group discussions, and brainstorming sessions provide rich data about students' existing schema, including critical misconceptions (Bransford, Brown, & Cocking, 2000).

Moderate Challenges

Ms. Martez believes that because students differ in their grasp of key concepts, she must modify her instruction to help them build knowledge, refine skills, and apply understandings on increasingly sophisticated tasks (Wiggins & McTighe, 1998). Assessment helps her modify instruction so that each student is appropriately challenged. She uses paper-and-pencil or performance-based formative assessments, including objective tests or quizzes, quickwrites, essays, and open-ended problems, varying the type according to the content being studied. She also develops a clear sense of what the culminating assessment will be when she first lays out the lesson or unit.

Rather than seeing assessment as an end-of-lesson or end-of-unit phenomenon, Ms. Martez incorporates it at the beginning, at the end, and everywhere in between.

Ms. Martez gives her students "task cards," which specify the steps in a learning process or experience. These cards include a set of directions for a task in order to facilitate independent learning and nurture autonomy. For example, each of Ms. Martez's learning groups had task cards with step-by-step directions to guide them through their assignments on greatest common factor. The task cards also frequently include rubrics that spell out performance expectations on assignments.

At the end of a lesson, students write in their journal a one-line description or an answer to a question about what they have learned in the lesson. Their responses are "exit tickets" for formative or ongoing assessment to help the teacher evaluate the effectiveness of a lesson design and keep instruction focused on key learning goals and individual needs.

Standards Testing

Teaching in a grade that requires state standardized assessments forces Ms. Martez to reconcile her "gotta get it covered and memorized by testing time" mentality and her belief in concept-centered differentiated instruction. She confesses to feeling conflicted about working wholeheartedly in two seemingly contradictory worlds of teaching and learning.

Three weeks before state standards testing, Ms. Martez asks students to go through their math books and select topics that they have mastered and those that need more work. She reflects on the results and decides to set up centers on such topics as

fractions, place value, geometry, and statistics, cycling students through centers related to their areas of need, and assigning "experts" to assist their peers.

Using Assessment to Target Learner Needs

Ms. Martez uses questioning and observing to differentiate instruction and ensure that her instruction is a good match for the varied needs of her students (Brimijoin, 2002). She adjusts questions or performance tasks to be more structured for those who are struggling with a concept and more abstract for those who have mastered the concept. Rather than seeing assessment as an end-of-lesson or end-of-unit phenomenon, Ms. Martez incorporates it at the beginning, at the end, and everywhere in between.

Ms. Martez invests much time and energy in mapping the "start and finish" by first constructing a big picture of assessment results that students bring with them. By the 5th grade at Redlands Elementary, students have one set of state standards test scores from 3rd grade and one set of nationally standardized scores from 4th grade. Ms. Martez enters all these scores on a spreadsheet. During individual conferences, Ms. Martez guides students in setting target goals for their progress and areas of emphasis for her instruction. At the end of the year, she enters all 5th grade scores from state standardized tests and calculates the percentage gains for each student and for the class overall.

Informal and formal data about student learning not only shape instruction but also determine its effectiveness.

At the end of this past year, 74 percent of her students passed the reading assessment, an overall gain of 27 percentage points over their 3rd grade test results; 58 percent passed math, a gain of 5 percentage points; 58 percent passed social studies, a gain of 24 percentage points; and 74 percent passed the science assessment, a gain of 32 percentage points (Brimijoin, 2002). Ms. Martez attributes the improvement in test score results chiefly to her use of pre-assessment, self-assessment, and ongoing assessment to differentiate instruction for individual learning needs:

The facts stuck because they were scaffolded into existing information, taught at the students' readiness levels, hooked in with interests, and nailed down with instruction targeted to the students' strongest learning styles.... Differentiation works in a standardized testing world.... We can't afford not to do it and expect to meet state standards, especially in low socioeconomic areas like Redlands. (Brimijoin, 2002, p. 263)

Ms. Martez uses the results of test score analysis to reflect on her teaching, comparing her curriculum design and instruction from one year to the next, noting strengths as well as weaknesses, and identifying questions that still need answering in order to refine her practice (Zeichner & Liston, 1996).

The students are also data collectors. They accept responsibility for monitoring their own progress and see that they have a role in shaping instruction. Ms. Martez weaves information gleaned from journal responses with formative quiz and test results. She sees assessment as a powerful tool to be used through the whole process of teaching and learning; one that demands the same kind of evaluation skills that good teachers use for effective management.

Ms. Martez advises other teachers that carefully articulated, continuous assessment that drives curriculum design "maximizes teaching time, streamlines instruction, and facilitates learning for all students." She insists that assessment is not "just another plate added to the 12-piece service," but a means of enhancing student and teacher performance.

Note

1. This article uses pseudonyms for the teacher and school.

References

Bransford, J., Brown, A., & Cocking, R. (Eds.). (2000). *How people learn: Brain, mind, experience, and school.* Washington, DC: National Academy Press.

Brimijoin, K. (2002). *A journey toward expertise in differentiation: A preservice and inservice teacher make their way.* Unpublished doctoral dissertation. University of Virginia, Charlottesville.

Bruner, J. (1963). *The process of education.* New York: Vintage Books.

Tomlinson, C. (1995). *Differentiating instruction for mixed-ability classrooms.* Alexandria, VA: ASCD.

Tomlinson, C. (1999). *The differentiated classroom: Responding to the needs of all learners.* Alexandria, VA: ASCD.

Wiggins, G., & McTighe, J. (1998). *Understanding by design.* Alexandria, VA: ASCD.

Zeichner, K., & Liston, D. (1996). *Reflective teaching: An introduction.* Mahwah, NJ: Lawrence Erlbaum Associates.

Kay Brimijoin is an assistant professor at Sweet Briar College, Sweet Briar, VA 24595; brimijoin@sbc.edu. **Ede Marquissee** teaches 6th grade at Summit Middle School, 4509 Homestead Road, Fort Wayne, IN 46814; emarquissee@sacs.k12.in.us. **Carol Ann Tomlinson** is a professor at the Curry School of Education, University of Virginia, Ruffner Hall, Charlottesville, VA 22904; cat3y@virginia.edu

UNIT 5

Motivation and Classroom Management

Unit Selections

Key Points to Consider

- Discuss several ways to motivate both at-risk and typical students. What difference is there?

- Why should motivational style be consistent with instructional techniques?

- How are motivation and classroom management related?

- Discuss several ways to discipline both typical students and those with exceptionalities.

- How are classroom management and discipline different? Discuss whether discipline can be developed within students, or whether it must be imposed by teachers, supporting your argument with data derived from your reading.

 Links: www.dushkin.com/online/
These sites are annotated in the World Wide Web pages.

Canada's Schoolnet Staff Room
http://www.schoolnet.ca/home/e/

The term *motivation* is used by educators to describe the processes of initiating, directing, and sustaining goal-oriented behavior. Motivation is a complex phenomenon, involving many factors that affect an individual's choice of action and perseverance in completing tasks. Furthermore, the reasons why people engage in particular behaviors can only be inferred; motivation cannot be directly measured.

Several theories of motivation, each highlighting different reasons for sustained goal-oriented behavior, have been proposed. We will discuss three of them: behavioral, humanistic, and cognitive. The behavioral theory of motivation suggests that an important reason for engaging in behavior is that reinforcement follows the action. If the reinforcement is controlled by someone else and is arbitrarily related to the behavior (such as money, a token, or a smile), then the motivation is extrinsic. In contrast, behavior may also be initiated and sustained for intrinsic reasons such as curiosity or mastery.

Humanistic approaches to motivation are concerned with the social and psychological needs of individuals. Humans are motivated to engage in behavior to meet these needs. Abraham Maslow, a founder of humanistic psychology, proposes that there is a hierarchy of needs that directs behavior, beginning with physiological and safety needs and progressing to self-actualization. Some other important needs that influence motivation are affiliation and belonging with others, love, self-es-

teem, influence with others, recognition, status, competence, achievement, and autonomy.

The dominant view of motivation in the educational psychology literature is the cognitive approach. This set of theories proposes that our beliefs about our successes and failures affect our expectations and goals concerning future performance. Students who believe that their success is due to their abilities and efforts are motivated toward mastery of skills. Students who blame their failures on inadequate abilities have low self-efficacy and tend to set ability and performance goals that protect their self-image.

In this unit's first selection, Martin Covington addresses the classic distinctions between intrinsic and extrinsic reinforcement. In the second article, Marge Scherer focuses on how to encourage a love of learning. She reflects on a conversation with Mihaly Csikszentmihalyi and his concept of "flow" in which a high level of challenge is met with the skills to meet the challenge. In the final article about motivation, Howard Margolis and Patrick McCabe show the interconnection between motivation and self-efficacy. They suggest that teachers can improve self efficacy by "stacking the deck for success," if they teach needed learning strategies and facilitative attributions, reinforce effort and persistence, and help students create personal goals.

No matter how effectively students are motivated, teachers always need to exercise management of behavior in the classroom. Classroom management is more than controlling the behavior of students or disciplining them following misbehavior. Instead, teachers need to initiate and maintain a classroom environment that supports successful teaching and learning. The skills that effective teachers use include preplanning, deliberate introduction of rules and procedures, immediate assertiveness, continual monitoring, consistent feedback to students, and specific consequences.

The next four articles address specific classroom management issues facing teachers today. The first article, "When Children Make Rules," shows how constructivism extends to classroom management. The next article by Robert and Jana Marzano emphasizes the importance of quality student-teacher relationships as a basis for classroom management. The third article presents proactive strategies for handling discipline problems that do occur, so that the situation is kept from escalating. The final article in this section speaks to the subject of corporal punishment in the classroom as a means of discipline, and how children's rights must be protected.

Intrinsic Versus Extrinsic Motivation in Schools: A Reconciliation

Abstract

   This article explores the nature of the relationships between intrinsic and extrinsic motivation in schools, and in particular examines critically the assertion that these processes are necessarily antagonistic. The weight of evidence suggests that rewards in the form of school grades and the focus of many students on doing well, gradewise, need not necessarily interfere with learning for its own sake. Educational implications of these findings are considered. One such implication is that focusing on students' interests can be a valuable motivational strategy.

Keywords:
   motivation; achievement; appreciation

Martin V. Covington[1]

Department of Psychology, University of California at Berkeley, Berkeley, California

   When psychologists speak of motivation, they typically refer to the reasons that individuals are aroused to action. Over the past 50 years, two quite different kinds of reasons have emerged in the thinking of psychologists: intrinsic and extrinsic reasons. Individuals are said to be driven to act for extrinsic reasons when they anticipate some kind of tangible payoff, such as good grades, recognition, or gold stars. These rewards are said to be extrinsic because they are unrelated to the action. In effect, the activity becomes a means to an end. By contrast, individuals are said to be intrinsically motivated when they engage in activities for their own sake. In this instance, the rewards reside in the actions themselves; that is, the actions are their own reinforcement. Put differently, in the case of intrinsic motivation, the repetition of an action does not depend as much

on some external inducement as on the satisfaction derived from overcoming a personal challenge, learning something new, or discovering things of personal interest.

   For generations, observers have extolled the virtues of learning for its own sake, not only because of the benefits of personal growth or enhanced well-being, but also because intrinsically based learning is the handmaiden to better, more efficient learning. For example, intrinsically engaged students are more likely than extrinsically driven students to employ deep-level, sophisticated study strategies in their work (Ames & Archer, 1988). Perhaps most noteworthy for establishing causal, not merely correlational, relationships are studies (e.g., Schunk, 1996) in which students were randomly assigned to varying achievement conditions. Those students who were

directed to work for the goals of mastery, exploration, and appreciation demonstrated greater task involvement and used more effective learning strategies than children who were directed to focus on their performance alone.

   At the same time, experts also lament the prospects of encouraging intrinsic engagement in a world controlled by extrinsic rewards (e.g., Kohn, 1993). My purpose here is to explore briefly the nature of the relationship between intrinsic and extrinsic motivation in schools, and in particular to examine critically the assertion that these processes are necessarily antagonistic, such that the will to learn for its own sake is inhibited or even destroyed by the offering of extrinsic rewards and incentives like school grades.

   It is important to be clear about what the issue is. The issue is not that offering tangible rewards will necessarily interfere with learning. To the contrary, offering students tangible rewards sometimes actually increases learning, especially if the assignment is seen as a chore or boring. Rather, the issue is whether offering rewards focuses undue attention on the tangible payoffs, thereby decreasing students' appreciation of what they are learning.

OBSTACLES TO INTRINSIC ENGAGEMENT

The potentially destructive impact of tangible rewards on the will to learn for its own sake has been documented in several ways. First, there is the prospect that once these rewards are no longer available, students will show little or no inclination to continue in their studies (Covington, 1998). Second, there is the possibility that offering rewards to students for doing what already interests them may also undercut personal task involvement. For example, if a teacher tries to encourage intrinsic values directly, say, by praising students for pursuing a hobby, then, paradoxically, these interests may actually be discouraged. This phenomenon is the so-called overjustification effect (Lepper, Greene, & Nisbett, 1973). According to one interpretation, such discouragement occurs because the value of an already justifiable activity becomes suspect by the promise of additional rewards—hence the term overjustification—so that the individual reasons, "If someone has to pay me to do this, then it must not be worth doing for its own sake."

The goal of fostering a love of learning is complicated not only by offering or withholding tangible rewards, but also by the scarcity of these rewards. In many classrooms, an inadequate supply of rewards (e.g., good grades) is distributed by teachers unequally, with the greatest number of rewards going to the best performers or to the fastest learners. This arrangement is based on the false assumption that achievement is maximized when students compete for a limited number of rewards. Although this may maximize motivation, students are aroused for the wrong reasons—to win over others and to avoid losing—and these reasons eventually lead to failure and resentment (Covington, 1998). In this competitive context, grades stand as a mark of worthiness, because it is widely assumed in our society that one is only as worthy as one's ability to achieve competitively.

If high grades not only are important for the tangible future benefits they bestow—being the gateway to prestigious occupations—but also serve as an indication of one's personal worth, then what becomes of the valuing of learning in the scramble for grades? Is not the valuing and appreciation of learning marginalized? No, apparently not. There can be little doubt that students also value learning, irrespective of the grades they receive (see Covington, 1999).

A RECONCILIATION

How can we resolve this apparent contradiction? The observations of students themselves provide some answers (Covington, 1999; Covington & Wiedenhaupt, 1997).

First, students readily acknowledge that they strive for the highest grades possible, but—and this is the important point—different students have different reasons for a grade focus. It is these reasons that in turn determine the degree to which students become intrinsically engaged. For instance, when students strive for high grades as a mark of approval, to impress other people, or to avoid failure, they will value learning only to the extent that it serves to aggrandize their ability status, not for any inherent attraction of the material itself. If, by contrast, students have a task-oriented purpose in striving for high grades (e.g., if they use grades as feedback for how they can improve and learn more), then they will appreciate their accomplishments for their positive proper-

ties. In effect, it is not necessarily the presence of grades per se, or even a dominant grade focus, that influences the degree to which learning is appreciated. Rather, students' valuing of what they learn depends on their initial reasons for learning and the meaning they attach to their grades. This implies that striving for good grades and caring for learning are not necessarily incompatible goals. The degree of compatibility of these goals is influenced by the reasons for learning.

Second, the degree to which students become intrinsically engaged in their schoolwork depends in part on whether they are achieving their grade goals, that is, whether they feel successful. On the one hand, being successful in one's studies promotes an appreciation for what one is learning. On the other hand, falling short of one's grade goals may intensify one's concentration on doing better (to the point that appreciation of the subject matter is excluded), divert attention to protecting one's sense of worth, or cause feelings of hopelessness about ever succeeding, feelings that bode ill for both the goal of appreciation and the goal of achievement. Thus, the degree of goal compatibility is also influenced by experiences of success and failure.

Third, students also indicate that they often manipulate academic circumstances to create a tolerable balance between grades and caring. The most frequent strategies involve making school more interesting by deliberately seeking out what is of interest to them, even in the case of boring assignments, or arranging a course of study, or even a college major, around personal interests. Thus, the compatibility of grades and caring is also influenced by personal interests.

From these observations, we can conclude that students are more likely to value what they are learning, and to enjoy the process, (a) when they are achieving their grade goals; (b) when the dominant reasons for learning are task-oriented reasons, not self-aggrandizing or failure-avoiding reasons; and (c) when what they are studying is of personal interest.

The role of personal interest in this equation is especially noteworthy. Although it is not surprising that people enjoy learning more about what already interests them, what is intriguing is the extent to which pursuing one's own interests offsets the potentially negative effects of receiving a disappointing grade. In fact, the evidence suggests that a student's appreciation for what he or she is learning is far greater when the student is failing but interested in the task than when the same student is succeeding, gradewise, but has little interest in the subject-matter content.

A related point concerning this equation also deserves comment. Receiving a good grade, especially for interesting work, increases, not decreases, intrinsic engagement. This finding seems to contradict the previously mentioned expectation that providing people with tangible payoffs for pursuing what already interests them will dampen their enthusiasm. Students themselves offer several plausible explanations for why these worries may be exaggerated, if not groundless. Based on their experiences, some students report anecdotally that doing well causes positive feelings like pride, which in turn increases their enthusiasm for learning. Other anecdotal observations suggest that doing well reduces worry about failing, so that students are freer to explore what is most interesting. And, according to yet other students, being successful stimulates them to study more, and the more they learn, the more interesting the material is likely to become. Whatever the explanation, it seems that the effects of tangible payoffs on intrinsic processes are far from simple.

EDUCATIONAL IMPLICATIONS

What practical steps do these findings suggest for how schools can

serve both the goal of disseminating knowledge and the goal of promoting an appreciation of what is learned in the face of an ever-present grade focus?

First, the most obvious implication is that a major instructional goal should be to arrange schooling around the personal interests of students. Second, obviously learning cannot always be arranged around personal preferences, nor can students always succeed. Nonetheless, instructional practices can alter the meaning of failure when it occurs. Basically, this step involves eliminating the climate of scarcity of rewards by defining success not in the relative sense of outperforming others, but rather absolutely, that is, in terms of whether students measure up to a given standard of performance, irrespective of how many other students do well or poorly (Covington & Teel, 1996). When well-defined standards of performance are provided, the failure to achieve them tends to motivate students to try harder because failure implies falling short of a goal, not falling short as a person.

Third, in addition to creating grading systems that encourage intrinsic reasons for learning, teachers should provide payoffs that actively strengthen and reward these positive reasons. Although students focus primarily on the prospects of getting a good grade, they are also more likely to invest greater time and energy (beyond what is necessary for the grade) in those tasks for which there are additional tangible, yet intrinsically oriented payoffs. These payoffs include the opportunity to share the results of their work with others, or the chance to explain more deeply and personally why what they learned was important to them. This suggestion implies that, far from being incompatible, intrinsic and extrinsic reasons for learning are both encouraged by tangible rewards, but by different kinds of tangible rewards. This proposition sheds an entirely new light on the concerns raised by many experts re-

garding the overjustification effect. It is not the offering of tangible rewards that undercuts personal task engagement so much as it is the absence of those kinds of payoffs that encourage and recognize the importance of being involved in and caring about what one is learning.

Finally, students are the first to acknowledge a conflict between the goals of striving for high grades and enjoying learning. However, the conflict arises, they say, not out of any incompatibility of goals. Rather, the demands of school leave little room to pursue either goal fully, let alone to pursue the two goals together. As a result, students must prioritize these objectives, a process that typically favors the goal of striving for grades, and they lament what they forfeit. But prioritizing is not the same as incompatibility. The recommendations made in this review can act to balance these priorities more in favor of intrinsic engagement and a love of learning.

Recommended Reading

Cameron, J., & Pierce, W. D. (1994). Reinforcement, reward and intrinsic motivation: A meta-analysis. *Review of Educational Research, 64*, 363–423.

Condry, J., & Koslowski, B. (1979). Can education be made "intrinsically interesting" to children? In D. Katz (Ed.), *Current topics in early childhood education* (Vol. II, pp. 227–260). Norwood, NJ: Ablex.

Cordova, D. I., & Lepper, M. R. (1996). Intrinsic motivation and the process of learning: Beneficial effects of contextualization, personalization and choice. *Journal of Educational Psychology, 88*, 715–730.

Covington, M. V. (1992). *Making the grade: A self-worth perspective on motivation and school reform.* New York: Cambridge University Press.

Elliot, A. J., & Harackiewicz, J. M. (1996). Approach and avoidance achievement goals and intrinsic motivation: A mediational analysis. *Journal of Personality and Social Psychology, 70*, 461–475.

Note

1. Address correspondence to Martin V. Covington, Department of Psychology, 3210 Tolman Hall, University of California at Berkeley, Berkeley, CA 94720-1650.

References

Ames, C., & Archer, J. (1988). Achievement goals in the classroom: Student learning strategies and motivation processes. *Journal of Educational Psychology, 80*, 260–267.

Covington, M. V. (1998). *The will to learn: A guide for motivating young people.* New York: Cambridge University Press.

Covington, M. V. (1999). Caring about learning: The nature and nurturing of subject-matter appreciation. *Educational Researchers, 34*, 127–136.

Covington, M. V., & Teel, K. M. (1996). *Overcoming student failure: Changing motives and incentives for learning.* Washington, DC: American Psychological Association.

Covington, M. V., & Wiedenhaupt, S. (1997). Turning work into play: The nature and nurturing of intrinsic task engagement. In R. Perry & J. C. Smart (Eds.), *Effective teaching in higher education: Research and practice, special edition* (pp. 101–114). New York: Agathon Press.

Kohn, A. (1993). *Punished by rewards.* New York: Houghton Mifflin.

Lepper, M. R., Greene, D., & Nisbett, R. E. (1973). Undermining children's intrinsic interest with extrinsic rewards: A test of the "overjustification" hypothesis. *Journal of Personality and Social Psychology, 28*, 129–137.

Schunk, D. H. (1996). Goal and self-evaluative influences during children's cognitive skill learning. *American Educational Research Journal, 33*, 359–382.

Do Students Care About Learning?

A Conversation with Mihaly Csikszentmihalyi

Learning to enjoy the intrinsic rewards of hard work is essential to successful human development, Mihaly Csikszentmihalyi, author of Becoming Adult: How Teenagers Prepare for the World of Work, *tells us. Here he talks with* Educational Leadership *about how to help students seek out the challenging and engaging activities that will propel them on their way toward becoming productive adults.*

Marge Scherer

In *your study, you identified students who stood out from the crowd because they, more than their peers, could find enjoyment in both work and play. You also found students who were disengaged and passive about most of the activities they participated in. What was the context of your longitudinal study?*

With the help from a grant from the Alfred P. Sloan Foundation, we identified 1,000 children who were in 6th, 8th, 10th, and 12th grades in 12 school districts from Orlando, Florida, to Long Beach, California, and everywhere in between. Nine years later, we are still following some of the participants as young adults, although a much smaller group of them.

We selected students randomly. We were not looking for children who enjoyed school or did not enjoy school. We just tried to get as much of a cross-section as possible. We developed questionnaires and interviewed these students, but we obtained most of our data through giving each student a programmable pager for a week. This pager would go off eight times a day, early morning to 11 P.M., at random moments. Whenever the pager signaled, the students would take out a little booklet and write where they were, what they were doing, what they were thinking about, their level of concentration, how happy they were, and how creative they felt when doing different activities.

They reported about 30 times during the week, so we received about 30,000 reports. And that allowed us to begin to see these children's experiences, the feelings and thoughts they had during the day, both at school and out of school. For instance, every time the pager went off, they had to say whether what they were doing was more like play, more like work, or like neither work nor play.

Was life more like work or play for these teenagers?

About 30 percent of the time they stated that it was like work; 30 percent of the time, they said that what they were doing was like play; 30 percent neither; and they reported that for 10 percent of their time, what they were doing was like both work and play.

In your follow-up studies, you concluded that students who often say that what they are doing is like both work and play are more likely to go on to college or make a successful transition to work.

Those students who say that whatever they do is more like work seem to do well in high school. Although they say that what they are doing is work and they don't enjoy it at the moment, they record on the response sheet that the activity is important

to their future. So they understand that, "Okay. This is work. It's not pleasant. But it will profit me in the future."

It's when they are participating in extracurricular activities that students most often say that they are both working and playing.

Those kids who say that what they do is mostly play enjoy their activities, but they don't think of them as being important for the future. But the best situation is when a person sees a life activity as both work and play. Unfortunately, only about 10 percent of the time do students report this experience. Some kids never report that they have this experience. The worst thing is to frequently feel that what you do is neither enjoyable right now nor good preparation for the future.

You say affluent students are more likely to say they are enjoying their activities than poorer students. Did you see any differences in attitudes among other groups of students?

Males much more than females say that what they do is play. Caucasian students play more than Asians, Hispanics, or African Americans. The survey has a lot of markers in terms of ethnicity, class, and gender. We found that those who see what they do as play get into better colleges after they leave high school. College selection procedures favor kids who do well academically but who also are engaged in original or interesting extracurricular activities.

It's when they are participating in extracurricular activities that students most often say that they are both working and playing.

What is it about extracurricular activities that makes them engaging to students?

Students say that they are doing something that is important to them. The activity is voluntary to a large extent. Kids can choose to do things that match their own interests and skills. So they are doing something fun. But at the same time they are doing work to adult specifications. If you work on the high school newspaper, you have to observe the deadlines and you produce something that is real.

Our youngest son, for instance, was uninterested in school until he began to hang out with the theater group and started building sets, doing the lighting and sound effects, painting the scenery, doing carpentry, and so forth. Once he did that, he became more able to focus on everything. And now he's teaching at MIT.

Flow describes the spontaneous, effortless experience you achieve when you have a close match between a high level of challenge and the skills to meet the challenge.

His academic classes did not offer him an opportunity to meet serious adult standards, but the extracurricular activity did.

Explain what you mean by the flow experience, the title of your earlier book.

Flow describes the spontaneous, effortless experience you achieve when you have a close match between a high level of challenge and the skills you need to meet the challenge. Flow happens when a person is completely involved in the task, is concentrating very deeply, and knows moment by moment what the next steps should be. If you're playing music, you know what note will come next, and you know how to play that note. You have a goal and you are getting feedback. The experience is almost addictive and very rewarding.

Small children are in flow most of the time as they learn to walk and talk and other new things. They choose what to do and they match their skills with challenges. Unfortunately, they begin to lose this feeling once they go to school because they can't choose their goals and they can't choose the level at which they operate. They become increasingly passive. We find that in Europe and the United States, about 15 percent of adults really can't remember any experience that seems like flow. A similar proportion, about 15 percent, claim that they have the flow experience several times a day.

We've published many articles on multiple intelligences and learning styles. Do you think people of a certain kind of intelligence are more likely to have the flow experience?

It depends on whether there are opportunities for your particular skill or intelligence. If you are musically inclined, for instance, and there is no opportunity to play music at your school and no other place to get the experience of playing, then you are at a disadvantage. In some cultures, there will be opportunities for one kind of intelligence more than for another.

The learning disability that may be an obstacle to experiencing flow is the inability to concentrate. Concentration is one of the hallmarks of the flow experience. If you have, for instance, an attention deficit, it may be difficult to get focused enough.

Have you found that any curriculum subjects lend themselves to more engagement than others?

Yes. There have been quite a few dissertations on this topic. Typically, students rate history the worst subject for engagement, whereas they rate anything having to do with computers high. And vocational subjects seem to be better than academic subjects for encouraging engagement.

Students get flow from group work, from individual tasks, and from quizzes much more often than they do from listening to the teacher or from watching audiovisuals.

We're in a testing culture now, with much emphasis on standards and high-stakes assessments. Is this new priority deflating students' love of learning, or is it beneficial because it offers challenges?

To the extent that the results of the tests are taken seriously, testing worries me. If a test

is fair and not above the heads of most of the kids, then students can take the test as a game and a challenge. Flow is easiest to experience when you are challenged, have clear goals, and get clear feedback. Now, if you're listening to a teacher, all of those things are missing. There's nothing to keep your attention focused. Whereas in a test, you have to pay attention. There is a challenge. The goals are clear. You can lose yourself in the activity. Unless it's way too difficult or way too easy, you can enjoy taking a test. But that doesn't mean that one should take any test very seriously because test results don't correlate much with anything.

Not with higher achievement or success in life?

Not that I know of. I would be interested in seeing the evidence that scores on tests correlate with happiness or success in life.

What recommendations do you have for teachers who want to structure instructional activities to achieve more flow or more engagement for students?

The more they can show the relevance of what they're doing to the life of the student, the better. That's the first and most obvious requirement. You also have to make clear the goal of every lesson. The student must know what he or she is supposed to achieve at the end. And teachers need a way to find out how well the students are learning. Computer-assisted teaching can be quite useful because there you can see your progress and you can change and correct your work as you move along. The fact that students feel positive about group activities suggests the need for more group work. There's too little group activity in high school except in science labs where two or three kids have to solve a problem or learn something together. There are many things that adults could do to make learning more engaging to students.

On the other hand, sometimes it seems to me that the best thing would be to forbid children to go to school until they can demonstrate that they have a real interest in something. Of course, such a system would be fair only if we had preschools for all children, where they could be exposed to a stimulating environment in a playful setting.

Education should be available to everyone, obviously. But education should not be an obligation, but rather a privilege that you earn by showing that you're curious about some part of the world. You get your education through that curiosity. The role of the teacher would then be to find the material that would allow the student to explore his or her curiosity. Because no matter what you're curious about, if you are really curious, you will have to learn everything else.

Whether the topic is bugs or stars or singing, there are connections. There is mathematics behind the music and chemistry behind the animals. Once the students are hooked on their interest, the teacher should be the gatekeeper to the enormous richness of information in the world. The role of the teacher is not to convey the same content to a captive audience, which becomes almost immediately aversive to most children.

I'm interested in how you became interested in the idea of flow. Was it an experience of your own that led you to find out more about it?

Essentially, I was interested in psychology. At the time, you couldn't get a degree in psychology by studying happiness or well-being, but creativity was something you could study.

So I studied creativity in artists. And I was struck by how these artists would get completely lost in what they were doing for long periods of time. And yet, once they finished the canvas, they never looked at it again. Most of them weren't trying to sell their art. The finished painting was an excuse for them to paint. The process of painting was the reward that motivated them.

So I started wondering, Does this happen in other aspects of life? It turned out that people play music for the same reason. They play music to go on the journey, not to reach the destination. In sports, it is the same. I thought that the experience that made the activity so rewarding would be different in music or chess or rock climbing. Instead, what was so surprising was how similarly everyone described how they felt, even though what they were doing was so different.

And for yourself, what are the activities that give you the experience of flow?

When I was in high school, I played chess competitively. I used to paint. I did serious rock climbing. Later, I wrote fiction for *The New Yorker*. All of these are wonderful flow activities. Now I get creative enjoyment mostly from work and from hiking here in Montana with the family.

What family characteristics are most conducive to inspiring a love of learning?

Modeling is the best strategy. If the kid grows up seeing that his parents and other adults have no interest in anything except making money, it's unlikely that he or she will learn that it's fun to study or learn new things.

It boils down to the essentials: support and challenge. By challenge I mean high expectations, high standards, allowing the child a lot of independence, exposing students to new opportunities whenever possible. Support means simply that the child feels that the family as a whole is interested in every member's welfare. If the mother comes home tired, the kids will notice it and try to help her and so forth.

When their families give them both support and challenge, children are more likely to choose harder subjects in high school, get better grades, end up in better colleges, and have higher self-esteem in college or after college. If they receive support only, the kids tend to be happy and feel better about themselves, but they're not necessarily ambitious. They don't try to advance in school. They don't take harder classes.

If the family offers a lot of challenges but does not provide support, then the kids tend to do well in school, but they're not very happy. And if they have neither support nor challenge from the family, then it's bad all around. Support and challenge impart different strengths. Challenge gives children vision and direction, focus and perseverance. Support gives the serenity that allows them freedom from worry and fear.

I was struck by how these artists would get completely lost in what they were doing for long periods of time.

Teenagers often have a great deal of anxiety that gets in their way when they tackle a challenge. What's the antidote to anxiety?

Well, there are several. One is tutoring or help in the subjects that provide the most anxiety; another is building up students' strengths. It's often the case that once the students find something that they are really good at, then the anxiety disappears in the other situations. The parents should monitor what the child is interested in and give opportunities to excel at those subjects.

Going back to our youngest son, we weren't the ones who helped him. Once he found that he was as good as or better than others at something, it gave him the feeling that he could do other things, too.

We have an idea in education that we have to work on our weaknesses. To a certain extent, that makes sense. But it makes even more sense to work on the strengths. Because once someone has developed strengths, then everything else becomes easier. Second, if you feel miserable studying mathematics and you spend all your time learning mathematics, chances are you will never be very good at it anyway. If the child is good at photography, allow him or her to explore and develop those strengths.

So you wouldn't be a fan of the core curriculum that requires all students to master certain culturally important content?

No, I think that's kind of silly. Look at our presidents. President Bush was a low *C* student all his life, and so was Clinton until he got to be a Rhodes scholar. It's kind of hypocritical to expect that all children should be good across the board when most adults aren't successful at everything.

The important thing is to stimulate the curiosity, reinforce the curiosity, and build on the strengths of the child. And then you have a vibrant, lively community instead of people who have been stuffed with information that they don't care about.

Of all the students you interviewed, do any stand out as special examples?

Hundreds. One could write a shelf of novels on the lives of these kids.

There was a boy from Kansas City who, at age 12, was really in bad shape. He hated school. He had nothing that he liked. His self-esteem was low. He was in trouble with the school. We thought he would end up having serious trouble.

Then, in his senior year, when we looked at his booklet, we noticed that he had completely changed. He was happy. He felt strong self-esteem. He'd write that he was especially happy when he was looking for a valve or pipes at the hardware store or when he was carrying some rocks to his truck. When he was doing these things, he felt really positive. And we couldn't understand what he was talking about.

Challenge gives children vision and direction, focus and perseverance. Support give the serenity that allows them freedom from worry and fear.

In the interviews, we asked him, What is this about looking for a valve or carrying rocks? He told us that he had a business building koi ponds. At some time in his junior year, he saw one of these Japanese fishponds in somebody's garden, and he became so fascinated that he built one in his own yard and one for his neighbor. And then he started building ponds commercially. At age 18, he bought a panel truck for his koi pond business. And he felt tremendous. He had to learn everything from plumbing to biology: how the fish live and what to feed them. He learned chemistry. He learned mathematics to understand water pressure and volume. Senior year he did great in school. He ended up going to a community college and taking technical courses. That is what can happen when a kid makes a connection between something inside and an opportunity outside. To me, that's how education should be. To educate means to lead out. And we don't lead kids out. We kind of stop them. To educate is to expose kids to many possibilities until they find a connection between what's really important to them and the world out there. And then we must nurture and cultivate that connection.

Did the act of writing the journals help the students in your study become more active in their pursuit of learning?

Definitely. Some psychologists use journal writing as therapy. Once you really have an idea of what you're doing, you have a chance to take charge of your behavior. Often kids are put in a dependent state in school; they are not supposed to take any initiative except in what the teachers want them to do. Television puts them in another kind of dependent state. Many come to tacitly believe that they have no say over their own development as human beings.

Writing things down and reflecting on them is one of those things that makes a person ask, Why am I doing these things when I feel so bad when I do them? Why don't I do more of those things that make me happy?

Mihaly Csikszentmihalyi is the D.J. and C.S. Davidson Professor of Psychology at the Drucker School of Management, Claremont Graduate University in Claremont, California. He is the author or coauthor of 15 books, among them *Flow: The Psychology of Optimal Experience* (Harper & Row, 1990) and, with Barbara Schneider, *Becoming Adult: How Teenagers Prepare for the World of Work* (BasicBooks, 2000). **Marge Scherer** is Editor in Chief of *Educational Leadership*; el@ascd.org.

Self-Efficacy

A Key to Improving the Motivation of Struggling Learners

HOWARD MARGOLIS and PATRICK P. McCABE

Self-efficacy . . . influence[s] task choice, effort, persistence, and achievement. Compared with students who doubt their learning capacities, those who have a sense of efficacy for [particular tasks] participate more readily, work harder, persist longer when they encounter difficulties, and achieve at a higher level. . . . Students do not engage in activities they believe will lead to negative outcomes. (Schunk and Zimmerman 1997, 36)

Many struggling learners resist academics, thinking that they lack the ability to succeed, even if they expend great effort. In other words, these struggling learners have low rather than high self-efficacy for academics. It is widely believed that without sufficiently high self-efficacy, or the belief that they can succeed on specific academic tasks like homework, many struggling learners will not make the effort needed to master academics. They will give up or avoid tasks similar to those previously failed (Baker and Wigfield 1999; Bandura 1993; Casteel, Isom, and Jordan 2000; Chapman and Tunmer 2003; Henk and Melnick 1995; Jinks and Morgan 1999; Lipson and Wixson 1997; Lynch 2002; Pajares 1996; Pintrich and Schunk 2002; Schunk and Zimmerman 1997; Walker 2003).

A key to reversing this perspective—getting struggling learners with low self-efficacy to invest sufficient effort, to persist on tasks, to work to overcome difficulties, to take on increasingly challenging tasks, and to develop interest in academics—is for teachers to systematically stress the development of high self-efficacy. Fortunately, research suggests that teachers can often strengthen struggling learners' self-efficacy by linking new work to recent successes, teaching needed learning strategies, reinforcing effort and persistence, stressing peer modeling, teaching struggling learners to make facilitative attributions, and helping them identify or create personally important goals (Ormrod 2000; Pajares 2003; Pajares and Schunk 2001; Pintrich and Schunk 2002; Schunk 1999; Zimmerman

2000a). For these strategies to be effective, however, struggling learners with low self-efficacy must succeed on the very type of tasks they expect to fail. This strongly suggests that classwork must be at their proper instructional level, and homework at their proper independent level (Culyer 1996; Lipson and Wixson 1997). Work should challenge rather than frustrate them (Strickland, Ganske, and Monroe 2002). It should strengthen expectations of success rather than failure. To achieve this, teachers need to (a) give struggling learners work at their proper instructional and independent levels, and (b) adhere to instructional principles likely to improve self-efficacy.

Frustration, Instructional, and Independent Levels

Perhaps the most important academic decision teachers make for struggling learners is determining the levels at which to instruct them. Swanson's (1999) findings support this contention. As part of a larger meta-analysis assessing the effectiveness of interventions for students with learning disabilities, he identified the instructional components that best predicted outcomes. Two of the more important components were controlling task difficulty and sequencing tasks from easy to difficult. His findings reflect recommendations that reading specialists have made for decades—instruct students at their proper instructional and independent levels and avoid the frustration level (Leslie and Caldwell 2001; McCormick 2003; Newcomer 1986).

Criteria for instructional, independent, and frustration level tasks are often defined by objective measures (e.g., the percent of words correctly identified in oral reading) and are influenced by each struggling learner's unique perceptions about what is frustrating or anxiety provoking. What one struggling learner finds challenging, another, with the same skills, can find frustrating and nightmarish. Challenge is also influenced by such factors as a struggling learner's ability to organize, initiate, monitor, and sustain activities. A task that one struggling learner has little difficultly structuring and organizing can overwhelm and frustrate another at the same academic level.

For struggling learners with expectations of failure, teachers should avoid tasks the learners find frustrating or anxiety provoking. If frequently encountered, such tasks will provoke dysfunctional but understandable avoidance reactions: refusal to start or complete work; off-task dawdling; unthoughtful, careless responses; distractibility and fidgetiness. Little learning will occur, and motivation will plummet. As Newcomer (1986) noted: "Continuing to expect a child to read material at his or her frustration level can create serious achievement and emotional problems" (26).

Although perceptions are personal and teachers may need to adjust instructional and independent level criteria for particular struggling learners, teachers should follow well-established guidelines for determining instructional and independent levels. In most cases, these guidelines set the stage for success.

For materials to be at a student's instructional reading level, students should quickly and correctly read aloud 90 to 95 percent of words in context and understand 70 to 89 percent of the text. Instructional level assumes that teachers will work with students, teaching vocabulary, skills, and strategies; monitoring and guiding practice; and structuring independent practice. For independent level materials, which students should find easier than instructional level materials, students should quickly and correctly read aloud 96 percent or more of the words in context and understand 90 percent or more of the text (McCormick 2003). Whenever students work by themselves, at their desks or at home, materials should be at their independent level. Giving instructional level homework to struggling learners is equivalent to giving them frustration level materials, as their independent work habits and skills are often poor and teachers are not there to teach, supervise, and support them.

Commercial informal reading inventories (IRIs) can help identify a struggling learner's instructional, independent, and frustration reading levels (Lipson and Wixson 1997; McCormick 2003). Although such IRIs are easy to administer, and some are supported by extensive validity data (Leslie and Caldwell 2001; McCabe and Margolis 1999), they lack the specificity of Curriculum-Based Assessment (CBA) for determining and monitoring struggling learners' reading levels in specific curriculum (Fewster and Macmillan 2002; Idol, Nevin, and Paolucci-Whitcomb 1999). One CBA strategy for identifying struggling learners' instructional and independent reading levels is to individually administer a hierarchical series of 100-word selections from the books the learners will likely read (Idol, Nevin, and Paolucci-Whitcomb 1999). By having learners read three different selections from each prospective book that matches their estimated reading abilities and comparing each learner's median performance for accuracy (number of words correctly read), rate (correct words per minute) and comprehension (percent of questions correctly answered) to locally derived norms, teachers can get relatively reliable indications of the challenge these books present (Idol, Nevin, and Paolucci-Whitcomb 1999; Fewster and Macmillan 2002).

Teachers also can use the cloze procedure to quickly estimate the learners' ability to understand specific reading materials. The procedure, which has learners silently read passages of 250 to 300 words, can be administered to individual students or whole classes. Unlike the materials from which the cloze passages were copied, the cloze passage replaces every fifth word with a blank space of even length (Lipson and Wixson 1997; Spinelli 2002). Students write in the missing words. Materials on which students accurately identify 44 to 56 percent of the missing words (synonyms are counted as incorrect) represent their instructional level, 57 percent or more their independent level, and 43 percent or less their frustration level (Spinelli 2002). These guidelines can help teachers identify materials that struggling learners can successfully read.

Instructional and independent levels are different for tasks and assignments that do not stress the fluent identification of words in context. Salvia and Ysseldyke (2001) consider correct response rates of 85 to 95 percent challenging and less than 85 percent "too difficult." They caution for "students with severe cognitive handicaps, rates of correct response of less than 90 percent may indicate that the material is too challenging for guided practice" (25).

By adhering to these guidelines and, when they're too demanding, reducing them and the length, complexity, and abstractness of the work to reflect struggling learners' actual difficulties, perceptions of difficulty, and feelings of anxiety, teachers can often strengthen learners' self-efficacy for academics. One strategy for determining the adaptations needed is FLIP (Schumm and Mangrum 1991), which asks students to evaluate materials for friendliness (F), language (L), interest (I), and prior knowledge (P). By using FLIP, or adapting it to different subject matter, materials, and assignments, teachers can design instruction that increases the probability of success.

Whenever instructional or independent level data are unclear and teachers have to choose between more or less difficult levels, they should choose the less difficult. As struggling learners' moderate efforts produce high rates of success, more challenging materials and tasks should replace easier ones. Otherwise, they will have little opportunity to learn anything new, may get bored, and may think that teachers have little confidence in their abilities.

Instructional Principles

Frequently Link New Work to Recent Successes

To effectively link new work to recent successes requires many recent successes. To create many, teachers need to "stack the deck for success" by adhering to the struggling learners' proper instructional and independent levels, "stimulating recall of prerequisite learning" (Borich 2000, 159), shortening and simplifying work, and limiting the number and length of assignments. The key is giving learners moderately challenging work they can succeed at, if they make a moderate effort.

One way to help assure that struggling learners get tasks likely to produce high rates of success is to systematically employ CBA and to continually monitor learners' success rates

FLIP question: "How difficult is the language in my reading assignment?"

Possible student responses:

- Many new words; complicated sentences
- Some new words; somewhat complicated sentences
- No new words; clear sentences

Source: Schumm and Mangrum 1991, 122.

FIGURE 1. Sample FLIP question and possible responses.

(Rieth and Evertson 1988). By administering brief CBA probes several times a month, to assess progress in learners' areas of difficulty (e.g., reading, writing, spelling), and designing instruction and assignments to match their achievement and readiness to handle similar or increasingly challenging tasks, teachers can increase the learners' probability of success (Alper, Ryndak, and Schloss 2001; Galagan 1985; Spinelli 2002).

Once struggling learners have recent successes to draw on, teachers can help them link new work to their previous successes by explicitly showing and asking them how the new work resembles those past successes and then reminding them of what they did to succeed. Examining prior successes also provides teachers an excellent opportunity to employ one or several other self-efficacy enhancing strategies: teaching struggling learners to evaluate their work and chart their successes; teaching them to attribute success to controllable factors like effort, persistence, and correct use of strategies; having them review and annotate portfolios of successful work; helping them identify or develop specific, short-term, realistic goals; and persuading them to keep trying (Henk and Melnick 1998; Ormrod 2000; Pintrich and Schunk 2002; Schunk 2003; Walker 2003).

Teach Needed Learning Strategies

Characteristically, struggling learners do not know how to approach academic tasks. They do not know what learning or cognitive strategies to use or how to use them (Ellis and Lenz 1996; Vaughn, Gersten, and Chard 2000). Thus, teachers need to explicitly and systematically teach them the secrets of learning—the strategies that produce success (Swanson 2000).

Explicit, systematic instruction involves sequencing materials and tasks from easy to difficult; modeling and explaining to struggling learners, in a simple step-by-step fashion what they need to do; providing feedback about what they are doing right and what they need to do differently; providing abundant opportunities for guided practice, with task-specific feedback about how to correct errors; and, when they have achieved a high degree of proficiency (e.g., 96 percent word recognition in context for reading [McCormick 2003] and 85 percent on non-word recognition tasks, such as subtraction problems [Joyce and Weil 1996]), having them practice independently. As

Vaughn, Gersten, and Chard (2000) concluded: "Teaching students how to apply a particular strategy should be overt, and students should have multiple opportunities to practice the strategy under quality feedback conditions before they are expected to use the strategy on their own" (105).

In addition to sequencing, modeling, explicit step-by-step directions, feedback, correction, and practice (Pintrich and Schunk 2002; Swanson 2000), teachers might increase struggling learners' expectations of success by involving them in cooperative learning activities which are well within their ability to achieve. They know they will discreetly get whatever help they need, and they view their group as friendly and internally noncompetitive (Alderman 1999; Henk and Melnick 1998; Schunk and Zimmerman 1997; Vermette 1998). Teachers might also increase struggling learners' expectations of success by giving them strategy reference cards to use whenever they want (Casteel, Isom, and Jordon 2000). Reference cards present and illustrate each step of a strategy in ways struggling learners can readily comprehend. If they use reference cards when learning a strategy, they are apt to feel comfortable with them. Because they determine when to use the cards, they can dispense with them when they want. By putting struggling learners in control of using the cards and modeling the use of the cards themselves, teachers can eliminate any stigma associated with them.

For struggling learners who believe they lack the ability to succeed and who avoid more than superficial involvement in schoolwork, explicit, systematic strategy instruction may lack the power to involve them in meaningful, engaging ways. In such situations, teachers (and in some cases, parents) need to provide extrinsic, age-appropriate reinforcers (e.g., stickers, small toys, free time, computer time) that struggling learners are willing to work for until they become interested in the work and develop a strong, sustaining belief that with moderate effort, they can succeed. To prevent extrinsic reinforcement from backfiring and to reduce or eliminate it within a few months, teachers need to adhere to several basic principles of reinforcement and instruction:

- Use the smallest, most natural reinforcers for which struggling learners will work.

- Vary reinforcers to avoid boredom; change reinforcers that no longer work.

- Start by reinforcing struggling learners every time they correctly apply the strategy; briefly explain why they earned the reinforcer.

- Gradually thin out the frequency of extrinsic reinforcement by reinforcing fewer instances of correct strategy application. Go slow—do not reduce reinforcement too quickly.

- From the beginning, pair tangible, extrinsic reinforcers with common social and verbal reinforcers (e.g., smiles, task-specific praise).

- Reinforce struggling learners in all environments and situations in which they should use the learning strategy and correctly use it (e.g., with different teachers or in different classes, reinforce correct strategy use).

- Listen to struggling learners to learn about their personal goals, values, interests, and problems and link schoolwork to these.
- Stress work that struggling learners find important, interesting, or curiosity arousing.

Reinforce Effort and Persistence

Social cognitive theory predicts that many struggling learners, students who have suffered countless academic difficulties and failures, will have low self-efficacy for academics (Henk and Melnick 1998; Jinks and Morgan 1999; Schunk and Zimmerman 1997; Walker 2003; Zimmerman 2000a). Consequently, they are less prone than successful learners to tackle tasks they perceive as difficult, invest significant effort in such tasks, persist in the face of difficulty, and perform at high levels (Bandura 1997; Ormrod 2000; Pajares 1996; Schunk 1999; Zimmerman 2000a).

To strengthen struggling learners' self-efficacy, teachers need to select tasks well within struggling learners' abilities, sequence tasks from easy to difficult, help struggling learners realize they have the skills to succeed, provide them with help and encouragement whenever needed, show them how to correct their mistakes, and introduce "difficult" tasks only when they are no longer difficult—when struggling learners have mastered the prerequisites on which success depends (Rosenshine 1983; Salvia and Ysseldyke 2001; Swanson 2000). In such situations, resistance will often evaporate, creating legitimate opportunities to reinforce effort and persistence.

Resistance, however, will not evaporate if the initial tasks are too lengthy, too complex, or too difficult. Thus, to create opportunities to reinforce effort and persistence, initial assignments should be challenging but well within the struggling learners' abilities. Success should require reasonable, moderate effort—not Herculean. Struggling learners should view tasks as doable, not impossible.

Doable tasks that struggling learners can successfully complete with moderate effort makes "effort feedback" credible and can enhance self-efficacy, motivation, and achievement (Schunk 2001). Effort feedback, however, can backfire, if struggling learners are frequently reinforced for the effort invested in repeating the same task. They may "doubt their capacities and wonder why they still have to work hard to succeed" (Schunk 2001, 139).

Stress Peer Modeling

Although teacher modeling is highly effective (Swanson 2000), peer models may be particularly effective in strengthening self-efficacy (Alderman 1999; Pajares and Schunk 2001; Schunk 1999, 2003). Fortunately, teachers who give students interesting work at their proper instructional and independent levels usually have several peer models to choose from, as such work encourages proper behavior.

Peer models can be mastery or coping models. Peer coping models have the advantage of showing struggling learners how other students, similar to them, make and overcome mistakes in acquiring and applying new skills and learning strategies. This fosters the belief, "She's like me. If she can do it, I can" (Schunk 2001).

To improve the effectiveness of peer coping models, teachers should

- choose an important skill or strategy that is likely to challenge but not frustrate models and struggling learners;
- break complicated skills and strategies into manageable components;
- select models who resemble the struggling learners and who they respect;
- have models explain their actions, in a simple step-by-step manner, while they work to learn and apply the skill or strategy;
- have models correct their mistakes and verbally attribute failures to controllable factors (e.g., poor effort) and successes to controllable factors (e.g., correctly using a strategy) and ability (e.g., "I read well enough to use the Multipass strategy");
- have struggling learners observe models reinforced, in a variety of appropriate situations, for correctly using the targeted skill or strategy; and
- reinforce struggling learners, in a variety of appropriate situations, for correctly using the targeted skill or strategy.

Teach Students to Make Facilitative Attributions

Attributions are people's explanatory beliefs about why things happen to them. They explain success and failure and influence future actions, including effort, persistence, and choices (Bandura 1997; Pajares and Schunk 2001; Zimmerman 2000b).

> The attributions that people assign to the things that happen to them . . . guide their future behavior.... [Students] may attribute their school successes and failures to ...aptitude or ability (how smart or proficient they are), effort (how hard they tried), other people (how well the teacher taught or how much their classmates like them), task difficulty (how "easy" or "hard" something is), luck, mood, illness, fatigue, or physical appearance. . . . If students erroneously attribute their failures to stable and uncontrollable causes, they are unlikely [emphasis added] to change their future behaviors in ways that will lead to greater success. (Ormrod 2000, 497-98)

To counteract the effects of erroneous attributions that destroy self-efficacy—reducing struggling learners' willingness to try, to make reasonable efforts, and to persist—teachers need to stress accurate, facilitative attributions throughout the day and teach struggling learners to do the same.

Facilitative attributions associate successes with controllable factors, such as effort, persistence, and the correct use of learning or cognitive strategies. They stress what students did (Composite explanation: "I succeeded because I tried very hard.... I stuck to it.... I followed the steps on my cue cards"). Similarly, they attribute poor performances and failures to the same controllable factors, but stress what students did not do (Composite explanation: "I failed because I didn't try hard enough…. I didn't stick to it…. I didn't follow the steps on my cue cards").

Facilitative attributions also link successes to ability, such as learned intelligence (e.g., "I'm smart about that now. I learned how to use Multipass to understand the tough parts of my science book"). In contrast, they divorce poor performance or failure from ability.

Many experts have recommended combining attribution statements with cognitive strategies (Borkowski, Weyhing, and Carr 1988; Chapman and Tunmer 2003; Fulk 1994; Mushinski Fulk and Mastropieri 1990; Pintrich and Schunk 2002; Schunk and Rice 1993; Shelton, Anastopoulos, and Linden 1985). In a sense, it provides the best of both by giving struggling learners the formula, the secret for achieving success—the strategy—and teaches them to take credit for using and sticking with the strategy. Mushinski Fulk and Mastroprini (1990) designed a model for integrating strategy and attribution instruction.

Help Students Create Personally Important Goals

Perhaps nothing is more motivating than combining personally important goals with the belief that with reasonable effort, they are achievable (Pintrich and Schunk 2002; Schunk 2001; Zimmerman 2000b). But not every goal is motivating. Not every goal will improve low self-efficacy. For goals to positively influence self-efficacy and motivation, they need to be personally important to struggling learners, short-term, specific, and achievable (Alderman 1999; Bandura 1997; Schunk 1999; Stipek 1998). Moreover, to sustain motivation, struggling learners need credible feedback that they are making substantial progress toward achieving their goal (Alderman 1999; Bandura 1997; Pajares and Schunk 2001; Schunk 1999, 2003).

Personally important goals are goals that students want to achieve, goals they think will make an important difference in their lives. Struggling learners are far more likely to work to achieve goals that are important to them (Slavin 1999), and which they think they can achieve, than goals they view as unimportant and beyond their abilities.

Short-term goals (e.g., "Get a B+ on next week's social studies test") work hand in hand with long-term goals (e.g., "Pass social studies so I'm eligible for the hockey team"). Long-term goals, goals that will take months or years to attain, express students' dreams, students' hopes. Short-term goals are subgoals; they are intermediate steps between the present and long-term goals. Struggling learners need short-term goals to prevent loss of motivation, caused by the remoteness of long-term goals. Without frequent, explicit, visible feedback that they are making progress on short-term goals, struggling learners often get discouraged, retreating from academics. Frequently noting progress improves self-efficacy and motivation (Schunk 1999, 2001).

Specific, short-term goals are easily measurable, allowing struggling learners and teachers to frequently evaluate progress against a clear standard. For example, struggling learners can easily judge whether they met these specific, short-term goals:

- Write two compositions that earn a "B" on the class writing rubric.

- Try out for the band.

Step 1: *Explain purpose.* Explain the purpose of the strategy. Make sure the student understands how the strategy will help her. Relate the purpose to the student's frame of reference so she sees value in learning the strategy.

Step 2: *Discuss effort.* Discuss with the student how she controls her own effort and the critical role effort plays in producing successful outcomes.

Step 3: *Model examples.* Apply the strategy correctly and incorrectly. Label the examples correct and incorrect.

Step 4: *Model attributions.* Model controllable attributions while engaging in the strategy (e.g., "I got the right answer because I first skimmed the chapter, read all the headings and subheadings, and tried hard. . . . I got the wrong answer because I rushed and didn't skim the whole chapter. I didn't try hard.")

Step 5: *Provide guided practice.* Give the student ample opportunity to practice the combined strategy-attribution sequence with timely task-specific feedback until she routinely gets the right answer, makes positive attributions about her efforts, and appears comfortable with the strategy (e.g., "Kelly, that's great. You got the right answer because you first skimmed the chapter and worked hard. You told yourself that putting the effort in improves your understanding.").

Step 6: *Provide independent practice.* Give the student ample opportunity to use the combined strategy-attribution sequences by herself. Monitor student behavior and offer task-specific feedback as needed (e.g., "Nice job Kelly. You worked hard and gave yourself credit for skimming the chapter before reading it. Your effort made a difference.").

Step 7: *Conduct formative evaluation.* Assess the student's progress and modify teaching strategies if difficulty is apparent (e.g., if Kelly has trouble skimming full chapters of some twenty pages, reduce skimming to a more manageable fraction and provide more frequent feedback).

Step 8: *Introduce a new strategy.* Once the student routinely uses the strategy correctly and takes credit for making adequate effort and using it correctly, introduce a slightly different strategy appropriate for the student's instructional level. Re-institute attribution retraining sequence with step 1.

Note: Adapted from B. M. Mushinski Fulk and M. A. Mastropieri 1990.

FIGURE 2. General steps for combined attribution retraining and strategy instruction.

Scene: The teacher reads a paragraph aloud to his class. The paragraph, on Martin Luther King's assassination, is projected onto a screen, from an overhead projector. As the teacher reads aloud, he illustrates the Paraphrasing Reading Strategy (Ellis 1996) by saying:

- I'm using the RAP strategy.

- The three steps are "R" for Read a paragraph, "A" for Ask yourself what the paragraph was about, and "P" for Put the main idea and two details in your own words.

- I read the paragraph. I'll check the "R" on my checklist.

FIGURE 3. A teacher think-aloud for a learning strategy checklist.

Although many struggling learners can monitor and evaluate their work, some cannot. Teachers can teach struggling learners to monitor their work by frequently demonstrating think-alouds when evaluating struggling learners' work (Tierney and Readance 2000; Walker 2003; Wilheim 2001), and teaching them to use simple self-evaluation forms, rubrics, learning strategy reference cards, and learning strategy checklists (Casteel, Isom, and Jordan 2000; Lipson and Wixson 1997; Walker 1997, 2003). Figure 3 illustrates how teachers might use a think-aloud with a learning strategy checklist.

Realistic goals, goals that struggling learners can achieve with moderate effort, are more motivating than excessively difficult or excessively easy goals. Excessively difficult goals lead to resistance or despair because struggling learners believe them impossible to achieve. In contrast, excessively easy goals offer no challenge. They are boring; when achieved, struggling learners do not feel more competent. One instance in which excessively easy goals may be appropriate, but only temporarily, is when struggling learners are reeling from sustained difficulty and failure and need successful experiences to begin restoring confidence.

If struggling learners lack personally important goals, or they are vague, teachers should help them formulate precise, personal goals. Otherwise, it is more difficult to meaningfully involve them in academics. Fortunately, many struggling learners appreciate the activity, as they, like most people, want something. The two keys are finding out what struggling learners want and helping them express it in explicit, visible, concrete terms.

One way to get the information needed to help struggling learners formulate personally important goals is to ask them to complete an interest inventory. Another, more personal way is to listen empathetically to them about anything they want to discuss. Teachers can then meet with them and use this information to collaboratively write down the struggling learners' long-term and related short-term goals. One strategy to better understand their goals, and to help them better understand their own goals, is for teachers and struggling learners to circle, discuss, illustrate, and define vague words—words that are difficult to visualize and describe. If the opportunity to help struggling learners develop personally important goals is unavailable, teachers might ask guidance counselors for assistance.

Once struggling learners have defined personally important, specific, realistic, short-term goals, and understand their relationship to their long-term goals and schoolwork, teachers and struggling learners need to frequently assess progress toward achieving these goals (Schunk, 2001). If struggling learners are making good progress, teachers and learners should discuss what they are doing to produce success; if progress is poor, how to improve the situation. Typically, as learners note progress, their self-efficacy and enthusiasm for learning improves.

Incorporate Other Motivational Factors

Motivation, or the willingness to initiate and sustain goal directed activity, is influenced by self-efficacy (Bandura 1993; Henk and Melnick 1998; Jinks and Morgan 1999; Pajares and Schunk 2001; Pintrich and Schunk 2002; Schunk and Rice 1993; Schunk and Zimmerman 1997; Zimmerman 2000b; Zimmerman and Martinez-Pons 1990). "If," as an old saying goes, "people don't think they can, they won't." The converse, however, is not true. Just because people think they can do something, does not mean they will. However, they will likely invest in activities they find interesting or valuable, if their environment is safe and supportive, and if difficulties do not lead to embarrassment or comparisons with more successful peers. Thus, attempts to increase self-efficacy must take place within emotionally safe, secure classes that emphasize motivational principles that create or nurture a desire to learn and achieve. Such classes are usually taught by enthusiastic, optimistic teachers who

- run well-organized classes;

- encourage students to use well-organized, well-stocked learning centers and libraries;

- treat students with respect;

- show interest in students;

- give students choices;

- relate curriculum to students' lives and interests, in and out of school;

- radiate interest in their lessons;

- stimulate and maintain curiosity;

- engage students in collaborative learning activities, such as cooperative learning and peer tutoring;

- encourage sharing;

- use a variety of teaching approaches, appropriate to lesson objectives;

- make expectations clear and realistic;

- provide help, whenever needed, in socially appropriate ways, that avoid student embarrassment;

- compare students' achievements to their past achievements, rather than to other students';

- stress cooperative rather than competitive activities;

- provide frequent, immediate, task-specific feedback, including corrective comments and justified praise;

- ensure that students have the prerequisite knowledge and skill to master new topics and assignments;

- emphasize what is right about students' work; and

- challenge rather than frustrate students.

Caveats

As Linnenbrink and Pintrich (2003) noted, "Psychology and educational psychology are probabilistic sciences. . . . [Because they examine] what occurs, on average, across situations, there may be . . . situations where the principles do not apply. . . . [Thus,] it is important that teachers use psychological research as a guide ...rather than a prescriptive device" (134). Consequently, teachers who employ this article's suggestions need to monitor their effects on struggling learners and continue to use and refine those suggestions that work and modify or abandon those that don't. More important than any single suggestion is addressing struggling learners' self-efficacy in informed, systematic ways.

Because self-efficacy is task-specific (e.g., affected by the level and complexity of the task and the social and physical context in which it must be completed), attempts to strengthen it need to focus on the specific task or academic subject in which struggling learners feel incompetent. It is quite possible, for example, that they feel highly confident in one subject (e.g., mathematics) and inadequate in another (reading). The distinction is often finer. In reading, some have confidence in their comprehension abilities with second grade materials but none in their second grade word recognition skills.

No one knows how high self-efficacy must be to improve poor effort, persistence, and academic performance. High self-efficacy, however, is not always good. Overconfident or cocky students may not invest the effort needed to do well (Zimmerman 2000b). Therefore, they need intrinsically interesting tasks that, within reason, challenge their abilities. If they are overconfident and uninterested in tasks, teachers need to link reinforcement to both effort and accomplishment (Pajares 2003; Pintrich and Schunk 2002).

To succeed, struggling learners often need teachers' assistance. If materials and tasks are at the learners' proper instructional and independent levels, the help needed should be minimal. If learners need excessive help, or have to invest a Herculean effort, the task is at their frustration level. In such situations, teachers need to modify tasks so struggling learners need only minimal help.

If teachers often give more help than struggling learners need, they may interpret this as a sign that teachers think they are incompetent (Schunk 2001). Thus, teachers need to carefully assess the amount of help needed and give struggling learners the least amount of help needed to achieve success.

Often, struggling learners' low self-efficacy is part of larger, more complex problems. Although the suggestions in this article can often improve self-efficacy, they will probably be most effective if incorporated into a comprehensive program that systematically addresses the struggling learners' priority needs. Moreover, some struggling learners have had so much failure in their lives, and have so many other problems, that efforts to improve self-efficacy will take a long time and an informed, coordinated, skilled effort on the part of teachers, related service personnel, and parents. Not addressing struggling learners' self-efficacy needs, however, is likely to impede educational progress (Bandura, 1993), as "students' self-beliefs about academic capabilities . . . play an essential role in their motivation to achieve" (Zimmerman 2000a, 89).

Conclusion

For students to meaningfully involve themselves in learning for sustained periods, sufficient self-efficacy is required. Understandably, many struggling learners believe that academics mean failure and frustration—they have low self-efficacy for academics.

To reverse this, teachers must recognize that low self-efficacy is not an immutable, global trait. Rather, it is a modifiable, task-specific set of beliefs derived largely from frequent failures. By matching task difficulty to struggling learners' instructional and independent levels, linking new work to recent successes, teaching them strategies that produce success, reinforcing effort and persistence, using peer models, stressing and teaching facilitative explanations for successes and failures, and helping them understand how schoolwork can help them achieve personally important goals, teachers can often strengthen struggling learners' self-efficacy. By doing so, teachers increase the likelihood that struggling learners will become more motivated, more involved, more persistent, and more successful learners.

REFERENCES

Alderman, M. K. 1999. *Motivation for achievement: Possibilities for teaching and learning.* Mahwah, NJ: Lawrence Erlbaum Publishers.

Alper, S., D. L. Ryndak, and C. N. Schloss. 2001. *Alternative assessment of students with disabilities in inclusive settings.* Boston: Allyn and Bacon.

Baker, L., and A. Wigfield. 1999. Dimensions of children's motivation for reading and their relations to reading activity and reading achievement. *Reading Research Quarterly* 34 (4): 452-57.

Bandura, A. 1993. Perceived self-efficacy in cognitive development and functioning. *Educational Psychologist* 28 (2): 117-48.

Bandura, A. 1997. *Self-efficacy: The exercise of control.* New York: Freeman.

Borich, G. D. 2000. *Effective teaching methods.* 4th ed. Merrill: Upper Saddle River, NJ.

Borkowski, J. G., R. S. Weyhing, and L. A. Carr. 1988. Effects of attributional retraining on strategy-based reading comprehension in learning-disabled students. *Journal of Educational Psychology* 80:46-53.

Casteel, C. P., B. A. Isom, and K. F. Jordan. 2000. Creating confident and competent readers: Transactional strategies instruction. *Intervention in School and Clinic* 36 (2): 67-74.

Chapman, J. W., and W. E. Tunmer. 2003. Reading difficulties, reading-related self-perceptions, and strategies for overcoming negative self-beliefs. *Reading and Writing Quarterly: Overcoming Learning Difficulties* 19 (1): 5-24.

Culyer, R. C. 1996. Making homework work. *Education Digest* 61(9): 52-53.

Ellis, E. S. 1996. Reading strategy instruction. In *Teaching adolescents with learning disabilities: Strategies and methods,* 61-125. Ed. D. D. Deshler, E. S. Ellis, and B. K. Lenz. 2nd ed. Denver: Love Publishing.

Ellis, E. S., and B. K. Lenz. 1996. Perspectives on instruction in learning strategies. In *Teaching adolescents with learning disabilities: Strategies and methods,* 9-60., ed. D. D. Deshler, E. S. Ellis, and B. K. Lenz. 2nd ed. Denver: Love Publishing.

Fewster, S., and P. D. Macmillian. 2002. School-based evidence for the validity of curriculum-based measurement of reading and writing. *Remedial and Special Education* 23 (3): 149-56.

Fulk, B. M. 1994. Mnemonic keyword strategy training for students with learning disabilities. *Learning Disabilities Research and Practice* 9 (3): 179-85.

Galagan, J. 1985. Psychoeducational testing: Turn out the light, the party's over. *Exceptional Children* 52:288-99.

Henk, W. A., and S. A. Melnick. 1995. The reader self-perception scale (RSPS): A new tool for measuring how children feel about themselves as readers. *Reading Teacher* 48:470-82.

———. 1998. Upper elementary-aged children's reported perceptions about good readers: A self-efficacy influenced update in transitional literacy contexts. *Reading Research and Instruction* 38 (1): 57-80.

Idol, I., A. Nevin, and P. Paolucci-Whitcomb. 1999. *Models of curriculum-based assessment: A blueprint for learning.* 3rd ed. Austin, TX: Pro-Ed.

Jinks, J., and V. Morgan. 1999. Children's perceived academic self-efficacy: An inventory scale. *The Clearing House* 72 (4): 224-30.

Joyce, B., and M. Weil. 1996. *Models of teaching.* 5th ed. Boston: Allyn and Bacon.

Leslie, L., and J. Caldwell. 2001. *Qualitative Reading Inventory-3.* NY: Longman.

Linnenbrink, E. A., and P. R. Pintrich. 2003. The role of self-efficacy beliefs in student engagement and learning in the classroom. *Reading and Writing Quarterly: Overcoming Learning Difficulties* 19 (2): 119-38.

Lipson, M. Y., and K. K. Wixson. 1997. *Assessment and instruction of reading disability: An interactive approach.* 2nd ed. NY: Longman.

Lynch, J. 2002. Parents' self-efficacy beliefs, parents' gender, children's reader self-perceptions, reading achievement and gender. *Journal of Research in Reading* 25 (1): 54-67.

McCabe, P., and H. Margolis. 1999. Developing reading programs: How the Qualitative Reading Inventory II can help consultants. *Journal of Educational and Psychological Consultation* 10 (4): 385-93.

McCormick, S. 2003. *Instructing students who have literacy problems.* 4th ed. Englewood Cliffs, NJ: Merrill.

Mushinski Fulk, B. M., and M. A. Mastropieri. 1990. Training positive attitudes. *Intervention in School and Clinic* 26 (2): 79-83.

Newcomer, P. L. 1986. *Standardized Reading Inventory* (manual). Austin, TX: Pro-Ed.

Ormrod, J. E. 2000. *Educational psychology: Developing learners.* 3rd ed. Upper Saddle River, NJ: Prentice Hall.

Pajares, F. 1996. Self-efficacy beliefs in academic settings. *Review of Educational Research* 66 (4): 543-78.

Pajares, F. 2003. Self-efficacy beliefs, motivation, and achievement in writing: A review of the literature. *Reading and Writing Quarterly: Overcoming Learning Difficulties* 19 (2): 139-58.

Pajares, F., and D. H. Schunk. 2001. Self-beliefs and school success: Self-efficacy, self-concept, and school achievement. In *Perception,* 239-66., ed. R. Riding and S. Rayner. London: Ablex Publishing.

Pintrich, P. R., and D. H. Schunk. 2002. *Motivation in education: Theory, research, and applications.* 2nd ed. Englewood Cliffs, NJ: Prentice Hall.

Rieth, H., and C. Evertson. 1988. Variables related to the effective instruction of difficult-to-teach children. *Focus on Exceptional Children* 20 (5): 1-8.

Rosenshine, B. 1983. Teaching functions in instructional programs. *Elementary School Journal* 83:335-51.

Salvia, J., and J. E. Ysseldyke. 2001. *Assessment.* 8th ed. Boston: Houghton Mifflin Company.

Schumm, J. S., and C. T. Mangrum II. 1991. FLIP: A framework for content area reading. *Journal of Reading* 35 (2): 120-24.

Schunk, D. H. 1999. Social-self interaction and achievement behavior. *Educational Psychologist* 34 (4): 219-27.

———. 2001. Social cognitive theory and self-regulated learning. In *Self-regulated learning and academic achievement: Theoretical perspectives,* 125-51., ed. B. J. Zimmerman and D. H. Schunk. Mahwah, NJ: Lawrence Erlbaum Associates.

———. 2003. Self-efficacy for reading and writing: Influence of modeling, goal setting, and self-evaluation. *Reading and Writing Quarterly: Overcoming Learning Difficulties* 19 (2): 159-72

Schunk, D. H., and J. M. Rice. 1993. Strategy fading and progress feedback: Effects on self-efficacy and comprehension among students receiving remedial reading services. *Journal of Special Education* 27:257-76.

Schunk, D. H., and B. J. Zimmerman. 1997. Developing self-efficacious readers and writers: The role of social and self-regulatory processes. In *Reading engagement: Motivating readers through integrated instruction,* 34-50., ed. J. T. Guthrie and A. Wigfield. Newark, DE: International Reading Association.

Shelton, T. L., A. D. Anastopoulos, and J. D. Linden. 1985. An attribution training program with learning disabled children. *Journal of Learning Disabilities* 18 (5): 261-65.

Slavin, R. E. 1999. *Educational psychology: Theory and practice.* 6th ed. Boston: Allyn and Bacon.

Spinelli, C. G. 2002. *Classroom assessment for students with special needs in inclusive settings.* Upper Saddle River, NJ: Merrill.

Stipek, D. 1998. *Motivation to learn: From theory to practice.* 3rd ed. Boston: Allyn and Bacon.

Strickland, D. S., K. Ganske, and J. K. Monroe. 2002. *Supporting struggling readers and writers: Strategies for classroom intervention 3-6.* Newark, DE: International Reading Association.

Swanson, H. L. 1999. Instructional components that predict treatment outcomes for students with learning disabilities: Support for a combined strategy and direct instruction model. *Learning Disabilities Research and Practice* 14 (3): 129-40.

Swanson, H. L. 2000. What instruction works for students with learning disabilities? Summarizing the results from a meta-analysis of intervention studies. In *Contemporary special education research: Synthesis of the knowledge base on critical instructional issues,* 1-30. ed.

R. Gersten, E. P. Schiller, and S. Vaughn. Mahwah, NJ: Lawrence Erlbaum Associates.

Tierney, R. J., and J. E. Readence. 2000. *Reading strategies and practices: A compendium.* 5th ed. Boston: Allyn and Bacon.

Vaughn, S., R. Gersten, and D. J. Chard. 2000. The underlying message in LD intervention research: Findings from research syntheses. *Exceptional Children* 67 (1): 99-114.

Vermette, P. J. 1998. *Making cooperative learning work.* Upper Saddle River, NJ: Merrill.

Walker, B. J. 1997. Discussions that focus on strategies and self-assessment. In *Lively discussions: Fostering engaged reading,* 183-204, ed. L. B. Gambrell and J. F. Almasi. Newark, DE: International Reading Association.

Walker, B. 2003. The cultivation of student self-efficiency in reading and writing. *Reading and Writing Quarterly: Overcoming Learning Difficulties* 19 (2): 173-87.

Wilheim, J. D. 2001. *Improving comprehension with think-aloud strategies.* New York: Scholastic Professional Books.

Zimmerman, B. J. 2000a. Self-efficacy: An essential motive to learn. *Contemporary Educational Psychology* 25:82-91.

————. 2000b. Attaining self-regulation: A social cognitive perspective. In *Handbook of self-regulation,* 13-39, ed. M. Boekaerts, P. R. Pintrich, and M. Zeidner. San Diego: Academic Press.

Zimmerman, B. J., and M. Martinez-Pons. 1990. Student differences in self-regulated learning: Relating grade, sex, and giftedness to self-efficacy and strategy use. *Journal of Educational Psychology* 82:51-59.

Howard Margolis is a professor of special education at Queens College of the City University of New York in Flushing. Patrick P. McCabe is an associate professor in the Graduate Literacy Education Program at St. John's University in Jamaica, New York.

When Children Make Rules

In constructivist classrooms, young children's participation in rule making promotes their moral development.

Rheta DeVries and Betty Zan

Sherice Hetrick-Ortman's kindergartners were passionate about block building. These children at the Freeburg Early Childhood Program in Waterloo, Iowa, lavished care on their complex structures and felt justly proud of their creations. Some of the children were concerned, however, about problems in the block area. They discussed the matter at group time and came up with some new rules to post in the block-building area:

- Keep hands off other people's structures.
- No knocking people's structures down.
- Four friends in the block area at one time.

When children care about a classroom problem such as this one and take part in solving it, they are more likely to view the resulting rules as fair. Having *made* the rules, they are more likely to observe them. Just as important, participating in the process of rule making supports children's growth as moral, self-regulating human beings.

Rules in schools have traditionally been made by teachers and given to children. Today, many teachers see the benefits of allowing children to have a voice in developing classroom rules. But if we are not careful, this involvement can be superficial and meaningless. How can we best involve children in making classroom rules?

Morality and Adult-Child Relationships

We speak from a constructivist point of view, inspired by the research and theory of Jean Piaget. In constructivist education, rule making is part of the general atmo-

sphere of mutual respect, and the goal is children's moral and intellectual development (DeVries & Zan, 1994).

Piaget (19832/1965) identified two types of morality that parallel two types of adult-child relationships: one that promotes optimal moral and intellectual development, and one that retards it. *Heteronomous* morality consists of conformity to external rules without question. Overly coercive relationships with adults foster this type of morality and can impede children's development of self-regulation. *Autonomous* morality, by contrast, derives from an internal need to relate to other people in moral ways. Cooperative relationships with adults foster this type of morality and help children develop high levels of self-regulation.

Obviously, children and adults are not equals. However, when the adult respects the child as a person with a right to exercise his or her will, their relationship has a certain psychological equality that promotes autonomy.

Piaget, of course, did not advocate complete freedom, and neither do we. Although constructivist teachers minimize the exercise of adult authority or coercion in relation to children, *minimize* does not mean *eliminate* (DeVries, 1999; DeVries & Edmiaston, 1999; DeVries & Kohlberg, 1987/1990). Rather, we strive for a balance that steadily builds the child's regulation of his or her own behavior.

Norms and Rules in Constructivist Classrooms

To investigate how constructivist teachers use external control and how they develop classroom norms and rules, we inter-

viewed the teachers at the Freeburg Early Childhood Program, a laboratory school serving children ages 3–7 in a predominantly low-income neighborhood. The school's aim is to demonstrate constructivist practices.

Norms Established by Teachers

We define *norms* as specific expectations that teachers establish for children's behavior—ways of behaving that everyone takes for granted as part of the culture of the classroom. A norm is usually unwritten and sometimes unspoken until someone violates it and the teacher takes corrective action. The Freeburg teachers' reflections revealed three kinds of norms that existed in their classrooms:

- *Safety and health norms* ensure children's well-being. Our teachers articulated these as non-negotiables. Examples include "No hurting others," "Lie down at rest time," "Keep shoes on outside," "No crashing trikes or other vehicles," and "Don't throw sand."
- *Moral norms* pertain to respect for people and animals. They often relate to fair treatment or distribution of goods. Examples of these are "Take fair turns," "Talk through a conflict until there is a resolution," "If you bring a live animal into the classroom, try to make it comfortable," and "No hurting animals."
- *Discretionary norms* consist of routines and procedures to make the classroom run smoothly and make learning possible. Kathy Morris, the teacher in the 3-year-olds' class, pointed out that

young children do not like chaos, and they need adults to figure out routines that work so that events run smoothly. Discretionary norms also include societal norms for politeness and individual responsibility that children need to know. Examples include "Sit with the group at group time," "Wait until all are seated at lunch before eating," and "Clean up your place after lunch."

All teachers must sometimes exert external control.

All teachers have safety and health norms, moral norms, and discretionary norms. These norms are acceptable and necessary uses of external authority in a constructivist classroom. But constructivist teachers carefully evaluate their reasons for norms and attempt to minimize the use of external control as much as possible.

Rules Made by Children

We define rules as formal agreements among teachers and children. Constructivist teachers often conduct discussions of problems that relate to their norms and engage children in making classroom rules that arise from these norms.

When teachers first suggest that children make rules, children often parrot such adult admonitions as "Never talk to strangers" or "Raise your hand and wait to be called on." This occurs especially when children are unaccustomed to a sociomoral atmosphere in which they feel free to express their honest opinions. Children may view rule making as another exercise in trying to figure out the right answer or say what they think the teacher wants to hear. The rules that they suggest may not reflect a real understanding of the need to treat others in moral ways. When children only mindlessly restate adults' rules, they have not engaged in true rule making.

Children who engage in true rule making sometimes reinvent rules that elaborate on already established norms. Although these elaborations are not entirely original, they still give the children feelings of autonomy in their power to create rules. For example, Gwen Harmon's 4-year-olds, working within the classroom norm "Don't hurt animals," developed the following practical and concrete rules regarding the chicks that they hatched in the classroom:

- Pick them up safely.
- Don't push them.

- Don't squeeze them.
- Don't put things in their box.
- Don't punch them.
- Don't put them on the light bulb.
- Don't drop them.
- Don't throw them.
- Don't pick them up by their wings.
- Don't color on them.
- Don't pull their heads off.

Reinvented rules demonstrate children's understanding of the moral norm because they translate the norm into children's own words and provide elaborations that make sense to them. Sometimes the elaborations are novel, dealing with situations that the teacher had not considered discussing. For example, in Beth Van Meeteren's 1st grade classroom, where the norm is to treat others with respect, children made the rule, "When people pass gas, do not laugh, or they will be upset or embarrassed."

Sometimes children develop entirely original rules. Unlike reinvented rules, invented rules reflect children's power to make decisions in the classroom. For example, Dora Chen's class of 4-year-olds invented a new rule in response to a problem they saw during one of their classroom routines. One day during clean-up, a child saw another child finishing a snack and felt that no one should eat snacks during clean-up time. He told the teacher, who raised the issue at group time. She asked, "What should our rule be?" After a 17-minute discussion in which the children suggested various possibilities, the teacher clarified the choice between "No snack during clean-up: throw it away" or "Finish snack before going outdoors." The children voted to throw away their unfinished snacks when clean-up started.

The new rule, driven by children's interest and concern, went beyond the teacher's concerns. Although the teacher preferred giving the children more time to finish their snacks, she believed that the children's solution was fair given the one-hour activity time in which to eat snacks.

Guidelines for Exerting External Control

Some people have the misconception that constructivist teachers are permissive and that external control never occurs in constructivist classrooms. In fact, all teachers must exert external control sometimes. From our discussions with teachers and our understanding of research and theory,

we have derived four general guidelines for the use of external control.

Provide a general and pervasive context of warmth, cooperation, and community. We draw inspiration for this guideline from the work of Jean Piaget, especially from *The Moral Judgment of the Child* (1932/1965). Many others, however, have come to this same conclusion starting from different theoretical perspectives (Nelson, 1996; Watson, 2003). In fact, almost all of the recent classroom management programs on the market, with the exception of Assertive Discipline, stress the importance of cooperation and community (Charles, 2002).

Act with the goal of students' self-regulation. A developmental perspective leads us to focus on the long term. We want to contribute to the development of autonomous, self-regulating human beings who can make decisions based on the perspectives of all involved. Therefore, compliance is not our primary goal. Of course, we all wish sometimes that children would be more compliant. But we constantly remind ourselves and one another that developing self-regulation takes time, and we celebrate significant events, such as when an aggressive child actually uses words for the first time to tell another child what he wants instead of slugging him.

Minimize unnecessary external control as much as is possible and practical. Constructivist teachers do use external control; in fact, they use it quite a bit. As Piaget states, "However delicately one may put the matter, there have to be commands and therefore duties" (1932/1965, p. 180). Teachers in constructivist classrooms, however, use external control of children consciously and deliberately, not impulsively or automatically. The teachers with whom we work constantly ask themselves whether the external regulation is absolutely necessary.

Through discussions with teachers Gwen Harmon, Shari McGhee, and Christie Sales, we have identified several situations that can lead to unnecessary control of children. Avoidable control-inducing situations occur when

- The classroom arrangement invites rowdy behavior.
- Children do not know the classroom routine.
- Too many transitions lead to too much waiting time.
- Crowding in a part of the classroom leads to conflicts.

- Group time goes on for too long; children become restless, and some act out.
- Activities are not sufficiently engaging to appeal to children's purposes, and children become aimless.
- The classroom does not contain enough materials, and children compete for what is available.
- Clean-up is poorly organized, and children resist cleaning up after activity time.
- A mismatch exists between the teacher's expectations and the children's competencies.
- The teacher attributes a character flaw to a child who misbehaves.

When external control is necessary, use the least amount necessary to secure compliance. Ideally, the constructivist teacher uses external control judiciously to make sure that the child's experience overall is a mixture increasingly in favor of the child's self-regulation. When external regulation becomes necessary, the teacher must preserve the child's dignity and autonomy—for example, by giving the child a choice and thus returning a degree of autonomy as soon as possible.

Meaningful Rule Making

For many years, we have advocated allowing young children to make classroom rules, arguing that such opportunities are part and parcel of a constructivist, democratic classroom. By encouraging children to make classroom rules, the teacher minimizes unnecessary external control and promotes the development of children's moral and intellectual autonomy.

To genuinely think for themselves and exercise autonomy, children must be given the power to make rules and decisions that both elaborate on classroom norms and break new ground. By actively seeking out appropriate opportunities and recognizing them when they arise in the daily life of the classroom, teachers can create classrooms that are fair and democratic.

References

Charles, C. (2002). *Building classroom discipline* (7th ed.). Boston: Allyn and Bacon.

DeVries, R. (1999). Implications of Piaget's constructivist theory for character education. In M. Williams & E. Schaps (Eds.), *Character education.* Washington, DC: Character Education Partnership.

DeVries, R., & Edmiaston, R. (1999). Misconceptions about constructivist education. *The Constructivist, 13*(3), 12–19.

DeVries, R., & Kohlberg, L. (1987/1990). *Constructivist early education.* Washington, DC: National Association for the Education of Young Children.

DeVries, R., & Zan, B. (1994). *Moral classrooms, moral children: Creating a constructivist atmosphere in early education.* New York: Teachers College Press.

Nelson, J. (1996). *Positive discipline.* New York: Ballantine Books.

Piaget, J. (1932/1965). *The moral judgment of the child.* London: Free Press.

Watson, M. (2003). *Learning to trust.* San Francisco: Jossey-Bass.

Rheta DeVries is a professor and Director of the Regents' Center for Early Developmental Education, University of Northern Iowa, 107 Schindler Education Center, Cedar Falls, IA 50701; (391) 273–2101; rheta.devries@uni.edu. **Betty Zan** is an assistant professor and Research Fellow at the Regents' Center for Early Developmental Education; (319) 273–2101; betty.zan@uni.edu.

The Key to Classroom Management

By using research-based strategies combining appropriate levels of dominance and cooperation and an awareness of student needs, teachers can build positive classroom dynamics.

Robert J. Marzano and Jana S. Marzano

Today, we know more about teaching than we ever have before. Research has shown us that teachers' actions in their classrooms have twice the impact on student achievement as do school policies regarding curriculum, assessment, staff collegiality, and community involvement (Marzano, 2003a). We also know that one of the classroom teacher's most important jobs is managing the classroom effectively.

A comprehensive literature review by Wang, Haertel, and Walberg (1993) amply demonstrates the importance of effective classroom management. These researchers analyzed 86 chapters from annual research reviews, 44 handbook chapters, 20 government and commissioned reports, and 11 journal articles to produce a list of 228 variables affecting student achievement. They combined the results of these analyses with the findings from 134 separate meta-analyses. Of all the variables, classroom management had the largest effect on student achievement. This makes intuitive sense—students cannot learn in a chaotic, poorly managed classroom.

Research not only supports the importance of classroom management, but it also sheds light on the dynamics of classroom management. Stage and Quiroz's meta-analysis (1997) shows the importance of there being a balance between teacher actions that provide clear consequences for unacceptable behavior and teacher actions that recognize and reward acceptable behavior. Other researchers (Emmer, Evertson, & Worsham, 2003; Evertson, Emmer, & Worsham, 2003) have identified important components of classroom management, including beginning the school year with a positive emphasis on management; arranging the room in a way conducive to effective management; and

identifying and implementing rules and operating procedures.

In a recent meta-analysis of more than 100 studies (Marzano, 2003b), we found that the quality of teacher-student relationships is the keystone for all other aspects of classroom management. In fact, our meta-analysis indicates that on average, teachers who had high-quality relationships with their students had 31 percent fewer discipline problems, rule violations, and related problems over a year's time than did teachers who did not have high-quality relationships with their students.

> The quality of teacher-student relationships is the keystone for all other aspects of classroom management.

What are the characteristics of effective teacher-student relationships? Let's first consider what they are not. Effective teacher-student relationships have nothing to do with the teacher's personality or even with whether the students view the teacher as a friend. Rather, the most effective teacher-student relationships are characterized by specific teacher behaviors: exhibiting appropriate levels of dominance; exhibiting appropriate levels of cooperation; and being aware of high-needs students.

Appropriate Levels of Dominance

Wubbels and his colleagues (Wubbels, Brekelmans, van Tartwijk, & Admiral,

1999; Wubbels & Levy, 1993) identify appropriate dominance as an important characteristic of effective teacher-student relationships. In contrast to the more negative connotation of the term *dominance* as forceful control or command over others, they define dominance as the teacher's ability to provide clear purpose and strong guidance regarding both academics and student behavior. Studies indicate that when asked about their preferences for teacher behavior, students typically express a desire for this type of teacher-student interaction. For example, in a study that involved interviews with more than 700 students in grades 4–7, students articulated a clear preference for strong teacher guidance and control rather than more permissive types of teacher behavior (Chiu & Tulley, 1997). Teachers can exhibit appropriate dominance by establishing clear behavior expectations and learning goals and by exhibiting assertive behavior.

Establish Clear Expectations and Consequences

Teachers can establish clear expectations for behavior in two ways: by establishing clear rules and procedures, and by providing consequences for student behavior.

The seminal research of the 1980s (Emmer, 1984; Emmer, Sanford, Evertson, Clements, & Martin, 1981; Evertson & Emmer, 1982) points to the importance of establishing rules and procedures for general classroom behavior, group work, seat work, transitions and interruptions, use of materials and equipment, and beginning and ending the period or the day. Ideally, the class should establish these rules and procedures through discussion and mutual consent by teacher and students (Glasser, 1969, 1990).

Along with well-designed and clearly communicated rules and procedures, the teacher must acknowledge students' behavior, reinforcing acceptable behavior and providing negative consequences for unacceptable behavior. Stage and Quiroz's research (1997) is instructive. They found that teachers build effective relationships through such strategies as the following:

- Using a wide variety of verbal and physical reactions to students' misbehavior, such as moving closer to offending students and using a physical cue, such as a finger to the lips, to point out inappropriate behavior.
- Cuing the class about expected behaviors through prearranged signals, such as raising a hand to indicate that all students should take their seats.
- Providing tangible recognition of appropriate behavior—with tokens or chits, for example.
- Employing group contingency policies that hold the entire group responsible for behavioral expectations.
- Employing home contingency techniques that involve rewards and sanctions at home.

Establish Clear Learning Goals

Teachers can also exhibit appropriate levels of dominance by providing clarity about the content and expectations of an upcoming instructional unit. Important teacher actions to achieve this end include

- Establishing and communicating learning goals at the beginning of a unit of instruction.
- Providing feedback on those goals.
- Continually and systematically revisiting the goals.
- Providing summative feedback regarding the goals.

The use of rubrics can help teachers establish clear goals. To illustrate, assume that a teacher has identified the learning goal "understanding and using fractions" as important for a given unit. That teacher might present students with the following rubric:

4 points. You understand the characteristics of fractions along with the different types. You can accurately describe how fractions are related to decimals and percentages. You can convert fractions to decimals and can explain how and why the process works. You can use fractions to understand and solve different types of problems.

3 points. You understand the basic characteristics of fractions. You know how fractions are related to decimals and percentages. You can convert fractions to decimals.

2 points. You have a basic understanding of the following, but have some small misunderstandings about one or more: the characteristics of fractions; the relationships among fractions, decimals, and percentages; how to convert fractions to decimals.

1 point. You have some major problems or misunderstandings with one or more of the following: the characteristics of fractions; the relationships among fractions, decimals, and percentages; how to convert fractions to decimals.

0 points. You may have heard of the following before, but you do not understand what they mean: the characteristics of fractions; the relationships among fractions, decimals, and percentages; how to convert fractions to decimals.

The clarity of purpose provided by this rubric communicates to students that their teacher can provide proper guidance and direction in academic content.

Exhibit Assertive Behavior

Teachers can also communicate appropriate levels of dominance by exhibiting assertive behavior. According to Emmer and colleagues, assertive behavior is

the ability to stand up for one's legitimate rights in ways that make it less likely that others will ignore or circumvent them. (2003, p. 146)

Assertive behavior differs significantly from both passive behavior and aggressive behavior. These researchers explain that teachers display assertive behavior in the classroom when they

- Use assertive body language by maintaining an erect posture; facing the offending student but keeping enough distance so as not to appear threatening and matching the facial expression with the content of the message being presented to students.
- Use an appropriate tone of voice, speaking clearly and deliberately in a

pitch that is slightly but not greatly elevated from normal classroom speech, avoiding any display of emotions in the voice.

- Persist until students respond with the appropriate behavior. Do not ignore an inappropriate behavior; do not be diverted by a student denying, arguing, or blaming, but listen to legitimate explanations.

Appropriate Levels of Cooperation

Cooperation is characterized by a concern for the needs and opinions of others. Although not the antithesis of dominance, cooperation certainly occupies a different realm. Whereas dominance focuses on the teacher as the driving force in the classroom, cooperation focuses on the students and teacher functioning as a team. The interaction of these two dynamics—dominance and cooperation—is a central force in effective teacher-student relationships. Several strategies can foster appropriate levels of cooperation.

Provide Flexible Learning Goals

Just as teachers can communicate appropriate levels of dominance by providing clear learning goals, they can also convey appropriate levels of cooperation by providing flexible learning goals. Giving students the opportunity to set their own objectives at the beginning of a unit or asking students what they would like to learn conveys a sense of cooperation. Assume, for example, that a teacher has identified the topic of fractions as the focus of a unit of instruction and has provided students with a rubric. The teacher could then ask students to identify some aspect of fractions or a related topic that they would particularly like to study. Giving students this kind of choice, in addition to increasing their understanding of the topic, conveys the message that the teacher cares about and tries to accommodate students' interests.

Teachers with effective classroom management skills are aware of high-needs students and have a repertoire of specific techniques for meeting some of their needs.

Take a Personal Interest in Students

Probably the most obvious way to communicate appropriate levels of cooperation is to take a personal interest in each student in the class. As McCombs and Whisler (1997) note, all students appreciate personal attention from the teacher. Although busy teachers—particularly those at the secondary level—do not have the time for extensive interaction with all students, some teacher actions can communicate personal interest and concern without taking up much time. Teachers can

- Talk informally with students before, during, and after class about their interests.
- Greet students outside of school—for instance, at extracurricular events or at the store.
- Single out a few students each day in the lunchroom and talk with them.
- Be aware of and comment on important events in students' lives, such as participation in sports, drama, or other extracurricular activities.
- Compliment students on important achievements in and outside of school.
- Meet students at the door as they come into class; greet each one by name.

Use Equitable and Positive Classroom Behaviors

Programs like Teacher Expectations and Student Achievement emphasize the importance of the subtle ways in which teachers can communicate their interest in students (Kerman, Kimball, & Martin, 1980). This program recommends many practical strategies that emphasize equitable and positive classroom interactions with all students. Teachers should, for example,

- Make eye contact with each student. Teachers can make eye contact by scanning the entire room as they speak and by freely moving about all sections of the room.
- Deliberately move toward and stand close to each student during the class period. Make sure that the seating arrangement allows the teacher and students clear and easy ways to move around the room.
- Attribute the ownership of ideas to the students who initiated them. For instance, in a discussion a teacher might say, "Cecilia just added to Aida's idea by saying that...."

- Allow and encourage all students to participate in class discussions and interactions. Make sure to call on students who do not commonly participate, not just those who respond most frequently.
- Provide appropriate wait time for all students to respond to questions, regardless of their past performance or your perception of their abilities.

Awareness of High-Needs Students

Classroom teachers meet daily with a broad cross-section of students. In general, 12–22 percent of all students in school suffer from mental, emotional, or behavioral disorders, and relatively few receive mental health services (Adelman & Taylor, 2002). The Association of School Counselors notes that 18 percent of students have special needs and require extraordinary interventions and treatments that go beyond the typical resources available to the classroom (Dunn & Baker, 2002).

Although the classroom teacher is certainly not in a position to directly address such severe problems, teachers with effective classroom management skills are aware of high-needs students and have a repertoire of specific techniques for meeting some of their needs (Marzano, 2003b). Figure 1 summarizes five categories of high-needs students and suggests classroom strategies for each category and subcategory.

- *Passive* students fall into two subcategories: those who fear *relationships* and those who fear *failure*. Teachers can build strong relationships with these students by refraining from criticism, rewarding small successes, and creating a classroom climate in which students feel safe from aggressive people.
- The category of *aggressive* students comprises three subcategories: *hostile, oppositional,* and *covert.* Hostile students often have poor anger control, low capacity for empathy, and an inability to see the consequences of their actions. Oppositional students exhibit milder forms of behavior problems, but they consistently resist following rules, argue with adults, use harsh language, and tend to annoy others. Students in the covert sub-category may be quite pleasant at times,

but they are often nearby when trouble starts and they never quite do what authority figures ask of them. Strategies for helping aggressive students include creating behavior contracts and providing immediate rewards and consequences. Most of all, teachers must keep in mind that aggressive students, although they may appear highly resistant to behavior change, are still children who are experiencing a significant amount of fear and pain.

- Students with *attention* problems fall into two categories: *hyperactive* and *inattentive.* These students may respond well when teachers contract with them to manage behaviors; teach them basic concentration, study, and thinking skills; help them divide tasks into manageable parts; reward their successes; and assign them a peer tutor.
- Students in the *perfectionist* category are driven to succeed at unattainable levels. They are self-critical, have low self-esteem, and feel inferior. Teachers can often help these students by encouraging them to develop more realistic standards, helping them to accept mistakes, and giving them opportunities to tutor other students.
- *Socially inept* students have difficulty making and keeping friends. They may stand too close and touch others in annoying ways, talk too much, and misread others' comments. Teachers can help these students by counseling them about social behaviors.

The most effective classroom managers did not treat all students the same; they tended to employ different strategies with different types of students.

School may be the only place where many students who face extreme challenges can get their needs addressed. The reality of today's schools often demands that classroom teachers address these severe issues, even though this task is not always considered a part of their regular job.

In a study of classroom strategies (see Brophy, 1996; Brophy & McCaslin, 1992), researchers examined how effective classroom teachers interacted with specific types of students. The study found that the most effective classroom managers did not

FIGURE 1 Categories of High-Needs Students

Category	Definitions & Source	Characteristics	Suggestions
Passive	Behavior that avoids the domination of others or the pain of negative experiences. The child attempts to protect self from criticism, ridicule, or rejection, possibly reacting to abuse and neglect. Can have a biochemical basis, such as anxiety.	**Fear of relationships:** Avoids connection with others, is shy, doesn't initiate conversations, attempts to be invisible. **Fear of failure:** Gives up easily, is convinced he or she can't succeed, is easily frustrated, uses negative self-talk.	Provide safe adult and peer interactions and protections from aggressive people. Provide assertiveness and positive self-talk training. Reward small successes quickly. Withhold criticism.
Aggressive	Behavior that overpowers, dominates, harms, or controls others without regard for their well-being. The child has often taken aggressive people as role models. Has had minimal or ineffective limits set on behavior. Is possibly reacting to abuse and neglect. Condition may have a biochemical basis, such as depression.	**Hostile:** Rages, threatens, or intimidates others. Can be verbally or physically abusive to people, animals, or objects. **Oppositional:** Does opposite of what is asked. Demands that others agree or give in. Resists verbally or nonverbally. **Covert:** Appears to agree but then does the opposite of what is asked. Often acts innocent while setting up problems for others.	Describe the student's behavior clearly. Contract with the student to reward corrected behavior and set up consequences for uncorrected behavior. Be consistent and provide immediate rewards and consequences. Encourage and acknowledge extracurricular activities in and out of school. Give student responsibilities to help teacher or other students to foster successful experiences.
Attention problems	Behavior that demonstrates either motor or attentional difficulties resulting from a neurological disorder. The child's symptoms may be exacerbated by family or social stressors or biochemical conditions, such as anxiety, depression, or bipolar disorders.	**Hyperactive:** Has difficulty with motor control, both physically and verbally. Fidgets, leaves seat frequently, interrupts, talks excessively. **Inattentive:** Has difficulty staying focused and following through on projects. Has difficulty with listening, remembering, and organizing.	Contract with the student to manage behaviors. Teach basic concentration, study, and thinking skills. Separate student in a quiet work area. Help the student list each step of a task. Reward successes; assign a peer tutor.
Perfectionist	Behavior that is geared toward avoiding the embarrassment and assumed shame of making mistakes. The child fears what will happen if errors are discovered. Has unrealistically high expectations of self. Has possibly received criticism or lack of acceptance while making mistakes during the process of learning.	Tends to focus too much on the small details of projects. Will avoid projects if unsure of outcome. Focuses on results and not relationships. Is self-critical.	Ask the student to make mistakes on purpose, then show acceptance. Have the student tutor other students.
Socially inept	Behavior that is based on the misinterpretation of nonverbal signals of others. The child misunderstands facial expressions and body language. Hasn't received adequate training in these areas and has poor role modeling.	Attempts to make friends but is inept and unsuccessful. Is forced to be alone. Is often teased for unusual behavior, appearance, or lack of social skills.	Teach the student to keep the appropriate physical distance from others. Teach the meaning of facial expressions, such as anger and hurt. Make suggestions regarding hygiene, dress, mannerisms, and posture.

Source: Marzano, R. J. (2003). *What works in schools: Translating research into action* (pp. 104–105). Alexandria, VA: ASCD.

treat all students the same; they tended to employ different strategies with different types of students. In contrast, ineffective classroom managers did not appear sensitive to the diverse needs of students. Although Brophy did not couch his findings in terms of teacher-student relationships, the link is clear. An awareness of the five general categories of high-needs students and appropriate actions for each can help teachers build strong relationships with diverse students.

Don't Leave Relationships to Chance

Teacher-student relationships provide an essential foundation for effective classroom management—and classroom management is a key to high student achievement. Teacher-student relationships should not be left to chance or dictated by the personalities of those involved. Instead, by using strategies supported by research, teachers can influence the dynamics of their classrooms and build strong teacher-student relationships that will support student learning.

References

Adelman, H. S., & Taylor, L. (2002). School counselors and school reform: New directions. *Professional School Counseling, 5*(4), 235–248.

Brophy, J. E. (1996). *Teaching problem students.* New York: Guilford.

Brophy, J. E., & McCaslin, N. (1992). Teachers' reports of how they perceive and cope with problem students. *Elementary School Journal, 93*, 3–68.

Chiu, L. H., & Tulley, M. (1997). Student preferences of teacher discipline styles. *Journal of Instructional Psychology, 24*(3), 168–175.

Dunn, N. A., & Baker, S. B. (2002). Readiness to serve students with disabilities: A survey of elementary school counselors. *Professional School Counselors, 5*(4), 277–284.

Emmer, E. T. (1984). *Classroom management: Research and implications.* (R & D Report No. 6178). Austin, TX: Research and Development Center for Teacher Education, University of Texas. (ERIC Document Reproduction Service No. ED251448)

Emmer, E. T., Evertson, C. M., & Worsham, M. E. (2003). *Classroom management for secondary teachers* (6th ed.). Boston: Allyn and Bacon.

Emmer, E. T., Sanford, J. P., Evertson, C. M., Clements, B. S., & Martin, J. (1981). *The classroom management improvement study: An experiment in elementary school classrooms.* (R & D Report No. 6050). Austin, TX: Research and Development Center for Teacher Education, University of Texas. (ERIC Document Reproduction Service No. ED226452)

Evertson, C. M., & Emmer, E. T. (1982). Preventive classroom management. In D. Duke (Ed.), *Helping teachers manage classrooms* (pp. 2–31). Alexandria, VA: ASCD.

Evertson, C. M., Emmer, E. T., & Worsham, M. E. (2003). *Classroom management for elementary teachers* (6th ed.). Boston: Allyn and Bacon.

Glasser, W. (1969). *Schools without failure.* New York: Harper and Row.

Glasser, W. (1990). *The quality school: Managing students without coercion.* New York: Harper and Row.

Kerman, S., Kimball, T., & Martin, M. (1980). *Teacher expectations and student achievement.* Bloomington, IN: Phi Delta Kappan.

Marzano, R. J. (2003a). *What works in schools.* Alexandria, VA: ASCD.

Marzano, R. J. (with Marzano, J. S., & Pickering, D. J.). (2003b). *Classroom management that works.* Alexandria, VA: ASCD.

McCombs, B. L., & Whisler, J. S. (1997). *The learner-centered classroom and school.* San Francisco: Jossey-Bass.

Stage, S. A., & Quiroz, D. R. (1997). A meta-analysis of interventions to decrease disruptive classroom behavior in public education settings. *School Psychology Review, 26*(3), 333–368.

Wang, M. C., Haertel, G. D., & Walberg, H. J. (1993). Toward a knowledge base for school learning. *Review of Educational Research, 63*(3), 249–294.

Wubbels, T., Brekelmans, M., van Tartwijk, J., & Admiral, W. (1999). Interpersonal relationships between teachers and students in the classroom. In H. C. Waxman & H. J. Walberg (Eds.), *New directions for teaching practice and research* (pp. 151–170). Berkeley, CA: McCutchan.

Wubbels, T., & Levy, J. (1993). *Do you know what you look like? Interpersonal relationships in education.* London: Falmer Press.

Robert J. Marzano is a senior scholar at Mid-continent Research for Education and Learning in Aurora, Colorado, and an associate professor at Cardinal Stritch University in Milwaukee, Wisconsin; (303) 796–7683; robertjmarzano@aol.com. His newest book written with Jana S. Marzano and Debra J. Pickering is *Classroom Management That Works* (ASCD, 2003). **Jana S. Marzano** is a licensed professional counselor in private practice in Centennial, Colorado; (303) 220–1151; janamarzan@aol.com.

Twelve Practical Strategies to Prevent Behavioral Escalation in Classroom Settings

SMITA SHUKLA-MEHTA and RICHARD W. ALBIN

Dan is a first-grade student at Edison Elementary with both academic and behavior problems. Although he has not met the classification criteria for special education eligibility, he does demonstrate high rates of off-task behavior and frequently argues with his teachers and other adults. One day during language arts, one of his peers, Samantha, got out of her seat to sharpen her pencil. Dan told Samantha very loudly that she was not supposed to get out of her seat. The teacher told Dan to mind his own business. Dan asked the teacher why Samantha could get up to sharpen her pencils but he could not do the same. The teacher said to Dan, "You need to copy the sentences from the board." Dan pushed his desk forward, made faces and said, "I don't want to!" The teacher walked up to Dan's desk, grabbed his arms and pulled him up from the chair, looked straight into his eyes and said, "One more word out of that mouth and I will send you to the Behavior Room." Dan said angrily, "I wish I was dead and I wish I could use my knife on you." He looked like he was about to cry. The teacher immediately informed the Principal and Dan was sent to Off Campus Detention (OCD) for 3 days. If he really had a knife, he would have been placed in OCD for the remaining days of the school year. This account of an actual incident is an example of behavioral escalation in the classroom.

When the term "behavioral escalation" is used, most people think of a crisis that involves injury to others or damage to physical property. However, in reality, although not every incident reaches crisis level proportions, it could end with a temporary removal of a student from the classroom or school. Examples of such behavior include: engaging the teacher in an argument, using verbal or gestural threats, coming too close to others, using intimidating tactics to coerce the teacher into withdrawing requests, throwing objects, walking out of the class-room or school without permission, resisting physical blocking or holds, or physically hitting others.

Every adult who has dealt with the problem behavior of students who "escalate," is able to give a physical description of the behavior. However, the task of defining behavioral escalation is a different matter altogether (Baer 1982; Evans, Meyer, Kurkjian, and Kishi 1988; Fox and Hoffman 2002; Shukla-Mehta and Albin 2002). Rarely do people think in terms of the structural pattern or the manner in which the various problematic responses are sequentially organized. For purposes of this article, behavioral escalation is defined as an event where a group of topographically (physically) different problem behaviors occur in a sequential pattern in which successive responses are of increasing severity or intensity (Albin, O'Brien, and Horner 1992; Colvin 1990; Lalli, Mace, Wohn, and Livezey 1995; Shukla and Albin 1996; Wahler and Fox 1982). Such sequences usually begin with less severe problems (e.g., whining, complaining, and arguing), many of which can be dealt with easily whereas others escalate and become more severe responses (e.g., throwing furniture, physical assault) that can even cause injury to people and/or damage to property (Shukla 1994).

Most classroom problems are minor and are easily resolved. Unfortunately, during behavioral escalation where both the teacher and student become engaged in a confrontation, classroom instruction comes to a standstill and other students in class become anxious or curious spectators (Hewitt 1999). Although this is true in both general and special education settings, it is more likely to occur in classrooms where the teacher is not properly trained to manage severe behavioral problems. Understandably, teachers want students to comply with requests rather than giving consequences for noncompliance. However, when both student and teacher escalate, students are eventually removed from the classroom for arguing, consistently challenging the teacher, or refusing to follow directions. In special educational settings, teachers may be more inclined to continue to redirect students to avoid behavioral escalation; however, instruction and engagement does end when someone gets hurt (Gunter and Jack 1994). Therefore, experts urge teachers to focus on preventing behavioral escalation rather than managing crisis situations once they occur. In the following discussion, we describe twelve practical strategies identified as empirically effective in preventing behavioral escalation. The strategies apply to general and special education classroom settings and can be useful across various school and non-school environments and with various age groups of children and adolescents.

Reinforce calm and on-task behaviors. Because most behavior is maintained by virtue of some kind of reinforcement (e.g., teacher attention, peer approval), teachers should immediately reinforce students when they display target behaviors like working calmly and being on-task through verbal praise or task assistance on a consistent basis. Teacher attention is a powerful tool. Teachers should not wait to attend to students until they display disruptive behavior; otherwise, inadvertently, problem behavior will be reinforced and will continue to occur in the future (Kennedy 2000). Teachers can walk around the classroom (i.e., use proximity control) and assist and reinforce students who are engaged in academic work (De Pry and Sugai 2002; Gunter, Shores, Jack, Rasmussen, and Flowers 1995). This will address one of the reasons students may seek to escape a task or access teacher attention by using problem behavior. Similarly, provide students with positive attention through a smile, gesture, touch, or a pleasant comment when they display unprompted socially appropriate behavior (e.g., helping a peer to complete a word problem). This will increase the likelihood of socially appropriate behavior instead of problem behavior (Carr, Bailey, Ecott, Lucker, and Weil 1998).

Know the triggers. Most student behavior is triggered (i.e., set off) by something. For example, students may start putting their books in the backpack when they look at the clock and see that only a few minutes are left until class is over. Anything that prompts an action from others is a trigger. For students, triggers for problem behavior may include difficult academic tasks (e.g., word problems involving fractions), less time available for task completion (e.g., 15 vocabulary words in 15 minutes), particular expressions by a teacher or peer (e.g., "Can't you get anything right?" [Albin et al. 1992; Baer 1997; Harrison and Gunter 1996]), or their own behavior (e.g., anxiety about an upcoming exam, not comprehending instruction, or fear of making mistakes [Skinner 1938]). Whenever possible, teachers should work to reduce or eliminate these triggers. For example, if academic task requests act as a trigger, teachers can make curricular or in-

structional adaptations, such as offering choices, extending the time for completing class assignments, providing assistance before the student gets frustrated, or providing the option of working with a peer buddy, depending on the specific problem situation (Dunlap, Kern-Dunlap, Clarke, and Robbins 1991; Gunter, Denny, and Venn 2000; Jolivette, Wehby, Canale, and Massey 2001; Shukla, Kennedy, and Cushing 1999). The best way to deal with such situations is to make these adaptations before behavior problems occur—proactively, not after the fact (Darch, Miller, and Shippen 1998). To be effective, the student must realize that these options are available and that he does not have to resort to inappropriate behavior to solve problems (Clare and Im 1999).

Similarly, teachers should also recognize events that trigger their own behavior (e.g., being questioned by a student, or excessive demands for help; Taylor and Romanczyk 1994). Knowledge of triggers for teacher behavior will allow them to regulate their own behavior and avoid a confrontation with students instead of being drawn into a verbal conflict when provoked (Colvin 2001; Omer 2001; Wahler and Dumas 1986).

Pay attention to anything unusual about the student's behavior. When the student arrives at school each day, note if the student appears distraught, anxious, or preoccupied. Often, previously unresolved problems (e.g., poor sleep, feeling sick, witnessing a fight between parents, or being anxious about an upcoming event) can undermine the otherwise positive effect of teacher reinforcers like praise (Horner, Day, and Day 1997; Kennedy and Meyer 1996). These events (called setting events) may be upsetting to students, so they are more likely to use problem behavior to access quiet space, rest, or low task demands (Kennedy and Meyer 1996). On such occasions when specific setting events play a role, assignment of low preference tasks, difficult or teacher-selected tasks, are more likely to trigger student behavior initiated to escape task demands (O'Reilly 1995). Again, it makes sense to afford students options before acting-out occurs rather than after its occurrence.

Do not escalate along with the student. When early behaviors in a sequence fail to produce the desired outcome (e.g., to avoid a difficult task or to get peer attention), students are more likely to display severe problem behavior (e.g., draw the teacher into a verbal argument [Hewitt 1999; Walker, Colvin, and Ramsey 1995]). This is especially true when in the past, the use of problem behavior may have resulted in escape from task related teacher requests through teacher capitulation or referring student to the office (i.e., a negative reinforcement history [Colvin 1990; Martens, Bradley, and Eckert 1997; Omer 2001; Patterson 1982; Patterson, Reid, and Dishion 1992; Wahler and Dumas 1986]). If students do succeed in drawing teachers into a verbal conflict, teachers should become cognizant of that fact and not escalate along with students. It is important for teachers to remain calm when provoked, especially if students have already lost self-control. Students try to provoke teachers by making comments like, "You can't make me do this," or "Well, I am done with my sentences and I ain't doing any more!" (Hewitt 1999). If teachers also lose self-control, then both persons will escalate together and act inappropriately (Colvin 2001). Teachers are models for socially appropriate behavior and should maintain that stature. Teachers should disengage (i.e., back off) from the confrontation. Depending on the stage and seriousness of the behavior, tactics such as humor (e.g., "Phew! We almost went to war over this!"), redirecting student attention (e.g., "Please review the punctuation on your sentences"), and giving students time or personal space (e.g., "… I will come back in a little bit to see if you need help") to think about their choices (Walker et al. 1995), may provide a break in the sequence of interactions (i.e., removing triggers). Such a break can succeed in preventing an escalation (Baer 1997).

Offer students opportunities to display responsible behavior. Most behavior is a matter of choice (Mace and Roberts 1993). Students choose to display a given behavior (e.g., complain about a peer) on the basis of their past experiences with using the behavior to obtain specific outcomes (e.g., get the teacher's attention and have the peer reprimanded [Fox and Hoffman 2002]). Thus, if the teacher continues to reprimand or redirect the peer, our student's complaining behavior would be reinforced. Such experiences over time create a "learning history," which affects the students' motivation for engaging in specific behaviors. However, if the teacher did not reprimand the peer following student complaints (i.e., put complaining on extinction), then it is likely that complaining will decrease. Students should be taught to take responsibility for their own behavior by making an informed choice on the basis of their knowledge of consequences for both acceptable and problem behavior. For example, when a student is agitated or difficult to redirect, teachers might offer the choice of moving to a quiet area to work, doing an alternative but related task, or asking for help until he or she feels calmer (Colvin 1993; Darch et al. 1998). Making any demand that the student stay on task or behave appropriately when he or she is very agitated will only serve to further escalate the situation. One option would be to verbally prompt the student regarding the right choice and clarify consequences for both the right and the wrong choices. We can do this successfully only if we have made it clear to students that asking for help or quiet time is preferred to acting out (Jayne, Schloss, Alper, and Menscher 1994).

However, if a student is very agitated or in an accelerated state, rational thinking may be difficult because of physiological arousal (e.g., adrenaline rush [Colvin 1993]). At this time, teachers should not attempt to promote appropriate behavior; instead, they should let the student know about the consequences of severe problem behavior such as physical assault or destruction of property. Later, teachers can debrief with the student privately so that the presence of peers (a potential source of peer attention) is not an issue in attempting to resolve the problem. Knowledge of the consequences at an early stage might prompt some students to make a responsible choice and discontinue problem behavior, but only if they possess the skill.

Intervene early in the sequence. Most students have several types of problem behaviors (e.g., complaining, getting out of seat, arguing), that they use to obtain the desired outcome (e.g., avoiding or escaping task requests). Some of these behaviors will be less severe (e.g., pushing task materials away) and others will be more severe (e.g., throwing or breaking task materials [Shukla and Albin 1996]). When less severe behaviors fail to produce the desired effect, some students will resort to more severe problem behaviors. This is how escalation occurs (Shukla 1994; Shukla-Mehta and Albin 2002). By intervening when less severe problem behaviors occur, teachers can avoid a potentially more serious incident.

Teachers should observe to see if there is an obvious pattern or sequence in which the different behaviors occur. Does a behavioral incident usually begin with one or two of the same behaviors each time (e.g., whining, complaining, or questioning the teacher)? Many times these are the early behaviors in the sequence and should be given our attention. When any of these early behaviors occur, teachers should anticipate the next few behaviors in the sequence and use effective strategies noted above to get the situation under control before the student loses control (Shukla 1994). Research and experience show that appropriate early intervention will usually prevent an escalation of behavior to crisis level proportions (Shukla and Albin 1996). Also, intervening after the occurrence of severe problem behavior by removing the student from the classroom might reinforce the student's escape-motivated problem behavior (Lalli, Casey, and Kates 1995).

Understand how such behavioral incidents ended in the past. Whether an incident is minor or major, how it ends will determine the likelihood of future occurrences. Teachers should evaluate the effectiveness of their strategy on the basis of the effect it has on a student's behavior (Horner, Sugai, Todd, and Lewis-Palmer 1999-2000). For example, if a student continues to disrespect the teacher during instruction by making lewd remarks, many schools require that the student be referred to the office. Temporary removal from the classroom could serve the purpose of escaping classroom instruction. Teachers should ask questions such as: Did I succeed in keeping the student focused on task, or did the student get his or her way (e.g., escape completion of class assignments)? If students got their way, then it is likely that they will continue to display such behaviors in the future because they seem to work—they were successful in producing the desired outcome even if the outcome is undesirable to the teacher (O'Neill et al. 1997).

Know the function of problem behaviors. Most students use problem behavior to either get access to something they find pleasant (e.g., peer or teacher attention, a desired item or activity, internal stimulation, or control of a situation), or to avoid or escape something they find unpleasant (e.g., a difficult task, a series of requests, or an nonpreferred teacher [O'Neill et al. 1997]). They will continue to use problem behavior until the desired outcome (reinforcer) is produced (Shukla-Mehta and Albin 2002). In such an instance, it is logical to assume that the various problem behaviors occur for the same function (or purpose [Sprague and Horner 1992]). The student may argue with the teacher, throw materials, or walk out of a class to escape or avoid the task demands of an assignment. However, the same student may use foul language, bully peers, or pass notes in class to get peer attention. Knowing the functions that problem behaviors serve for students is the key to the effective selection of intervention strategies for managing such behaviors (Day, Horner, and O'Neill 1994; Lalli and Kates 1998; O'Neill et al. 1997).

Use good judgment about which behaviors to punish. It is important to make sure that the consequence matches the severity of the problem behavior. In other words, do not use severe punishment (e.g., verbal humiliation or spanking) for mildly disruptive behavior problems (e.g., walking out of seat or pushing task materials away) (Horner et al. 1990) or the same consequence (e.g., in-school suspension) for all types of problem behavior (e.g., talking, arguing, getting out of seat, or hitting a peer [Sugai, Sprague, Horner, and Walker 2000]). Particularly within special education settings, the use of severe punishment for early occurring, less severe problem behaviors may decrease their occurrence momentarily, but lead to an escalation at some other point in the future—a few minutes, a few hours, or a few days later (Colvin 1993). In such a situation, aggression is induced by punishment (Goh and Iwata 1994). When the needs of students are not met, the problem situation still remains unresolved, increasing the likelihood of an escalation in behavior.

Use extinction procedures wisely. The technical definition of extinction is the withdrawal of the consequent stimulus that previously maintained the problem behavior. In other words, extinction pertains to removing or not delivering a specific consequence following the occurrence of a behavior, that in the past, consistently served to reinforce the behavior (i.e., maintained its occurrence). For example, a student uses foul language (behavior) during instruction and the teacher sends the student to the behavior specialist (consequence) on the assumption that the student will not display similar behavior in future. However, if this behavior continues to occur on a daily basis, it is likely that the consequence (escape from the instructional situation) is reinforcing the student's problem behavior. To illustrate, if the teacher wanted to put foul

language on extinction, she would stop sending the student out of the classroom (i.e., remove the reinforcer). Instead, she would use an alternative strategy, for example, teach the student to request assistance for difficult tasks (Durand and Carr 1992).

Teachers advertently or inadvertently use extinction for less severe behavior problems such as complaining or shouting to reduce its occurrence by ignoring the behavior. They believe that if they ignore such behaviors, the student will stop complaining or shouting. However, if these behaviors are maintained by escape, complaining or shouting will stop but the student will escalate to more severe behavior like throwing books or pushing the desk (Shukla and Albin 1996). This is because extinction for less severe behaviors in the sequence may stop their occurrence but motivate the student to engage in more severe behaviors that have produced the desired outcome (Goh and Iwata 1994), leading to an escalation in behavior.

Most experts agree that it is better to use extinction in combination with differential reinforcement of alternative (communication) responses that are more socially acceptable (Carr and Durand 1985; Lalli et al. 1995; Shukla and Albin 1996). For instance, a student argues with the teacher about a grade assigned for a class project because in the past such coercive tactics resulted in changing to a higher grade. If the teacher does not change the grade (i.e., uses extinction), the student may stop arguing and instead press his or her parents to file a complaint against the teacher (more serious behavior). Before that happens, the teacher should use this opportunity to prompt an alternative and socially appropriate response (e.g., asking questions politely, describing logic) instead of arguing. When the student complies, the teacher should provide immediate reinforcement (e.g., "Thanks for asking so politely") and acknowledge appropriate behavior. (The grade may or may not be changed.) This will help to prevent an escalation in behavior while giving the student an opportunity to communicate effectively with the teacher.

Teach students socially appropriate behavior to replace problem behavior. All of the strategies we have described can be successful in preventing a behavioral escalation, but there is no substitute for teaching students socially appropriate behavior or skills to replace problem behavior (Derby et al. 1997; Day et al. 1994; Durand and Carr 1992; Horner and Day 1991; Lalli, Mace, Wohn, and Livezey 1995; Shukla and Albin 1996; Sprague and Horner 1992). Teachers should use their knowledge of the main reasons for the occurrence of behavioral problems and teach alternative social and communication skills that will succeed in producing the same effect as problem behavior does for the student. For example, teach the student to ask for help instead of complaining when a difficult task is assigned. Then, when the student requests help, the teacher must provide assistance immediately and consistently. If not, the student will revert back to complaining because asking for help does not seem to produce the desired effect.

Teach academic survival skills and set students up for success. There is little question that academic failure is positively correlated with behavioral problems (Bulgren and Carta 1993; Cooper and Speece 1990). Teachers who teach academic survival skills to students (Snyder and Bambara 1997) and promote their active engagement (Martens, Lochner, and Kelly 1992), are less likely to be challenged with disruptive behavior (De Pry and Sugai 2002). Also, the use of effective instructional strategies has been known to increase student success and encourage more socially appropriate classroom behavior. Some examples include the use of response cards (Armendariz and Umbreit 1999), where students have the option to write their response to teacher questions on a dry-erase board and raise it up for the teacher to check. This allows the teacher to know the accuracy of the student's response. Alternatively, teachers may also use index cards with previously prepared answers to specific questions, and the student raises the index card with the correct response. The use of guided notes (Lazarus 1991) is also an effective tool. Guided notes are helpful for students who find it difficult to take notes at the speed at which the teacher lectures. Thus, the teacher provides students with notes from her lectures with key words, terminologies, and summary points left blank. The students are required to fill in the blank spaces by paying attention to the lecture notes on the overhead transparencies. This tool makes it easier to take notes. Teachers could also reduce task difficulty by making adaptations in curricula such as using books on tape, incorporating paragraph or chapter summaries, providing vocabulary lists, and similar such techniques. Teachers should also use proactive instructional methods such as pre-correction (Colvin, Patching, and Sugai 1993). Teachers anticipate the mistakes that students might make, either academically or behaviorally, and present a prompt before the error, making it more likely that the student will attend to that prompt and be successful. For example, if a math teacher knows that one of her students has difficulty figuring out the formula for solving fraction problems, she can provide some prompts (e.g., "Remember the rule about the lowest common denominator"). Such a prompt will guide the student to follow the logical path and determine the correct answer.

The various events surrounding the escalation of student behavior problems can pose significant challenges, but they are preventable. If we study carefully the behavioral patterns of students and identify the purpose of problem behavior, then we will be more successful in implementing proactive and preventive strategies. The key is to anticipate the occurrence of events and to use effective preventive strategies instead of falling into the trap of relying on punishment to control student behavior (Horner et al. 1990). Above all, teaching academic survival skills and social skills, just like any other academic content, is essential to ensuring successful student outcomes. The higher the rate of student success, the less likely the student is to engage in problem behavior (Todd, Horner, and Sugai 1999).

REFERENCES

Albin, R. W., M. O'Brien, and R. H. Horner. 1992. Analysis of an escalating sequence of problem behaviors: A case study. *Research in Developmental Disabilities* 16:133-47.

Armendariz, F., and J. Umbreit. 1999. Using active responding to reduce disruptive behavior in a general education classroom. *The Journal of Positive Behavior Interventions* 1:152-58.

Baer, D. M. 1982. The imposition of structure on behavior and the demolition of behavioral structures. In *Response structure and organization: The 1981 Nebraska symposium on motivation,* edited by J. Bernstein, 217-254. Lincoln: University of Nebraska Press.

Baer, D. M. 1997. Some meanings of antecedent and environmental control. In *Environment and behavior*, edited by D. M. Baer and E. M. Pinkston, 15-29. Boulder, CoIo.: Westview Press.

Bulgren, J. A., and J. J. Carta. 1993. Examining the instructional contexts of students with learning disabilities. *Exceptional Children* 59:182-91.

Carr, E. G., and V. M. Durand. 1985. Reducing behavior problems through functional communication training. *Journal of Applied Behavior Analysis* 18:111-26.

Carr, J. E., J. S. Bailey, C. L. Ecott, K. D. Lucker, and T. M. Weil. 1998. On the effects of noncontingent delivery of differing magnitudes of reinforcement. *Journal of Applied Behavior Analysis* 31:313-22.

Clare, C. M., and A. Im. 1999. Choice vs. preference: The effects of choice and no choice of preferred and non-preferred spelling tasks on the academic behavior of students with disabilities. *Journal of Behavioral Education* 9:239-53.

Colvin, G. 2001. *Defusing anger* [Video]. Available from IRIS Media, 258 East 10th Avenue, Suite B, Eugene, OR 97401.

Colvin, G. 1993. *Managing acting-out behavior*. Eugene, Ore.: Behavior Associates.

_____. 1990. Procedures for preventing serious acting out behavior in the classroom. *Association for Direct Instruction News* 9, 27-30.

Colvin, G., B. Patching, and G. Sugai. 1993. Precorrection: An instructional approach for managing predictable problem behaviors. *Intervention in School and Clinic* 28:143-50.

Cooper, D. H., and D. L. Speece. 1990. Maintaining at-risk children in regular education settings: Initial effects of individual differences and classroom environment. *Exceptional Children* 54:117-28.

Darch, C., A. Miller, and P. Shippen. 1998. Instructional classroom management: A proactive model for managing student behavior. *Beyond Behavior* 9:18-27.

Day, H. M., R. H. Horner, and R. E. O'Neill. 1994. Multiple functions of problem behaviors: Assessment and intervention. *Journal of Applied Behavior Analysis* 27:279-89.

De Pry, R. L., and G. Sugai. 2002. The effect of active supervision and pre-correction on minor behavioral incidents in a sixth grade general education classroom. *Journal of Behavioral Education* 11:255-67.

Derby, K. M., D. P. Wacker, W. Berg, A. DeRaad, S. Ulrich, J. Asmus, et al. 1997. The long-term effects of functional communication training in home settings. *Journal of Applied Behavior Analysis* 30:507-31.

Dunlap, G., L. Kern-Dunlap, S. Clarke, and F. R. Robbins. 1991. Functional assessment, curricular revision, and severe problem behavior problems. *Journal of Applied Behavior Analysis* 24:387-97.

Durand, V. M., and E. G. Carr. 1992. An analysis of maintenance following functional communication training. *Journal of Applied Behavior Analysis* 25:777-94.

Evans, I. M., L. H. Meyer, J. A. Kurkjian, and G. S. Kishi. 1988. An evaluation of behavioral interrelationships in child behavior therapy. In *Handbook of behavior therapy in education*, edited by J. C. Witt, S. N. Elliot, and F. M. Gresham, 89-215. New York: Plenum.

Fox, S., and M. Hoffman. 2002. Escalation behavior as a specific case of goal-directed activity: A persistence paradigm. *Basic & Applied Social Psychology* 24:273-85.

Goh, H., and B. A. Iwata. 1994. Behavioral persistence and variability during extinction of self-injury maintained by escape. *Journal of Applied Behavior Analysis* 27:173-74.

Gunter, P. L., and S. L. Jack. 1994. Effects of challenging behaviors of students with EBD on teacher instructional behavior. *Preventing School Failure* 38:35-40.

Gunter, P. L., R. L. Shores, S. E. Jack, S. K. Rasmussen, and J. Flowers. 1995. On the move: Using teacher/student proximity to improve students' behaviors. *Teaching Exceptional Children* 28:12-14.

Harrison, J. S., and P. L. Gunter. 1996. Teacher instructional language and negative reinforcement: A conceptual framework for working with students with emotional and behavioral disorders. *Education and Treatment of Children* 19:183-96.

Hewitt, M. B. 1999. The control game: Exploring oppositional behavior. *Reclaiming Children and Youth* 8:30-33.

Horner, R. H., and H. M. Day. 1991. The effects of response efficiency on functionally equivalent competing behaviors. *Journal of Applied Behavior Analysis* 24:719-32.

Horner, R. H., H. M. Day, and J. R. Day. 1997. Using neutralizing routines to reduce problem behaviors. *Journal of Applied Behavior Analysis* 30:601-14.

Horner, R. H., G. Dunlap, R. E. Koegel, E. G. Carr, W. Sailor, J. Anderson, et al. 1990. Toward a technology of "nonaversive" behavioral support. *Journal of the Association for Persons With Severe Handicaps* 15:125-32.

Homer, R. H., G. Sugai, A. W. Todd, and T. Lewis-Palmer. 1999-2000. Elements of behavior support plans: A technical brief. *Exceptionality* 8:205-15.

Jayne, D., P. J. Schloss, S. Alper, and S. Menscher. 1994. Reducing disruptive behavior by training students to request assistance. *Behavior Modification* 18:320-38.

Jolivette, K., J. H. Wehby, J. Canale, and N. G. Massey. 2001. Effects of choice-making opportunities on the behavior of students with emotional and behavioral disorders. *Behavioral Disorders* 26:131-45.

Kennedy, C. H. 2000. When reinforcers for problem behavior are not readily apparent. *Journal of Positive Behavior Interventions* 2:195-201.

Kennedy, C. H., and K. A. Meyer. 1996. Sleep deprivation, allergy symptoms and negatively reinforced behavior. *Journal of Applied Behavior Analysis* 29:133-35.

Lalli, J. S., S. Casey, and K. Kates. 1995. Reducing escape behavior and increasing task completion with functional communication training, extinction, and response chaining. *Journal of Applied Behavior Analysis* 28:261-68.

Lalli, J. S., and K. Kates. 1998. The effect of reinforcer preference on functional analysis outcomes. *Journal of Applied Behavior Analysis* 31:79-90.

Lalli, I. S., F. C. Mace, T. Wohn, and K. Livezey. 1995. Identification and modification of a response-class hierarchy. *Journal of Applied Behavior Analysis* 28:551-59.

Lazarus, B. D. 1991. Guided notes, review, and achievement of secondary students with learning disabilities in main-stream content courses. *Education and Treatment of Children* 14:112-27.

Mace, F. C., and M. L. Roberts. 1993. Factors affecting selection of behavioral interventions. In *Communicative alternatives to challenging behavior: Integrating functional assessment and intervention strategies*, edited by J. Reichle and D. P. Wacker, 113-133. Baltimore: Paul H. Brookes.

Martens, B. K., T. A. Bradley, and T. L. Eckert. 1997. Effects of reinforcement history and instructions on the persistence of student engagement. *Journal of Applied Behavior Analysis* 30:569-72.

Martens, B. K., D. G. Lochner, and S. Q. Kelly. 1992. The effects of variable-interval reinforcement on academic engagement. A demonstration of matching theory. *Journal of Applied Behavior Analysis* 25:143-51.

Omer, H. (2001), Helping parents deal with children's acute disciplinary problems without escalation: The principle of nonviolent resistance. *Family Process* 40:53-66.

O'Neill, R. E., R. H. Horner, R. W. Albin, J. R. Sprague, K. Storey, and S. J. Newton. 1997. *Functional assessment and program development for problem behavior: A practical handbook*. Pacific Grove, Calif: Brooks-Cole.

O'Reilly, M. F. 1995. Functional analysis and treatment of escape-maintained aggression correlated with sleep deprivation. *Journal of Applied Behavior Analysis* 28:225-26.

Patterson, G. 1982. *Coercive family process: A social learning approach to family intervention*. Eugene, Ore.: Castalia.

Patterson, G. R., J. B. Reid, and T. J. Dishion. 1992. *Antisocial boys*. Eugene, Ore.: Castalia.

Shores, R. E., P. L. Gunter, and S. L. Jack. 1993. Classroom management strategies: Are they setting events for coercion? *Behavioral Disorders* 18:92-102.

Shukla, S. 1994. Escalating sequences of problem behaviors: Analysis and intervention. Unpublished doctoral dissertation, University of Oregon, Eugene.

Shukla, S., and R. W. Albin. 1996. Effects of extinction alone and extinction plus functional communication training on covariation of problem behaviors. *Journal of Applied Behavior Analysis* 29:565-68.

Shukla, S., C. H. Kennedy, and L. S. Gushing. 1999. Intermediate school students with severe disabilities: Supporting their social participation in general education classrooms. *The Journal of Positive Behavior Interventions* 1:130-40.

Shukla-Mehta, S., and R. W. Albin. 2002. Strategies for preventing behavioral escalation: From theory to practice. *Behavioral Development Bulletin* 1:19-33.

Skinner, B. F. 1938. *The behavior of organisms*. New York: Appleton-Century Crofts.

Snyder, M. C., and L. M. Bambara. 1997. Teaching secondary students with learning disabilities to self-manage classroom survival skills. *Journal of Learning Disabilities* 30:534-43.

Sprague, J. R., and R. H. Horner. 1992. Covariation within functional response classes: Implications for treatment of severe problem behavior. *Journal of Applied Behavior Analysis* 25:735-45.

Sugai, G., J. R. Sprague, R. H. Horner, and H. M. Walker. 2000. Preventing school violence: The use of office discipline referrals to assess and monitor school-wide discipline interventions. *Journal of Emotional and Behavioral Disorders* 8:94-101.

Taylor, J. C., and R. G. Romanczyk. 1994. Generating hypotheses about the function of student problem behavior by observing teacher behavior. *Journal of Applied Behavior Analysis* 27:251-65.

Todd, A. W., R. H. Horner, and G. Sugai. 1999. Self-monitoring and self-recruited praise: Effects on problem behavior, academic engagement, and work completion in a typical classroom. *The Journal of Positive Behavior Interventions* 1:66-76.

Wahler, R. G., and J. E. Dumas. 1986. Maintenance factors in coercive mother-child interactions: The compliance and predictability hypotheses. *Journal of Applied Behavior Analysis* 19:13-22.

Wahler, R. G., and J. J. Fox. 1982. Response structure in deviant child-parent relationships: Implications for family therapy. In *Response structure and organization. The 1981 Nebraska symposium on motivation*, edited by D. J. Bernstein, 1-46. Lincoln: University of Nebraska.

Walker, H. M., G. Colvin, and R. Ramsey. 1995. *Antisocial behavior in school: Strategies and best practices*. Pacific Grove, Calif.: Brookes/Cole.

Smita Shukla-Mehta is an associate professor in the College of Education and Psychology at the University of Texas at Tyler, and Richard W. Albin is an associate professor in the Department of Educational and Community Services at the University of Oregon, Eugene.

From *The Clearing House,* November/December 2003. Reprinted by permission of the Helen Dwight Reid Educational Foundation. Published by Heldref Publications, 1319, Eighteenth St., NW, Washington, DC 20036-1802. Copyright © 2003.

Corporal Punishment
Legalities, Realities, and Implications

PATRICIA H. HINCHEY

For some time now, I have been talking to practitioners about corporal punishment in schools, especially middle and high schools. Practitioner responses to my questions about the legal status of paddling and other physical discipline in their states have fallen into two categories: surprise that I would ask about the subject as if practices such as paddling still existed anywhere, and surprise that I would ask about the topic as if paddling weren't common in every school in the country. Most teachers appear to assume that the status of corporal punishment in their own school or state is a national standard—a perception that is far from contemporary reality. The following quiz will help readers determine the reliability of their own perceptions relating to this topic:

True or False?

- The issue of corporal punishment has reached the United States Supreme Court, which has upheld the practice as constitutional.

- Military personnel and criminals have the right to due process before corporal punishment can be imposed; as a matter of federal law, schoolchildren, on the contrary, do not.

- Early in his term in office, President George W. Bush promoted legislation that would protect educators who had beaten children form lawsuits. Both teachers' unions, the NEA (National Education Association) and the NFT (National Federation of Teachers), opposed this legislation, intended to protect their members.

- Researchers have demonstrated that corporal punishment can constitute a form of sexual abuse.

However unlikely it may seem to many readers, the answer in every case is "true."

U.S. Courts and Corporal Punishment

The Supreme Court case that now provides the foundation for corporal punishment policies is *Ingraham v. Wright* (1977). Two students, James Ingraham and Roosevelt Andrews, suffered severe paddlings in their Florida junior high school that left Ingraham needing medical attention for severe pain and bruising and Andrews unable in one instance to use his arm for a week. Their suit argued that the paddlings were unconstitutional, in violation of the Eighth Amendment's prohibition of cruel and unusual punishment and also of the Fourteenth Amendment's guarantee of due process. The Court, however, rejected both arguments. Because corporal punishment has long been common among parents and school officials alike, the Court found, it could not be classified as "cruel and unusual." Moreover, the Court found that the Eighth Amendment is intended to protect criminals, not schoolchildren, and that children who suffered severe punishment could gain redress by prosecuting officials on such charges as assault and battery, a recourse thought to be sufficient protection for children.

Although many parents and students have indeed sought legal redress for severe beatings, they rarely win in court—

making it especially difficult to understand why President Bush has supported a legislative effort to prohibit lawsuits against educators (Breaking 2001; Spare 2001). Courts have found in favor of schools and teachers even when the punishment they imposed included paddling a nine-year-old seven times within half an hour; sticking a straight pin into a student's arm; confining children in closets and other small, dark spaces; slamming them into walls; and stuffing and/or taping children's mouths (Hyman and Snook 1999). Parents have also been dismayed to lose cases filed after a child was paddled without parental permission. Unless a school chooses to abide by parental wishes, parents in states where corporal punishment is legal can protect their children from beatings only by removing them from schools that employ paddling.

Sometimes the offenses against children are so egregious that it seems unbelievable that courts would find for schools and against the family, but it routinely happens. For example, one seventeen-year-old female, who was both an honor student and a senior with no prior record of misbehavior, skipped school. This young adult was forced to bend over a desk and submit to several blows inflicted by an adult male coach whom she had trusted until the incident. For the girl, consequences included not only the physical pain of the beating, but also menstrual hemorrhaging and long-lasting emotional trauma. Despite arguments that the case involved not only physical but also sexual abuse, the school won the case (Hyman and Snook 1999). In fact, over and over again corporal punishment has been linked to sexual abuse, although many state legislators who could outlaw the practice apparently remain unmoved by such arguments (see Donahue 2001, for example, or Johnson 1994, and others listed on Project NoSpank's Web page "Spanking Can Be Sexual Abuse," available at <http://nospank.net/101.htm >).

Nor is any special consideration offered to students with disabilities, for whom courts have upheld paddling, isolation, and mouth taping as punishments. In one case, a disabled student was forced to do exercise so rigorous that it led to his death (Hyman and Snook 1999). Rather than finding such incidents a cause for restraining corporal punishment, legislators have blithely moved forward toward solidifying educators' legal right to impose physical punishment on students with disabilities. In June 2001, a bill enabling discipline of the disabled was introduced by U.S. Senator Jeff Sessions of Alabama and passed the United States Senate.

As the following examples illustrate, courts rarely punish abusive educators in states that allow corporal punishment.

Worldwide and Nationwide Legality

It is perhaps telling that the United States is one of two countries worldwide that have not yet ratified the Convention on the Rights of the Child, adopted by the United Nations General Assembly in November 1989. The other is Somalia. The document calls for multiple protections of the human rights of children, including the right to be protected from violence.

As other countries of the world move toward greater and greater protection of their children, with Northern Ireland and Scotland strengthening laws against corporal punishment in 2001, the United States retains its dubious distinction of being one of very few developed countries whose national policy allows corporal punishment in schools. Over one hundred organizations joined forces to call this fact to national attention in a widely publicized letter to the president of the United States: "Throughout the developed, industrial world, and in many developing nations, the use of corporal punishment against schoolchildren is forbidden. No European country permits the practice" (Open Letter to the President, available at <http://nospank.net/endcp.htm>). Organizations signing the letter included the American Academy of Pediatrics, the National Congress of Parents and Teachers Association, the National Mental Health Association, the American Psychological Association, the American Association of Physicians for Human Rights, the National Association of School Psychologists, the American School Counselor Association, and the National Committee for Prevention of Child Abuse.

However, the organizations' plea that the president "instruct the Secretary of the U.S. Department of Education to take expeditious and forceful action to deny federal assistance to any school, school district, or other educational entity that authorizes the use of corporal punishment" has fallen on deaf ears. The effort has also been undermined both by President Bush's support for legislation protecting those who beat children and by Senator Session's efforts to make sure that all children are equally subject to such beatings. A *Houston Chronicle* story reported the case of several Canadian parents who moved to Ohio and Indiana to escape the Canadian law prohibiting the use of such objects as paddles, sticks, and belts to inflict punishment on children. In Ohio and Indiana, parents (and others) are free to strike children with such instruments (Clairborne 2001).

For those concerned about the physical safety and mental health of children, the good news is that legislators in twenty-seven states and the District of Columbia have heeded the research and advice of pediatricians, parents, educators, and others and have passed state laws prohibiting corporal punishment in schools. However, that leaves children in nearly half of all states still subject to the abuses of corporal punishment with little or no practical means of prevention or redress. The box identifies states that continue to allow physical punishment of schoolchildren, despite its dangers.

Although defenders of corporal punishment argue that few incidents are excessive, a review of news reports indicates otherwise—and that the extreme cases are sufficiently horrifying to justify exclusion of corporal punishment, whatever the rate of incidence.

States That Allow Corporal Punishment

*Alabama	*Mississippi
Arizona	*Missouri
*Arkansas	New Mexico
Colorado	North Carolina
Delaware	Ohio
Florida	*Oklahoma
*Georgia	Pennsylvania
Idaho	South Carolina
Indiana	*Tennessee
Kansas	*Texas
Kentucky	Wyoming
*Louisiana	

Note: *States listed in the top ten pupil-battering states in both the 1996–97 and 1997–98 Elementary and Secondary School Civil Rights Compliance Reports.

Source: Danger Zones: States in the U.S. that Permit Pupil-Beating, Jordan Riak, .<http://nospank.net/eddpts.htm>

The Realities of Corporal Punishment in the United States

All of the following incidents were reported in newspapers during 2001. In the context of cases with results as severe as death, some cases seem almost trivial by comparison. Still, it is likely that most parents would be greatly upset by the actions of a California teacher who, despite a ban on corporal punishment, taped a first-grader's mouth shut and threatened to tie her up (McLellan 2001); and of an Arizona teacher who tried to force a sixth-grader to chew gum already chewed by others and saved in a jar for the purposes of this punishment (Mother 2001). Such bodily indignities, however, are the least of what a child may suffer in school, as other reported incidents nationwide reveal.

An Oklahoma Christian school teacher struck a 12-year-old with a 3-foot long dowel because he was passing notes in class and inflicted bruises that hospital doctors characterized as "severe" (Martin 2001). A parent in Louisiana was unsuccessful in filing a criminal action against an assistant principal who broke a paddle on a 13-year-old (Shackleford 2001). A parochial school director in Florida was arrested after using a wooden board to paddle an 8-year-old, leaving a mark some 4 inches wide and 6 inches long and welts as high as a quarter of an inch (Port 2001). In another Florida incident, a dean at an elementary school was found guilty of misdemeanor battery for excessively beating an 8-year-old; he was required to take an anger-management course and subsequently returned to his role as school leader—although after this incident, the school did ban corporal punishment (Hustead 2001). In Michigan, another state where

corporal punishment is legally restricted, a 15-year-old freshman football player did not return to school for weeks after he received 10 blows with a paddle that eventually cracked. Some six or seven other player were also hit, one approximately 12 or 13 times (Potts 2001). In Tennessee, a school employee faced criminal charges after hitting a 15-year-old in the arm with a baseball bat (Armstrong 2001).

A national antispanking group called for a civil rights audit of students in Mobile, Alabama because black children in recent years have received 65 to 70 percent of all paddlings there, although they make up slightly less than half of all students. Statistics also indicated that on the whole, for the 1998–99 school year, 73 percent of paddlings administered statewide in Alabama were to the black students who make up only 41 percent of its total school population (Catalanello 2001).

If all reports related to religious schools and alternative "boot-camp" type schools were included, this list would be much longer.

Implications: What Teachers Can Do

When I work with education students, tomorrow's teachers, I try to impress on them that becoming a professional educator means accepting responsibility for protecting the rights and interests of children in classrooms. To do less is to fall short of the trust placed in us by our students, their parents, and our profession. A classroom teacher who is willing to take even one of the following steps is, on the other hand, acting to meet professional responsibilities.

1. Become familiar with the information made available by Parents and Teachers against Violence in Education (PTAVE) and by Temple University's National Center for the Study of Corporal Punishment and Alternatives (NCSCPA). Web sites sponsored by these organizations offer a complete library of resources, including news and research articles. The more teachers know about corporal punishment, the better they can counter arguments for it with evidence of the danger it poses to children.

- PTAVE's Project No Spank, <http://nospank.net/>
- Temple University's NCSCPA, <http://temple.edu/education/nespca/NCSCPA.html>

2. Become familiar with print resources as well. Among the most important books on corporal punishment is Hyman and Snook's *Dangerous Schools: What We Can Do About the Physical and Emotional Abuse of Our Children*. Although that book is possibly the most important print resource detailing the dangers of physical punishment, there are several others that also can be helpful:

- Greven, P. 1991. Spare the child: The religious roots of punishment and the psychological impact of physical abuse. New York: Random House.
- Straus, M., and D. Donnelly. 1993. Beating the devil out of them: Corporal punishment in American families. San Francisco: Jossey-Bass.
- Males, M. 1996. The scapegoat generation: America's war on adolescents. Monroe, MA: Common Courage Press.

3. Monitor Project No Spank. Because this is one of the most important sources of information for children's advocates, signing on to its mailing list can be an important step in staying informed and involved.

4. Accept the need to be political in a variety of ways, in a variety of arenas. Develop relationships with colleagues, parents, administrators, school board members and politicians who have the power to help change policy and laws. Find allies and work with them to bring change on local and state levels, using voting power judiciously.

Educate your colleagues at every opportunity. Raise your concerns with other teachers and share what you know about the dangers of corporal punishment. Have them read what you have read, and try to enlist their support and build a strong core of opposition.

Promote efforts to be sure your school is safe for children. Research local policy. If corporal punishment is allowed, consider working for change; meanwhile, try to determine if guidelines are being followed and promote compliance if they are not. In schools where corporal punishment is not permitted, try to determine if the reality of classroom life conforms to regulations; if you find discrepancies, do what you can to spark awareness and promote adherence to policy.

Seek union support. If you are in a local union affiliated with the National Education Association (NEA), ask union representatives to begin publicizing the NEA stance against corporal punishment because of its dangers. The NEA was, in fact, the first major national education organization that called for banning corporal punishment in a 1992 resolution (NEA 1998). If you are affiliated with the American Federation of Teachers, work to persuade that union to join in the NEA public stance.

Enlist the help of your parents and teachers association. Be sure that local chapters are familiar with *Corporal punishment: Myths and realities* (National PTA, 1991) <http://nospank.net/pta.htm>. This National PTA document discusses the dangers of corporal punishment.

Parting Thoughts

As teachers, we must always act as advocates for children's welfare. We have many avenues to help ensure that schools are safe for children—or to protest and publicize existing dangers loudly and frequently, seeking a change in policy. To help end the legal beatings of children in schools teachers must become thoroughly educated on the issue and then assume the role of change agents, pursuing restraint and reform at every opportunity. Certainly parents, administrators, and school board members share teachers' commitment to the welfare of children. By learning and then sharing the extensive evidence against corporal punishment, teachers may be able to counter the ubiquitous argument that "a little swat on the behind never hurt anybody." Lawmakers and courts have failed to ensure that schools are safe places for the children entrusted to our care. These children cannot afford teachers to fail as their advocates and protectors as well.

Key words: corporal punishment, teachers as advocates, abuse, child welfare

REFERENCES

Armstrong accused of hitting teen with baseball bat. 2001. Associated Press State & Local Wire. 6 September. Retrieved 28 January 2002, from Lexis-Nexis database.

Bragg, R. 2001. Christian school questioned over discipline for wayward. *New York Times.* 5 July. Retrieved 28 January 2002, from <http://nospank.net/n-i03.htm>

Breaking the hickory stick. 2001. Editorial, *New York Times,* Late Edition (East Coast): A.16. 7 May.

Catalanello, R. 2001. National group seizes on racial disparity in punishment at Mobile schools. *Mobile Register.* 21 July. Retrieved 28 January 2002, from <http://nospank.net/n-i13.htm>.

Clairborne, W. 2001. Canadians from sect flee to U.S. over right to spank. 2 August. *Houston Chronicle:* 7.

Donahue, J. 2001. Spanking as sexualized abuse. *Counseling Today.* May. Retrieved 29 October 2001 from <http://nospank.org/donahue.htm>.

Hustead, J. 2001. "Excessive" spanking gets Dawkins probation. 10 April. *Press Journal* (Vero Beach, FL): A3.

Hyman, I., and P. Snook. 1999. *Dangerous schools: What we can do about the physical and emotional abuse of our children.* San Francisco: Jossey-Bass.

Johnson, T. 1994. The sexual dangers of spanking children. Retrieved 29 October 2001, from <http://nospank.org/s-dngr.htm>.

Martin, L. 2001. Teacher charged with injury. *Tulsa World.* 11 October. Retrieved 25 January 2002, from Lexis-Nexis database.

McLellan, D. 2001. Tustin district bars substitute who allegedly taped girl's mouth shut. *Los Angeles Times:* B3. 22 May.

Mother says child was ordered to chew someone else's used gum. 2001. *Associated Press State & Local Wire.* 12 April. Retrieved 28 January 2002, from Lexis-Nexis database.

National Education Association (NEA). 1998. *Child Abuse and Neglect.* Retrieved 20 February 2002, from <http://www.nea.org/issues/safescho/childabus.html>.

Parents and Teachers Against Violence in Education (PTAVE). *Project No Spank.* Retrieved 29 October 2001, from <http://www.nospank.net>.

Port Charlotte school director arrested for paddling student. 2001. *Associated Press State & Local Wire*. 3 July. Retrieved 28 January 2002, from Lexis-Nexis database.

Potts, L. February 5, 2001. Football coach accused of paddling student is suspended. *Associated Press State & Local Wire*. Retrieved January 28, 2002, from Lexis-Nexis database.

Shackleford, C. 2001. Principal won't face charges over paddling. *Chattanooga Times:* B2. 13 September.

Spare the rod: Washington shouldn't encourage corporal punishment, 2001. Editorial in Pittsburgh *Post-Gazette*. 21 May. Retrieved 25 January 2002, from `<http://nospank.net/n-h81.htm>`.

Stockwell, J. 2001. Boy's death at school a homicide. *Washington Post*. 5 July. Retrieved 28 January 2002, from `<http://nospank.net/n-i04.htm>`.

Patricia H. Hinchey is an associate professor of education at Penn State University.

From *The Clearing House*, January/February 2003. Reprinted with permission of the Helen Dwight Reid Foundation. Published by Heldref Publications, 1319 Eighteenth St. NW, Washington, DC 20036-1802. © 2003.

UNIT 6
Assessment

Unit Selections

Key Points to Consider

- What fundamental concepts from contemporary learning and motivation theories have specific implications for how teachers assess their students? Are such practices consistent with what is promulgated with standardized tests?

- What are some important principles for using standardized tests scores to improve instruction? What are some limitations of standardized tests?

- Many educators believe that schools should identify the brightest, most capable students. What are the assessment implications of this philosophy? How would low achieving students be affected?

- What principles of assessment should teachers adopt for their own classroom testing? Is it necessary or feasible to develop a table of specifications for each test? How do we know if the test scores teachers use are reliable and if valid inferences are drawn from the scores? How can teachers make time to involve students in self-assessment?

 Links: www.dushkin.com/online/
These sites are annotated in the World Wide Web pages.

Awesome Library for Teachers
  http://www.neat-schoolhouse.org/teacher.html
Kathy Schrocks's Guide for Educators: Assessment
  http://school.discovery.com/schrockguide/assess.html
Phi Delta Kappa International
  http://www.pdkintl.org
Washington (State) Center for the Improvement of Student Learning
  http://www.k12.wa.us/

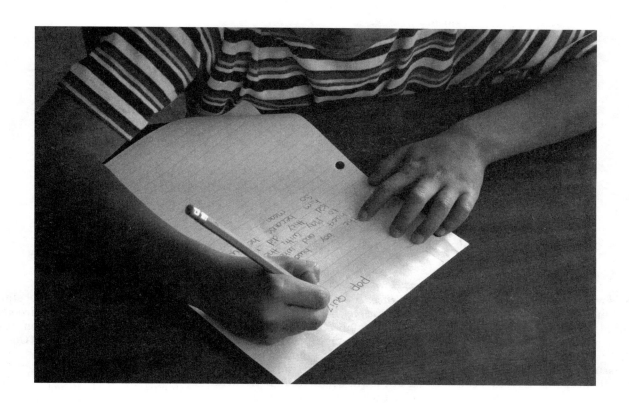

In which reading group does Jon belong? How do I construct tests? How do I know when my students have mastered the course objectives? How can I explain test results to Mary's parents? Teachers answer these questions, and many more, by applying principles of assessment. Assessment refers to procedures for measuring and recording student performance and constructing grades that communicate to others levels of proficiency or relative standing. Assessment principles constitute a set of concepts that are integral to the teaching-learning process. Indeed, a significant amount of teacher time is spent in assessment activities, and with more accountability there is a greater emphasis on assessment.

Assessment provides a foundation for making sound evaluative judgments about students' learning and achievement. Teachers need to use fair and unbiased criteria in order to assess student learning objectively and accurately and make appropriate decisions about student placement. For example, in assigning Jon to a reading group, the teacher will use his test scores as an indication of his skill level. Are the inferences from the test results valid for the school's reading program? Are his test scores consistent over several months or years? Are they consistent with his performance in class? The teacher should ask and then answer these questions so that he or she can make intelligent decisions about Jon. On the other hand, will knowledge of the test scores affect the teacher's perception of classroom performance and create a self-fullfilling prophesy? Teachers also evaluate students in order to assign grades, and the challenge is to balance "objective" test scores with more sub-

jective, informally gathered information. Both kinds of evaluative information are necessary, but both can be inaccurate and are frequently misused.

The articles in this section focus on two contemporary issues in assessment—the use of high-stakes standardized tests and classroom assessment that is integrated with teaching.

The first article in this unit provides an overview of what we have learned over many years about the impact of standardized testing on teaching and learning. The next two articles discuss the importance of standards-based testing and how this kind of testing may be related to classroom instruction. It has become increasingly clear that high-stakes testing will be required, and understanding the limitations as well as negative consequences of this kind of testing is needed.

W. James Popham, a longstanding expert in testing, argues for much more emphasis on classroom assessment. This suggested emphasis is provided in the next three articles in this unit. The first describes a landmark series of investigations called "Working Inside the Black Box." Researchers provide a detailed account of how formative classroom assessment can provide better grading of students, more effective use of student self-assessment, and improved learning. Richard Stiggins, another expert in testing, then argues for student self-assessment as a technique that engages students in learning and provides excellent formative feedback to teachers. In the last article Guskey shows how classroom assessments can be integrated with teaching to support corrective instruction that targets the improvement of student learning.

The Lessons of High-Stakes Testing

Research shows that high-stakes tests can affect teaching and learning in predictable and often undesirable ways.

By Lisa M. Abrams and George F. Madaus

Today's widespread implementation of standards-based reform and the federal government's commitment to test-based accountability ensure that testing will remain a central issue in education for the foreseeable future. Test results can provide useful information about student progress toward meeting curricular standards. But when policymakers insist on linking test scores to high-stakes consequences for students and schools, they often overlook lessons from the long history of research.

The Current Landscape

The most recent round of high-stakes testing grew out of the standards-based reform movement that began in the early 1990s. This reform effort gave rise to state-level accountability systems characterized by four components (Hamilton, Stecher, & Klein, 2002):

• *Content standards* that communicate the desired knowledge and skills;

• *Tests* designed to measure the progress toward achieving the content standards;

• *Performance targets,* which identify criteria used to determine whether schools and students have reached the desired level of achievement; and

• *Incentives,* such as rewards and sanctions based on the attainment of the performance targets.

Every state has now instituted a statewide testing program and curricular standards or frameworks—except Iowa, where local districts develop their own standards and benchmarks. The state tests vary substantially in difficulty, content, item format, and, especially, the sanctions attached to test performance. For example, Massachusetts, New York, Texas, and Virginia use test results to award high school diplomas. Other states—Missouri, Rhode Island, and Vermont, for example—use students' performance on the state test to hold schools, rather than students, accountable. Still others, including Iowa, Montana, Nebraska, and North Dakota, currently attach no sanctions to test performance (Edwards, 2003).

The 2001 reauthorization of the Elementary and Secondary Education Act, also known as No Child Left Behind (NCLB), carries testing and accountability requirements that will substantially increase student testing and hold all schools accountable for student performance. This legislation marks a major departure from the federal government's traditional role regarding elementary and secondary education. It requires that states administer reading and math tests annually in grades 3-8 and dur-

ing one year in high school starting in 2005-2006. These requirements will affect almost 25 million students each school year (National Center for Education Statistics, 2002).

NCLB requires states to meet adequate yearly progress (AYP) goals to ensure school accountability for student achievement on state tests. Schools that fail to achieve AYP goals face demanding corrective actions, such as replacement of school staff, implementation of new curriculum, extension of the school day or academic year, parental choice options, and, finally, complete reorganization.

Lessons We Should Have Learned

The current emphasis on testing as a tool of education reform continues a long tradition of using tests to change pedagogical priorities and practices. In the United States, this use of testing dates back to 1845 in Boston, when Horace Mann, then Secretary of the Massachusetts State Board of Education, replaced the traditional oral exam with a standardized written essay test. Internationally, high-stakes testing extends as far back as the 15th century in Treviso, Italy, where teacher salaries were linked to student examination performance (Madaus & O'Dwyer, 1999).

A 1988 examination of the effects of high-stakes testing programs on teaching and learning in Europe and in the United States (Madaus, 1988) identified seven principles that captured the intended and unintended consequences of such programs. Current research confirms that these principles still hold true for contemporary statewide testing efforts.

Principle 1: The power of tests to affect individuals, institutions, curriculum, or instruction is a perceptual phenomenon. Tests produce large effects if students, teachers, or administrators believe that the results are important. Policymakers and the public generally do believe that test scores provide a reliable, external, objective measure of school quality. They view tests as symbols of order, control, and attainment (Airasian, 1988).

Today's high-stakes testing movement relies on the symbolic importance of test scores. Forty-eight states currently require schools to provide the public with "report cards" (Edwards, 2003). Goldhaber and Hannaway (2001) found that the stigma associated with a school receiving a low grade on the state report card was a more powerful influence on Florida teachers than were the school-level sanctions imposed for poor test results.

Principle 2: The more any quantitative social indicator is used for social decision making, the more likely it will be to distort and corrupt the social process it is intended to monitor. In other words, placing great importance on state tests can have a major influence on what takes place in classrooms, often resulting in an emphasis on test preparation that can compromise the credibility or accuracy of test scores as a measure of student achievement.

We can assess whether this principle still applies today by examining the relationship between rising state test scores and scores on other achievement tests. Both old and new studies of this relationship (for example, Amrein & Berliner, 2002; Haladyna, Nolen, & Haas, 1991; Klein, Hamilton, McCaffrey, & Stecher, 2000; Linn, 1998) show that improvements in the state test scores do not necessarily reflect general achievement gains.

We can also find examples of this second principle in two recent surveys of teachers' opinions. In one national study, roughly 40 percent of responding teachers reported that they had found ways to raise state-mandated test scores without, in their opinion, actually improving learning (Pedulla et al., 2003). Similarly, in a Texas survey, 50 percent of the responding teachers did not agree that the rise in TAAS scores "reflected increased learning and high-quality teaching" (Hoffman, Assaf, & Paris, 2001, p. 488).

Principle 3: If important decisions are based on test results, then teachers will teach to the test. Curriculum standards and tests can focus instruction and provide administrators, teachers, and students with clear goals. A substantial body of past data and recent research, however, confirms that as the stakes increase, the curriculum narrows to reflect the content sampled by the test (for example, Jones et al., 1999; Madaus, 1991; McMillan, Myran, & Workman, 1999; Pedulla et al., 2003; Stecher, Barron, Chun, & Ross, 2000).

New York State, where the state department of education is requiring schools to spend more time on the NCLB-tested areas of reading and math, provides an example of how such pressure encourages schools to give greater attention to tested content and decrease emphasis on nontested content. According to one school principal, "the art, music, and everything else are basically out the window… something has to go" (Herszenhorn, 2003).

Principle 4: In every setting where a high-stakes test operates, the exam content eventually defines the curriculum. Pressure and sanctions associated with a state test often result in teachers using the content of past tests to prepare students for the new test. Several studies have documented that an overwhelming majority of teachers feel pressure to improve student performance on the state test. For example, 88 percent of teachers surveyed in Maryland and 98 percent in Kentucky believed that they were under "undue pressure" to improve student performance (Koretz, Barron, Mitchell, & Keith, 1996a, 1996b). As an outgrowth of this pressure, the amount of instructional time devoted to specific test preparation often increased.

More recent studies have found that teachers are spending a sizable amount of instructional time and using a variety of test-specific methods to prepare students for their state tests (Herman & Golan, n.d.; Hoffman, Assaf, & Paris, 2001). In North Carolina, 80 percent of elementary teachers surveyed "spent more than 20 percent of their total instructional time practicing for the end-of-grade tests" (Jones et al., 1999, p. 201). A national survey found that teachers in high-stakes states were four times more likely than those in low-stakes settings to report spending more than 30 hours a year on test preparation activities, such as teaching or reviewing topics that would be on the state test, providing students with items similar to those on the test, and using commercial test-preparation materials from previous years for practice (Pedulla et al., 2003).

> The current emphasis on testing as a tool of education reform continues a long tradition of using tests to change pedagogical priorities and practices.

Principle 5: Teachers pay attention to the form of the questions of high-stakes tests (short-answer, essay, multiple-choice, and so on) and adjust their instruction accordingly. A wide variety of research confirms that test format does influence instruction in both positive and negative ways.

Studies in states that require students to formulate and provide written responses to test questions show an increased emphasis on teaching writing and higher-level thinking skills (Taylor, Shepard, Kinner, & Rosenthal, 2003). For example, in Kentucky, 80 percent of teachers surveyed indicated that they had increased their instructional emphasis on problem solving and writing as a result of the portfolio-based state test (Koretz, Barron, Mitchell, & Keith, 1996a).

In several studies, teachers have reported decreases in the use of more time-consuming instructional strategies and lengthy enrichment activities (Pedulla et al., 2003; Taylor et al., 2003). Further, a recent study found that the format of the state test may adversely affect the use of technology for instructional purposes: One-third of teachers in high-stakes states said that they were less likely to use computers to teach writing because students were required to construct handwritten responses on the state test (Russell & Abrams, in press).

Principle 6: When test results are the sole or even partial arbiter of future education or life choices, society treats test results as the major goal of schooling rather than as a useful but fallible indicator of achievement. Almost 100 years ago, a chief inspector of schools in England described this principle in a way that resonates today:

> Whenever the outward standard of reality (examination results) has established itself at the expense of the inward, the ease with which worth (or what passes for such) can be measured is ever tending to become in itself the chief, if not sole, measure of worth. And in proportion as we tend to value the results of education for their measurableness, so we tend to undervalue and at last to ignore those results which are too intrinsically valuable to be measured. (Holmes, 1911, p. 128)

In the next five years, almost half of U.S. states will require students to pass a state-mandated test as a requirement for graduation (Edwards, 2003). As a result, a passing score on the state test is the coin of the realm for students, parents, teachers, and administrators. The social importance placed on state test scores ensures that students' successful performance on the state test is the ultimate goal for schools. Local press coverage on school pass rates and anecdotal evidence that scores on the state test may influence local real estate sales show the importance of test performance as a surrogate for education quality.

Principle 7: A high-stakes test transfers control over the curriculum to the agency that sets or controls the exam. State standards-based reform efforts leave the details and development of testing programs to state departments of education and whomever the department contracts with to construct the test. This system shifts the responsibility for determining curricular priorities and performance standards away from local school administrators or classroom teachers and often results in a one-size-fits-all curriculum and test.

Falmouth, Massachusetts, provides a recent noteworthy example of how a high-stakes state test can override local control. Under the threat of losing state funding and the licensure of the school principal and superintendent, the Falmouth School Committee reversed a decision to award diplomas to special-needs students who failed the Massachusetts state exam, thus shattering the hopes of a student seeking admittance to a nonacademic culinary degree program (Myers, 2003).

From High-Stakes Tests to Multiple Measures

No one denies the importance of accountability. The relationship between test scores and accountability, however, is not as simple as most people think. The seven principles formulated in 1988 have been acted out in state after state in the past 15 years and clearly reveal the serious flaws in the practice of using a single high-stakes measure to hold all students and schools accountable.

Cut-off scores that place students in such performance categories as *needs improvement, basic, proficient, or advanced* are arbitrary. The subjective methods used to categorize students into performance categories often lack validity (Horn, Ramos, Blumer, & Madaus, 2000). Further, most policymakers and the public do not understand the psychometric underpinnings of the tests. Issues that might seem trivial to them, such as the assumptions made when running computer programs that produce scaled scores, and even basic decisions about rounding, have significant consequences when categorizing students.

We need to enhance state testing programs by including multiple measures of student achievement.

Like any measurement tool that produces a number—such as blood pressure gauges, complex laboratory tests, radar detectors, breathalyzers, and fingerprinting—test scores are fallible. Yet most state laws do not consider margin of error when interpreting a student's scores.

Misguided executive decisions, poorly conceived legislation, understaffing, unrealistic reporting deadlines, and unreasonable progress goals can cause numerous errors in test scores (Rhoades & Madaus, 2003). In addition, scoring or programming errors can result in incorrect scores. Winerip (2003) describes the impact of human error on one Florida 3rd grader. When the tests of 71 3rd grade students who scored below the passing cut-off score were hand-scored, the process unearthed a scoring machine error that marked a question wrong for this student because of an erasure. "Instantly, Raven was transformed from 3rd-grade dufe to a state-certified 4th grader" (p. B9).

In addition, any single test can only sample knowledge and cannot give a full picture of what students know and can do. As an illustration, Harlow and Jones's interviews with students (2003) showed that on the science portion of the Third International Mathematics and Science Study (TIMSS), the students had more knowledge about concepts than their written answers had demonstrated for more than half of the test questions. Conversely, the interviews suggested that for one-third of the items, students lacked a sound understanding of the information assessed even though they had given the correct response.

A fundamental principle in social science research is to always use at least two methods when studying social science phenomena because relying on only one method can produce misleading results. We need to enhance state testing programs by including multiple measures of student achievement. Measuring in a variety of ways does not mean giving students multiple opportunities to take the same test, but rather incorporating other methods of measurement or additional criteria, such as teacher judgments, when making decisions about grade promotion and graduation.

As districts, schools, and teachers respond to federal and state test-based accountability policies, we must step back from a blind reliance on test scores. We need to acknowledge that tests, although useful, are also fallible indicators of achievement. We also need to recognize that when test scores are linked to high-stakes consequences, they can weaken the learning experiences of students, transform teaching into test preparation, and taint the test itself so that it no longer measures what it was intended to measure.

In classrooms, teachers provide many opportunities for students to demonstrate their knowledge and skills. Likewise, we should insist that test scores never be used in isolation, but that schools incorporate other indicators of what students know and can do—especially teacher judgment—before making high-stakes decisions about the education of students.

Teachers are spending a sizable amount of instructional time to prepare students for their state tests.

References

Airasian, P. W. (1988). Symbolic validation: The case of state-mandated, high-stakes testing. *Educational Evaluation and Policy Archives, 10*(4), 301-313.

Amrein, A. L., & Berliner, D. C. (2002). High-stakes testing, uncertainty, and student learning. *Education Policy Analysis Archives, 10*(18). [Online]. Available: http://epaa.asu.edu/epaa/v10n18

Edwards, V. (Ed.). (2003, Jan. 9). *Quality Counts 2003: If I can't learn from you... (Education Week Special Report), 12*(17). Bethesda, MD: Editorial Projects in Education.

Goldhaber, D., & Hannaway, J. (2001). *Accountability with a kicker: Observations on the Florida A+ Plan.* Paper presented at the annual meeting of the Association of Public Policy and Management, Washington, DC.

Haladyna, T., Nolen, S., & Haas, N. (1991). Raising standardized achievement test scores and the origins of test score pollution. *Educational Researcher, 20*(5), 2-7.

Hamilton, L., Stecher, B., & Klein, S. (Eds). (2002). *Making sense of test-based accountability in education.* Santa Monica, CA: Rand.

Harlow, A., & Jones, A. (2003, July). *Why students answer TIMSS science test items the way they do.* Paper presented at the annual conference of the Australian Science Education Research Association, Melbourne, Victoria, Australia.

Herman, J., & Golan, S. (n.d.). *Effects of standardized testing on teachers and learning* (CSE Technical Report 334). Los Angeles: National Center for Research on Evaluation, Standards, and Student Testing.

Herszenhorn, D. (2003, July 23). Basic skills forcing cuts in art classes. *The New York Times*, p. B1.

Hoffman, J., Assaf, L., & Paris, S. (2001). High-stakes testing in reading: Today in Texas, tomorrow? *The Reading Teacher, 54*(5), 482-494.

Holmes, E. (1911). *What is and what might be.' A study of education in general and elementary in particular.* London: Constable.

Horn, C., Ramos, M., Blumer, I., & Madaus, G. (2000). *Cut scores: Results may vary.* Chestnut Hill, MA: National Board on Educational Testing and Public Policy, Boston College.

Jones, M., Jones, B., Hardin B., Chapman, L., Yarbough, T., & Davis, M. (1999). The impact of high-stakes testing on teachers and students in North Carolina. *Phi Delta Kappan, 81*(3), 199-203.

Klein, S., Hamilton, L., McCaffrey, D., & Stecher, B. (2000). What do test scores in Texas tell us? *Education Policy Analysis Archives, 8*(49). [Online]. Available: http://epaa.asu.edu/epaa/v8n49

Koretz, D., Barron, S., Mitchell, K., & Keith, S. (1996a). *Perceived effects of the Kentucky instructional results information system* (KIRIS)(MR-792PCT/FF). Santa Monica, CA: Rand.

Koretz, D., Barron, S., Mitchell, K., & Keith, S. (1996b). *Perceived effects of the Maryland school performance assessment program* (CSE Technical Report 409). Los Angeles: National Center for Research on Evaluation, Standards, and Student Testing.

Linn, R. (1998). *Assessments and accountability* (CSE Technical Report 490). Boulder, CO: CRESST/University of Colorado at Boulder.

Madaus, G. (1988). The influence of testing on the curriculum. In L. Tanner (Ed.), *Critical issues in curriculum* (pp. 83-121). Chicago: University of Chicago Press.

Madaus, G. (1991, January). *The effects of important tests on students: Implications for a national examination or system of examinations.* Paper prepared for the American Educational Research Association Invitational Conference on Accountability as a State Reform Instrument, Washington, DC.

Madaus, G., & O'Dwyer, L. (1999). A short history of performance assessment: Lessons learned. *Phi Delta Kappan, 80*(9), 688-695.

McMillan, J., Myran, S., & Workman, D. (1999, April 19-23). *The impact of mandated statewide testing on teachers' classroom assessment and instructional practices.* Paper presented at the annual meeting of the American Educational Research Association, Montreal, Quebec, Canada.

Myers, K. (2003, July 16). A dream denied: Aspiring chef rethinks her future as Falmouth school board bows to state pressure on MCAS. *Cape Cod Times.* Available: www.capecodonline.com

National Center for Education Statistics. (2002). *Digest of educational statistics* 2001. Washington, DC: Government Printing Office.

Pedulla, J., Abrams, L., Madaus, G., Russell, M., Ramos, M., & Miao, J. (2003). *Perceived effects of state-mandated testing programs on teaching and learning: Findings from a national survey of teachers.* Chestnut Hill, MA: National Board on Educational Testing and Public Policy, Boston College.

Rhoades, K., & Madaus, G. (2003). *Errors in standardized tests: A sys-*

temic problem. Chestnut Hill, MA: National Board on Educational Testing and Public Policy, Boston College.

Russell, M., & Abrams, L. (in press). Instructional uses of computers for writing: The impact of state testing programs. *Teachers College Record*.

Stecher, B., Barron, S., Chun, T., & Ross, K. (2000). *The effects of the Washington state education reform on schools and classrooms* (CSE Technical Report 525). Los Angeles:

National Center for Research on Evaluation, Standards, and Student Testing.

Taylor, G., Shepard, L., Kinner, F., & Rosenthal, J. (2003). *A survey of teachers' perspectives on high-stakes testing in Colorado: What gets taught, what gets lost* (CSE Technical Report 588). Los Angeles: CRESST.

Winerip, M. (2003, July 23). Rigidity in Florida and the results. *The New York Times,* p. B9.

Lisa M. Abrams (617-552-0665; abramsli@bc.edu) is a doctoral candidate and a research associate at the Center for the Study of Testing, Evaluation, and Education Policy, and **George F. Madaus** (617–552-4521;madaus@bc.edu) is a professor and Boisi Chair in Education and Public Policy, Boston College, 323 Campion Hall, Chestnut Hill, MA 02467.

Are We Measuring Student Success with High-Stakes Testing?

by Kathleen Anderson Steeves,
Jessica Hodgson,
and Patricia Peterson

A researcher, whether scientific, political, or educational, will tell you that evaluative measures begin with a working theory of the expected outcome. If high-stakes standardized exams and tests of similar ilk are intended to measure student success, why then have we not seen more discussion and careful thought placed on understanding what the outcomes of such testing actually mean and say about our students? What, in effect, do such tests actually set out to measure in our children?

Should we not, as teachers, administrators, and community leaders, be more worried about the measures and results of these annual "intelligence" tests that are increasingly being used to label students? FairTest (2002) recently noted that the United States already tests more children more often than any other nation. As a FairTest (1998) survey concluded, "There are more regulations governing the food we feed our pets than the tests used to make decisions about our children."

Should we not, as educators, insist on the time to step back and answer some fundamental questions? What is a successful student? What constitutes successful student habits, knowledge, abilities, and work? How can high-stakes testing be used more appropriately as a powerful tool for teachers to assist student learning?

Should we not open the debate about whether high-stakes tests, as they currently exist in most states, are accurate measures of what we want our students to be able to do before grade promotion or graduation? Do we want to stay on a path of instruction in which decisions are made about student intelligence, teacher ability, and school value based on a one-time test of general knowledge that has not been clearly defined or examined? As a country adopting more standardized testing, should we not see if its outcomes meet its admittedly high goals?

As educators who see the real effects of the tests on a daily basis, we believe that redefining and reexamination is overdue. Only after reevaluation and setting the parameters for student success can we go on to say definitively that such tests adequately measure the intended variables. This reevaluation must be undertaken before current testing trends, which may label students unfairly and inaccurately, become further entrenched in our society as the all-encompassing measure of a good student.

HISTORICAL DEFINITIONS OF THE SUCCESSFUL STUDENT

Though the specific details of student success have varied throughout the history of education—from the Puritan's scripture-citing prodigy to the Industrial Revolution's well-oiled cog of a learner—certain variables have remained intact (McNergney and Herbert 1995). As Goodlad (1984, 36) stated, there are a "broad array of educational goals in four [predominant] areas that have emerged in this country over more than 300 years." Though not nationally recognized, these four areas have become educationally institutionalized. They represent a logical first step in the search for the "successful" student, including, as Goodlad (1984, 51) noted, "A. Academic Goals (including: 1. Mastery of Basic Skills and Fundamental Processes, and 2. Intellectual Development); B. Vocational Goals; C. Social, Civic, and Cultural Goals; and D. Personal Goals."

According to Goodlad (1984), both parents and teachers have ranked academic goals of schooling as their top priority. These goals consisted of enabling students to: read, write, and solve basic arithmetic problems; acquire ideas from reading and listening; learn to communicate ideas through writing and speaking; utilize available sources of information; employ problem-solving skills, principles of logic, and different modes of inquiry; use and evaluate knowledge through critical and independent skills; accumulate a general fund of knowledge; and develop a positive attitude toward intellectual development.

Of the eight sub-skills constituting academic success, only one—enabling students to "accumulate a general fund of knowledge"—suggests that student success is connected to the mere "knowing" (or testing) of general information. Instead, Goodlad's goals point to a student's ability to "do" as the keystone to academic success. Words like "acquire," "problem-solve," "utilize," "analyze," and "inquire" rest at the helm of a student's successful navigation and eventual completion of school.

Currently, standards in all disciplines *are* academically rigorous. In describing their own standards for student success, national learning organizations have defined success in terms of what the student can "do":

- Apply reflective thinking and decision making when analyzing current civic/social events (National Council for the Social Studies 1993).
- Develop the abilities that characterize science as inquiry (Center for Science, Mathematics, and Engineering Education 1996).
- Investigate, make sense of, and construct meanings from new situations; make and provide arguments for conjectures; and use a flexible set of strategies to solve problems from both within and outside mathematics (National Council of Teachers of Mathematics 1989).
- Apply a wide range of strategies to comprehend, interpret, evaluate, and appreciate texts, including drawing on prior experience, interactions with other readers and writers, knowledge of word meaning of other texts (National Council of Teachers of English 1996).
- Use English to communicate in social settings, to achieve academically in all content areas and in socially and culturally appropriate ways (Teachers of English to Speakers of Other Languages 1997).

Indeed, teacher conceptions of the "successful" student appear to be aligned with those of the community, parents, and employers, each defining success as a student's ability to solve problems, seek solutions, and create and understand meaningful texts. A research study of employers in Oxon Hill, Maryland (Walker 1999), found that employers, like teachers, defined a successful student as one able to acquire and apply knowledge, such as: 1) locating and using meaningful information, 2) deciphering written and spoken language, 3) employing English in a context-appropriate manner, and 4) working with others in a professional manner.

Members of the National Education Goals Panel (1994) imagined successful students as those "practicing the scientific method, solving problems as a group, analyzing data, expressing their findings in writing, and defending their analysis in discussion." Educators such as Theodore R. Sizer and Ernest Boyer have envisioned similar learning environments and roles for the "successful" student. For Sizer (1992, 72), "The residue of serious learning is a mixture of awareness and logic. One exercises qualities of the mind with specifics, but the qualities themselves are the end to be pursued." In short, the goal of learning for Sizer is not the knowledge garnered but rather the process of learning to garner it. As Boyer (in Fiske 1991, 65), former president of the Carnegie Foundation for the Advancement of Teaching, has argued, "The key to problem solving is not to figure out the answer to a question that someone else hands you, but to define the right problem. An educated person

today is someone who knows the right questions to ask." When so many seem to agree on the current definition of a successful student, what's the problem?

HIGH-STAKES TESTING IN PRACTICE

Since U.S. educators first invented the modern standardized norm-referenced test, as Debra Meier (2000, 25) recently declared:

> *Our students have been taking more tests more often than any nation on the face of the earth, and schools and districts have been going public with test scores starting almost from the moment children enter school. From the third- or fourth-grade level (long before any of our international counterparts bother to test children) we have test data for virtually all schools, by race, class, and gender. We know exactly how many kids did better or worse in every subcategory. We have test data for almost every grade thereafter in reading and math, and to some degree in all other subjects. This has been the case for nearly half a century.*

Current trends in testing, though still tentative because there has not been enough time for in-depth study, include: use of multiple-measure assessments, emphasis on reading, and some sort of transitional accountability system as an interim step to mandatory state testing (Anderson, Fiester, Gonzales, and Pechman 1996). According to FairTest (2002), as of 1999, 17 states had graduation tests and five more were planning to implement such tests. Of the 15 states south of the Mason-Dixon line, 11 required students to pass graduation tests. In all, 39 states give either a criterion-referenced or norm-referenced test to determine their students' proficiency level. Almost all states are in the process of implementing proficiency tests of some kind, a process required now by the new federal education legislation. Illustrations from several jurisdictions provide a snapshot of some of the issues for teachers and students in this high-stakes testing trend.

In the District of Columbia, principals' and teachers' evaluations are initially to be based on student scores and improvement on the Stanford-9 (SAT-9) test battery, a multiple choice test adopted in 1996 to measure student achievement in reading and mathematics. A committee that included several teachers argued that the SAT-9 test matched the district's public schools curriculum, which is now aligned with national standards. The SAT-9 is available with various sets of empirical, normative information; ironically, none of the individual tests apply specifically to urban school districts (Harcourt Brace Educational Measurement 1999).

In Maryland, the state's School Performance Assessment Program (MSPAP), established in 1990 as the result of the Governor's Commission on School Performance, tests students' mastery in math, reading, and writing. Tasks require students to respond to questions or directions that lead to a solution to a problem, a recommendation, a decision, an explanation, or a rationale for the students' response to the task or question (Maryland State Department of Education [MSDOE] 1998). Once hailed for offering one of the first "performance-based" school tests in the nation, few states have followed Maryland's lead with MSPAP (Argetsinger and Nakashima 1998), finding such tests to be too expensive and time-consuming. MSPAP critics have complained that the test is used only to rate schools and does not measure individual student performance. An analysis of the 2001 MSPAP scores for the eighth-grade exam showed a dramatic decline in scores that left educators without an explanation. As a result, schools were given an option as to whether to use it or not. Questions were raised about the test's validity and the reliance on one test as a measure of teacher and school success (Shulte 2002). Starting with the class of 2004, high school students will be required to pass the Maryland Functional tests in content courses as a requirement for graduation (MSDOE 1998).

Massachusetts has spent $20 million on the development of the Massachusetts Comprehensive Assistance System, which will be required of all tenth-graders beginning in 2003. The state test will include multiple-choice and open-response questions. A newly formed group, the Coalition for Authentic Reform in Education, is actively opposing the notion that one test should be the only measure of student achievement (Public Broadcasting Service [PBS] 2002).

In Virginia, public schools began using the Standards of Learning (SOL) tests to assess students and schools in 1998. Students are tested in English, mathematics, history/social studies, science, and computer/technology in grades 3, 5, and 8 and at the end of core courses in high school. Beginning with the class of 2004, passing the SOL tests will be a determinant of earning a high school diploma. In addition, by 2006, a school's accreditation will depend on a 70 percent student-passing percentage on the SOL tests (Virginia Department of Education [VDOE] 1999–2001). In the second year of testing, 93 percent of public schools failed to reach the approved benchmark. The state was considering ways to adjust its timetable to implement sanctions (Mathews 1999). At this point, about half of the schools have achieved a passing rate on the required core SOL exams—though ESL students' scores were not included (VDOE 2001). In an effort to comply with expected requirements of President Bush's (2001) "No Child Left Behind" federally backed education legislation, Virginia is moving to expand the SOL testing to grades 4, 6, and 7.

HIGH-STAKES TESTING MAY FAIL STUDENTS AND TEACHERS

If these high-stakes tests are to be the measure of students, as well as of schools, it is imperative that we assess the effect of such testing on student academic success. When our country looks blindly to one test to tell us all we hope to know about students, teachers, and schools, then educators must demand a closer look at the actual meaning of these test results. Many educators know the flaws in the system firsthand. For example, when important consequences—such as student graduation and school accreditation—are linked to high-stakes testing, teachers are likely to respond by "teaching to the test" (Gordon and Reese 1997, 346). To ensure that students pass the assessment, teachers cover material that they believe will most likely be included on the test. However, teaching to these high-stakes tests has several negative consequences for both teachers and students.

When teaching to the test, the test does not become an assessment of a student's mastery of content; it is, instead, a powerful curricular tool. The teacher is forced to make instructional decisions that are not based on prior professional experience, or what is of academic importance, or what is in the best interest of the student; instead, decisions are based on what is most likely to be included on a standardized test (Shepard 1991). In essence, the test becomes a teacher's filter for making instructional decisions. As the curriculum becomes more narrow, content and skills that are not on the standardized assessment are eliminated. In fact, teachers feel pressure to make sure classroom activities correspond to material on the assessment even though they may know other materials will better prepare students for success in the world.

Gordon and Reese (1997) conducted a study on the effects of high-stakes testing on teachers in Texas. In this case, the high-stakes assessment became the object of instruction rather than the outcome of previous instruction. The Texas Assessment of Academic Skills (TAAS) evaluates schools based on the results of the assessment and gives cash awards to schools with high test scores, while poorly performing schools face "sanctions and intervention" (Gordon and Reese 1997, 348). These researchers found that one way Texas teachers have responded to high-stakes testing is to emphasize skills on the test. Teachers tended to spend more time on "drill and practice" and less time on "hands-on activities" found in the curriculum standards. Teachers in Texas complained that the TAAS made them accountable in terms of teaching TAAS-related content, but it did not make them accountable in terms of being effective teachers (Gordon and Reese 1997). Critics of the state's testing procedures have noted that dropout rates have increased, as has cheating (PBS 2002).

Gary Natriello (in Benning 1999), a professor at Columbia University's Teachers College, has argued that the new emphasis on testing may discourage teachers from entering the field because they really want to shape young minds rather than raise a test score by a point or two. Furthermore, schools—especially in urban settings—already have difficulty filling teaching positions. If the broad application of high-stakes test scores demoralizes the teachers currently working, and discourages potential teachers from applying, student achievement ultimately suffers.

Students are likewise affected by high-stakes testing. One of the most troubling effects of high-stakes testing is that it "can force students to leave school before they have to take the examination, or after failing it" (Madaus 1991, 229). Another effect is that the performance of principals and superintendents is often linked to the number of students who reach the bar set by the state. Unfortunately, this situation may mean it is in an administrator's best interest to eliminate systematically from the test those students who probably wouldn't make the bar and to keep enrolled discipline-problem students who will get high scores on the test. In fact, in efforts to increase school performance on high-stakes testing, some schools have relied on increased special education placement and retention in grade. This system allows schools to control, to some extent, the student population whose test scores are reflected in school scores (Allington and McGill-Franzen 1992).

Whatever philosophical perspective one has toward high-stakes testing, it is clear that these tests have a significant effect on both teachers and students. In narrowing the curriculum, changing instructional strategies, and impacting the classroom and student demographics, high-stakes testing negatively alters the educational environment for teachers and students.

There is no evidence that passing the current tests equates to student success. Actually, for many, it may even mean the opposite.

Overall, educators understand that the emphasis these tests place on lower-level skills is not in line with what discipline-based organizations are asking their teachers to do in meeting content standards. Given the increased focus on nationwide standards, it must be asked whether schools *are* supplying their students with the skills and knowledge necessary to become "successful." There is no evidence that passing the current tests equates to student success. Actually, for many, it may even mean the opposite. These questions must then be asked: Are we producing students who can problem-solve, analyze, and ask the right questions? Are we evaluating them accordingly? Are these popular and increasingly endorsed "high-stakes" tests, which neatly tell us who has succeeded and who has failed, attuned to our definition of a successful student or to the philosophy of success that shapes current practice?

RETHINKING HOW WE MEASURE SUCCESS

With the current rush toward adoption of high-stakes testing forms that align with state standards, we must encourage important and necessary public discussion about the outcomes and what we are actually trying to assess in our students today (U.S. Department of Education 1998). As schools hurriedly move toward the narrow use of standardized tests to determine eligibility for graduation and school and teacher evaluation, we argue that it still has not been made clear what these tests really measure and if they actually come close to identifying our society's agreed-upon definition of a successful student.

It is necessary to reopen the discussion on testing, not as a measure to be removed, but as something that must be reexamined for what test results actually do mean and how the billions in testing dollars could be spent best in assessing our students. We must begin a discussion about what a successful student is and whether a revamped test or a restructured system of accounting for the results could more accurately measure this success.

As part of the call to reenergize this important discussion, various issues must be considered. The discussion has begun in a number of states, but it must be expanded.

How do we increase the validity of these tests? Most research employs a margin of error. Why is that not true in high-stakes tests? A student scoring one point below the cut-off score (defined in no logical way) gets no credit, while the student scoring at the cut-off point or one point above gets full credit and is promoted.

Which standards are we using to measure success? All content areas include important skills and knowledge, but what consistent measure of comparison is being used (state, county, district, or national standards)?

What are the long-term effects of high-stakes testing on students who do not graduate or drop out before they fail yet again? Do we have the collective will across the board in urban, suburban, and rural schools to use the test data to make a difference and assist students who need additional instructional time and resources to achieve the standards?

In the end, we must ask one another if we have developed a clear, agreed-upon definition of a successful student so that we may really put required resources into achieving success for all students. We must be certain that the promise to "leave no child behind" is not just overlooked by current community leaders and politicians who herald the tests unchanged. We must insist that high-stakes, standardized testing becomes less a political tool for finger pointing and assessing student and school failure and more of a reasoned way to help pinpoint why these students are failing and where resources are needed to produce the truly successful students we all want!

REFERENCES

Allington, R. L., and A. McGill-Franzen. 1992. Does high-stakes testing improve school effectiveness? *ERS Spectrum* 10(2): 3–12.

Anderson, L., L. Fiester, M. Gonzales, and E. Pechman. eds. 1996. *Improving America's schools: Newsletter on issues on school reform* (Spring). Washington, D.C.: Improving America's Schools Association. Available at: *http://www.ed.gov/pubs/IASA/newsletters/standards.*

Argetsinger, A., and E. Nakashima. 1998. In Md., the 'bubble' test has burst: Analytical exam gains favor over multiple-choice format. *Washington Post,* 11 May, A1.

Benning, V. 1999. Teachers wary of new exams. Poll finds support for D.C. program. *Washington Post,* 5 July, A1.

Bush, G. W. 2001. No child left behind. Washington, D.C.: U.S. Department of Education. Available at *http://www.ed.gov/offices/OESE/esea/nclb/titlepage.html.*

Center for Science, Mathematics, and Engineering Education, 1996. *National science education standards.* Washington, D.C.: National Academy Press.

FairTest: The National Center for Fair & Open Testing. 1998. FairTest applauds National Research Council report opposing high-stakes tests and endorsing tougher regulation of exam use. Press release, 3 Sept. Cambridge, Mass.: FairTest. Available at *http://www.fairtest.org/pr/nrc-pr.htm.*

FairTest:The National Center for Fair & Open Testing. 2002. Will more testing improve schools? Fact sheet. Cambridge, Mass.: FairTest. Available at: *http://www.fairtest.org.facts/Will%20More%20Testing%20Improve%20Schools.html.*

Fiske, E. B. 1991. *Smart schools, smart kids. Why do some schools work?* New York: Simon & Schuster.

Goodlad, J. I. 1984. *A place called school: Prospects for the future.* New York: McGraw-Hill.

Gordon, S. P., and M. Reese. 1997. High-stakes testing: Worth the price? *Journal of School Leadership* 7(4): 345–68.

Harcourt Brace Educational Measurement. 1999. Stanford-9 Achievement Test Series: It's like nothing you've ever seen before. San Antonio: HBEM.

Madaus, G. F. 1991. The effects of important tests on students. *Phi Delta Kappan 73*(3): 226–31.

Maryland State Department of Education. 1998. Maryland school performance report, 1998: State and school systems. Annapolis: MSDOE. ERIC ED 429 348.

Mathews, J. 1999. Va. schools may get reprieve on standards. *Washington Post,* 16 September, B1.

McNergney, R. F., and J. M. Herbert. 1995. *Foundations of education: The challenge of professional practice.* Boston: Allyn & Bacon.

Meier, D. 2000. *Will standards save public education?* Boston: Beacon Press.

National Council for the Social Studies. 1993. Social studies online: Standards and position statements. Washington, D.C.: NCSS.

National Council of Teachers of English. 1996. *Standards for the English Language Arts.* Urbana, Ill.: NCTE and the International Reading Association.

National Council of Teachers of Mathematics. 1989. Curriculum standards for grades 9–12. Reston, VA: NCTM. Available at *http://standards.nctm.org/Previous/CurrEvStds/currstand9-12.htm.*

Public Broadcasting Service. 2002. Frontline: Testing our schools. Television program, 28 March.

Shepard, L. A. 1991. Will national tests improve student learning? *Phi Delta Kappan 73*(3): 232–38.

Shulte, B. 2002. County questions drop in MSPAP scores: Despite new initiatives, district's results decline. *Washington Post,* 31 January, T14.

Sizer, T. R. 1992. *Horace's School: Redesigning the American high school.* Boston: Houghton Mifflin.

Teachers of English to Speakers of Other Languages. 1997. ESL standards for pre-K–12 students. Alexandria, Va.: TESOL. ERIC ED 420 991.

U.S. Department of Education. 1998. Turning around low-performing schools. A guide for state and local leaders. Washington, D.C.: USDE. ERIC ED 420 119.

Virginia Department of Education. 1999–2001. Standards of learning discussion forum. SOLs unfair to students. Richmond: VDOE. Available at: *http://www.vdoe.vipnet.org/messages/23/36.html?996190534.*

Virginia Department of Education. 2001. Spring 1999 Standards of Learning test results. Richmond: VDOE. Available at: *http://www.pen.k12.va.us/sol99.*

Walker, L. 1999. A community case study. GWU class, Teacher Education, SPED #233, Professor West, Washington, D.C.

Kathleen Anderson Steeves is Associate Professor of History/Social Studies Education at George Washington University in Washington, D.C. Her research interests include secondary history and social studies, education reform and standards, teacher leadership, and the history of education.

Jessica Hodgson teaches social studies at Chantilly High School in Fairfax County, Virginia. She is currently involved in research on using writing as a learning tool in the history classroom.

Patricia Peterson teaches 7th- and 8th-Grade English at Garner-Patterson Middle School in Washington, D.C. Her focus is on literacy development through poetry, music, and service learning. Ms. Peterson recently established a student Poetry Club connecting students with community artists and writers.

From *The Educational Forum*, Spring 2002, pp. 228-235. © 2002 by Kappa Delta Pi, International Honor Society in Education. Reprinted by permission.

The Seductive Allure of Data

Most state accountability tests fail to produce the kinds of data that will improve teaching and learning. Teachers can get the data they need from classroom assessments—if they know how to design instructionally useful tests.

W. James Popham

The word *data*, at least to most educators, simply reeks of goodness. Although probably less heart-warming than *children, smaller classes*, and *summer vacation*, the term *data* inclines most educators to think good thoughts laced with notions of evidence, science, and rigor. Indeed, the theme of this issue of *Educational Leadership* reflects educators' belief that data play a central role in improving student achievement. In any education lexicon these days, the term *data* is inarguably one of our most positively loaded nouns.

Data Scorned?

But *data* shouldn't elicit automatic obeisance from right-thinking educators. Indeed, we should spurn some data. In the following analysis, I intend to dismiss certain sorts of data. I want educators to realize that the wrong kinds of data, even if warmly applauded by many, can actually stifle teachers' pursuit of accurate evidence regarding their students' achievement.

Currently, teachers are buffeted by messages that the often undecipherable test results they receive are, in fact, the data they need to make instructional decisions. Is it any wonder when, after trying in vain to make sense of such opaque test data, many teachers simply quit believing in the instructional utility of data? To avoid becoming disillusioned with all data, teachers must learn how to distinguish between instructionally delightful and instructionally dismal data.

At the Top of the Heap: Test Data

Although all sorts of data might help to improve instruction, the most important data in the United States these days are *test data*—particularly data describing students' performance on achievement tests. That's because schools increasingly employ those data to evaluate educators' effectiveness.

State-determined achievement tests increasingly serve as the centerpiece of state accountability systems. But data from most states' accountability tests, unfortunately, have almost no value for improving teaching and learning. More dangerously, such tests lull educators into believing that they have appropriate data when, in fact, they do not. As a consequence, many educators fail to ask for more meaningful, instructionally valuable data that would help them teach students better.

Instructionally Beneficial Data

Instructionally beneficial data can only come from instructionally useful tests. Here are five attributes of an instructionally useful test, which apply to large-scale assessments as well as to teacher-made classroom assessments.

Significance. An instructionally useful test measures students' attainment of a worthwhile curricular aim—for instance, a high-level cognitive skill or a substantial body of important knowledge. It makes no sense to assess students' mastery of such trifling knowledge as esoteric scientific terms or dates associated with obscure historical events. (I suppose that someone might come up with a cogent argument for asking students to memorize state capitals. I've never been able to.)

Teachability. An instructionally useful test measures something teachable. Teachability means that most teachers, if they deliver reasonably effective instruction aimed at the test's assessment targets, can get most of their students to master what the test measures. For instance, an instructionally useful test should not measure students' innate intelligence. In standardized achievement tests, we frequently encounter items requiring students to engage in such spatial visualization tasks as mentally "folding" letters or geometric shapes into two equal halves. Such tasks clearly depend on a student's inherited visualization aptitude.

Similarly, certain high-level inference skills are extraordinarily difficult to teach because the cognitive processes central to those skills usually depend on the idiosyncratic nature of a particular student's prior experiences. It simply makes no sense to assess students' mastery of essentially unteachable outcomes.

Describability. A useful test provides or is directly based on sufficiently clear descriptions of the skills and knowledge it measures so that teachers can design properly focused instructional activities. These descriptions must not only be provided in plain language, but must also be sufficiently succinct so that they are not off-putting to busy teachers.

If a test is based on an already clearly described set of content standards, and if teachers can tell which of those content standards the test will cover, then no further descriptive information is needed. But if the content standards are not clear enough to unambiguously let teachers identify those curricular targets, then lucid descriptions of what the test will assess must accompany any instructionally useful test. A content standard such as "Students will read a variety of different types of texts" communicates little of instructional value to the teacher.

It makes no sense to assess students' mastery of ill-defined curricular targets or to force teachers to play an annual guessing game about which of the state's content standards the statewide accountability tests will assess.

Reportability. An instructionally useful test yields results at a specific enough level to inform teachers about the effectiveness of the instruction they provide. A national commission has urged that any education accountability test report its results on a standard-by-standard basis for individual students (Commission on Instructionally Supportive Assessment, 2001). Such per-standard reporting of results would enable teachers to identify those parts of their instruction that were successful or unsuccessful on the basis of students' post-instruction test data.

It makes no sense to provide teachers with data so general that those teachers cannot evaluate and improve their own instructional efforts. Similarly, it makes no sense for assessors to contend that they have assessed the complete array of a state's content standards when, in fact, they have measured some standards either by only a handful of items or by no items at all.

Nonintrusiveness. In clear recognition that testing time takes away from teaching time, an instructionally useful test shouldn't take too long to administer—it should not intrude excessively on instructional activities. For instance, if a state-level test of students' reading skills is administered each spring, it should be administrable in one, or at most two, class periods. Longer tests simply soak up too much instructional time. It makes no sense to test students interminably, diverting several weeks of precious instructional time each year to assessment.

In review, we are most likely to obtain instructionally useful data through the use of instructionally useful tests. The five attributes of an instructionally useful test are its significance, teachability, describability, reportability, and nonintrusiveness. The data derived from an instructionally useful test will enable teachers to do a better job of instructing their students. And that, after all, should be the reason we test students in the first place.

Detecting Dismal Data

As suggested earlier, tests that don't produce instructionally useful data can disincline educators to demand data that are instructionally beneficial. In the following three common assessment situations, the wrong kinds of data—provided by the wrong kinds of tests—have diminished the quality of education that we provide to our students.

Nationally Standardized Achievement Tests

Today's nationally standardized tests miss the mark dramatically with respect to three of the attributes of instructionally useful assessment:

- *Describability.* All nationally standardized achievement tests have been constructed according to a traditional measurement approach aimed at providing a comparative picture of students' relative performances. The developers try to devise a "one-size-fits-all" test and describe it in a manner that will make it attractive to many potential purchasers. As a result, nationally standardized tests don't include properly tied-down descriptions of what they assess. Teachers can't aim their instruction accurately if they have murky assessment targets.

- *Teachability.* In order to produce the score spread on which comparative score interpretations depend, nationally standardized tests contain many instructionally insensitive items that are linked to students' socioeconomic status or inherited academic aptitudes. It is particularly difficult for teachers to increase students' performance on such items.

- *Reportability.* Nationally standardized achievement tests almost always report their results at levels of generality altogether unsuitable for teachers' day-to-day instructional decision making. Some national tests do a better job than others when it comes to reporting students' results. But in no case do these tests provide data that teachers can easily use to appraise their own instructional effectiveness.

I believe that nationally standardized achievement tests have a role in education. Both parents and teachers can benefit from data indicating a student's relative strengths and weaknesses. But the genuine instructional yield of nationally standardized tests is much more modest than the publishers of these tests would have us believe.

Standards-Based Tests

There is a charade currently going on in the way the United States carries out its education assessment activities. Its name is "standards-based assessment." Standards-based tests supposedly measure students' mastery of a state's officially approved content standards—the skills and knowledge constituting the state's curricular aims. Yet because most states have adopted too many content standards and stated them too vaguely, most states' standards-based tests just don't do a decent job determining a student's mastery of those standards.

Pretending that a one- or two-hour state test can provide a meaningful fix on a student's mastery of myriad, often fuzzy content standards is patently hypocritical. Today's standards-based assessments constitute a serious violation of any sort of truth-in-advertising precept. Standards-based tests don't measure what they pretend to measure.

The data yielded by today's standards-based tests have another equally serious shortcoming. Those data almost never provide any indication of *which* content standards a student has or hasn't mastered. In the absence of such data, how can teachers tell which parts of their instruction they need to modify?

Teachers don't learn much of instructional value when the standards-based test results tell them that Johnny is "not proficient" with respect to his mastery of a set of 17 language arts content standards. Teachers cannot discern which of the 17 content standards their students have mastered (hence, which standards have been well taught) and which of the 17 content standards their students have not mastered (hence, which standards have not been well taught).

So most of today's standards-based tests fall down seriously on several attributes of an instructionally useful test. They often lack significance because, in a fruitless effort to measure all of a state's sprawling content standards, they simply do not assess students' mastery of the most important content. Standards-based tests also get low grades on describability—they usually fail to describe their assessment targets satisfactorily, because these tests are based on a plethora of too many, insufficiently clear content standards. And perhaps most seriously, standards-based tests often lack reportability—they fail to provide standard-by-standard reports to teachers, students, or students' parents.

Teachers' Classroom Assessments

Given the enormous pressure placed on teachers these days to boost their students' scores on external exams, teachers understandably tend to give less attention to their own classroom assessments. That's a mistake—but only if the teacher's classroom tests are instructionally useful.

Teachers can judge the instructional utility of their classroom assessments by using the same five attributes of an instructionally useful test that I just applied to large-scale external exams. Teachers should ask themselves the following questions:

- Do my classroom assessments measure genuinely worthwhile skills and knowledge?
- Will I be able to promote my students' mastery of what's measured in my classroom assessments?

- Can I describe what skills and knowledge my classroom tests measure in language sufficiently clear for my own instructional planning?
- Do my classroom assessments yield results that allow me to tell which parts of my instruction were effective or ineffective?
- Do my classroom tests take up too much time away from my instruction?

Clearly, the answers to these questions will vary from teacher to teacher. Generally, teachers who employ their classroom assessments most appropriately adopt a "less is more" approach. They focus on measuring only a modest number of curricular aims, but make certain that those aims deal with genuinely significant outcomes that students can master with adequate instruction. As a dividend of focusing on a smaller number of significant outcomes, those outcomes can then be clearly described to help the teacher target instruction and assessment.

Teachers must deal with one additional consideration if they intend to use their classroom data to supplement results from external exams: Unless classroom tests provide credible data, skeptics will rush to dismiss the results as "self-interested home cooking." I'm not talking about tests that teachers use only to inform themselves about their ongoing instruction, but rather about the more significant sorts of data that schools use to judge a teacher's instructional effectiveness.

One straightforward way for teachers to collect credible evidence of their own effectiveness is to use a pretest/posttest design in which they give identical assessments at the start of a semester and again at its conclusion. Students must use the same kind of paper if the test calls for a constructed response (such as writing an essay). Students do not date their responses. The teacher codes the pretests and posttests so they can be subsequently identified, and then mixes them all together so that a scorer cannot discern which responses are pretests and which are posttests.

Data from most states' accountability tests, unfortunately, have almost no value for improving teaching and learning.

At this point the teacher calls on a nonpartisan scorer (for instance, another teacher or a parent) to blind-score the students' responses. Only after all the shuffled papers have been scored does the teacher sort them into pretests and posttests. The improvement between the pretests and posttests constitutes credible evidence of the teacher's instructional success (Popham, 2001).

What Can Educators Do?

In response to today's increasingly important assessment concerns, I suggest a two-stage course of action. First, educators should disregard data from any test that isn't instructionally useful. Second, they should push for the installation of instructionally useful tests so that the data that those assessments yield will lead to better-taught students.

Although most of today's standards-based tests are not instructionally useful, that need not be the case. A national commission recently described how to create accountability tests that are both accurate and instructionally useful (Commission on Instructionally Supportive Assessment, 2001). Many states assess students' written composition competence by requiring students to generate original writing samples, which are then evaluated according to scoring guides (rubrics) based on teachable criteria. Almost all of today's writing samples are instructionally beneficial. If you live in a state where such instructionally useful tests do not exist, lobby aggressively for their introduction.

If you live in a state that uses nationally standardized achievement tests for accountability purposes, try your hardest to get them replaced with more appropriate, instructionally useful accountability tests.

Teachers should also bring common sense to the scrutiny of their own classroom assessments. In general, a quest for assessment sanity will lead teachers to adopt a less-is-more measurement approach. However, if the resultant data will be used for instructional evaluation, then teachers must collect those data in a manner sufficiently credible to persuade even non-believers of the data's validity.

To educators, the wrong data can often be seductively appealing. But the right data will, in fact, help teachers do a better job with students. *Those* are the data we need.

References

Commission on Instructionally Supportive Assessment. (2001). *Building tests that support instruction and accountability: A guide for policymakers.* Washington, DC:

Author. [Online]. Available: www.nea.org/accountability/buildingtests.html

Popham, W. J. (2001). *The truth about testing: An educator's call to action.* Alexandria, VA: ASCD.

W. James Popham is a professor emeritus at the University of California, Los Angeles, Graduate School of Education and Information Studies; wpopham@ucla.edu.

Working Inside the Black Box:

Assessment for Learning in the Classroom

In their widely read article "Inside the Black Box," Mr. Black and Mr. Wiliam demonstrated that improving formative assessment raises student achievement. Now they and their colleagues report on a follow-up project that has helped teachers change their practice and students change their behavior so that everyone shares responsibility for the students' learning.

BY PAUL BLACK, CHRISTINE HARRISON, CLARE LEE, BETHAN MARSHALL, AND DYLAN WILIAM

IN 1998 "Inside the Black Box," the predecessor of this article, appeared in this journal.[1] Since then we have learned a great deal about the practical steps needed to meet the purpose expressed in the article's subtitle: "raising standards through classroom assessment."

In the first part of "Inside the Black Box," we set out to answer three questions. The first was, Is there evidence that improving formative assessment raises standards? The answer was an unequivocal yes, a conclusion based on a review of evidence published in over 250 articles by researchers from several countries.[2] Few initiatives in education have had such a strong body of evidence to support a claim to raise standards.

This positive answer led naturally to the second question: Is there evidence that there is room for improvement? Here again, the available evidence gave a clear and positive answer, presenting a detailed picture that identified three main problems: 1) the assessment methods that teachers use are not effective in promoting good learning, 2) grading practices tend to emphasize competition rather than personal improvement, and 3) assessment feedback often has a negative impact, particularly on low-achieving

students, who are led to believe that they lack "ability" and so are not able to learn.

However, for the third question—Is there evidence about how to improve formative assessment?—the answer was less clear. While the evidence provided many ideas for improvement, it lacked the detail that would enable teachers to implement those ideas in their classrooms. We argued that teachers needed "a variety of living examples of implementation."

THE JOURNEY:
LEARNING WITH TEACHERS

Since 1998, we have planned and implemented several programs in which groups of teachers in England have been supported in developing innovative practices in their classrooms, drawing on the ideas in the original article. While this effort has amply confirmed the original proposals, it has also added a wealth of new findings that are both practical and authentic. Thus we are now confident that we can set out sound advice for the improvement of classroom assessment.

THE KMOFAP PROJECT

To carry out the exploratory work that was called for, we needed to collaborate with a group of teachers willing to take on the risks and extra work involved, and we needed to secure support from their schools and districts. Funding for the project was provided through the generosity of the Nuffield Foundation, and we were fortunate to find two school districts—Oxfordshire and Medway, both in southern England—whose supervisory staff members understood the issues and were willing to work with us. Each district selected three secondary schools: Oxfordshire chose three coeducational schools, and Medway chose one coeducational school, one boys' school, and one girls' school. Each school selected two science teachers and two mathematics teachers. We discussed the plans with the principal of each school, and then we called the first meeting of the 24 teachers. So in January 1999, the King's—Medway-Oxfordshire Formative Assessment Project (KMOFAP) was born.

Full details of the project can be found in our book, *Assessment for Learning: Putting It into Practice.*[3] For the present purpose, it is the outcomes that are important. The findings presented here are based on the observations and records of visits to classrooms by the King's College team, records of meetings of the whole group of teachers, interviews with and writing by the teachers themselves, and a few discussions with student groups. Initially, we worked with science and mathematics teachers, but the work has been extended more recently to involve teachers of English in the same schools and teachers of other subjects in other schools.

SPREADING THE WORD

Throughout the development of the project, we have responded to numerous invitations to talk to other groups of teachers and advisers. Indeed, over five years we have made more than 400 such contributions. These have ranged across all subjects and across both primary and secondary phases. In addition, there has been sustained work with some primary schools. All of this gives us confidence that our general findings will be of value to all, although some important details may differ for different age groups and subjects. Furthermore, a group at Stanford University obtained funding from the National Science Foundation to set up a similar development project, in collaboration with King's, in schools in California. Extension of our own work has been made possible by this funding. And we also acknowledge support from individuals in several government agencies who sat on the project's steering group, offered advice and guidance, and helped ensure that assessment for learning (see "Assessment for Learning," below) is a central theme in education policy in England and Scotland.

THE LEARNING GAINS

From our review of the international research literature, we were convinced that enhanced formative assessment would produce gains in student achievement, even when measured in such narrow terms as scores on state-mandated tests. At the outset we were clear that it was important to have some indication of the kinds of gains that could be achieved in real classrooms and over an ex-

ASSESSMENT FOR LEARNING

▲ Assessment for learning is any assessment for which the first priority in its design and practice is to serve the purpose of promoting students' learning. It thus differs from assessment designed primarily to serve the purposes of accountability, or of ranking, or of certifying competence. An assessment activity can help learning if it provides information that teachers and their students can use as feedback in assessing themselves and one another and in modifying the teaching and learning activities in which they are engaged. Such assessment becomes "formative assessment" when the evidence is actually used to adapt the teaching work to meet learning needs.

tended period of time. Since each teacher in the project was free to choose the class that would work on these ideas, we discussed with each teacher what data were available within the school, and we set up a "mini-experiment" for each teacher.

Each teacher decided what was to be the "output" measure for his or her class. For grade-10 classes, this was generally the grade achieved on the national school-leaving examination taken when students are 16 (the General Certificate of Secondary Education or GCSE). For grade-8 classes, it was generally the score or level achieved on the national tests administered to all 14-year-olds. For other classes, a variety of measures were used, including end-of-module-test scores and marks on the school's end-of-year examinations.

Many teachers do not plan and conduct classroom dialogue in ways that might help students to learn.

For each project class, the teacher identified a comparison class. In some cases this was a parallel class taught by the same teacher in previous years (and in one case in the same year). In other cases, we used a parallel class taught by a different teacher or, failing that, a nonparallel class taught by the same or a different teacher.

When the project and the control classes were not strictly parallel, we controlled for possible differences in prior achievement by the use of "input" measures, such as school test scores from the previous year or other measures of aptitude.

This approach meant that the size of the improvement was measured differently for each teacher. For example, a grade-10 project class might outperform the comparison class by half a GCSE grade, but another teacher 's grade 8 project class might outscore its control class by 7% on an end-of-year exam. To enable us to aggregate the results, we adopted the common measuring stick of the "standardized effect size," calculated by taking the difference between the scores of the experimental and control groups and then dividing this number by the standard deviation (a measure of the spread in the scores of the groups).

For the 19 teachers on whom we had complete data, the average effect size was around 0.3 standard deviations. Such improvements, produced across a school, would raise a school in the lower quartile of the national performance tables to well above average. Thus it is clear that, far from having to choose between teaching well and getting good test scores, teachers can actually improve their students' results by working with the ideas we present here.

HOW CHANGE CAN HAPPEN

We set out our main findings about classroom work under four headings: questioning, feedback through grading, peer- and self-assessment, and the formative use of summative tests. Most of the quotations in the following pages are taken directly from pieces written by the teachers. The names of the teachers and of the schools are pseudonyms, in keeping with our policy of guaranteeing anonymity.

QUESTIONING

Many teachers do not plan and conduct classroom dialogue in ways that might help students to learn. Research has shown that, after asking a question, many teachers wait less than one second and then, if no answer is forthcoming, ask another question or answer the question themselves.[4] A consequence of such short "wait time" is that the only questions that "work" are those that can be answered quickly, without thought—that is, questions calling for memorized facts. Consequently, the dialogue is at a superficial level. As one teacher put it:

> I'd become dissatisfied with the closed Q & A style that my unthinking teaching had fallen into, and I would frequently be lazy in my acceptance of right answers and sometimes even tacit complicity with a class to make sure none of us

had to work too hard. … They and I knew that if the Q & A wasn't going smoothly, I'd change the question, answer it myself, or only seek answers from the "brighter students." There must have been times (still are?) where an outside observer would see my lessons as a small discussion group surrounded by many sleepy onlookers.
> —*James*, Two Bishops School

The key to changing such a situation is to allow longer wait time. But many teachers find it hard to do this, for it requires them to break their established habits. Once they change, the expectations of their students are challenged:

> Increasing waiting time after asking questions proved difficult to start with due to my habitual desire to "add" something almost immediately after asking the original question. The pause after asking the question was sometimes "painful." It felt unnatural to have such a seemingly "dead" period, but I persevered. Given more thinking time, students seemed to realize that a more thoughtful answer was required. Now, after many months of changing my style of questioning, I have noticed that most students will give an answer and an explanation (where necessary) without additional prompting.—*Derek*, Century Island School

One teacher summarized the overall effects of her efforts to improve the use of question-and-answer dialogue in the classroom as follows:

Questioning

• My whole teaching style has become more interactive. Instead of showing how to find solutions, a question is asked and pupils are given time to explore answers together. My year 8 [grade 7] target class is now well-used to this way of working. I find myself using this method more and more with other groups.

No hands

• Unless specifically asked, pupils know not to put their hands up if they know the answer to a question. All pupils are expected to be able to answer at any time even if it is an "I don't know."

Supportive climate

• Pupils are comfortable with giving a wrong answer. They know that these can be as useful as correct ones. They are happy for other pupils to help explore their wrong answers further.
—*Nancy*, River-side School

Increasing the wait time can help more students become involved in discussions and increase the length of their replies. Another way to broaden participation is to ask students to brainstorm ideas, perhaps in pairs, for two to three minutes before the teacher asks for contributions. Overall, a consequence of such changes is that teachers learn more about the students' prior knowledge and about any gaps and misconceptions in that knowledge, so that teachers' next moves can better address the learners' real needs.

To exploit such changes means moving away from the routine of limited factual questions and refocusing attention on the quality and the different functions of classroom questions. Consider, for example, the use of a "big question": an open question or a problem-solving task that can set the scene for a lesson and evoke broad discussion or prompt focused small-group discussions. However, if this strategy is to be productive, both the responses that the task might generate and the ways of following up on these responses have to be anticipated. Collaboration between teachers to exchange ideas and experiences about good questions is very valuable. The questions themselves then become a more significant part of teaching, with attention focused on how they can be constructed and used to explore and then develop students' learning. Here's one teacher's thinking on the matter:

> I chose a year-8, middle-band group and really started to think about the type of questions I was asking—were they just instant one-word answers—what were they testing—knowledge or understanding—was I giving the class enough time to answer the question, was I quickly accepting the correct answer, was I asking the girl to explain her answer, how was I dealing with a wrong answer? When I really stopped to think, I realized that I could make a very large difference to the girls' learning by using all their answers to govern the pace and content of the lesson. —*Gwen*, Waterford School

Effective questioning is also an important aspect of the impromptu interventions teachers conduct once the students are engaged in an activity. Asking simple questions, such as "Why do you think that?" or "How might you express that?" can become part of the interactive dynamic of the classroom and can provide an invaluable opportunity to extend students' thinking through immediate feedback on their work.

Overall, the main suggestions for action that have emerged from the teachers' experience are:

• More effort has to be spent in framing questions that are worth asking, that is, questions that explore issues that are critical to the development of students' understanding.

• Wait time has to be increased to several seconds in order to give students time to think, and everyone should be expected to have an answer and to contribute to the discussion. Then all answers, right or wrong, can be used to develop understanding. The aim is thoughtful improvement rather than getting it right the first time.

• Follow-up activities have to be rich, in that they create opportunities to extend students' understanding.

Put simply, the only point of asking questions is to raise issues about which a teacher needs information or about which the students need to think. When such changes have been made, experience demonstrates that students become more active participants and come to realize that learning may depend less on their capacity to spot the right answer and more on their readiness to express and discuss their own understanding. The teachers also shift in their role, from presenters of content to leaders of an exploration and development of ideas in which all students are involved.

FEEDBACK THROUGH GRADING

When giving students feedback on both oral and written work, it is the nature, rather than the amount, of commentary that is critical. Research experiments have established that, while student learning can be advanced by feedback through comments, the giving of numerical scores or grades has a negative effect, in that students ignore comments when marks are also given.[5] These results often surprise teachers, but those who have abandoned the giving of marks discover that their experience confirms the findings: students do engage more productively in improving their work.

Many teachers will be concerned about the effect of returning students' work with comments but no scores or grades. There may be conflicts with school policy:

> My marking has developed from comments with targets and grades, which is the school policy, to comments and targets only. Pupils do work on targets and corrections more productively if no grades are given. Clare [Lee] observed on several occasions how little time pupils spent reading my comments if there were grades given as well. My routine is now, in my target class, i) to not give grades, only comments; ii) to give comments that highlight what has been done well and what needs further work; and iii) to give the minimum follow-up work expected to be completed next time I mark the books.
> —*Nancy*, Riverside School

Initial fears about how students might react turned out to be unjustified, and neither parents nor school inspectors have reacted adversely. Indeed, the provision of comments to students helps parents to focus on the learning issues rather than on trying to interpret a score or grade. We now believe that the effort that many teachers devote to grading homework may be misdirected. A numerical score or a grade does not tell students how to improve their work, so an opportunity to enhance their learning is lost.

A commitment to improve comments requires more work initially, as teachers have to attend to the quality of the comments that they write on students' work. Collaboration between teachers in sharing examples of effective comments can be very helpful, and experience will lead to more fluency. There is, however, more involved because comments become useful feedback only if students use them to guide further work, so new procedures are needed.

> After the first INSET [inservice training meeting] I was keen to try out a different way of marking books to give pupils more constructive feedback. I was keen to try and have a more easy method of monitoring pupils' response to my comments without having to trawl through their books each time to find out if they'd addressed my comments. I implemented a comment sheet at the back of my year-8 class' books. It is A4 [letter] in size, and the left-hand side is for my comments, and the right-hand side is for the pupils to demonstrate by a reference to the page in their books where I can find the evidence to say whether they have done the work. . . . The comments have become more meaningful as the time has gone on, and the books still take me only one hour to mark. — *Sian,* Cornbury Estate School

We have encountered a variety of ways of accommodating the new emphasis on comments. Some teachers have ceased assigning scores or grades at all, some teachers enter scores in their own record books but do not write them in the students' books, others give a score or grade only after a student has responded to the teacher's comments. Some teachers spend more time on certain pieces of work to ensure that they obtain good feedback and, to make time for this, either do not mark some pieces, or look at only a third of their students' books each week, or involve the students in checking the straightforward tasks.

A particularly valuable method is to devote some lesson time to rewriting selected pieces of work, so that emphasis can be put on feedback for improvement within a supportive environment. This practice can change students' expectations about the purposes of class work and homework.

As they tried to create useful feedback comments, many of the project teachers realized that they needed to reassess the work that they had asked students to undertake. They found that some tasks were useful in revealing students' understandings and misunderstandings, while others focused mainly on conveying information. So some activities were eliminated, others modified, and new and better tasks actively sought.

Overall the main ideas for improvement of feedback can be summarized as follows:

• Written tasks, alongside oral questioning, should encourage students to develop and show understanding of the key features of what they have learned.

• Comments should identify what has been done well and what still needs improvement and give guidance on how to make that improvement.

• Opportunities for students to respond to comments should be planned as part of the overall learning process.

The central point here is that, to be effective, feedback should cause thinking to take place. The implementation of such reforms can change both teachers' and students' attitudes toward written work: the assessment of students' work will be seen less as a competitive and summative judgment and more as a distinctive step in the process of learning.

PEER ASSESSMENT AND SELF-ASSESSMENT

Students can achieve a learning goal only if they understand that goal and can assess what they need to do to reach it. So self-assessment is essential to learning.[6] Many teachers who have tried to develop their students' self-assessment skills have found that the first and most difficult task is to get students to think of their work in terms of a set of goals. Insofar as they do so, they begin to develop an overview of that work that allows them to manage and control it for themselves. In other words, students are developing the capacity to work at a metacognitive level.

In practice, peer assessment turns out to be an important complement to self-assessment. Peer assessment is uniquely valuable because students may accept criticisms of their work from one another that they would not take seriously if the remarks were offered by a teacher. Peer work is also valuable because the interchange will be in language that students themselves naturally use and because students learn by taking the roles of teachers and examiners of others.[7] One teacher shared her positive views of peer assessment:

> As well as assessing and marking (through discussion and clear guidance) their own work, they also assess and mark the work of others. This they do in a very mature and sensible way, and this has proved to be a very worthwhile experiment. The students know that homework will be checked by themselves or another girl in the class at the start of the next lesson. This has led to a well-established routine and only on extremely rare occasions have students failed to complete the work set. They take pride in clear and well-presented work that one of their peers may be asked to mark. Any disagreement about the answer is thoroughly and openly discussed until agreement is reached.
> —*Alice,* Waterford School

The last sentence of this teacher's comments brings out an important point: when students do not understand an explanation, they are likely to interrupt a fellow student when they would not interrupt a teacher. In addition to this advantage, peer assessment is also valuable in placing the work in the hands of the students. The teacher can be free to observe and reflect on what is happening and to frame helpful interventions:

> We regularly do peer marking—I find this very helpful indeed. A lot of misconceptions come to the fore, and we then discuss these as we are going over the homework. I then go over the peer marking and talk to pupils individually as I go round the room.
> —*Rose*, Brownfields School

However, self-assessment will happen only if teachers help their students, particularly the low achievers, to develop the skill. This can take time and practice:

> The kids are not skilled in what I am trying to get them to do. I think the process is more effective long term. If you invest time in it, it will pay off big dividends, this process of getting the students to be more independent in the way that they learn and to take the responsibility themselves.
> —*Tom*, Riverside School

One simple and effective idea is for students to use "traffic light" icons, labeling their work green, yellow, or red according to whether they think they have good, partial, or little understanding. These labels serve as a simple means of communicating students' self-assessments. Students may then be asked to justify their judgments in a peer group, thus linking peer assessment and self-assessment. This linkage can help them develop the skills and the detachment needed for effective self-assessment.

Another approach is to ask students first to use their "traffic light" icons on a piece of work and then to indicate by hands-up whether they put a green, yellow, or red icon on it. The teacher can then pair up the greens and the yellows to help one another deal with their problems, while the red students meet with the teacher as a group to deal with their deeper problems. For such peer-group work to succeed, many students will need guidance about how to behave in groups, including such skills as listening to one another and taking turns.

In some subjects, taking time to help students understand scoring rubrics is also very helpful. Students can be given simplified versions of the rubrics teachers use, or they can be encouraged to rewrite them or even to create their own. Again, peer assessment and self-assessment are intimately linked. Observers in several language arts classrooms saw children apply to their own work lessons they had learned in peer assessment. A frequently heard comment was "I didn't do that either" or "I need to do that too."

Students' reflection about their understanding can also be used to inform future teaching, and their feedback can indicate in which areas a teacher needs to spend more time. A useful guide is to ask students to "traffic light" an end-of-unit test at the beginning of the unit: the yellow and red items can be used to adjust priorities within the teaching plan. Our experience leads us to offer the following recommendations for improving classroom practice:

• The criteria for evaluating any learning achievements must be made transparent to students to enable them to have a clear overview both of the aims of their work and of what it means to complete it successfully. Such criteria may well be abstract, but concrete examples should be used in modeling exercises to develop understanding.

• Students should be taught the habits and skills of collaboration in peer assessment, both because these are of intrinsic value and because peer assessment can help develop the objectivity required for effective self-assessment.

• Students should be encouraged to keep in mind the aims of their work and to assess their own progress toward meeting these aims as they proceed. Then they will be able to guide their own work and so become independent learners.

The main point here is that peer assessment and self-assessment make distinct contributions to the development of students' learning. Indeed, they secure aims that cannot be achieved in any other way.

THE FORMATIVE USE OF SUMMATIVE TESTS

The practices of self-assessment and peer assessment can be applied to help students prepare for tests, as in tackling the following problem:

> [The students] did not mention any of the reviewing strategies we had discussed in class. When questioned more closely, it was clear that many spent their time using very passive revision [reviewing] techniques. They would read over their work doing very little in the way of active revision or reviewing of their work. They were not transferring the active learning strategies we were using in class to work they did at home.
> —*Tom*, Riverside School

To remedy this situation, students can be asked to "traffic light" a list of key words or the topics on which the test will be set. The point of this exercise is to stimulate the students to reflect on where they feel their learning is secure, which they mark green, and where they need to concentrate their efforts, in yellow and red. These traffic lights then form the basis of a review plan. Students can be asked to identify questions on past tests that probe their "red" areas. Then they can work with textbooks and in peer groups to ensure that they can successfully answer those questions.

The aftermath of tests can also be an occasion for formative work. Peer marking of test papers can be helpful, as with normal written work, and it is particularly useful if students are required first to formulate a scoring rubric—an exercise that focuses attention on the criteria of quality relevant to their productions. After peer marking, teachers can reserve their time for discussion of the questions that give widespread difficulty, while peer tutoring can tackle those problems encountered by only a minority of students.

One other finding that has emerged from research studies is that students trained to prepare for examinations by generating and then answering their own questions outperformed comparable groups who prepared in conventional ways.[8] Preparing test questions helps students develop an overview of the topic:

> Pupils have had to think about what makes a good question for a test and in doing so need to have a clear understanding of the subject material. As a development of this, the best questions have been used for class tests. In this way, the pupils can see that their work is valued, and I can make an assessment of the progress made in these areas. When going over the test, good use can be made of group work and discussions between students concentrating on specific areas of concern.
> —*Angela*, Cornbury Estate School

Developments such as these challenge common expectations. Some have argued that formative and summative assessments are so different in their purpose that they have to be kept apart, and such arguments are strengthened when one experiences the harmful influence that narrow, high-stakes summative tests can have on teaching. However, it is unrealistic to expect teachers and students to practice such separation, so the challenge is to achieve a more positive relationship between the two. All of the ways we have described for doing so can be used for tests in which teachers have control over the setting and the marking. But their application may be more limited for tests in which the teacher has little or no control.

Overall, the main possibilities for improving classroom practice by using summative tests for formative purposes are as follows:

• Students can be engaged in a reflective review of the work they have done to enable them to plan their revision effectively.

• Students can be encouraged to set questions and mark answers so as to gain an understanding of the assessment process and further refine their efforts for improvement.

• Students should be encouraged through peer assessment and self-assessment to apply criteria to help them understand how their work might be improved. This may include providing opportunities for students to rework examination answers in class.

The overall message is that summative tests should become a positive part of the learning process. Through active involvement in the testing process, students can see that they can be the beneficiaries rather than the victims of testing, because tests can help them improve their learning.

REFLECTIONS: SOME UNDERLYING ISSUES

The changes that are entailed by improved assessment for learning have provoked us and the teachers involved to reflect on deeper issues about learning and teaching.

LEARNING THEORY

One of the most surprising things that happened during the early INSET sessions was that the participating teachers asked us to run a session on the psychology of learning. In retrospect, perhaps we should not have been so surprised at this request. After all, we had stressed that feedback functioned formatively only if the information fed back to the learner was used by the learner in improving performance. But while one can work out after the fact whether or not any feedback has had the desired effect, what the teachers needed was a way to give their students feedback that they knew in advance was going to be useful. To do that they needed to build up models of how students learn.

So the teachers came to take greater care in selecting tasks, questions, and other prompts to ensure that students' responses actually helped the teaching process. Such responses can "put on the table" the ideas that students bring to a learning task. The key to effective learning is then to find ways to help students restructure their knowledge to build in new and more powerful ideas. In the KMOFAP classrooms, as the teachers came to listen more attentively to the students' responses, they began to appreciate more fully that learning was not a process of passive reception of knowledge, but one in which the learners were active in creating their own understandings. Put simply, it became clear that, no matter what the pressure to achieve good test scores, learning must be done by the student.

Students came to understand what counted as good work through exemplification. Sometimes this was done through focused whole-class discussion around a particular example; at other times it was achieved through the use of sets of criteria to assess the work of peers.

Engaging in peer assessment and self-assessment is much more than just checking for errors or weaknesses. It involves making explicit what is normally implicit, and thus it requires students to be active in their learning. As one student wrote:

> After a pupil marking my investigation, I can now acknowledge my mistakes easier. I hope that it is not just me who learned from the investigation but the pupil who marked it did also. Next time I will have to make my explanations clearer, as they said "It is hard to understand."…
> I will now explain my equation again so it is clear.

The students also became much more aware of when they were learning and when they were not. One class, which was subsequently taught by a teacher not emphasizing assessment for learning, surprised that teacher by complaining: "Look, we've told you we don't understand this. Why are you going on to the next topic?" While students who are in tune with their learning can create difficulties for teachers, we believe that these are exactly the kinds of problems we should want to have.

SUBJECT DIFFERENCES

From hearing about research and discussing ideas with other colleagues, the teachers built up a repertoire of generic skills. They planned their questions, allowed appropriate wait time, and gave feedback that was designed to cause thinking. They ensured that students were given enough time during lessons to evaluate their own work and that of others.

However, after a while it became clear that these generic strategies could go only so far. Choosing a good question requires a detailed knowledge of the subject, but not necessarily the knowledge that is gained from advanced study in a subject. A high level of qualification in a subject is less important than a thorough understanding of its fundamental principles, an understanding of the kinds of difficulties that students might have, and the creativity to be able to think up questions that stimulate productive thinking.[9] Furthermore, such pedagogical content knowledge is essential in interpreting responses. That is, what students say will contain clues to aspects of their thinking that may require attention, but picking up on these clues requires a thorough knowledge of common difficulties in learning the subject. Thus, while the general principles of formative assessment apply across all subjects, the ways in which they manifest themselves in different subjects may differ. We have encountered such differences in making comparisons between teachers of mathematics, science, and language arts.

In mathematics, students have to learn to use valid procedures and to understand the concepts that underpin them. Difficulties can arise when students learn strategies that apply only in limited contexts and do not realize that they are inadequate elsewhere. Questioning must then be designed to bring out these strategies for discussion and to explore problems in understanding the concepts so that students can grasp the need to change their thinking. In such learning, there is usually a well-defined correct outcome. In more open-ended exercises, as in investigations of the application of mathematical thinking to everyday problems, there may be a variety of good solutions. Then an understanding of the criteria of quality is harder to achieve and may require joint discussion of examples and of the abstract criteria that they exemplify.

In science, the situation is very similar. There are many features of the natural world for which science provides a "correct" model or explanation. However, outside school, many students acquire different ideas. For example, some students come to believe that animals are living because they move but that trees and flowers are not because they don't. Or students may believe that astronauts seem almost weightless on the moon because there is no air present. Many of these "alternative conceptions" can be anticipated, for they have been well documented. What has also been documented is that the mere presentation of the "correct" view has been shown to be ineffective. The task in such cases is to open up discussion of such ideas and then provide feedback that challenges them by introducing new pieces of evidence and argument that support the scientific model.

There are other aspects for which an acceptable outcome is less well defined. As in mathematics, open-ended investigations call for different approaches to formative assessment. Even more open are issues about social or ethical implications of scientific achievements, for there is no "answer." Thus such work has to be "open" in a more fundamental way. Then the priority in giving feedback is to challenge students to tease out their assumptions and to help them to be critical about the quality of any arguments.

Peer assessment and self-assessment have a long history in language arts. Both the nature of the subject and the open outcome of many of the tasks characteristically make such practices central to one of the overall aims of the discipline, which is to enhance the critical judgment of the students.

A second important function of peer assessment and self-assessment was introduced by Royce Sadler, who argued that criteria alone are unhelpful in judging the quality of a piece of work or in guiding progression, because there will always be too many variables.[10] The key lies in knowing how to interpret the criteria in any particular case, which involves "guild knowledge." Teachers acquire this knowledge through assessing student work, and it is this process that allows them to differentiate between grades and to gain a sense of how progress is achieved. Peer assessment and self-assessment provide similar opportunities for students to be apprenticed into the guild, provided the criteria of quality are clearly communicated.

The priority in giving feedback is to challenge students to tease out their assumptions and to help them be critical about the quality of arguments.

In language arts, as in science and mathematics, attention needs to be paid to the central activities. Those that are the most successful are those rich tasks that provide students with an opportunity either to extend their understanding of a concept within the text or to "scaffold" their ideas before writing. Characteristically, these include small-group and pair work, with the results often being fed back into a whole-class discussion. Again, this type of work is not uncommon in language arts, the skill being to make the task sufficiently structured to scaffold learning but not so tightly defined as to limit thinking. Such activities not only provide students with a chance to develop their understanding through talk, but they also provide the teacher with the opportunity to give feedback during the course of a lesson through further questioning and guidance. The better the quality of the task, the better the quality of the interventions.

Differences between learning tasks can be understood in terms of a spectrum. At one end are "closed" tasks with a single well-defined outcome; at the other are "open" tasks with a wide range of acceptable outcomes. Tasks in language arts—for example, the writing of a poem—are mainly at the open end. But there are closed components even for such tasks—for example, the observance of grammatical or genre conventions. Tasks in, say, mathematics are more often closed, but applications of mathematics to everyday problems can require open-ended evaluations. Thus, in varying measure, the guidance needed for these two types of learning work will be needed in all subjects.

Despite these differences, experience has shown that the generic skills that have been developed do apply across subjects. One of the project's science teachers gave a talk to the whole staff about his experiences using some of the generic skills that we've been discussing and subsequently found how such practices distributed themselves throughout the disciplines:

> Art and drama teachers do it all the time, so do technology teachers (something to do with open-ended activities, long project times, and perhaps a less cramped curriculum?). But an English teacher came up to me today and said, "Yesterday afternoon was fantastic. I tried it today with my year 8s, and it works. No hands up, and giving them time to think. I had fantastic responses from kids who have barely spoken in class all year. They all wanted to say something, and the quality of answers was brilliant. This is the first time for ages that I've learnt something new that's going to make a real difference to my teaching."
> —*James*, Two Bishops School

MOTIVATION AND SELF-ESTEEM

Learning is not just a cognitive exercise: it involves the whole person. The need to motivate students is evident, but it is often assumed that offering such extrinsic rewards as grades, gold stars, and prizes is the best way to do it. However, there is ample evidence to challenge this assumption.

Students will invest effort in a task only if they believe that they can achieve something. If a learning exercise is seen as a competition, then everyone is aware that there will be losers as well as winners, and those who have a track record as losers will see little point in trying. Thus the problem is to motivate everyone, even though some are bound to achieve less than others. In tackling this problem, the type of feedback given is very important. Many research studies support this assertion. Here are a few examples:

- Students who are told that feedback "will help you to learn" learn more than those who are told that "how you do tells us how smart you are and what grades you'll get." The difference is greatest for low achievers.[11]
- Students given feedback as marks are likely to see it as a way to compare themselves with others (ego involvement); those given only comments see it as helping them to improve (task involvement). The latter group outperforms the former.[12]

Students given marks are likely to see it as a way to compare themselves with others; those given only comments see it as helping them to improve. The latter group outperforms the former.

- In a competitive system, low achievers attribute their performance to lack of "ability"; high achievers, to their effort. In a task-oriented system, all attribute performance to effort, and learning is improved, particularly among low achievers.[13]
- A comprehensive review of research studies of feedback found that feedback improved performance in 60% of the studies. In the cases where feedback was not helpful, the feedback turned out to be merely a judgment or grade with no indication of how to improve.[14]

In general, feedback given as rewards or grades enhances ego involvement rather than task involvement. It can focus students' attention on their "ability" rather than on the importance of effort, thus damaging the self-esteem of low achievers and leading to problems of "learned helplessness."[15] Feedback that focuses on what needs to be done can encourage all to believe that they can improve. Such feedback can enhance learning, both directly through the effort that can ensue and indirectly by supporting the motivation to invest such effort.[16]

THE BIG IDEA:
FOCUS ON LEARNING

Our experiences in the project all point to the need to rethink a teacher's core aim: enhancing student learning. To achieve this goal calls for a willingness to rethink the planning of lessons, together with a readiness to change the roles that both teacher and students play in supporting the learning process.

A LEARNING ENVIRONMENT: PRINCIPLES AND PLANS

Improvement in classroom learning requires careful forethought.

> Actually thinking about teaching has meant that I have been able to come up with ideas and strategies to cope with whatever has arisen and has contributed greatly to my professional development. I now think more about the content of the lesson. The influence has shifted from "What am I going to teach and what are the pupils going to do?" toward "How am I going to teach this and what are the pupils going to learn?"
> —*Susan*, Waterford School

One purpose of a teacher's forethought is to plan to improve teaching actions. So, for example, the planning of questions and activities has to be in terms of their learning function.

> I certainly did not spend sufficient time developing questions prior to commencing my formative training. . . . Not until you analyze your own questioning do you realize how poor it can be. I found myself using questions to fill time and asking questions which required little thought from the students. When talking to students, particularly those who are experiencing difficulties, it is important to ask questions which get them thinking about the topic and will allow them to make the next step in the learning process.
> —*Derek*, Century Island School

Of equal importance is concern for the quality of the responses that teachers make, whether in dialogue or in feed-back on written assignments. Effective feedback should make more explicit to students what is involved in a high-quality piece of work and what steps they need to take to improve. At the same time, feedback can enhance students' skills and strategies for effective learning.

There is also a deeper issue here. A learning environment has to be "engineered" to involve students more actively in the learning tasks. The emphasis has to be on students' thinking and making that thinking public. As one teacher put it:

> There was a definite transition at some point, from focusing on what I was putting into the process, to what the students were contributing. It became obvious that one way to make a significant sustainable change was to get the students doing more of the thinking. I then began to search for ways to make the learning process more transparent to the students. Indeed, I now spend my time looking for way s to get students to take responsibility for their learning and at the same time making the learning more collaborative.
> —*Tom*, Riverside School

Collaboration between teachers and students and between students and their peers can produce a supportive environment in which students can explore their own ideas, hear alternative ideas in the language of their peers, and evaluate them.

> One technique has been to put the students into small groups and give each student a small part of the unit to explain to [his or her] colleagues. They are given a few minutes' preparation time, a few hints, and use of their exercise books. Then each student explains [his or her] chosen subject to the rest of the group. Students are quick to point out such things as, "I thought that the examples you chose were very good as they were not ones in our books. I don't think I would have thought of those." Or "I expected you to mention particles more when you were explaining the difference between liquids and gases." These sessions have proven invaluable—not only to me, in being able to discover the level of understanding of some students, but to the students too.
> —*Philip*, Century Island School

An additional advantage of such an environment is that a teacher can work intensively with one group, challenging the ideas and assumptions of its members, knowing that the rest of the class members are also working hard.

So the main actions to be taken to engineer an effective learning environment are:

- Plan classroom activities to give students the opportunity to express their thinking so that feedback can help develop it;
- formulate feedback so that it guides improvement in learning;
- use activities that demand collaboration so that everyone is included and challenged and train students to listen to and respect one another's ideas; and
- be sure that students are active participants in the lessons and emphasize that learning may depend less on their capacity to spot the right answer and more on their readiness to express and discuss their own understanding.

A LEARNING ENVIRONMENT: ROLES AND EXPECTTIONS

It is one thing to plan new types of classroom activity and quite another to put them into practice in ways that are faithful to the aims they were developed to serve. Here there are no recipes to follow in a uniform way. *Inside the Black Box* was clear in stating that the effective development of formative assessment would come about only if "each teacher finds his or her own ways of incorporating the lessons and ideas that are set out above into her or his own patterns of classroom work."

A second principle is that the learning environment envisaged requires a classroom culture that may well be unfamiliar and disconcerting for both teachers and students. The effect of the innovations implemented by our teachers was to change the "classroom contract" between the teacher and the student—the rules that govern the behaviors that are expected and seen as legitimate by teachers and students.

The students have to change from behaving as passive recipients of the knowledge offered by the teacher to becoming active learners who can take responsibility for and manage their own learning.

For the teachers, courage is necessary. One of the striking features of the project was that, in the early stages, many participants described the new approach as "scary" because they felt they were going to lose control of their classes. Toward the end of the project, they spoke not of losing control but of sharing responsibility for the students' learning with the class—exactly the same process but viewed from two very different perspectives. In one perspective, the teachers and students are in a delivery/recipient relationship; in the other, they are partners in pursuit of a shared goal:

> What formative assessment has done for me is made me focus less on myself but more on the children. I have had the confidence to empower the students to take it forward.
> —*Robert*, Two Bishops School

What has been happening here is that everybody's expectations—that is, what teachers and students think that being a teacher or being a student requires you to do—have been altered. While it can seem daunting to undertake such changes, they do not have to happen suddenly. Changes with the KMOFAP teachers came slowly and steadily, as experience developed and confidence grew in the use of the various strategies for enriching feedback and interaction. For example, many teachers started by using questions to encourage thinking. Then they improved their oral and written feedback so that it brought thinking forward and went on to develop peer and self-assessment.

To summarize, expectations and classroom culture can be changed:

• by changing the "classroom contract" so that all expect that teacher and students work together for the same end: the improvement of everyone's learning;

• by empowering students to become active learners, thus taking responsibility for their own learning;

• by incorporating the changes in the teacher's role one step at a time, as they seem appropriate; and

• by sustained attention to and reflection on ways in which assessment can support learning.

WHAT YOU CAN DO

To incorporate some of the ideas about formative assessment into your own practice, the first step is to reflect on what you are now doing. Discussion with colleagues and observation of one another's lessons can help spark such reflection.

A next step must be to try out changes. Wholesale change can be too risky and demanding, so it is often best to think of one thing you feel confident to try—be it "traffic lights," peer assessment, improved questioning, whatever—and simply try it. If you are a teacher in a middle school or high school, try it with just one group. Or if you are an elementary teacher, try it in just one subject area. We found that, as teachers gained confidence in the power of allowing students to say what they know and what they need to know, the teachers decided that they should extend assessment for learning to the whole of their teaching.

Taking on further strategies will then lead to further progress. When several colleagues are collaborating, each starts with a different strategy and then shares findings. This process should lead to the explicit formulation of an "action plan," comprising a range of strategies to be used, in combination, preferably starting with a class at the beginning of the school year. The first reason to start at the beginning of the year is so that there can be time to accustom both teacher and students to a new way of working. The second is that it can be very difficult to change the established habits and routines in the middle of a year. The experience of a year's sustained work, with only a few classes, preferably alongside similar efforts by colleagues, can provide a firm basis for subsequent adoption of new practices on a wider scale.

Collaboration with a group trying out similar innovations is almost essential. Mutual observation and the sharing of ideas and experiences about the progress of action plans can provide the necessary support both with the tactics and at a strategic level. Support for colleagues is particularly important in overcoming those initial uncertainties when engaging in the risky business of changing the culture and expectations in the classroom.

As for any innovation, support from administrators is essential. One way administrators can support change of this kind is to help peer groups of teachers find time to meet on a regular basis. Opportunities should also be found for teachers to report to faculty and staff meetings.

The work of any group experimenting with innovations is an investment for the whole school, so that support should not be treated as indulgence for idiosyncratic practices. Indeed, such work should be integrated into a school improvement plan, with the expectation that the dissemination of fruitful practices will follow from the evaluation of a group's experiences.

There may be a need to review school policies: an example would be a policy that, by demanding a grade on every piece of homework, prevents the serious use of comments.

At the same time, there may be a need to review current school policies because such policies can actually constrain the use of formative assessment. A notable example would be a policy that, by demanding that a score or grade be given on every piece of homework, prevents the serious use of comments. Five of the six schools in the KMOFAP project have, following the experience of their science and mathematics teachers, modified their policies to allow "comment only" marking; for two of these, the modification was that no scores or grades be given on homework throughout the school. In another example, a "target setting" system that required very frequent review was inhibiting any change in learning methods that might slow down immediate "progress" in order to produce medium-to long-term gains in learning skills. Those engaged in innovations may need formal exemption from such policies.

Thus support, evaluation, and subsequent dissemination of innovation in assessment for learning will be planned in a coherent way only if the responsibility for strategic over-sight of the development is assigned to a member of the school leadership team. Our experience supports the view that to realize the promise of formative assessment by leaving a few keen individuals to get on with it would be unfair to them, while to do it by imposing a policy that requires all teachers to immediately change their personal roles and styles would be absurd.

What is needed is a plan, extending over at least three years, in which a few small groups are supported for a two year exploration. These groups then form a nucleus of experience and expertise for disseminating their ideas throughout the school and for supporting colleagues in making similar explorations for themselves.

Notes

1. Paul Black and Dylan Wiliam, "Inside the Black Box: Raising Standards Through Classroom Assessment ," *Phi Delta Kappan*, October 1998, pp. 139-48. A version of this article has been published and widely sold in the United Kingdom. A booklet, published in 2002, has also been widely distributed in the UK. It covers the same issues as the article and bears the same title with the same authors. Both booklets, and further booklets in this series, are published by NFER-NELSON.

    Only a few references to the literature are given here. Further information about publications and other resources can be obtained on the King's College website in the pages of the King's Formative Assessment Group. Some of the publications can be downloaded from this site: www.Kel.ac.uk/education/research/Kal.html.

2. Paul Black and Dylan Wiliam, "Assessment and Classroom Learning," *Assessment in Education*, March 1998, pp. 7-71.

3. Paul Black, Christine Harrison, Clare Lee, Bethan Marshall, and Dylan Wiliam, *Assessment for Learning: Putting It into Practice* (Buckingham, U.K.: Open University Press, 2003).

4. Mary Budd Rowe, "Wait Time and Rewards as Instructional Variables , Their Influence on Language, Logic, and Fate Control," *Journal of Research in Science Teaching*, vol. 11, 1974, pp. 81-94.

5. Ruth Butler, "Enhancing and Undermining Intrinsic Motivation; The Effects of Task-Involving and Ego-Involving Evaluation on Interest and Performance," *British Journal of Educational Psychology*, vol. 58, 1988, pp. 1-14.

6. Royce Sadler, "Formative Assessment and the Design of Instructional Systems," *Instructional Science*, vol. 18, 1989, pp. 119-44.

7. Royce Sadler, "Formative Assessment: Revisiting the Territory," *Assessment in Education*, vol. 5, 1998, pp. 77-84.

8. See, for example, Paul W. Foos, Joseph J. Mora, and Sharon Tkacz, "Student Study Techniques and the Generation Effect," *Journal of Educational Psychology*, vol. 86, 1994, pp. 567-76; and Alison King, "Facilitating Elaborative Learning Through Guided Student-Generated Questioning ," *Educational Psychologist*, vol. 27, 1992, pp. 111-26.

9. See, for example, Mike Askew et al., *Effective Teachers of Numeracy: Final Report*(London: King's College London, School of Education, 1997). In this study, there was no correlation between the progress made by elementary school students in arithmetic and the highest level of mathematics studied by the teacher. Indeed, there was a nonsignificant negative correlation between the two. The students who made the most progress were taught by teachers without high levels of subject knowledge, but who emphasized the connections between mathematics concepts.

10. Sadler, "Formative Assessment and the Design of Instructional Systems."

11. Richard S. Newman and Mahna T. Schwager, "Students' Help Seeking During Problem Solving: Effects of Grade, Goal, and Prior Achievement," *American Educational Research Journal*, vol. 32, 1995, pp. 352–76.

12. Ruth Butler, "Task-Involving and Ego-Involving Properties of Evaluation: Effects of Different Feedback Conditions on Motivational Perceptions, Interest, and Performance ," *Journal of Educational Psychology*, vol. 79, 1987, pp. 474-82.

13. Rhonda G. Craven, Herbert W. Marsh, and Raymond L. Debus, "Effects of Internally Focused Feedback on Enhancement of Academic Self-Concept," *Journal of Educational Psychology*, vol. 83, 1991, pp. 17-27.

14. Avraham N. Kluger and Angelo DeNisi, "The Effects of Feedback Interventions on Performance: A Historical Review, a Meta-Analysis, and a Preliminary Feedback Intervention Theory," *Psychological Bulletin*, vol. 119, 1996, pp. 254-84.

15. Carol S. Dweck, "Motivational Processes Affecting Learning," *American Psychologist* (Special Issue: Psychological Science and Education), vol. 41, 1986, pp. 1040-48.

16. Carol S. Dweck, *Self-Theories: Their Role in Motivation, Personality, and Development* (Philadelphia: Psychology Press, 2000).

PAUL BLACK is a professor emeritus, Department of Education and Professional Studies, King's College London, where CHRISTINE HARRISON is a lecturer in science education. CLARE LEE is a teacher advisor for the Warwickshire County Council. BETHAN MARSHALL is a lecturer in English education, Department of Education and Professional Studies, School of Education, King's College London. DYLAN WILIAM is director of the Learning and Teaching Research Center, Educational Testing Service, Princeton, N.J. They wish to thank the Medway and Oxfordshire local education authorities and the schools directly involved in the project described here, especially the teachers who shouldered the greatest burdens. The work on which this article is based was supported by grants from the Nuffield Foundation and from the U.S. National Science Foundation, as part of the Stanford University Classroom Assessment Project to Improve Teaching and Learning (CAPITAL). But the opinions expressed are those of the authors. © 2004, Dylan Wiliam.

Classroom Assessment for Learning

Classroom assessment that involves students in the process and focuses on increasing learning can motivate rather than merely measure students.

Stephen Chappuis and Richard J. Stiggins

Imagine classroom assessment as a healthy part of effective teaching and successful learning. At a time when large-scale, external assessments of learning gain political favor and attention, many teachers are discovering how to engage and motivate students using day-to-day classroom assessment for purposes beyond measurement. By applying the principles of what is called *assessment for learning*, teachers have followed clear research findings of the effects that high-quality, formative assessment can have on student achievement.

We typically think of assessment as an index of school success rather than as the cause of that success. Unfortunately, largely absent from the traditional classroom assessment environment is the use of assessment as a tool to promote greater student achievement (Shepard, 2000). In general, the teacher teaches and then tests. The teacher and class move on,

leaving unsuccessful students, those who might not learn at the established pace and within a fixed time frame, to finish low in the rank order. This assessment model is founded on two outdated beliefs: that to increase learning we should increase student anxiety and that comparison with more successful peers will motivate low performers to do better.

By contrast, assessment for learning occurs during the teaching and learning process rather than after it and has as its primary focus the ongoing improvement of learning for all students (Assessment Reform Group, 1999; Crooks, 2001; Shepard, 2000). Teachers who assess for learning use day-to-day classroom assessment activities to involve students directly and deeply in their own learning, increasing their confidence and motivation to learn by emphasizing progress and achievement rather than failure and defeat (Stig-

gins, 1999; 2001). In the assessment for learning model, assessment is an instructional tool that promotes learning rather than an event designed solely for the purpose of evaluation and assigning grades. And when students become involved in the assessment process, assessment for learning begins to look more like teaching and less like testing (Davies, 2000).

Student-Involved Assessment

Research shows that classroom assessments that provide accurate, descriptive feedback to students and involve them in the assessment process can improve learning (Black and Wiliam, 1998). As a result, assessment for learning means more than just assessing students often, more than providing the teacher with assessment results to revise instruction. In assessment for learning, both teacher and student use classroom assessment information to modify teaching and learning activities. Teachers use assessment information formatively when they

- Pretest before a unit of study and adjust instruction for individuals or the entire group.
- Analyze which students need more practice.
- Continually revise instruction on the basis of results.
- Reflect on the effectiveness of their own teaching practices.
- Confer with students regarding their strengths and the areas that need improvement.
- Facilitate peer tutoring, matching students who demonstrate understanding with those who do not.

We tend to think of students as passive participants in assessment rather than engaged users of the information that assessment can produce. What we should be asking is, How can students use assessment to take responsibility for and improve their own learning?

Student involvement in assessment doesn't mean that students control decisions regarding what will or won't be learned or tested. It doesn't mean that they assign their own grades. Instead, student involvement means that students learn to use assessment information to manage their own learning so that they understand how they learn best, know exactly where they are in relation to the defined learning targets, and plan and take the next steps in their learning.

Student-involved assessment means that students learn to use assessment information to manage their own learning.

Students engage in the assessment for learning process when they use assessment information to set goals, make learning decisions related to their own improvement, de-

velop an understanding of what quality work looks like, self-assess, and communicate their status and progress toward established learning goals. Students involved in their own assessment might

- Determine the attributes of good performance. Students look at teacher-supplied anonymous samples of strong student performances and list the qualities that make them strong, learning the language of quality and the concepts behind strong performance.
- Use scoring guides to evaluate real work samples. Students can start with just one criterion in the guide and expand to others as they become more proficient in scoring. As students engage in determining the characteristics of quality work and scoring actual work samples, they become better able to evaluate their own work. Using the language of the scoring guide, they can identify their areas of strength and set goals for improvement—in essence, planning the next steps in their learning.
- Revise anonymous work samples. Students go beyond evaluating work to using criteria to improve the quality of a work sample. They can develop a revision plan that outlines improvements, or write a letter to the creator of the original work offering advice on how to improve the sample. This activity also helps students know what to do before they revise their own work.
- Create practice tests or test items based on their understanding of the learning targets and the essential concepts in the class material. Students can work in pairs to identify what they think should be on the test and to generate sample test items and responses.
- Communicate with others about their growth and determine when they are nearing success. Students achieve a deeper understanding of themselves and the material that they are attempting to learn when they describe the quality of their

own work. Letters to parents, written self-reflections, and conferences with teachers and parents in which students outline the process they used to create a product allow students to share what they know and describe their progress toward the learning target. By accumulating evidence of their own improvement in growth portfolios, students can refer to specific stages in their growth and celebrate their achievement with others.

Effective Teacher Feedback

"You need to study harder." "Your handwriting is very nice." "Good job." Traditionally, teachers use such statements to register their approval or disapproval of student performance. But such evaluative feedback, long a classroom staple, is of limited value for improving student learning and can actually have negative effects on students' desire to learn. And grades, those traditional coded symbols and markings—B-, 71 percent, 4/10, Satisfactory, F— actually communicate even less about what students have done well or need to do to improve. By contrast, teacher comments that focus on student work and not on individual student characteristics can increase students' motivation and desire to learn.

Black and Wiliam (1998) point to the benefits of replacing judgmental feedback with specific, descriptive, and immediate feedback. When the goal is to increase student motivation and learning, productive feedback tells students what they are doing right, pinpointing strengths and helping learners develop those strengths even further. For some students, receiving this feedback in writing and having time to reflect on it is sufficient. Other students need face-to-face teacher feedback to reinforce what they have done well.

Effective teacher feedback describes why an answer is right or wrong in specific terms that students understand. Students can also generate their own descriptive feedback by comparing their work with teacher-provided exemplars or posted samples. They can then compare their own feedback with that of their teacher.

Descriptive feedback should provide ways for students to improve in clear, constructive language. Instead of simply labeling student errors or omissions, effective feedback guides students to better performance throughout the learning process. Useful comments focus specifically on improving only one area at a time.

Finally, teacher feedback for learning draws an even bigger picture by telling students where they are now relative to the defined learning targets—and where teachers ultimately want them to be. By modeling for students a variety of suggestions designed to narrow the gap between where they are and where they should be headed, teachers can help students learn to generate their own strategies for improvement.

The Skills of Self-Assessment

Eventually, we want students to be able to direct their own learning. Yet it often seems unclear just how students will achieve this goal. Assessment for learning helps students become self-directed learners by developing their self-assessment skills. The principles of assessment for learning are interrelated: Just as involving students in the assessment process helps make assessment more like instruction, students need to learn to self-assess so that they can use the descriptive feedback from the teacher to its best advantage. Sadler (1989) and Atkin, Black, and Coffey (2001) describe a model of formative assessment in which learners continually ask themselves three questions as they self-assess.

Where Am I Trying to Go?

Students need clearly articulated, concise learning targets to be able to answer this first question. Learning is easier when learners understand what goal they are trying to achieve, the purpose of achieving the goal, and the specific attributes of success. Teachers should continually help students clarify the intended learning as the lessons unfold—not just at the beginning of a unit of study. Teachers share learning intentions with students when they

- Phrase objectives in terms that begin with "We are learning to…" or "I can…"
- Ask students to read the objectives aloud and ask clarifying questions.
- Separate what they want students to do—the instructions for completing the task—from what they want students to learn. Otherwise, the directions might overshadow the intended learning.
- Inform students why they need to learn what comes next and how it connects to previous and future learning.
- Display the learning objectives in the classroom.
- Provide students with examples of outstanding work as well as samples of lesser quality so that they can see the differences.
- Ask students to rephrase the learning targets or describe what attainment of a target looks like (Arter & Busick, 2001; Clarke, 2001).

Where Am I Now?

Students can practice comparing their work to models of high-quality work and trying to identify the differences. They can use teacher feedback from formative assessments to gather evidence of what they know and can do relative to the defined learning target. They can use teacher questions designed to prompt students to reflect on what they have learned individually relative to the intended learning. All of these strategies help students ascertain—and, even more important, learn *how* to ascertain—where they are and where they need to be, an awareness that is central to their ultimate success.

Teachers share learning intentions with students when they separate what they want students to do—the instructions for completing the task— from what they want students to learn.

How Do I Close the Gap?

Assessment for learning helps students know what to do to move from their current position to the final learning goal. To meet learning goals, students must participate fully in creating the goals, analyzing assessment data, and developing a plan of action to achieve the next goal (Clarke, 2001).

Students should learn question-and-answer strategies that they can use to close the gap: What do I need to change in my work to improve its quality? What specific help do I need to make these changes? From whom can I get help? What resources do I need?

Sadler (1989) notes that a steady flow of descriptive feedback to students encourages continual self-assessment around what constitutes quality. Keeping students connected to a vision of quality as the unit of study progresses helps them close the gap by formulating their next steps in learning.

All Students Learning Well

The habits and skills of self-assessment are within the grasp and capabilities of almost every student. Students take greater responsibility for their own learning when they regularly assess themselves (Shepard, 2001). In the hands of trained teachers, assessment for learning breeds confidence in learning. It provides students with opportunities for monitoring and communicating to others their own progress.

Educators open the door to using assessment in more productive ways when they acknowledge that students respond differently to the use of test scores as threats of punishment or promises of reward. Those who succeed keep striving; those who fail may give up. By contrast, most students respond positively to classroom assessment environments that promote success rather than simply measure it.

Students demonstrate unprecedented score gains on standardized assessments when their teachers apply the principles of assessment for learning in the classroom (Black and Wiliam, 1998). With appropriate training, teachers can improve the accuracy of their day-to-day assessments, make their feedback to students descriptive and informative, and increase the involvement of students in the entire assessment process. In this way, classroom assessment for learning becomes a school improvement tool that helps create responsible, engaged, and self-directed learners.

References

Arter, J. A., & Busick, K. U. (2001). *Practice with student-involved classroom assessment*. Portland, OR: Assessment Training Institute.

Assessment Reform Group. (1999). *Assessment for learning: Beyond the black box*. Cambridge, England: University of Cambridge.

Atkin, J. M., Black, P., & Coffey, J. (2001). *Classroom assessment and the National Science Education Standards*. Washington, DC: National Academy Press.

Black, P., & Wiliam, D. (1998). Inside the black box: Raising standards through classroom assessment. *Phi Delta Kappan, 80*(2), 139-148.

Clarke, S. (2001). *Unlocking formative assessment*. London: Hodder and Stoughton.

Crooks, T. (2001). *The validity of formative assessments*. Leeds, England: British Educational Research Association.

Davies, A. (2000). *Making classroom assessment work*. Merville, British Columbia, Canada: Connections Publishing.

Sadler, R. (1989). Formative assessment and the design of instructional systems. *Instructional Science, 18*, 119-144.

Shepard, L. A. (2000). The role of assessment in a learning culture. *Educational Researcher, 29*(7), 4-14.

Shepard, L. A. (2001, July). *Using assessment to help students think about learning*. Keynote address at the Assessment Training Institute Summer Conference, Portland, OR.

Stiggins, R. J. (1999). Assessment, student confidence, and school success. *Phi Delta Kappan, 81*(3), 191–198.

Stiggins, R. J. (2001). *Student-involved classroom assessment* (3rd ed.). Upper Saddle River, NJ: Merrill-Prentice Hall.

Stephen Chappuis is Director of Professional Development and **Richard J. Stiggins** is President and Founder of the Assessment Training Institute, 317 SW Alder St., Ste. 1200, Portland, OR 97204; (800) 480–3060; ati@assessmentinst.com.

How Classroom Assessments Improve Learning

Teachers who develop useful assessments, provide corrective instruction, and give students second chances to demonstrate success can improve their instruction and help students learn.

Thomas R. Guskey

Large-scale assessments, like all assessments, are designed for a specific purpose. Those used in most states today are designed to rank-order schools and students for the purposes of accountability—and some do so fairly well. But assessments designed for ranking are generally not good instruments for helping teachers improve their instruction or modify their approach to individual students. First, students take them at the end of the school year, when most instructional activities are near completion. Second, teachers don't receive the results until two or three months later, by which time their students have usually moved on to other teachers. And third, the results that teachers receive usually lack the level of detail needed to target specific improvements (Barton, 2002; Kifer, 2001).

The assessments best suited to guide improvements in student learning are the quizzes, tests, writing assignments, and other assess-ments that teachers administer on a regular basis in their classrooms. Teachers trust the results from these assessments because of their direct relation to classroom instructional goals. Plus, results are immediate and easy to analyze at the individual student level. To use classroom assessments to make improvements, however, teachers must change both their view of assessments and their interpretation of results. Specifically, they need to see their assessments as an integral part of the instruction process and as crucial for helping students learn.

Despite the importance of assessments in education today, few teachers receive much formal training in assessment design or analysis. A recent survey showed, for example, that fewer than half the states require competence in assessment for licensure as a teacher (Stiggins, 1999). Lacking specific training, teachers rely heavily on the assessments offered by the publisher of their textbooks or instructional materials. When no suitable assessments are available, teachers construct their own in a haphazard fashion, with questions and essay prompts similar to the ones that their teachers used. They treat assessments as evaluation devices to administer when instructional activities are completed and to use primarily for assigning students' grades.

To use assessments to improve instruction and student learning, teachers need to change their approach to assessments in three important ways.

Make Assessments Useful
For Students
Nearly every student has suffered the experience of spending hours preparing for a major assessment, only to discover that the material that he or she had studied was different from what the teacher chose to emphasize

on the assessment. This experience teaches students two unfortunate lessons. First, students realize that hard work and effort don't pay off in school because the time and effort that they spent studying had little or no influence on the results. And second, they learn that they cannot trust their teachers (Guskey, 2000a). These are hardly the lessons that responsible teachers want their students to learn.

Nonetheless, this experience is common because many teachers still mistakenly believe that they must keep their assessments secret. As a result, students come to regard assessments as guessing games, especially from the middle grades on. They view success as depending on how well they can guess what their teachers will ask on quizzes, tests, and other assessments. Some teachers even take pride in their ability to out-guess students. They ask questions about isolated concepts or obscure understandings just to see whether students are reading carefully. Generally, these teachers don't include such "gotcha" questions maliciously, but rather—often unconsciously—because such questions were asked of them when they were students.

Classroom assessments that serve as meaningful sources of information don't surprise students. Instead, these assessments reflect the concepts and skills that the teacher emphasized in class, along with the teacher's clear criteria for judging students' performance. These concepts, skills, and criteria align with the teacher's instructional activities and, ideally, with state or district standards. Students see these assessments as fair measures of important learning goals. Teachers facilitate learning by providing students with important feedback on their learning progress and by helping them identify learning problems (Bloom, Madaus, & Hastings, 1981; Stiggins, 2002).

Critics sometimes contend that this approach means "teaching to the test." But the crucial issue is, What determines the content and methods of teaching? If the test is the primary determinant of what teachers teach and how they teach it, then we are indeed "teaching to the test." But if desired learning goals are the foundation of students' instructional experiences, then assessments of student learning are simply extensions of those same goals. Instead of "teaching to the test," teachers are more accurately "testing what they teach." If a concept or skill is important enough to assess, then it should be important enough to teach. And if it is not important enough to teach, then there's little justification for assessing it.

For Teachers

The best classroom assessments also serve as meaningful sources of information for teachers, helping them identify what they taught well and what they need to work on. Gathering this vital information does not require a sophisticated statistical analysis of assessment results. Teachers need only make a simple tally of how many students missed each assessment item or failed to meet a specific criterion. State assessments sometimes provide similar item-by-item information, but concerns about item security and the cost of developing new items each year usually make assessment developers reluctant to offer such detailed information. Once teachers have made specific tallies, they can pay special attention to the trouble spots—those items or criteria missed by large numbers of students in the class.

In reviewing these results, the teacher must first consider the quality of the item or criterion. Perhaps the question is ambiguously worded or the criterion is unclear. Perhaps students misinterpreted the question. Whatever the case, teachers must determine whether these items adequately address the knowledge, understanding, or skill that they were intended to measure.

If teachers find no obvious problems with the item or criterion, then they must turn their attention to their teaching. When as many as half the students in a class answer a clear question incorrectly or fail to meet a particular criterion, it's not a student learning problem—it's a teaching problem. Whatever teaching strategy was used, whatever examples were employed, or whatever explanation was offered, it simply didn't work.

Analyzing assessment results in this way means setting aside some powerful ego issues. Many teachers may initially say, "I taught them. They just didn't learn it!" But on reflection, most recognize that their effectiveness is not defined on the basis of what they do as teachers but rather on what their students are able to do. Can effective teaching take place in the absence of learning? Certainly not.

Some argue that such a perspective puts too much responsibility on teachers and not enough on students. Occasionally, teachers respond, "Don't students have responsibilities in this process? Shouldn't students display initiative and personal accountability?"

Indeed, teachers and students share responsibility for learning. Even with valiant teaching efforts, we cannot guarantee that all students will learn everything excellently. Only rarely do teachers find items or assessment criteria that every student answers correctly. A few students are never willing to put forth the necessary effort, but these students tend to be the exception, not the rule. If a teacher is reaching fewer than half of the students in the class, the teacher's method of instruction needs to improve. And teachers need this kind of evidence to help target their instructional improvement efforts.

Follow Assessments with Corrective Instruction

If assessments provide information for both students and teachers, then they cannot mark the end of learning. Instead, assessments must be followed by high-quality, corrective instruction designed to remedy whatever learning errors the assessment identified (see Guskey, 1997). To charge ahead knowing that students have not learned certain concepts or skills well would be foolish. Teachers must therefore follow their assessments with instructional alternatives that present those concepts in new ways and engage students in different and more appropriate learning experiences.

Teachers need to see their assessments as an integral part of the instruction process and as crucial for helping students learn.

High-quality, corrective instruction is not the same as reteaching, which often consists simply of restating the original explanations louder and more slowly. Instead, the teacher must use approaches that accommodate differences in students' learning styles and intelligences (Sternberg, 1994). Although teachers generally try to incorporate different teaching approaches when they initially plan their lessons, corrective instruction involves extending and strengthening that work. In addition, those students who have few or no learning errors to correct should receive enrichment activities to help broaden and expand their learning. Materials designed for gifted and talented students provide an excellent resource for such activities.

Developing ideas for corrective instruction and enrichment activities can be difficult, especially if teachers believe that they must do it alone, but structured professional development opportunities can help teachers share strategies and collaborate on teaching techniques (Guskey, 1998, 2000b). Faculty meetings devoted to examining classroom assessment results and developing alternative strategies can be highly effective. District-level personnel and collaborative partnerships with local colleges and universities offer wonderful resources for ideas and practical advice.

Occasionally, teachers express concern that if they take time to offer corrective instruction, they will sacrifice curriculum coverage. Because corrective work is initially best done during class and under the teacher's direc-

tion, early instructional units will typically involve an extra class period or two. Teachers who ask students to complete corrective work independently, outside of class, generally find that those students who most need to spend time on corrective work are the least likely to do so.

As students become accustomed to this corrective process and realize the personal benefits it offers, however, the teacher can drastically reduce the amount of class time allocated to such work and accomplish much of it through homework assignments or in special study sessions before or after school. And by not allowing minor errors to become major learning problems, teachers better prepare students for subsequent learning tasks, eventually need less time for corrective work (Whiting, Van Burgh, & Render, 1995), and can proceed at a more rapid pace in later learning units. By pacing their instructional units more flexibly, most teachers find that they need not sacrifice curriculum coverage to offer students the benefits of corrective instruction.

Give Second Chances to Demonstrate Success

To become an integral part of the instructional process, assessments cannot be a one-shot, do-or-die experience for students. Instead, assessments must be part of an ongoing effort to help students learn. And if teachers follow assessments with helpful corrective instruction, then students should have a second chance to demonstrate their new level of competence and understanding. This second chance helps determine the effectiveness of the corrective instruction and offers students another opportunity to experience success in learning.

Writing teachers have long recognized the many benefits of a second chance. They know that students rarely write well on an initial attempt. Teachers build into the writing process several opportunities for students to gain feedback on early drafts and then to use that feedback to revise and improve their writing. Teachers of other subjects frequently

balk at the idea, however—mostly because it differs from their personal learning experiences.

Some teachers express concern that giving students a second chance might be unfair and that "life isn't like that." They point out that that a surgeon doesn't get a second chance to perform an operation successfully and a pilot doesn't get a second chance to land a jumbo jet safely. Because of the very high stakes involved, each must get it right the first time.

But how did these highly skilled professionals learn their craft? The first operation performed by that surgeon was on a cadaver—a situation that allows a lot of latitude for mistakes. Similarly, the pilot spent many hours in a flight simulator before ever attempting a landing from the cockpit. Such experiences allowed them to learn from their mistakes and to improve their performance. Similar instructional techniques are used in nearly every professional endeavor. Only in schools do student face the prospect of one-shot, do-or-die assessments, with no chance to demonstrate what they learned from previous mistakes.

All educators strive to have their students become lifelong learners and develop learning-to-learn skills. What better learning-to-learn skill is there than learning from one's mistakes? A mistake can be the beginning of learning. Some assessment experts argue, in fact, that students learn nothing from a successful performance. Rather, students learn best when their initial performance is less than successful, for then they can gain direction on how to improve (Wiggins, 1998).

Other teachers suggest that it's unfair to offer the same privileges and high grades to students who require a second chance that we offer to those students who demonstrate a high level of learning on the initial assessment. After all, these students may simply have failed to prepare appropriately. Certainly, we should recognize students who do well on the initial assessment and provide opportunities for them to extend their learning through enrichment activities. But those students who do well on a second assessment have also learned well. More important, their poor performance on the first assessment may not have been their fault. Maybe the teaching strategies used during the initial instruction were inappropriate for these students, but the corrective instruction proved more effective. If we determine grades on the basis of performance and these students have performed at a high level, then they certainly deserve the same grades as those who scored well on their first try.

Assessments can help improve education, but as long as we use them only as a means to rank schools, and students, we will miss their most powerful benefits.

A comparable example is the driver's license examination. Many individuals do not pass their driver's test on the first attempt. On the second or third try, however, they may reach the same high level of performance as others did on their first. Should these drivers be restricted, for instance, to driving in fair weather only? In inclement weather, should they be required to pull their cars over and park until the weather clears? Of course not. Because they eventually met the same high performance standards as those who passed on their initial attempt, they receive the same privileges. The same should hold true for students who show that they, too, have learned well.

Similar Situations
Using assessments as sources of information, following assessments with corrective instruction, and giving students a second chance are steps in a process that all teachers use naturally when they tutor individual students. If the student makes a mistake, the teacher stops and points out the mistake. The teacher then explains that concept in a different way. Finally, the teacher asks another question or poses a similar problem to ensure the student's understanding before going on. The challenge for teachers is to use their classroom assessments in similar ways to provide all students with this sort of individualized assistance.

Successful coaches use the same process. Immediately following a gymnast's performance on the balance beam, for example, the coach explains to her what she did correctly and what could be improved. The coach then offers specific strategies for improvement and encourages her to try again. As the athlete repeats her performance, the coach watches carefully to ensure that she has corrected the problem.

Successful students typically know how to take corrective action on their own. They save their assessments and review the items or criteria that they missed. They rework problems, look up answers in their textbooks or other resource materials, and ask the teacher about ideas or concepts that they don't understand. Less successful students rarely take such initiative. After looking at their grades, they typically crumple up their assessments and deposit them in the trash can as they leave the classroom. Teachers who use classroom assessments as part of the instructional process help all of their students do what the most successful students have learned to do for themselves.

The Benefits of Assessment
Using classroom assessment to improve student learning is not a new idea. More than 30 years ago, Benjamin Bloom showed how to conduct this process in practical and highly effective ways when he described the practice of mastery learning (Bloom, 1968, 1971). But since that time, the emphasis on assessments as tools for accountability has diverted attention from this more important and fundamental purpose.

Assessments can be a vital component in our efforts to improve education. But as long as we use them only as a means to rank schools and students, we will miss their most powerful benefits. We must focus instead on helping teachers change the way they use assessment results, improve the quality of their classroom assessments, and align their assessments with valued learning goals and state or district standards. When teachers' classroom assessments become an integral part of the instructional process and a central ingredient in their efforts to help students learn, the benefits of assessment for both students and teachers will be boundless.

References
Barton, P. E. (2002). *Staying on course in education reform.* Princeton, NJ: Statistics & Research Division, Policy Information Center, Educational Testing Service.

Bloom, B. S. (1968). Learning for mastery. *Evaluation Comment (UCLA-CSEIP), 1*(2), 1-12.

Bloom, B. S. (1971). Mastery learning. In J. H. Block (Ed.), *Mastery learning: Theory and practice.* New York: Holt, Rinehart & Winston.

Bloom, B. S., Madaus, G. F., & Hastings, J. T. (1981). *Evaluation to improve learning.* New York: McGraw-Hill.

Guskey, T. R. (1997). *Implementing mastery learning* (2nd ed.). Belmont, CA: Wadsworth.

Guskey, T. R. (1998). Making time to train your staff. *The School Administrator, 55*(7), 35-37.

Guskey, T. R. (2000a). Twenty questions? Twenty tools for better teaching. *Principal Leadership, 1*(3), 5-7.

Guskey, T. R. (2000b). *Evaluating professional development.* Thousand Oaks, CA: Corwin Press.

Kifer, E. (2001). *Large-scale assessment: Dimensions, dilemmas, and policies.* Thousand Oaks, CA: Corwin Press.

Sternberg, R. J. (1994). Allowing for thinking styles. *Educational Leadership, 52*(3), 36-40.

Stiggins, R. J. (1999). Evaluating classroom assessment training in teacher education programs. *Educational Measurement: Issues and Practice, 18*(1), 23-27.

Stiggins, R. J. (2002). Assessment crisis: The absence of assessment for learning. *Phi Delta Kappan, 83*(10), 758-765.

Whiting, B., Van Burgh, J. W., & Render, G. F. (1995). *Mastery learning in the classroom.* Paper presented at the annual meeting of the American Educational Research Association, San Francisco.

Wiggins, G. (1998). *Educative assessment.* San Francisco: Jossey-Bass.

Thomas R. Guskey is Professor of Education Policy Studies and Evaluation, College of Education, University of Kentucky, Taylor Education Bldg., Lexington, KY 40506; guskey@uky.edu.

From *Educational Leadership,* February 2003, pp. 6-11. Copyright © 2003 by Thomas Guskey. Reprinted by permission of the author.

Index

Index

Test Your Knowledge Form

We encourage you to photocopy and use this page as a tool to assess how the articles in *Annual Editions* expand on the information in your textbook. By reflecting on the articles you will gain enhanced text information. You can also access this useful form on a product's book support Web site at *http://www.dushkin.com/online/*.

NAME:

DATE:

TITLE AND NUMBER OF ARTICLE:

BRIEFLY STATE THE MAIN IDEA OF THIS ARTICLE:

LIST THREE IMPORTANT FACTS THAT THE AUTHOR USES TO SUPPORT THE MAIN IDEA:

WHAT INFORMATION OR IDEAS DISCUSSED IN THIS ARTICLE ARE ALSO DISCUSSED IN YOUR TEXTBOOK OR OTHER READINGS THAT YOU HAVE DONE? LIST THE TEXTBOOK CHAPTERS AND PAGE NUMBERS:

LIST ANY EXAMPLES OF BIAS OR FAULTY REASONING THAT YOU FOUND IN THE ARTICLE:

LIST ANY NEW TERMS/CONCEPTS THAT WERE DISCUSSED IN THE ARTICLE, AND WRITE A SHORT DEFINITION:

We Want Your Advice

ANNUAL EDITIONS revisions depend on two major opinion sources: one is our Advisory Board, listed in the front of this volume, which works with us in scanning the thousands of articles published in the public press each year; the other is you—the person actually using the book. Please help us and the users of the next edition by completing the prepaid article rating form on this page and returning it to us. Thank you for your help!

ANNUAL EDITIONS: Educational Psychology 05/06

ARTICLE RATING FORM

Here is an opportunity for you to have direct input into the next revision of this volume.
We would like you to rate each of the articles listed below, using the following scale:

1. **Excellent: should definitely be retained**
2. **Above average: should probably be retained**
3. **Below average: should probably be deleted**
4. **Poor: should definitely be deleted**

Your ratings will play a vital part in the next revision.
Please mail this prepaid form to us as soon as possible.
Thanks for your help!

RATING	ARTICLE
	1. Good Teachers, Plural
	2. Teachers as Leaders
	3. What Urban Students Say About Good Teaching
	4. Helping Children Cope With Loss, Death, and Grief: Response to a National Tragedy
	5. Shaping the Learning Environment: Connecting Developmentally Appropriate Practices to Brain Research
	6. To Be Successful—Let Them Play!
	7. What Empathy Can Do
	8. Differing Perspectives, Common Ground: The Middle School and Gifted Education Relationship
	9. 'Mom, Will Kaelie Always Have Possibilities?'—The Realities of Early Childhood Inclusion
	10. Into the Mainstream: Practical Strategies for Teaching in Inclusive Environments
	11. Challenges of Identifying and Serving Gifted Children With ADHD
	12. Raising Expectations for the Gifted
	13. Celebrating Diverse Minds
	14. When Should Bilingual Students Be in Special Education?
	15. Cultural Influences on the Development of Self-Concept: Updating Our Thinking
	16. Students Remember…What They Think About
	17. Beyond Learning By Doing: The Brain Compatible Approach
	18. Ability and Expertise: It's Time to Replace the Current Model of Intelligence
	19. It's No Fad: Fifteen Years of Implementing Multiple Intelligences
	20. Caution–Praise Can Be Dangerous
	21. Webs of Skill: How Students Learn
	22. Invitations to Learn
	23. Promoting Academic Achievement Through Social and Emotional Learning
	24. Teachers Bridge to Constructivism
	25. Constructivism and Block Scheduling: Making the Connection

RATING	ARTICLE
	26. What is High-Quality Instruction?
	27. The Integration of Instructional Technology Into Public Education: Promises and Challenges
	28. Using Data to Differentiate Instruction
	29. Intrinsic Versus Extrinsic Motivation in Schools: A Reconciliation
	30. Do Students Care About Learning? A Conversation with Mihaly Csikszentmihalyi
	31. Self-Efficacy: A Key to Improving the Motivation of Struggling Learners
	32. When Children Make Rules
	33. The Key to Classroom Management
	34. Twelve Practical Strategies to Prevent Behavioral Escalation in Classroom Settings
	35. Corporal Punishment: Legalities, Realities, and Implications
	36. The Lessons of High-Stakes Testing
	37. Are We Measuring Student Success With High-Stakes Testing?
	38. The Seductive Allure of Data
	39. Working Inside the Black Box: Assessment for Learning in the Classroom
	40. Classroom Assessment for Learning
	41. How Classroom Assessments Improve Learning

(Continued on next page)

BUSINESS REPLY MAIL
FIRST CLASS MAIL PERMIT NO. 551 DUBUQUE IA

POSTAGE WILL BE PAID BY ADDRESEE

McGraw-Hill/Dushkin
2460 KERPER BLVD
DUBUQUE, IA 52001-9902

ABOUT YOU

Name

Date

Are you a teacher? ☐ A student? ☐
Your school's name

Department

Address   City   State   Zip

School telephone #

YOUR COMMENTS ARE IMPORTANT TO US!

Please fill in the following information:
For which course did you use this book?

Did you use a text with this ANNUAL EDITION? ☐ yes ☐ no
What was the title of the text?

What are your general reactions to the *Annual Editions* concept?

Have you read any pertinent articles recently that you think should be included in the next edition? Explain.

Are there any articles that you feel should be replaced in the next edition? Why?

Are there any World Wide Web sites that you feel should be included in the next edition? Please annotate.

May we contact you for editorial input? ☐ yes ☐ no
May we quote your comments? ☐ yes ☐ no